# REAL WORLD PAGEMAKER 4

THE BANTAM ITC SERIES

# REAL WORLD PAGEMAKER 4

## *Industrial Strength Techniques*

*Macintosh Edition*

OLAV MARTIN KVERN

STEPHEN ROTH

**BANTAM BOOKS**
NEW YORK · TORONTO · LONDON · SYDNEY · AUCKLAND

REAL WORLD PAGEMAKER 4:
INDUSTRIAL STRENGTH TECHNIQUES
MACINTOSH EDITION

A Bantam Book/May 1990

Cover art © Gary Kelley. Originally commissioned by
David Bartels for St. Louis Union Station.

Interior design by Nancy Sugihara

For information address: Bantam Books.

ISBN 0-553-34874-4

Published simultaneously in the United States and Canada

---

Bantam Books are published by Bantam Books, a
division of Bantam Doubleday Dell Publishing
Group, Inc. Its trademark consisting of the words
"Bantam Books" and the portrayal of a rooster, is
Registered in U.S. Patent and Trademark Office and
in other countries. Marca Registrada, Bantam Books,
666 Fifth Avenue, New York, New York 10103

---

PRINTED IN THE UNITED STATES OF AMERICA

0 9 8 7 6 5 4 3 2 1

# *Pharoahs and Thunder Lizards*

Be forewarned: This is not a book that's going to sit on your shelf looking impressive. It's going to spend its days open on your desk, always within easy reach. Before long, its pages are going to be dog-eared from use, the binding will crack from repeated openings, and a tribe of paper clips and Post-It notes will invade its chapters, serving as guides to your favorite tricks.

Because this isn't a book like all those other computer books you've seen. After all, how many computer books promise to make you into a "a raging, inexorable thunder lizard of a page maker?" In fact, it's not a computer book at all. It's a *publishing* book—a distinction that's crucial to the success it achieves. What you're about to learn in the pages ahead isn't the mechanics of running a piece of software. You'll be making pages.

But *Real World PageMaker 4* has more to recommend it than simply the right attitude. Steve Roth and Ole Kvern bring to the table more combined PageMaker experience than you're likely to find anywhere else, in print or out.

Steve was my predecessor as editor at *Personal Publishing*. He's knowledgeable, tough, and the straightest shooter in town (sometimes too straight: I'm still taking heat for the time Steve referred—in print—to a major software vendor's pride and joy as "dog meat").

Ole is senior documentation designer at Aldus. But don't let that prissy title fool you. At Aldus, Ole is the Pharoah of PageMaker—the guy the tech-support team turns to when everyone else is stumped.

Together, they form a remarkable duo: the tough outsider and the savvy insider. And they're funny to boot.

So remember: If you just want something that will look impressive on your shelf, maybe you should try one of those other books. Or better yet, buy another copy of *Real World PageMaker*. Steve and Ole won't mind a bit.

Daniel Brogan
Editor-in-Chief
*Personal Publishing*

# *About 97,515 Words Ago…*

"So what should we do?"

"Let's write a PageMaker book."

"Is there anything new to say about PageMaker?"

"Oh…I guess not."

When we first discussed writing a PageMaker book, we decided that there just wasn't enough material that hadn't been covered elsewhere. About a week later, one of us called the other. We'd been thinking the same thing: that the PageMaker techniques we routinely used and talked about weren't covered in the manuals, and weren't covered in any of the books on the market.

We finally realized that like the authors of every other PageMaker book to date, we had been seduced by PageMaker's fluid interface—by its reach-out-and-touch-it, warm-and-fuzzy look and feel. Even though we use dozens of tricky techniques in PageMaker day in and day out, we'd been lulled into complacency, fooled into thinking that there wasn't much to say beyond the standard PageMaker book's waltz through the menus.

We'd also started to believe something we'd heard—from the advertisements of PageMaker's competitors, from software reviewers for magazines, from Apple Computer, and even from Aldus: that PageMaker is easy to learn, has an elegant user interface, and excels at producing a wide variety of documents, but just isn't as powerful as the competition. Just isn't suited for high-end users. Or just isn't good enough for professional typographers.

## *Going Deep*

We wrote this book because we wanted to show that PageMaker is not only easy to learn and use, but is also deep and powerful. PageMaker's user interface itself empowers users by being elegant, pleasant, and operating in an intuitively obvious fashion. Like the Macintosh, there's far more to PageMaker than its surface. There's a diabolically powerful engine inside for laying out pages, newsletters, magazines, books, and encyclopedias.

So we thought some more. We started building lists of the devious techniques that we use. We searched back issues of all the magazines, scoured the online services, went through all the other PageMaker books, talked to every PageMaker aficionado we know (and we know lots), and came up with enough material to convince us that we really had a book.

That exercise convinced us of something else, as well: PageMaker users really need this book. Unlike the plethora of excellent, in-depth, tip-laden books on Ventura Publisher, PageMaker books are almost all of the how-to-design-your-newsletter variety. There is no compendium of the techniques that hundreds of thousands of PageMaker users have developed over the last five years. And no book really dives into PageMaker's hidden depths—precise positioning, Aldus Prep, Aldus Printer Description files, and modifying PageMaker with ResEdit.

In fact, not one of the books we looked at explains satisfactorily how PageMaker handles leading—an important topic, to say the least. There are huge, gaping holes in the material available on using PageMaker, patched only sporadically by tip-and-tricks and how-to columns in various magazines. The tips in this book go a long way, we hope, toward filling those holes.

**PageMaker and
the Real World**

We didn't want to just put together a list of tips, though. If you're coming to visit us once, we're happy to tell you to turn left at the second tree and right at the fire hydrant (the press-this-key approach to computer books). If you're living in the neighborhood, though, you'd better get a map and learn your way around. We wanted to create the definitive roadmap and explanation of how PageMaker works—how it "thinks" about pages—and how you can best work within its metaphors.

Finally—and perhaps this is the most important—we wanted to make clear throughout the book that PageMaker doesn't exist in a vacuum. There are hundreds of things that affect you when you're building PageMaker pages—from the way you've got your Macintosh system set up, to the printing method you're using, to your colleague across the office who yells out "Hey, Harry! I've got an update of that sidebar!" and tosses you a disk. All the PageMaker expertise in the world means nothing if it's not informed by knowledge of the whole publishing process, and how to make that process smooth and seamless.

Because we want you to understand PageMaker's role in the publishing process, you'll find some lengthy conceptual discussions here—discussions of how PageMaker works, how the Macintosh works, how publishing works, and how they all work together in the real world. The idea is to develop your own PageMaker expertise—building the comprehensive body of knowledge that becomes so ingrained that it looks and feels like intuition.

**On Becoming
a Monster**

Intuition is often the subconscious product of bitter experience. We have developed our intuitive approaches to PageMaker through intensive use of the product (expletives deleted). We've been through the tight deadlines, the pages that, for some reason, refused to print, and the files that wouldn't open. We've produced piles of published pages several stories tall (including more than 2,100 pages using prerelease versions of PageMaker 4—not a pretty sight).

Along the way, we've been able to pass on our experience to dozens of others, creating new monster PageMaker users—sometimes in less than a week. Now, with this book, we want to do the same for you. We want to make you to PageMaker what Godzilla was to Tokyo—a raging, inexorable thunder lizard of a page maker, letting nothing stand in your way.

## *About this Book*

We've tried to address many different types of PageMaker users in this book—from newcomers with strong backgrounds in typography and design, to long-time PageMaker pros who still probably don't know all the tricks hidden away in the program, to beginners who want to get started on the right foot—using the program the way the pros do.

This book is for PageMaker users who want to use the program right—the way it was designed to work—and for those who want to make it do double back flips. Unfortunately, those two goals are not always compatible.

PageMaker's design encourages a certain working style, and it's nice to you when you adopt that style. Pages come together smoothly, and page elements act the way they're supposed to act. Wherever possible, we espouse methods that work well within PageMaker's metaphors and that PageMaker can handle with ease. These techniques are much preferable to fighting the program, trying to do things in ways that confuse or enrage PageMaker.

At the same time, we often need to do things that PageMaker wasn't designed to do. You'll find a number of tips and tricks herein that make Aldus engineers blanch. Some of those techniques are not elegant, and a few are downright hacks ("greasy," our tech reviewer said). They essentially solve problems by fooling PageMaker into doing things it doesn't really know how to do.

Just because some of our techniques seem complicated, though, that doesn't necessarily mean they're not proper ways to use Page-Maker. If you take the time to work through them, and get a feel for how they operate within PageMaker's working style, you'll go a long way toward developing your own relationship with PageMaker, and learning your own ways of cajoling it into amazing and previously untried machinations.

**Organization**

The organization of this book is simple—just like most of the chapter titles. We begin with the basics—building your system and whipping PageMaker into line—then move on to the main subject areas—words, pictures, printing, color, and using PageMaker in a workgroup. Here's a rundown of the chapters.

***Chapter 1: What's New in PageMaker 4.*** The latest release of PageMaker adds dozens of new features, and new ways to use existing features. This chapter is written mainly for PageMaker 3 users who are moving up to version 4 and want a quick overview of the new features. If you want to go deeper, we've included page references for each feature, directing you to lengthier discussions in later chapters.

***Chapter 2: Building a PageMaker System.*** There's a lot more to using PageMaker than just using PageMaker. From the Macintosh System to fonts, desk accessories, and utilities, there are dozens of little tools that comprise a complete PageMaker system. This chapter talks about putting all those pieces together into a working package, and describes our favorite tools and utilities.

***Chapter 3: Making PageMaker Mind.*** This chapter explains how PageMaker works, and how you can best work with it. It covers the pasteboard, the Toolbox, selecting, moving, and sizing page elements, and modifying PageMaker to work the way you do.

***Chapter 4: Words.*** Words are the basic building blocks of most Page-Maker publications. This chapter covers stories, text blocks, paragraph and character formatting, style sheets, and text editing tools, with a dose of special type effects for emphasis.

***Chapter 5: Pictures.*** Words alone can make for dull publications. This chapter talks about creating graphics in PageMaker, bringing them in from other programs, and working your will on them no matter where they come from.

***Chapter 6: Printing.*** When you come right down to it, printing is what

PageMaker is all about. This chapter covers all the options in the Print dialog box, plus ways to modify PageMaker's PostScript, APD files, and even Aldus Prep.

***Chapter 7: Color.*** You can get color out of PageMaker in several ways—by printing on a color printer, producing spot color overlays, or running PageMaker PostScript through a process separation program. This chapter explains the best ways to specify color in PageMaker, and the best ways to produce and reproduce that color.

***Chapter 8: Workgroup Publishing.*** Using PageMaker proficiently is one thing. Using it proficiently with two, five, or fifty other people is something else again. This chapter discusses PageMaker's place in the workgroup environment, and focuses on PageMaker's new tools for keeping track of source files.

***Chapter 9: How We Made this Book.*** We used many, if not most, of the techniques discussed in this book in making the book itself. This chapter details the production process for *Real World PageMaker 4*, including a fully-documented style sheet with its associated QuicKeys.

***Appendix: Resources.*** The appendix lists all the products mentioned in the book, and provides addresses and phone numbers for the companies from which they are available.

## Finding What You Need

We've tried to organize the book so you can get at the information in several ways. You can read the book from beginning to end, of course (being the authors, we highly recommend this method). For the less hardy (or foolhardy), we've divided the chapters with heads hanging in the margins. You can scan through those heads, or look through the table of contents that follows this preface. All the first- and second-level heads are included there along with the chapter heads, so you can jump right to the topic that interests you.

We've also encapsulated all of our favorite techniques in tips—easily recognizable, because they start with the word "Tip." There's a list of tips following the table of contents. Finally, if you just have one question about using PageMaker, or are trying to remember where you saw something, you can resort to the index in the back of the book.

If we get enough requests, in the next edition we're going to use an *Information Anxiety*-style table of contents (we call it that because it's been made popular by Richard Saul Wurman's book by that name), with little write-ups of each chapter right there in the contents. We decided against using one in this book because Steve thinks they promote information anxiety rather than assuaging it. Ole disagrees. Send your ballot now.

## Conventions

We wanted this book to be as immediately accessible and intuitively obvious as PageMaker, so we've avoided clogging it up with lots of little icons and typographic cues that nobody can understand without an explanation. We did face the difficulty of identifying items in PageMaker, however—dialog boxes, menus and menu items, options, commands, etc. To make it easy, we've established one simple convention: If we identify an item when we name it (the Preferences dialog box, the Snap to rulers option, 400% page view), we simply leave it at that. If we don't identify the item, we put quotes around it (with "Snap to rulers" on, zoom to "400%," select "Image control"). The only exceptions are standard Mac commands (Save, New, Open, etc.), which don't need quotation marks. It's so simple that you probably didn't even need to read this section.

We've tried to avoid gratuitous jargon, but there's one term we couldn't avoid: h-menu. This refers to hierarchical menus—the ones that pop off the side of other menus. We just couldn't bear to call them hierarchical menus throughout the book, and besides, everyone calls them h-menus. Just be thankful we didn't call dialog boxes "DBs."

## Disclaimer

Kids! Don't try this at home! Some of the techniques described in this book are truly industrial strength, and like the person pouring molten metal at the steel mill, you should either know what you're doing, or be prepared to accept the consequences of your actions before you attempt them. In particular, the sections on modifying PageMaker or any of the other files packaged with PageMaker should be approached with caution. Here are several rules to keep in mind when you're using *Real World PageMaker 4*.

***Always work on copies of files, never on the originals.*** If you don't keep a backup file, how will you be able to retrace your steps when something goes wrong? And never work on a "live" file—especially the System file—with ResEdit. Even though ResEdit is socially acceptable these days, it's still not a tool to be used lightly.

***Don't call Aldus technical support if something you read in this book doesn't work.*** They're the best in the business, but they're not responsible for what we've written, and shouldn't be expected to support it. Instead, write to us c/o Bantam Computer Books, and we'll try to put changes and fixes in future editions (we're expecting the 23rd edition to be published sometime in 2027). We want to provide you the most powerful set of PageMaker tools, but we assume you will use them responsibly, and at your own risk.

***Think of others.*** If you modify screen fonts, Aldus Prep, APD, kerning, or tracking files, remember to protect other users on your network or your service bureau by making sure your modified files aren't used inadvertently by others. Few things can cause more trouble for your publishing cohorts than an APD file that you've changed without telling anyone and without saving it under another name. And nothing is more of a bother to an imagesetting service bureau than having to restart their RIP because of a renegade Aldus Prep.

## Acknowledgments

We hate to end on such an admonitory note, so we'll resort to thanks and congratulations. Congratulations to everyone at Aldus for delivering a great product in spite of incredible pressures, and thanks in particular to Ben Bauermeister, jwhiting, John "that's almost certainly a bug" Nelson, Mitch "Deep Page" Boss, Doug Stuart, Matt Crosby, Tim Roth, Robin Briggs, Ann Sauer, Sheri Hargus, Eric McCashey, Laura Urban Perry, Harry C. Edwards, Stacy "those keys are fixed now, really!" Robinson, and to John V. and Patricia Callander Hedtke. Very special thanks to Jan C. Wright and Tracy Tobin, the other surviving members of the original Documentation Graphics team, and to Kate Schaefer and Glenn Hackney for the loan of their Mac IIcx. Our deep and abiding thanks to the founding members of Aldus—Paul Brainerd, Jeremy Jaech, Mark Sundstrom, Mike Templeman, and Dave Walter—for creating PageMaker and thereby empowering designers, illustrators, writers, and editors everywhere.

Thanks also go to Mike Roney, one of the few computer book editors who deserves the title (he's even on MCI Mail); Terry Nasta, a managing editor who more than manages; Mark Davison, engineer extraordinaire, who gave the book a thorough (!) technical review; Chuck Cantellay and the whole staff of Seattle ImageSetting for handling some horrendous Lino jobs (especially Peter Curry, who helped us nurse the book out of the Lino); Susie Hammond for her sharp eye and warm heart; and Leslie Simons, for charm, wit, and on occasion, brutally honest assessments of this book's writing (it's better for it). We owe so many people so many favors that we've probably missed a few. If you're among them, thanks. We couldn't have done it without you.

Ole Kvern
Steve Roth

# Overview

# Contents

CHAPTER 2

**CHAPTER 3**

## *Making PageMaker Mind*  49

CHAPTER  4

## *Words*  85

CHAPTER 6

CHAPTER 7

# Tips

## *Words*

## *Pictures*

## *Printing*

## *Color*

## Workgroup Publishing

# *What's New in PageMaker 4*

If you want to find out quickly what's new in PageMaker 4, this chapter is for you. It's also a good pathway into the book as a whole. We've divided the new features into four categories—words, pictures, books, and general features, and each feature discussion ends with a page reference telling you where to look for more details.

## *Words*

Most of the changes in PageMaker 4 are in the areas of text and type. This latest version removes almost every limitation that typophiles railed against in earlier versions, and adds a nice complement of word-processing tools.

**Story Editor**

Triple-clicking on a text block in PageMaker launches the Story editor, and a whole new view of the story appears—the Story view. Story view provides quite a robust text-editing environment, unencumbered by the need to fit copy to your layout. You can just scroll through the story and edit it, without PageMaker having to recompose the story with every keystroke. You can see local style changes such as bold and italic in Story view, and the style bar on the left shows you what style is applied to each paragraph. See page 183.

In addition to a better environment for text editing, the Story editor also adds searching, replacing, and spell checking.

***Find and change.*** The Find and Change functions in PageMaker 4 are very similar to Word's, but they go much further. You can use special codes to find and change all of PageMaker's special characters, for instance—thin spaces, discretionary hyphens, etc. You can also search for certain formatting attributes—paragraph style, font, size, and type style—and change them to other attributes.

You can even combine character- and attribute-based changes, to change the formatting for any occurrence of "PageMaker," for instance, to 16-point Brush Script. PageMaker will do any of this finding or changing throughout the publication, the story, or the selected range of text. See page 186.

***Spell checking.*** The other major feature of the Story editor is spell checking. It uses the same dictionaries as the hyphenation routines, so you can fine-tune both at once. See page 187.

## Text Block Tools

There are two new features for working with text blocks in PageMaker 4. You can rotate text blocks, and get a better idea of how selected blocks are threaded to other blocks due to improved icons in the top and bottom windowshade handles.

***Text rotation.*** You can rotate text blocks in 90-degree increments, as long as they're not threaded to other text blocks, and as long as all the text in that story has been placed. See pages 103, 37.

***Windowshade icons.*** PageMaker 3 showed a + sign in a windowshade if the text continued (whether that continued text had been placed or not), a blank handle at the beginning of a story, and a # sign at the end. In PageMaker 4, you get a little more information, and the conventions have changed a bit. A blank windowshade handle means there's no more text preceding or following that text block. These appear at the beginning and end of stories. A + sign means that there's more placed text preceding or following the text block—it's threaded to another text block. A down arrow (the "overset indicator") in a bottom windowshade handle means there's more text in the story that hasn't been placed yet. See page 88.

## Text Place Filters

The filters that PageMaker uses to place various kinds of text files are much improved in this version, and there are more of them (hold down Option and select "About PageMaker" from the Apple menu to get a list of your installed text filters). They're also easier to install. You just copy the filter into the Aldus Filters folder.

***Microsoft Word.*** The Word filter now lets you control a number of aspects of the file as it's placed—how PageMaker handles page breaks, for instance, and table of contents and index entries. It also imports Word's footnote references correctly. See page 210.

***Rich Text Format.*** The new RTF filter lets you import and export files in this extremely robust ASCII text format. Everything that you can specify in a Microsoft Word document can be coded as ASCII using RTF, including styles, local formatting, and graphics. See page 215.

## Character Formatting

A good portion of the typographic improvements in PageMaker 4 relate to character formatting. You can specify a wider range of type sizes and leading with better accuracy than in PageMaker 3; adjust the width of characters, expanding and condensing the type; adjust the size and position of super- and subscripts, and the size of small caps; and kern more accurately, using a more flexible and powerful approach than was used in PageMaker 3.

***Type sizes.*** You can now specify type from 4 to 650 points in increments of .1 point.

***Leading.*** The finest leading increment PageMaker 3 could handle was half a point. In PageMaker 4, you can specify leading in .1-point increments, from 1 to 1300 points. See page 108.

***Set width.*** You can now condense and expand type horizontally in 1 percent increments, from 5 to 250 percent. See page 150.

***Type options.*** The new Type options dialog box lets you adjust the size and position of sub- and superscripts, and the size of small caps. While it seems mundane, it allows for some amazing type effects that formerly required careful manual positioning. See page 152.

***Manual kerning accuracy and approach.*** Where PageMaker 3 applied manual kerning by inserting invisible "kerning" characters between letter pairs, PageMaker 4 makes manual kerning a character attribute; kerning values apply to the space following a character. Kerning accuracy has been improved to .01-em increments. Manual kerning is now cumulative with automatic kerning; PageMaker adds the manual kerning to the automatic kerning. See page 155.

***Range Kerning.*** You can select a range of text in PageMaker 4 and apply manual kerning to all the character pairs in that text. See page 157.

***Tracking.*** There are five different tracking levels that apply to selected ranges of text. This automatically sets type looser or tighter depending on the size of the type. Tracking tables are supplied for the PostScript "plus" set of typefaces and a few others. At least one third-party tracking editor is available. See page 139.

## Paragraph Formatting

There are probably more changes in paragraph formatting than in any other portion of PageMaker 4. You can specify automatic rules above and below paragraphs; control letter and word spacing parameters on a paragraph level (rather than PageMaker 3's story level); force-justify a paragraph; control hyphenation more comprehensively; control tabs more conveniently and accurately; insert a new-line character that doesn't begin a new paragraph; align paragraphs to a baseline grid; control widows and orphans; keep paragraphs together; specify page and column breaks before paragraphs; and ask PageMaker to highlight lines that break your spacing and/or keep-together rules.

***Paragraph rules.*** If you want a paragraph to have a rule line above or below, PageMaker will do it for you automatically, so the rule moves with the paragraph. You have control over the thickness, position, and color of the lines. See page 140.

***Word and letter spacing.*** Word and letter spacing controls now work on the paragraph level, so you can fine-tune these adjustments for different types of paragraphs. Subheads can have different settings from body copy, for instance. See page 137.

***Force justification.*** The Force justify alignment option justifies the last line of a paragraph (including one-line paragraphs) to the width of the text block. See page 123.

***Next style.*** With this new feature, you can set up your styles to automatically change to another style when you press Return. This is handy, for instance, if you know that para1 style always follows a level 3 style. If you're doing most of your text entry in PageMaker, this is a great enhancement. See page 174.

***Hyphenation controls.*** You can now limit the number of consecutive hyphens, set hyphenation to manual, dictionary, or algorithmic (or any combination of those three methods), and use multiple hyphenation dictionaries in a publication. See page 193.

***Tab handling.*** When you call up the Indents/tabs dialog box, it aligns the ruler zero point to the left edge of the text block (if the left edge is visible in the window), making it much easier to align tabs visually. You can select a tab in the Indents/tabs dialog box and specify a new position, alignment, or leader character instead of removing the tab and adding a new one, and you can type numeric values for tab positions, in addition to moving tabs with the mouse. PageMaker now aligns decimal-tabbed figures properly, even when some of the figures are enclosed in parentheses. See page 124.

***New line.*** Pressing Command-Return inserts a new-line character, just like in Word. This lets you break a line without creating a new paragraph with all its attendant attributes (first-line indent, space before, paragraph rule, etc.), and break justified paragraphs without forcing the line flush left. See page 126.

***Align to grid.*** The Align to grid option (for some reason it's hidden in the paragraph Rule options dialog box) forces the succeeding paragraph to align to a leading grid that you specify, measured from the top of the text block. See page 118.

***Widow and orphan control.*** You can specify the minimum number of lines in a paragraph that PageMaker should keep together at the tops and bottoms of columns. See page 147.

***Keeps and breaks.*** The Keep lines together and Keep with next *n* lines options let you keep a paragraph together on a page, or keep it together with a given number of lines in the ensuing paragraph. See page 146.

***Show loose/tight lines and keeps violations.*** These options (in the Preferences dialog box) ask PageMaker to highlight on screen any violations of the rules you've set up for word and letter spacing, and for keeping paragraphs together. See page 138.

## Pictures

There are only two changes to graphics handling in PageMaker 4, but they are perhaps the most significant new features. You can insert graphics into text, and wrap text around items from the master pages. In addition, PageMaker 4 includes almost all the color features from Color Extension

**Inline Graphics**

In addition to the stand-alone, independent graphics that PageMaker has always offered, you can now insert a graphic within text, so it moves as the text reflows. Inline graphics act just like characters in the text (with some exceptions), so you can use them for special characters such as keycaps within a line, or for larger graphics that constitute paragraphs in their own right. PageMaker imports and exports inline graphics within Microsoft Word and RTF files. See page 263.

**Wrapping Around Master Items**

When you apply text wrap to items on the master page, text will adhere to that wrap on every page that has master items displayed. This lets you customize your text flow behavior, for instance to exclude certain page areas such as companion columns or header regions. This feature is especially useful for autoflowing larger documents. See page 279.

**Color**

All of the color features from PageMaker 3.02 Color Extension are included in PageMaker 4, with the exception of the Colors button in the Preferences dialog box, which let you customize on-screen colors to more closely match printed output. Since you might have missed Color Extension, we'll summarize the new color features.

*Larger palette of colors.* You can define up to 32,767 colors in PageMaker 4.

*Printing to color PostScript printers.* You can print color pages on color PostScript printers such as the QMS ColorScript.

*Place color TIFF images.* PageMaker 4 can place and print 8- and 24-bit color TIFFs.

*Pantone colors.* You can choose colors from a palette of PMS (Pantone Matching System) colors.

*Open Prepress Interface.* When you print PageMaker 4 publications to disk using the As separations option in the PostScript print options dialog box, OPI comments are included in the PostScript output . This means that you can produce process color separations of your pages using a separation program (such as Aldus PrePrint), or you can take your pages to an OPI-equipped color prepress service bureau, which will merge high-quality separations of scanned images into the page film.

Besides incorporating these PageMaker 3.02 Color Extension features, PageMaker 4 also adds the ability to print selected spot color overlays.

## *Books*

You can create publications up to 999 pages in length in PageMaker 4, though with the new Book tools, you won't need or want to. In the Book publication list dialog box, you set up a list of PageMaker pubs that make up your book, in the order you want them to appear. This doesn't allow for automatic page numbering from chapter to chapter (you still need to specify the starting page number explicitly for each pub), but it does allow for chain printing (with some limitations), and automatic generation of tables of contents and indices.

**Table of Contents**

There's a new paragraph attribute in PageMaker 4, "Include in table of contents." You generally turn this on for chapter heads, and perhaps first- and second-level heads. When your book is finished, you ask PageMaker to build a table of contents. It creates a new story, compiling all the paragraphs for which the Include in table of contents attribute is set, and inserts the page number for each. It either loads a text place gun with the new story or replaces a previously created table of contents story. It builds new styles and applies them to the different table of contents levels as it builds the story, so you can adjust the styles and format the table of contents quickly. See page 199.

**Indexing**

Long-document users, rejoice: PageMaker 4's indexing tools are the best we've ever seen. You'll still need to do all of the thinking—because that's just the way the task of indexing works—but PageMaker does all of the tedious bookkeeping: tracking page numbers (including ranges of pages), and keeping an eye on cross-references. See page 201.

## *General Features*

PageMaker 4 sports a number of general improvements, not least of which is an increase in speed over PageMaker 3. Pages draw faster, text recomposes faster, and, through the Story editor, text entry speed has increased by an order of magnitude. Besides performance improvements, PageMaker 4 offers a new and powerful Paste technique; keeps track of the source files you've used to create your publication through the Links command; adds new options for numbering pages; and adds a context-sensitive online help system. The Table Editor application, included in the PageMaker 4 package, creates simple tables.

**Paste**

It doesn't seem like there's much you can do with the Macintosh Paste command, but PageMaker 4 does a lot. If you simply copy and paste an item, PageMaker either pastes the copy on top of the original with a slight offset, or it pastes it in the middle of the screen. If you hold down Option as you choose Paste from the Edit menu, you invoke Page-Maker 4's "power paste" feature.

When you Option-paste, PageMaker pastes the item at exactly the same position on the page as it was cut or copied from—even if you've changed pages or page view (as long as part—more than about 10 percent—of that position is still visible). That's handy, but it gets better. If you Option-paste an item, move it a given distance, then Option-paste again, the new copy is offset by that same distance. With Option-paste, step-and-repeat duplication is a breeze. See page 75.

**Links**

The Links command on the File menu is one of the most important new features in PageMaker 4. Using "Links," you can keep track of the files you've placed in your publication, see whether a file has been modified since you placed it, choose whether to include a copy of the file in your publication, set the file to replace automatically if the source file has been modified, and locate files in a workgroup publishing environment. If you've ever had problems with revision control, the Links command is for you. See page 350.

**Page Numbering**

PageMaker 4 will number pages alphabetically (upper- or lowercase), with Roman numerals (upper- or lowercase), and with good old Arabic numerals. If your page numbers are broken out by chapter (1-15, 4-23, etc.), you can designate a page-number prefix for PageMaker to insert when creating tables of contents and indices. See page 62.

**Help**

PageMaker 4's online help is context-sensitive. If you want information on the Export command, for example, you can invoke Help by pressing the Help key on your keyboard, then choose the command from the menu using the ? cursor. A screen containing information on the Export command will appear. You can also choose Help from the Windows menu to get a listing of Help topics. See page 84.

**Table Editor**

The PageMaker 4 package includes an application for creating and editing tables called Table Editor (pretty catchy, eh?). If you need to create simple, black-and-white tables, Table Editor could be for you. Table Editor can export its tables as tab-delimited text or as a PICT-type graphic for placement in a PageMaker publication. See page 133.

## Going to Pages

PageMaker 4 is a big program, and getting bigger all the time. We're going to leave it for a moment though. In the next chapter we'll discuss building a Macintosh system that provides the foundation for working with PageMaker, and all the tools that go into such a system.

# Building a PageMaker System

If you're building a house, you don't set the walls down on mud. You build forms, position steel rods for reinforcement, and pour cement for the foundation. Your Macintosh system should provide the same kind of solid foundation for PageMaker. If your System's damaged, infected with viruses, or lacks the fonts you need, you'll have a hard time building solid publications. There are several things you'll want to take care of before you ever double-click on the PageMaker icon. The first part of this chapter discusses ways to configure and supercharge your Macintosh system to work with PageMaker.

Page-building, just like house-building, requires the proper tools. PageMaker doesn't exist in a vacuum, after all. You *can* build pages with PageMaker and nothing else, but most people use PageMaker together with a whole suite of programs. To begin with, you need a word processor (we use Microsoft Word, and recommend it), but you probably also need a drawing program (use FreeHand if you can afford it), and possibly a paint program, gray-scale editing program, and any of four dozen little utilities.

In the second part of this chapter we discuss our favorite tools and utilities, trying our hardest to limit our discussion to those tools and techniques that really do relate to PageMaker. (We refer you to the general Macintosh and desktop publishing magazines for reviews of word processors, drawing, and painting programs. They're too big and too numerous to cover here.) Before we get to the tools themselves, though, let's discuss the Macintosh system—the foundation on which your PageMaker publishing edifice is built.

## *About the Macintosh*

In the last three years, we've seen incredible developments in Macintosh software and hardware that have added power and flexibility to the machine. Sometimes, these advances have been made at the price of the Macintosh's ease of use. The once-clear vision of the Macintosh as a computer "for the rest of us" has become clouded.

While the machine is miles ahead of its competition (machines running OS/2, Windows, GEM, or MS-DOS) in terms of ease of use, there's still a mound of abstruse, esoteric information to plow through before you can tap the true power of the Macintosh. Now there are Macintosh wizards, just as there are DOS wizards and UNIX wizards. There may be some basic human craving for technical expertise, for knowing more than the next person. We don't know. We do know that, if you have some question about your Macintosh system, and can't find the answer in this book, you should ask your local Mac guru (everyone needs a guru).

Good books on the Macintosh include *The Macintosh Bible* (Goldstein & Blair) and *Encyclopedia Macintosh* (Sybex). The first is the biggest seller, but the latter is the biggest (782 pages for $24.95—cheaper per page than this book). *Encyclopedia Macintosh* is by Craig Danuloff and Deke McClelland, whose PageMaker book was, until this one came out, hands-down the best on the market. (It just goes to show you how authors can improve from their humble beginnings of filling desktop publishing books with clip art and typeface samples.)

**PageMaker 4 and the Macintosh**

PageMaker 4 runs on all Macintoshes with 1 MB of RAM. Performance on machines with 128 K ROMs, however (upgraded 128Ks, 512Ks, and

512Kes), is pretty unbearable. If you own one of the older machines, think about upgrading further, with a 68020 or 68030 accelerator board (most have the 256 K ROMs that came out with the SE and the II) and more RAM (these boards also usually have SIMM slots for easier RAM expansion). If you're in a workgroup publishing environment, consider retiring the 512Ks to the role of AppleShare administrator, running as servers for your network (see "File Transfer Methods" in Chapter 8, *Workgroup Publishing*). There is still life in the older machines!

## *The Macintosh System*

It's not sexy. It doesn't have racing stripes. It doesn't produce flashy, multimedia presentations. It doesn't, in fact, *do* anything that you can see. But it does make PageMaker and desktop publishing possible. The System file and the Macintosh ROM provide the *stuff* that makes the Macintosh go. Without that stuff, your Macintosh would behave like… well…like an IBM PC.

### ▼ *Tip: The System File and the System Folder*

Remember that the System file and the system folder are different things. The System file (the program that tells the Macintosh that it's a Macintosh) is stored in the system folder. This confuses lots of people.

### ▼ *Tip: One System*

If you have more than one System file on your Mac, you're playing with fire. Nothing contributes to crashes more than multiple Systems (and besides, they eat disk space). You should have one System file, in your one system folder, along with all the other system resources.

If you get a new program and they tell you to copy everything on every disk onto your hard disk (including their system folder), ignore them. They're boneheads.

**System Resources**

You can extend the Macintosh System by adding resources—fonts, desk accessories (DAs), INITs, CDEVs, FKEYs, and Sounds (we'll discuss each below). Once the resources are installed, PageMaker and other programs can use them to do their jobs. If we continue with our metaphor of the System as the foundation of a building, the installable resources are like plumbing, gas lines, or the electrical wiring—except they're lots easier to install. We couldn't get by without them (though Ole thinks Steve rather overdoes a good thing).

There are two ways to add resources to your system. You use different methods for different resources.

- Copy the resources into your system folder. You use this method for downloadable printer fonts, INITs, and CDEVs.

- Install the resource in your System file. This is the method you use for screen fonts, desk accessories, FKEYs, and Sounds. We'll cover this method first.

**Font/DA Mover, Suitcase II, and MasterJuggler**

You can install fonts and DAs in your System file with the Font/DA Mover utility (it comes on your Apple System disks). Files containing these resources are called suitcases, and the icon representing them looks like a little suitcase.

On one side of the Font/DA Mover window, open your System file. Open the suitcase containing the resources on the other side, and copy the resources over (Figure 2-1). You can also remove selected resources from the System or suitcase files.

Now that we've told you how to install resources in your System, here's another piece of advice: don't do it. When you get lots of fonts and DAs installed in your System, it gets huge, unwieldy, and volatile. Even worse, there are serious limits on how many fonts (circa 200) and DAs (15) you can install in your System file. So you end up adding and removing fonts every time you start working on a new design. And we don't know how anyone could get by with only 15 desk accessories. We recommend that you only use the Font/DA Mover to create suitcase files containing sets of fonts and DAs, and exercise caution whenever you do that (more below).

**Figure 2-1**
Font/DA Mover copying
fonts into the System file

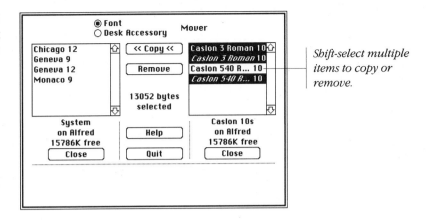

*Shift-select multiple
items to copy or
remove.*

The solution to these font and DA limitations is to use either of two programs—Suitcase II or MasterJuggler. These programs let you keep your System file virtually empty. You keep all your fonts and DAs in suitcase files, which you can load and unload on the fly, whenever you need them. So you might have a suitcase containing Garamond fonts, another containing Optima, and another that has all your favorite utility DAs. You can really be organized.

MasterJuggler and Suitcase II both work as desk accessories, so you can call them up to load or unload suitcases whenever you need to. You really must have one of these programs. Power users prefer MasterJuggler because of its superior user interface and its great pop-up menu for launching programs or switching between currently active programs in MultiFinder. Suitcase II has one big advantage: it will find PostScript typefaces even if they're not loose in your system folder, even—and this is the difference—when it's Adobe Type Manager that's looking for them. With MasterJuggler, you have to have the typefaces loose in the system folder or ATM won't find them. Suitcase II's manual also has the best discussion we've seen of the whole Macintosh font-numbering nightmare that we attempt to unravel below.

### ▼ *Tip: Pare Down Your System*

Once you're using Suitcase II or MasterJuggler, you can prune fonts and DAs out of your System with Font/DA Mover. You need to leave at least one DA in the System (we keep Chooser, Control Panel, and Key

Caps in there), and you have to keep certain sizes of Chicago, Geneva, and Monaco for use by programs in menus, dialog boxes, etc.

In Font/DA Mover, select all the fonts in your System and click the Remove button. The program will refuse to remove the ones that have to stay there, but you'll be rid of all the rest. Be careful that you don't throw away fonts you haven't backed up. Alternatively, you can copy them into a separate suitcase that you can load with either Suitcase II or MasterJuggler.

---

### ▼ Tip: Creating New Suitcase Files

This is simple, but people constantly have difficulty with it. You can create a new suitcase file to contain one or more fonts and/or DAs in the following manner (Figure 2-2).

1. Launch Font/DA Mover.

**Figure 2-2**
Creating a new suitcase
with Font/DA Mover

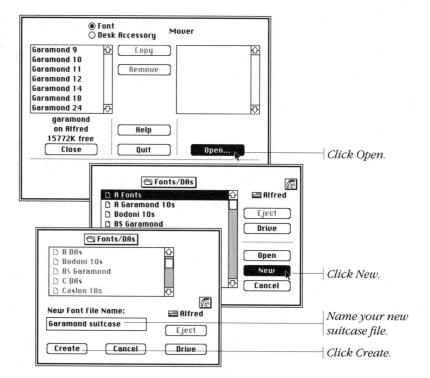

Click Open.

Click New.

Name your new
suitcase file.

Click Create.

2. On the left, open the suitcase or System file containing the resources you want to copy.

3. On the right, click Open.

4. Font/DA Mover asks you what file to open. You don't want to open an existing file, so click New to create a new one. Font/DA Mover asks you for a file name for the suitcase file. Type a name and click the Create button.

5. Copy resources into the new suitcase.

6. Click Quit.

You've just created a new suitcase containing only the resources you want. You can load the suitcase with Suitcase or MasterJuggler.

## *Of Fonts and Faces*

Take a deep breath. Macintosh fonts are fairly simple to work with, but they're hard to explain. For every rule you make, there's an exception.

Fonts on the Macintosh usually have two parts. One part displays on your screen (the screen font), and one part prints on your printer (the printer font). You load screen fonts with Font/DA Mover, Suitcase II, or MasterJuggler, as we explained above. Printer fonts (usually PostScript downloadable fonts) go in your system folder, where the Macintosh can find them when it's time to print.

You can compress suitcase files with Suitcase II and MasterJuggler, so you can gain disk space that's been taken up since you learned about the joy of having lots of fonts and DAs.

**Screen Fonts**

Screen, or bitmapped, fonts are made up of bits—patterns of pixels turned on and off, just like in a MacPaint file. Since they're made up of dots, screen fonts get way ugly when you try to scale them. If you want to use 9-point Chicago for something and have it look (reasonably) decent, you've got to have a 9-point Chicago screen font installed. If you don't, the Mac scales some other size, which is a mistake with bitmapped fonts. All the dots get messed up and illegible.

Many people don't realize it, but there are screen fonts for all the variations in a typeface—bold, italic, and bold italic. You only need to have one screen font—the roman (nonbold, nonitalic) version—for every font you use. You can still specify bold, italic, and bold italic without having a special screen font, and PageMaker will find the correct printer font.

If you're using Adobe Type Manager and/or NFNTs (both discussed below), you'll get a good representation of the way the printed font will appear. Otherwise, you'll see a version of the font generated from the roman screen font. It doesn't look as good as if you specify a specialized screen font (B Times Bold, for example), but spacing and line breaks display correctly.

If you're not using ATM or NFNTs, you can specify the specialized screen font for a bold, italic, or bold italic typeface. The type looks better on the screen, but you're liable to run into problems if you take your file to an imagesetting service bureau, because the service bureau is probably using NFNTs (for more on conflicts between NFNT and non-NFNT installations, read on).

## Printer Fonts

Unlike bitmapped fonts, PostScript typefaces are scalable. The printer typeface file contains scalable character outlines, not fixed-size bitmaps. You can specify any size of a particular typeface, and you'll only need one PostScript printer font. Unlike screen fonts, however, you do need a different printer font for each variant of the font. You won't have any problem with the typefaces that are resident in your printer (Times, Helvetica, et al.), but downloaded PostScript typefaces require special treatment. Garamond Italic, for example, requires a different face than Garamond Bold Italic. For the skinny on how PageMaker handles printer fonts and downloading with PostScript devices, see "PageMaker and Downloaded Fonts" in Chapter 6, *Printing*.

## Exceptions

So far, things are pretty clear. There are bitmapped screen fonts, and scalable PostScript printer fonts. You see the screen fonts on screen, and the printer fonts on printout. Now for the exceptions.

***ATM.*** Adobe Type Manager (discussed below) finds the PostScript outlines on disk and builds bitmapped fonts on the fly for screen display (for font sizes not currently in the System), and for output on non-PostScript printers.

***Bitmapped fonts.*** Not all fonts have both a screen and printer version. Some send the printer the same font as you see on your screen. We call these bitmapped fonts. Our old favorites—New York, Chicago, and San Francisco—are all bitmapped fonts, designed for the Macintosh's 72-dpi screen display and the ImageWriter's 72-dpi output.

***Resident fonts.*** You may not need to store the printer font on your Macintosh if the printer fonts are in your printer's ROM, or have been downloaded to your printer's hard disk. In this case, you only need the screen font (unless you're using ATM).

***High-res bitmaps.*** With some printers (the LaserWriter II SC, for example), you have a 72-dpi bitmapped font for screen display, and use a higher-resolution (usually 300-dpi) bitmapped font for printing. If you're using bitmapped printer fonts, you'll need to have a printer font for each size of type you use in your publications. Integral multiples work okay (specifying 24-point type when you have a 48-point screen font), but otherwise the scaling gets pretty ugly.

***Non-PostScript outlines.*** Some non-PostScript printers—notably GCC's Personal LaserPrinter (PLP) and WriteMove—use non-PostScript outline printer fonts rather than the high-resolution bitmapped printer fonts used by the LaserWriter II SC, or the PostScript outlines used with PostScript printers. These outline fonts work like PostScript printer fonts, however. You can even use the same "Plus" set of screen fonts. The PLP software knows to substitute its fonts where necessary.

***Outlines and shadows.*** Outlined and shadowed printer fonts do not exist for most PostScript typefaces, so PageMaker generates outline and shadowed versions during printing. Whether an outlined or shadowed version of a font can be generated by PageMaker depends on settings found in the FOND resource (see *Inside LaserWriter* for more information on the FOND resource's style mapping table). These settings depend entirely on the mood of the type designer, and vary widely from typeface to typeface.

***Bold and italic.*** For some PostScript fonts for which no bold, italic, or bold italic version exists (Zapf Dingbats, for instance), PageMaker generates a bold, italic, or bold italic version of the font during printing. See the previous item on outlines and shadows for more information.

***Royal fonts.*** Just to muddy the waters, Apple has extended Quick-Draw font technology for System 7 to include scalable outline fonts. This font technology is called Royal, and may appear before the official release of System 7. We haven't seen any of these fonts yet, but we understand they'll work about the same way as PostScript fonts with ATM. It remains to be seen how they will work with PostScript devices.

## Font Names and Numbers

In the early days, there weren't many fonts for Macintoshes, and there weren't many people moving their documents off their own machines. Each font was given an ID number attached to its FONT resource when it was copied into the System with the Font/DA Mover, and Macintosh applications called fonts by their local System number.

Everything was fine until 1) the font market exploded, 2) people started sharing documents, and 3) people started taking their documents to service bureaus for imagesetting or laser printing. The problem was that font #22 on your System might be totally different from font #22 on the service bureau's System. Ole once designed an instrument panel with MacDraw on his Macintosh at home. He used Helvetica for all of the labels for the controls. When it came out of a Linotronic 100, all of the knobs and buttons were labelled with Cairo. This happens all the time.

With FONT IDs, there are unavoidable conflicts, because there are only 255 possible FONT ID numbers. If Font/DA Mover encounters a conflict between two fonts, it simply renumbers one of them. Pretty soon, everyone has different font IDs. Apple eventually realized that this was a problem, and created a new font resource—NFNT (pro-nounced En-font). The NFNT resource can accommodate 32,767 distinct font IDs, and font manufacturers have now assigned uniqu NFNT IDs to each of their fonts. Or they should have. By the time yo read this, just about every font should be available in NFNT form

These days, most desktop publishing applications (par ticularly Page-Maker and FreeHand) call fonts by their name, not their number Names are always (or almost always) unique, so font substitution isn' as much of a problem. But imagesetting service bureaus still have t deal with files from applications (like Persuasion) that call fonts by their ID numbers, and have, therefore, switched to NFNTs.

NFNTs should solve the whole font substitution problem, but there's a catch. When you copy fonts to a System file (or to an existing suitcase file) using the Font/DA Mover, you run a risk. If the utility finds a font with the same ID already installed, it will renumber the font you're trying to move. It will *not* renumber fonts being moved to a new or empty suitcase. What this means: use NFNT font suitcases and either Suitcase II or MasterJuggler!

NFNTs also shorten your Font h-menu (or the pop-up in the Type specifications dialog box) by listing only the roman screen font, rather than clogging it up with "B Times Bold." You specify bold and italic versions of the font with the Type styles h-menu, key commands, or the Type styles check boxes in the Type specifications dialog box, rather than choosing the specific screen font from the menu.

### ▼ Tip: Use Font/DA Mover 3.8 or Later

Versions of Font/DA Mover prior to version 3.8 did not know how to handle NFNTs. Always use 3.8 or later.

### ▼ Tip: Don't Use Specialized Screen Fonts with NFNTs

If you've installed NFNTs *and* still have specialized, non-NFNT fonts installed, you run the risk of getting Courier or a bitmap out of the printer every time you format type using the bold, italic, or bold italic screen font. Again, use NFNT screen fonts, and lose the specialized, non-NFNT fonts.

## *Other Resources*

Fonts are the most complex resource you have to deal with on the Mac. While you can enter great depths with the other resources, their basic installation and operation is pretty straightforward. We'll run through the different classes of resources, then get into examples of our favorites in the last part of this chapter.

### Desk Accessories

DAs are little programs that you choose from the Apple menu. Sometimes they're not so little. There are full-blown drawing, painting, word-processing, and utility applications hidden away in some desk accessories, not to mention important productivity boosters like our favorite, Neko.

Like fonts, you store desk accessories in suitcases. You can install them, remove them, and copy them with the Font/DA Mover, and load and unload them with Suitcase II or MasterJuggler.

### INITs and CDEVs

When you start up your Macintosh, it looks through the system folder for files of two types—type INIT and type CDEV (they're not acronyms, they're file types). If you place one of these resources in the system folder and restart your Mac, the System loads them into memory, where they hang out waiting to do something. Some INITs just stay in the background, keeping track of deleted files and such, without your ever having to know they're there. Others wait for you to call them into action. CDEVs (Control Panel devices—like a subclass of INITs) let you control their operation through the Control Panel.

INITs and CDEVs are great; being able to use them is one of the big advantages of the Macintosh (memory-resident programs on IBMs are a total pain). They eat memory, though, sometimes cause compatibility problems (usually with each other), and can be a terrible nuisance when you're trying to diagnose a problem.

### ▼ *Tip: Use an INIT Controller*

There are several INITs on the market that let you control other INITs and CDEVs at startup—notably Aask by CE Software (who else?) and INIT Picker by Microseeds. Both of these programs do a great job of turning INITs on and off (otherwise, you have to drag the INITs out of your system folder), reordering INIT launching sequences, and uncovering INIT compatibility problems. You still have to restart before any changes take effect, though.

If you're having a problem that you think might be INIT-related, turn off all of your INITs using one of these programs, restart, and see if the problem persists. If it does, the problem is not INIT-related. If not, try turning on one INIT at a time, restarting, and checking the problem. Eventually, the problem will re-appear, and you'll know which INIT is guilty. Remember, though, that your problem might be with the amount of RAM you have available, or some conflict *between* INITs, rather than one misbehaving INIT.

---

**FKEYs**

FKEYs (which sort of stands for "function keys," in programmer-speak) sit around waiting for you to hit a particular key combination. Then they do something. The only one we use is Switch-A-Roo (see below).

To be truthful, FKEYs are kind of archaic. There's nothing you can do with them that you can't do with INITs, but FKEYs are harder to install. You open the FKEY with ResEdit (discussed below), select and copy the FKEY resource, open the System file or a suitcase, and paste in the FKEY. If you put it in a suitcase, you can load it with Suitcase II or MasterJuggler, which can be more convenient than using an INIT, because you have to reboot to load an INIT.

**Sounds**

Yes, you can add sounds if you feel the urge. Steve is partial to Curly Joe saying, "woo woo woo." Ole likes the sound of a glass ball scraping across a piece of styrofoam. Actually, we both use the simple beep.

## *These Are a Few of Our Favorite Things*

As we said, the Macintosh system is not as simple and straightforward as it once was. There are dozens of different tools out there that quickly become indispensable. What follows is a rundown of our favorites. We'll be referring to these programs throughout the book, so if you find at some point that you don't know what we're talking about, come back to this section.

We've divided these tools into categories—tools for text and type, art, PostScript, and general utilities, but as is so often the case, the categories don't always fit perfectly. Most type tools, for instance, have a lot to do with PostScript. And it's often difficult to draw the line between type and graphics (type can act like a graphic, and graphics can be included in typefaces). So if you don't find a given tool where you expect it to be, refer to the table of contents in the beginning of the book. Manufacturers and products are listed in the appendix.

## *File Tools*

Since PageMaker's biggest job is bringing together many different types of files, we often find ourselves rooting around on disks and inside files trying to get them to act the way we want them to act. The tools covered in this section work on three levels—manipulating complete files (copying, moving, finding, etc.), changing their attributes (type, creator, etc.), and working inside those files to extract or modify parts.

**Apple File Exchange**

We've seen an amazing number of people who knew that their Macintosh IIcx (or any other Mac with the SuperDrive) could read MS-DOS formatted 3-½-inch disks, but couldn't figure out how to get it to accept the DOS disk.

It's simple. Run Apple File Exchange (it comes on the Apple System disks), *then* insert the disk. Once that's done, your Mac can read the disk. The Apple File Exchange comes with several filters (or translators), and more are available from various sources, notably

DataViz's MacLink Plus and MacLink Plus PC packages. If you're working with lots of MS-DOS files, these filters can make the process of bringing these barbarian files into the civilized Mac environment almost painless.

You can also use Apple File Exchange and its filters locally, to translate MS-DOS files you've brought from a DaynaFile MS-DOS drive, modem, or direct serial connection to a PC.

**Boomerang**

Boomerang is a very handy freeware INIT, written by Hiroaki Yamamoto (who must be crazy—or just altruistic—to give away software this good). Boomerang changes the way you work with file listing dialog boxes (like Open, Place, and Save—Figure 2-3). It remembers where you've been, what files you've opened, and what applications you've used. If you're working with multiple disks or file servers, or are flipping back and forth between applications, files, and folders (in desktop publishing, who isn't?), Boomerang is for you.

**Figure 2-3**
Boomerang menus

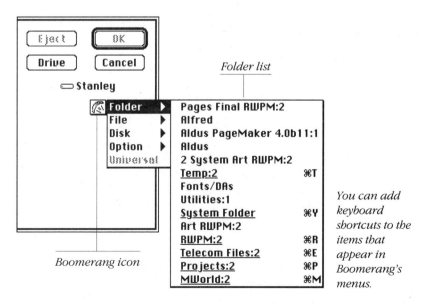

Folder list

You can add keyboard shortcuts to the items that appear in Boomerang's menus.

Boomerang icon

Once Boomerang is running, a small pop-up menu appears in file selection dialog boxes. Pop up the menu, and you'll be able to choose disks, files, and folders you've used recently, or tap some of

Boomerang's special features. You can even assign Command keys to your most commonly used files and folders, so you can open a file on a different disk, four layers deep in folders, without ever touching the mouse (you barely even see the dialog box).

It seems we're always trying to save files before we have a folder to put them in. Ordinarily, we'd have to back out of the Save as dialog box, add a folder with DiskTop (discussed below), choose Save as again, and direct the file to the new folder. With Boomerang, we just choose "New folder," name the folder, and save the file.

**CanOpener**

CanOpener (Abbott Publishing) comes as both an application and a DA, but the two are so close to functionally equivalent that we always use the DA (Figure 2-4). As you'd expect from its name, CanOpener opens files and extracts information, and can write the information out as TEXT and PICT files. It's often the only way to get text and graphics out of a damaged file.

**Figure 2-4**
CanOpener

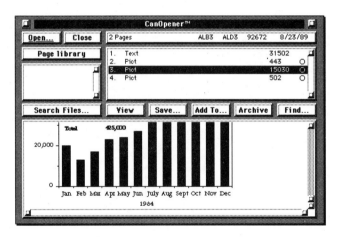

*You can extract text and graphics from this damaged PageMaker file.*

▼ *Tip: From PageMaker to FreeHand*

Among other things, CanOpener is, at present, the best way to move formatted text from PageMaker to Aldus FreeHand, which is a great thing to do. FreeHand is the most powerful single-page layout program on the market, unbeatable for complex process-color pages, but it lacks paragraph formatting features and the ability to import formatted text. If you simply copy PageMaker text blocks to the Clipboard and paste them into FreeHand, the text usually explodes, spattering the page with characters. While you can work around this (use "Select all" and set letter and word spacing to 0), it's easier to use CanOpener.

1. Lay out your text in PageMaker.
2. Copy the text blocks to the Clipboard.
3. Paste the contents of the Clipboard into the Scrapbook.
4. Open the Scrapbook file with CanOpener.
5. Use CanOpener to save the Scrapbook image as a PICT file.
6. Open and convert the PICT file with FreeHand.

Note that FreeHand breaks each line into a separate text block, and even breaks text blocks between kerned characters, including autokerning pairs (Figure 2-5).

**Figure 2-5**
PageMaker text block moved into FreeHand with CanOpener

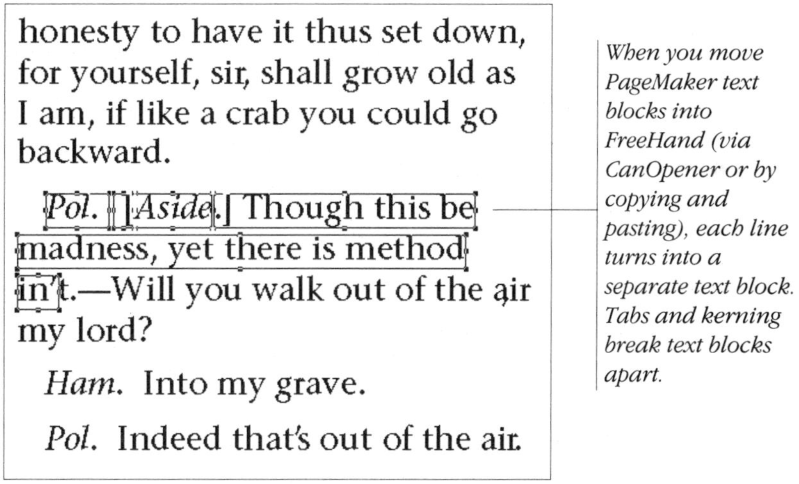

honesty to have it thus set down, for yourself, sir, shall grow old as I am, if like a crab you could go backward.

*Pol.* []*Aside.*] Though this be madness, yet there is method in't.—Will you walk out of the air my lord?

*Ham.* Into my grave.

*Pol.* Indeed that's out of the air.

*When you move PageMaker text blocks into FreeHand (via CanOpener or by copying and pasting), each line turns into a separate text block. Tabs and kerning break text blocks apart.*

**DiskTop**

DiskTop, from CE Software, is one of our favorite Swiss Army knives. It's a DA that does many of the things you'd normally do from the Finder—copying and deleting files, formatting disks, and scanning directories, but DiskTop adds several features that Finder doesn't have.

*A great Find command.* You could easily, for example, search for every file containing ".pm4," having file type "ALD4," and created between January 1, 1990 and January 5, 1990—and find them all. You choose which mounted disks to search.

*A true Move command.* (Former UNIX hacks, rejoice!) In the Finder, if you want to move a file from one drive to another, you have to copy the file to the new drive, then delete the original file. Using DiskTop's Move command, you simply move the file from one drive to another. DiskTop takes care of deleting the original file for you.

*An extended Get Info command.* You can use this to check and change file type, creator, and a number of other file variables (like whether the file is visible, or locked). We constantly have to change file types, as you'll see throughout the book, so DiskTop is worth the price for this capability alone.

*Better keyboard control of Finder functions.* If you open a folder in the Finder and type the first few letters of a file's name, does the Finder select the file? No. DiskTop does.

*Application launching.* If you double-click on a file with the type PICT and the creator MDRW and MacDraw isn't available, the Finder displays an alert informing you that it can't find the application. DiskTop, in the same situation, asks you what program you'd like to use to open the document (in this case, you could choose FreeHand, SuperPaint, Canvas, etc.).

*Tidiness.* We don't know if this appeals to everybody, but looking through folders in the Finder can become a nightmare—you end up with a desktop cluttered with open folders. When you browse with DiskTop, only one folder is open at a time, and when you close DiskTop, you close the folder.

*Speed.* Moving from folder to folder, copying files, and deleting files are all accomplished much faster in DiskTop.

### ▼ *Tip: Pausing a Search in DiskTop*

When you're searching for a file with DiskTop, pressing Spacebar pauses the search without returning you to the main DiskTop screen. It took us a long time before we discovered that one.

### ▼ *Tip: Get Technical*

You can use DiskTop's Preferences dialog box to set your level to Technical, Normal, or Locked Normal. The Technical level means that DiskTop will display more information on the files it lists, and it also activates DiskTop's Get Info feature so you can change file types, creators, and attributes. Set your DiskTop Level preference to Technical, even if you're not.

### ▼ *Tip: Adding to DiskTop's Menu*

If you frequently find yourself moving between two or three files or applications but don't want to claw your way through folders or across drives to find them every time, you can install the files in DiskTop's menu. When you choose an application in DiskTop's menu, DiskTop launches the application. Choosing the file name in the menu selects that file and opens it, launching an application to open the file if necessary. If an application capable of opening the file is currently running, DiskTop simply opens the file.

There are other good ways to move back and forth between folders or disks (ShortCut, Boomerang), and other ways to attach files to application-launching menus (OnCue, MasterJuggler). If you don't have one of those tools, though, DiskTop does the job.

**ResEdit**

To really take control of Macintosh files, you must have ResEdit, a program provided by Apple (get it from a user group or online service) that lets you edit the resources of Macintosh files.

In the dark ages (1986), ResEdit was seen as an incarnation of evil, of Satan, of the seething chaos that lies beneath mortal reality. Covens of ResEdit users formed, and under a leering, gibbous moon, made dire sacrifices to the dark god of resources. Decent folk stayed home nights, keeping constant vigil over their applications, lest they become hacked and corrupt.

Today, in the bright, clear light of reason, we see that what was once shunned as witchcraft is simply the misunderstood roots of our science. Further, ResEdit has improved immensely. You can now use it to modify applications to your liking without ever cracking the cover(s) of *Inside Macintosh*.

To understand ResEdit, you have to understand that Mac files have split personalities. They have data forks and resource forks. With most applications, the program code itself and all the canned resources that the program calls on (messages, dialog boxes, icons, menus, keyboard shortcuts, etc.) are in the resource fork. If you can change the resources in the resource fork, you can change the program (see "Modifying PageMaker's Menus with ResEdit" in Chapter 3, *Making PageMaker Mind*). ResEdit lets you modify programs without programming.

Documents have data and resource forks, as well. A viewable EPS (encapsulated PostScript) graphic file, for instance, has all the PostScript code for printing the image in the data fork, and a PICT representation in the resource fork for viewing on screen and printing on non-PostScript printers. You'll find several tips showing you how to edit the resource and data forks of graphic files (EPS and PICT) in Chapter 5, *Pictures*.

There are lots of great things you can do with ResEdit. Ole has several others that he wanted to add, but he couldn't think of what they have to do with PageMaker.

## *Text and Type Tools*

Text is not type, but it does have potential. As you'll see in Chapter 4, *Words*, we're pretty adamant about getting your text and type set up correctly before it ever lands on a PageMaker page. The tools here are the primary ones we use to massage, edit, and mold text into type.

**Adobe Type Manager**

If you want to see smooth characters on screen and on output from non-PostScript printers, Adobe Type Manger (ATM) is for you. It's an inexpensive, slick little INIT that generates bitmapped fonts (for screen and printer) from type 1 PostScript typeface outlines. (Type 1 fonts come from Adobe, Linotype, Agfa-Compugraphic, and Monotype, and by the time you read this, probably everyone else. Currently, most non-Adobe fonts are type 3. ATM can't read them, so you have to rely on fixed-size screen fonts for display.)

With ATM, the type on your screen looks smoother—closer to the way it will appear when printed—even when you zoom in close. The screen display of kerning, for example, is far better with ATM than without (i.e., you can actually adjust kerning on screen, rather than having to print the page six or eight times before you get it right). Non-PostScript printers can use the generated characters to print PostScript typefaces with good quality.

ATM is very simple to use. Just drag it into your system folder and restart. Once that's done, you can adjust ATM's settings by clicking the ATM icon in the Control Panel. You can adjust the size of ATM's font cache, but remember that the larger you make the font cache, the more RAM ATM uses; the smaller you make the font cache, the longer it takes ATM to display your fonts.

### ▼ Tip: Choosing Lines or Characters

If your final output will be on a PostScript device, you'll want to use ATM's Preserve line spacing option so that line and page breaks won't change when you open pubs created without ATM. If you're depending on ATM for printing, on the other hand, you will probably want to choose the Preserve character shapes option—especially if your non-PostScript printer is producing characters with slightly clipped ascenders or descenders.

**Key Caps**

Are you ever at a loss for which key to type to get some obscure character in Zapf Dingbats (or our favorite, Bullets & Boxes)? Just call up the Key Caps DA (it comes on the Mac System disks). Then choose the font from the Key Caps menu, and push the Shift and Option keys until you find the character you want (Figure 2-6). Not all the PostScript characters are available from the Mac keyboard—fractions, for instance—but we haven't figured out any good way of getting at them.

**Figure 2-6**
Key Caps with Bullets &
Boxes selected

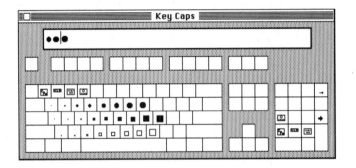

**Macify**

Macify is a little public-domain utility (Figure 2-7) that converts text files into text files you can be proud of. First, it strips the linefeeds following carriage returns out of DOS text files (when you see little boxes at the beginning of every paragraph in one of these files, you'll know what we're talking about).

**Figure 2-7**
Macify

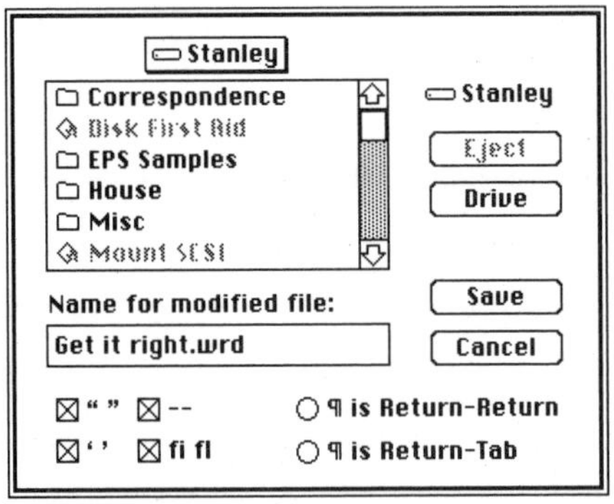

Beyond just stripping linefeeds, though, Macify also converts straight quotes to curved quotes, double hyphens to em dashes, and fi and fl to ligatures (fi and fl; even PageMaker's Place filters won't handle this conversion for you). Macify only works with text-only files, but it sure is handy with those.

**Quote Init**

PageMaker converts straight quotes and double hyphens to curved ("sexed") quotes and em dashes on import, but it doesn't insert them automatically as you type. Quote Init (actually it's a CDEV), a shareware program by Lincoln Stein, does it for you, although sometimes it's a bit unpredictable. That's okay, because you can toggle any of its automatic conversions on and off with a Command key, and then type in your special characters the old-fashioned way (see the discussion of Key Caps earlier in this chapter). Not only does it handle quotes and dashes, it automatically generates ligatures for fi, fl, oe, and ae as you type (Figure 2-8). Between Quote Init, Macify, and PageMaker's Place filters, you can make pretty darn sure that there are no straight quotes in your pubs (unless you want them).

**Figure 2-8**
Quote Init

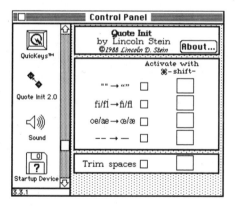

**Vantage**

Vantage, from Preferred Software, is a DA word processor that reads and writes text-only files. It's great for cleaning up files that have come from non-Macintosh environments (stripping linefeeds from DOS files, for example), running fast search-and-replaces, and doing text-only style tagging. Vantage can also work directly with text on the Clipboard; if you copy some text out of PageMaker and then open Vantage, the text is there waiting for you.

**▼ *Tip: Changing Case with Vantage***

We usually tell people who are generating text files for us to place in PageMaker that they should type everything in upper- and lowercase (Ulc), because we can always change the case of the type using the Case pop-up menu in the Type specifications dialog box. We wouldn't have to say this if people would stop emphasizing words using ALL CAPS, a bad habit left over from the days of Selectrics. But never mind that. They haven't stopped underlining things, either.

When you've placed a file and find text that's been entered as all caps, try the following.

1. Copy the text to the Clipboard.

2. Open Vantage, leaving the text selected in PageMaker.

3. In Vantage's view of the Clipboard, select the text you want to change, and choose a case option from the Vantage menu ("Lower Case," [sic] for example).

4. Close Vantage and paste the changed text over the text that's still selected in PageMaker.

To change the text to initial capitals, choose "Capitalize Words" or "Capitalize Sentences" after choosing "Lower Case." You could even create a Sequence QuicKey to do this for you if you had to face the problem often (see "QuicKeys" later in this chapter).

**Varityper Utilities**

When Varityper entered the PostScript imagesetter market, we wondered whether they'd do a better job than Linotype. One good sign is the set of four excellent font utility DAs that they've developed and distributed for free. They're especially useful for service bureaus, but anyone who handles mountains of fonts will be glad to have them.

***FontConflicts.*** This DA lets you compare the fonts installed on two different systems, to see if there are any conflicts (i.e., if you'll get font substitution when you move files from one to the other). It's great if you need it.

***FontMagic.*** Use this DA to see all your installed screen fonts (in the System only, or also in loaded suitcases), on screen or printed out. Or it gives you statistics on all those fonts—styles, sizes, IDs, and whether they're FONT or NFNT IDs.

***FontWizard.*** It does a lot of the same things as FontMagic, but FontWizard gives you a bit more variety in how it displays fonts on screen, and will check to see if the font is resident in the printer.

***PSFontFinder*** will scan through a PostScript file and try to find which fonts are called for. It's not completely reliable, because different people and applications write PostScript differently, but it works well with PageMaker-generated PostScript. It's great for service bureaus, who want to see what fonts are called for in PostScript dumps.

## *Art Tools*

Without graphics, a publication is just words. While words are fine and good things, pictures add a needed spice to publications. With the growth of icon-based systems like the Macintosh, we're looking forward to a return to hieroglyphic writing, which will heal the schism that has existed between words (left-brain) and pictures (right-brain) since the decline of ancient Egyptian civilization.

We use a number of art tools to prepare graphics for use in Page-Maker. Naturally, we use major graphics applications like Aldus FreeHand and Adobe Photoshop, but we also use lots of smaller applications for everything from file conversion to touching up screen shots to creating specialized fonts. See Chapter 5, *Pictures*, for more on working with graphics in PageMaker.

**Art Browser**

If you have a lot of EPS files lying around on disk, it's easy to forget what's in them (especially if your file names aren't very descriptive). Art Browser (Figure 2-9), a DA that Adobe Systems developed and distributes for free, lets you look at those graphics. It's a pain because you have to restart the DA every time you open a new file, but at least you can see what an EPS looks like without placing it on a page.

**Figure 2-9**
Art Browser

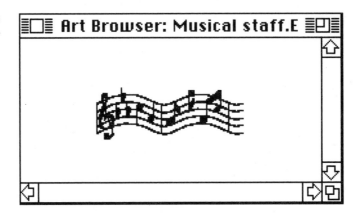

**The Art Importer**    The Art Importer, from Altsys (makers of Fontographer and FreeHand), turns EPS and PICT graphics (that don't contain bitmaps) into PostScript fonts. What's the use in that? Think about it—are there graphics that you use frequently? Corporate logos, special symbols, and so on? Graphics you have to place time after time and drag into position (or place inline) over and over again? If you make these graphics into a font, your life gets a lot easier. Just select the font, type a key, and the corporate logo appears. Creating the font is simply a matter of pasting or importing your graphics into a grid of 16 characters (you can't make fonts with more characters than that in Art Importer). Then Art Importer creates screen fonts and a downloadable PostScript typeface. The screen fonts are far from wonderful, but the PostScript typefaces print at full resolution, as you'd expect.

That's just scratching the surface of what you can do with The Art Importer. Suppose you're producing documentation for a software company (like someone we know). When keystrokes were called for in the text, you could have your writers enter "<command>" in their text files. When you import the text files into PageMaker, you can search for "<command>" and replace it with a character containing an illustration of a Command key from a font made up of EPS renderings of Macintosh keyboard keys.

The Art Importer offers one other advantage to PageMaker users.

You can't rotate graphics in PageMaker, but you can rotate type. So if you make a graphic into type, you can rotate the graphic in PageMaker (Figure 2-10).

**Figure 2-10**
Rotating a graphic
with Art Importer

*There's no way you can rotate this EPS graphic in Page-Maker…*

*…unless you turn it into a character in a font, type it in a text block…*

*…and rotate the text block.*

**Capture**

Apple provides a way to take pictures of the Macintosh screen—the standard Command-Shift-3 FKEY that's in the System. The trouble is, not everything you can display on a Macintosh screen can be captured with the stock FKEY. And when you shoot a picture of a color screen on a Mac IIcx, you get a black-and-white image, rotated 90 degrees.

Several companies have produced screen capture programs for the Macintosh, and we've found that Capture, from Mainstay, flawlessly captures everything we need from a Macintosh screen (except the cursor), and takes up very little of our precious RAM. (Exposure, from Preferred Publishers, is an amazing screen-capture/editing program that we used for most of the art in this book, but it takes up more than 200 K of RAM. Capture takes up less than 20 K.)

To use Capture, you just press Command-Shift-3 (the same key combination as the Macintosh System's screen capture FKEY), drag a selection rectangle over the part of the screen you want to capture, and Capture copies the screen image to the Clipboard. Hold down Option before you release the mouse button, and Capture writes the image to a PICT file. To make up for its inability to capture the cursor, Mainstay ships a Scrapbook file full of different cursors that you can add to Capture's screen shots.

### ▼ Tip: Getting at Cursors

If you need to use a cursor from some program in your screen shots, open the program with ResEdit and look around for the cursor resource. It's often called CRSR or curs. Copy the cursors that you find in there, and paste them into a paint program.

---

**DeskPaint**

DeskPaint is a DA paint program from Zedcor that we use constantly. It has some handy tools for working with paint-type graphics (type PNTG), and there's nothing better for touching up TIFFs (bitmaps in the Tagged Image File Format). DeskPaint only handles bilevel TIFFs, though; it doesn't yet understand gray-scale images.

### ▼ Tip: Determining and Changing Resolution with DeskPaint

When you need to know the resolution of a TIFF, open it with DeskPaint and choose the About DeskPaint menu option (if you can't open the TIFF directly because it's a gray-scale or color TIFF, place the TIFF in PageMaker, then copy it to the Clipboard and open DeskPaint. DeskPaint converts the TIFF to a bilevel TIFF, but the resolution remains the same). The screen that appears contains information on the currently open file, including its resolution (Figure 2-11). If you want to change the resolution of the image, type a new value in the Resolution text edit box, and DeskPaint changes the file to the new

**Figure 2-11**
Using DeskPaint
to determine the
resolution of a TIFF

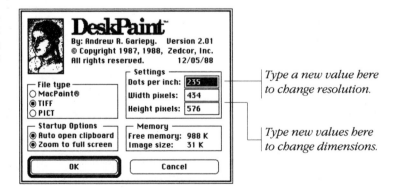

*Type a new value here to change resolution.*

*Type new values here to change dimensions.*

resolution. If you're working with a paint-type graphic, DeskPaint changes the file type to TIFF as it changes the resolution. You don't really add or remove any dots by doing this; DeskPaint just changes the size of the image.

---

### ▼ Tip: Automatically Cropping an Image in DeskPaint

To reduce the size of your TIFF images, try cropping the image in DeskPaint. Command-click with the Lasso tool to select the smallest bounding box containing the image, then double-click on the Cropping tool. DeskPaint deletes all of the white space around the object. Save the image, and you'll find that it's smaller without the white space.

---

**SmartArt**

SmartArt, from Emerald City Software, is a program for generating a variety of PostScript effects from canned PostScript art, and for creating EPS graphics. Many people see SmartArt as something like a clip art package, and it's great for that, as long as the available art and effects fill your needs (you can't modify the effects yourself by going into the PostScript code). But for us it's more like a stripped-down version of LaserTalk. We know at least one person who used SmartArt to write the PostScript part of a major application.

SmartArt sends PostScript code to your PostScript printer, and brings back and displays a screen image. You can then save the PostScript and screen image together as a displayable EPS file. For more on this, see "Using SmartArt to Create a Screen Rendition of a Straight EPS File" in Chapter 5, *Pictures*.

**Xris-Xros**

Xris-Xros, from file translation master Max Taylor's Taylored Software, converts any page you've printed to disk using the Apple LaserWriter driver into Illustrator 1.1 format EPS. Why is this great? It's a good way to take Word files, for example, into Illustrator or FreeHand, and it's the only way to get formatted PageMaker text into Illustrator.

## *PostScript Tools*

If you use PageMaker professionally, you probably also use PostScript. If you don't use PostScript, you have our admonitions—to start using PostScript. You can't tap the full power of PageMaker without it. The tools here are all for downloading PostScript to PostScript printers. Any one of them suffices, but we use them all, depending on what we want to download, and why.

**Adobe Font Downloader, LaserWriter Font Utility**

These two applications send PostScript to your PostScript printer or imagesetter over AppleTalk. You can use them to download fonts to your printer's RAM or hard drive, and to send PostScript files to your printer. They'll both give you a list of the fonts available in your printer's RAM or on its hard drive, and they'll both perform housekeeping tasks like rebooting the printer. Nothing fancy, just necessary. We prefer the LaserWriter Font Utility (Figure 2-12) when we're downloading fonts to a printer with a hard disk, but when we need to download to a printer's RAM, we use LaserStatus.

**Figure 2-12**
LaserWriter Font Utility

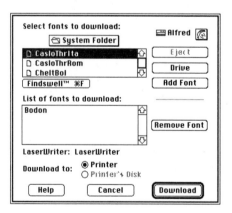

**LaserStatus**

LaserStatus, from CE Software, is a desk accessory PostScript downloading program. It's also great for seeing what your printer's doing. It monitors the printer's status at all times while it's open, and there's an Information button that queries the printer for its type and PostScript version number, available memory, and resident fonts (Figure 2-13).

**Figure 2-13**
LaserStatus and
the LaserStatus
information window

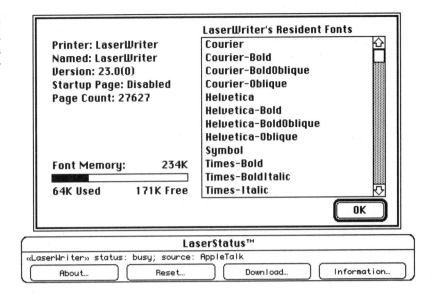

**Tip: Set 'em Up Joe**

On LaserStatus' Download menu, there's a Configure command. Choose it to enter a sequence of files to send to your printer.

You can save the sequence of files to a LaserStatus "set" file, then start the set running while you go do something fun. Or you can give the set to your imagesetting service bureau so that they don't have to think about how to run your job. They just choose to download the set, and LaserStatus sends all the specified files (Figure 2-14).

**Figure 2-14**
Downloading from
LaserStatus

*Housekeeping files
make sure the imageset-
ter is set up properly
for each job.*

*Font files*

*Postscript dumps of
PageMaker files*

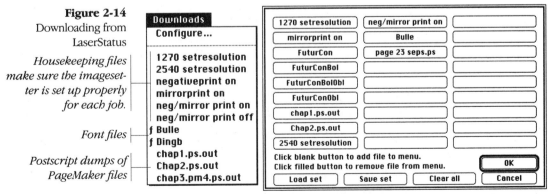

*You can create sets of files that LaserStatus will
download one after another.*

**LaserTalk**

LaserTalk from Emerald City Software is *the* indispensable application for working with PostScript files. LaserTalk turns your Macintosh into a terminal on your PostScript printer, so you can examine the inner workings of your printer's RAM as it processes the PostScript you send it. You can step through PageMaker PostScript files that won't print, check your hacks to Aldus Prep, and if you're so inclined, examine the stacks, dictionaries, and current device status. If you're serious about mucking around in PostScript, you need LaserTalk.

**SendPS**

The original PostScript downloading utility, SendPS is distributed free by Adobe via user groups, online services, and clandestine, late-night handoffs—the usual methods. SendPS isn't anything special, but it does save anything that comes back from the printer to a text file, so you can look at it later. LaserTalk it ain't, but the price is right.

## *General Utilities*

There are innumerable great tools and utilities for the Macintosh. Many of them have some relevance to PageMaker, however tangential. We've chosen to mention the ones below because we refer to them elsewhere in the book. Please don't write to complain that we failed to mention the most important Macintosh tool ever created. This section could be a whole book in itself, but then we'd be writing *Encyclopedia Macintosh* or *The Macintosh Bible,* not *Real World PageMaker 4.*

**Easy Access**

The Easy Access INIT is a part of the Apple System software. It's probably in your system folder, unless you've removed it, since the system installer script puts it there.

Invoke Easy Access by pressing Command-Shift-Clear (on the numeric keypad). When Easy Access is on, keys on the numeric keypad move the cursor and perform several functions usually done with the mouse (Figure 2-15). Note that the mouse is still active when Easy Access is on.

**Figure 2-15**
Easy Access keys

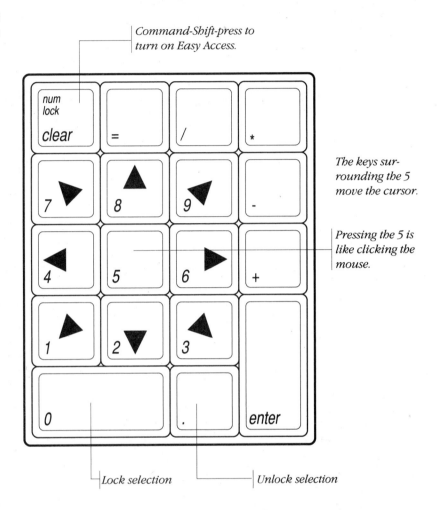

Command-Shift-press to
turn on Easy Access.

The keys sur-
rounding the 5
move the cursor.

Pressing the 5 is
like clicking the
mouse.

Lock selection        Unlock selection

Tapping one of the cursor movement keys moves the cursor one pixel; holding down the key moves the cursor continuously. The longer you hold down the cursor movement key, the faster the cursor moves. Usually, you'll want to tap the keys to move the cursor one pixel at a time, since continuous movement is hard to control.

**Neko**

Neko, from Kenji Gotoh, is probably *the* business productivity tool of the 90s. And it's free. In a small window, an animated cat chases your cursor, which can be a mouse, a fish, or a bird. There are several settings for the speed of the pursuing cat. The cat falls asleep when it catches the cursor, or scratches against the edges of the window when you move the cursor outside the window. What can we say? We like very slow cats, chasing fish (Figure 2-16).

**Figure 2-16**
Neko

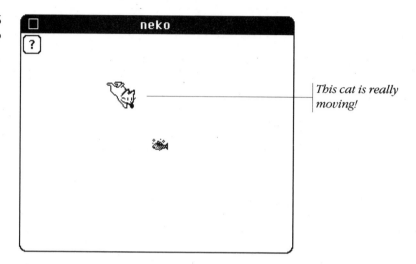

This cat is really moving!

**QuicKeys**

One of the best PageMaker-enhancers on the market is QuicKeys, from CE Software (if this book is beginning to sound like an ad for CE Software, there's good reason for it—their stuff is great). With QuicKeys, you can assign keystrokes to actions—making menu selections, entering text, and so on. You can then automate procedures you use every day by stringing sets of keystrokes together and executing them by pressing a single key. QuickKeys saved us hundreds of hours creating this book alone.

While there are other programs out there for making keyboard macros—notably Tempo II, AutoMac III (many people got this along with Word 4, and use it because they have it), and, on your Apple System disks, MacroMaker—we've found QuicKeys to be the best of the lot, particularly in the areas of creating and editing key sequences. Still, all of these are good products, and most of the tricks we describe here and throughout the book could be converted to work with any of these programs.

You can create many different kinds of QuicKeys for different purposes, as shown in Table 2-1.

**Table 2-1 Types of QuicKeys**

| QuicKey Type | What it Does |
| --- | --- |
| Text | Enter text |
| File | Launch a file |
| Menu/DA | Choose a menu item or DA |
| Alias | Make one key command act like another |
| Clicks | Record mouse motions and clicks |
| Sequences | Chain keys together |
| Buttons | Search for and click buttons in dialog boxes |
| Mousies | Move, click, and drag the mouse |
| Specials | Enter typographic open and close quotes automatically, shut down your Mac, etc. |
| Date/Time | Enter the date and/or time in a pleasingly complete variety of ways |
| FKEYs | Execute FKEYs |

Given these options, you can perform a truly mind-boggling number of actions. There are a couple of limitations, however. You can't nest Sequence QuicKeys inside other Sequence QuicKeys, and there are no conditional controls. "Do this until I click the mouse," "Do this if you find this," or "Do this *n* times" would be terrific additions to an already terrific package.

We've had to restrain ourselves in writing this section (and throughout the book, where we're always tempted to detail our sick QuicKeys). There are so many things you can do with QuicKeys that we could easily devote a chapter to it. Or more. Ole is wishing for a keyboard with another modifier key (besides Shift, Control, Command, Option). We could call it the QuicKey.

The first things that come to mind to include are the simple ones—

things you do every day, over and over again, like selecting a certain font, leading, or point size for some piece of local formatting. Suppose, for example, you always add a Zapf Dingbats character to the end of stories in a newsletter, then change the point size of the character to 6 points. Here's how to do it with QuicKeys.

1. Make a Menu/DA QuicKey that chooses Zapf Dingbats from the font h-menu. It's a lot easier with QuicKeys to choose an h-menu item than it is to go through the Type specifications dialog box. At the time this was written, QuicKeys had a hard time handling long pop-up menus in dialog boxes.

2. Make another Menu/DA QuicKey that chooses 6 from the font size h-menu.

3. Make a Text QuicKey that types the character or characters you want to use. (We like Option-7 in Zapf Dingbats for ends of stories.)

4. Create a Sequence QuicKey that executes all of these QuicKeys.

You should now have a QuicKey that changes the font to Zapf Dingbats, changes the size to 6-point, and types the character. If you're like either of us, you'll probably sit back and press the key a few times, just to see the characters enter themselves, like magic, on your screen. But wait a minute! Couldn't you add another keystroke that took you to the end of the story, then typed that string of characters? You bet.

5. Add a Literal keystroke to your sequence—Command-3 (on the numeric keypad). This takes you to the end of the story containing the text entry point. (For more on moving through text, see "Moving Through and Selecting Text" in Chapter 4, *Words*).

▼ *Tip: A Workaround That Isn't*

You'd think that you could get around QuicKeys' inability to nest Sequence QuicKeys inside other Sequence QuicKeys by creating a Sequence, creating an Alias for it, then repeatedly calling the Alias inside the other Sequence. This doesn't work. QuicKeys simply beeps as if to say, "Good idea, but not this time."

**▼ *Tip: Punch In and Out with QuicKeys***

QuicKeys is shipped with a bunch of predefined goodies, including a number of Date/Time entry keys. You can use these to keep track of how long you've been working on a PageMaker publication.

1. Create a Date/Time QuicKey that enters the date.
2. Create a Date/Time QuicKey that enters the time.
3. Create a Sequence QuicKey that presses both of the keys you just defined.
4. Open a PageMaker publication and create a text block somewhere off the page.
5. Press the Sequence QuicKey to enter the date and time.
6. Now, every time you open or close the publication, place a text insertion point at the end of the text block with the date and time in it, and press your QuicKey. QuicKeys will enter a new date and time, and you'll be able to see how much time you've spent working on the publication.

This is also handy for keeping track of when a publication was last modified. If you really want to be slick, add a QuicKey that zooms out to Fit in world view, selects the Text tool, clicks an insertion point in the text block containing your Date/Time log, and moves the cursor to the end of the text block before entering the new time and date.

**▼ *Tip: Swap QuicKey Sets with QuickAccess***

You can create as many QuicKey sets as you like, then load them into memory using a utility program called QuickAccess that is distributed with QuicKeys. You can have particular sets for particular publication files, just as you can have different sets for different programs.

**Switch-A-Roo**

If you have a color monitor and graphics board and find yourself switching back and forth between color settings (or between color and monochrome displays), you need the Switch-A-Roo FKEY. It's available from all the usual nefarious sources, with (we hope) instructions on how to install it with ResEdit.

## *Living with Your System*

Living with a system setup is sort of like living with a person. It takes a while to get used to their foibles and idiosyncrasies, and to adapt your patterns around those peculiarities. Sometimes you're furious at them, while at other times you can't imagine how you'd get by without them.

Happily, though, your Macintosh system is not like a person in most other ways. It doesn't think, talk, or make noise during movies. It never gets mad at you (though sometimes it seems to), and it doesn't respond to flattery, bribery, or cajoling humor. When it does, we'll be able to stop writing books, and let the Mac write them for us.

# Making PageMaker Mind

They say there's no such thing as a bad dog, only different dogs. You may not feel that way, but one thing is certain: everyone sets up and uses PageMaker differently. We all have our own ways of making PageMaker mind.

Your copy of PageMaker should heel, fetch, speak, and print to disk exactly as you think it should. Otherwise, the darn thing just sits around eating disk space and scaring the neighbor's kids. Training your copy of PageMaker takes time and effort, but you'll end up with a version of PageMaker that'll bring your pipe, your slippers, and, we can only hope, your newspaper.

## Rules to Live By

In this chapter we'll cover techniques that apply to working with PageMaker in general—from master pages to getting help. Some of the material covered here may seem elementary; we urge you to read it anyway. We're trying to communicate ways of thinking about the program that will help you solve your own PageMaker problems and develop your own PageMaker tips and tricks.

To begin with, there are several maxims we've developed during those brief periods when we weren't rushing to make deadlines. All of them are intended to make it so that you don't have to rush to make deadlines.

***Be lazy.*** Computers are supposed to take the drudgery out of life. If you find yourself doing the same thing over and over again, you can probably make the computer do it for you, so you can do something fun. Also, people tend to tire of doing the same thing over and over again, and make mistakes. Computers don't. Although automating processes seems time-consuming at first—it can be tough creating QuicKeys macros, for example—it's well worth doing for the time it'll save you in the future.

And if you're in a position to hire people, be smart: hire the lazy.

***Keep it simple.*** We don't mean that you should keep the design of your publication simple, but that you should keep the PageMaker implementation of that design as simple as possible. Accomplish your design goals using the smallest number of PageMaker elements possible. Large numbers of text blocks, lines, stories, and boxes slow PageMaker to a crawl. Extraneous items placed on the pasteboard and text blocks that are too wide or full of extra carriage returns are other things that can slow (or knock) you down. And besides, you don't want to have to remember all that stuff.

***Keep it organized.*** Pick a system for producing a publication and stick to it. Set up files, folders, and font suitcases in some fashion that makes sense to you and then use them consistently. If you're working in a group, make sure everyone understands the file organization, has copies of and uses identical font suitcases, and keeps their files updated. There are few experiences more painful in desktop publishing than taking the wrong version of your publication to an imagesetting service bureau, or taking the wrong versions of linked graphics files.

***Make it repeatable.*** Approach each publication with the idea that you'll be revising it sometime in the future, even if you think you won't.

If you've been lazy, kept the publication simple, and kept the publication files organized, you'll have most of the work done the next time you open the file.

**Use styles.** Paragraph styles are the key to keeping your text formats repeatable, and they make experimenting easier and faster.

**Avoid things you can't see.** This is one rule that you'll want or need to break in some cases, but in general, don't put things on your pages that you can't see. You'll trip over them every time.

**Experiment.** We know it takes time to learn a new way of doing things, like using a new keyboard shortcut. Take the time. Try out new things. You won't remember them all, but some of them will stick, and you'll have a better, faster way of doing something.

**If it doesn't work, poke at it.** It sounds dumb, but it's the most important rule. Try doing the same thing again; sometimes it'll work. If, for example, you're having trouble printing a page, try proof printing. If the page prints, you'll know something's wrong with the graphics. Just keep on poking at it until it works. And finally—we know this sounds absurd but it often works—try having someone else do the same thing.

## Getting Ready

With those rules in mind, you still need to make sure you're set up before you ever get into PageMaker. Even if you weren't a boy scout (we weren't), always be prepared.

**Is your system ready?** Is your printer set up to print? Are the fonts you want to use loaded? (If you open a publication that uses fonts you haven't loaded, you'll have to close it, load fonts, then reopen the publication— a time-consuming bother.) If your system isn't set up, go to the previous chapter, go directly to the previous chapter, do not pass Go, do not collect $200. There are few things more frustrating than reworking an entire publication because you've changed your system configuration. Do it now.

***Are the files you want to place in PageMaker really ready to place?*** You can save an enormous amount of time if your text and graphics files are in good shape before you take them into PageMaker. It's far better, for example, to have a piece of art that is exactly what you want than to place something in PageMaker and try to "fix it up" with PageMaker lines and boxes—getting the alignment right is tough.

It's also better to import a graphic that is exactly the portion of the image you want, rather than importing a graphic and cropping it. Make the changes with the graphics applications you used to create the artwork whenever possible.

Similarly, if your text files are styled and/or tagged, you won't have to style (or format) each paragraph in PageMaker. Text files should have been proofed and corrected. Even with the Story editor, it's still easier to make text changes in a word processor than in PageMaker. For more on preparing your files for PageMaker, check out Chapters 4, *Words,* and 5, *Pictures.*

***Where are your hands?*** Most of the serious PageMaker users we've seen—even the southpaws—keep the right hand on the mouse while the left hand hovers over the left end of the keyboard. You may find that another arrangement works better for you, but you should know that most of the Control-Option-Command-Shift combinations you'll want to use are found around the left end of the keyboard.

Of course, we show you how to change PageMaker's keyboard shortcuts using ResEdit or QuicKeys, so you can customize your copy of PageMaker to suit whatever personal, idiosyncratic, and sick preferences you might have (see "QuicKeys" in Chapter 2, *System,* and the tip "Modifying PageMaker's Menus with ResEdit" later in this chapter).

## Changing PageMaker's Defaults

Do you often find yourself choosing "Preferences" under the Edit menu so that you can change your unit of measurement to picas, rather than inches? Or having to change your paper size setting from

"Letter" to a custom size you often use? Setting the the line width to "Hairline"? Let's fix that.

You can change almost all of PageMaker's default settings—page size, styles, units of measurement, paragraph specs, colors, typeface, point size, etc. This is a good thing, because the defaults that Page-Maker ships with are mostly useless. With no document open, just go through and change the menus and dialog boxes to your preferred settings. Every change you make will be recorded in "PM 4 Defaults"—a file in your PageMaker folder.

For example, in the Preferences dialog box, we always change the default measurement to "Picas." Ole sets the ruler guides to "Back," so that he doesn't have to keep dragging the rulers aside to get to things that are behind them. Steve prefers them in front, since he can always Command-click to select objects that are behind the ruler guides. And get rid of those default styles (keep clicking "Remove" in the Define styles dialog box until you've eradicated them). They'll just confuse you later if you don't, because you're bound to have a different style named "Headline" that gets mixed up with the "Headline" in PageMaker's default styles list.

Changing PageMaker's defaults is one of the easiest and best ways to save yourself time. We'll explain our preferred defaults throughout the book; you'll have to decide whether your preferences are the same, or whether you want to be wrongheaded and recalcitrant.

### ▼ Tip: Modifying PageMaker 4's Menus with ResEdit

It's easy to add Command-key shortcuts to PageMaker 4, and change the existing ones,  using ResEdit (see Figure 3-1).

1. Start ResEdit and open a copy of your PM4 RSRC file (back up your original PM4 RSRC file first, and take the copy out of your PageMaker 4 folder).

2. Open the resource named MENU (you can just type "me" and ResEdit will find the resource for you).

3. Open the various menu resources until you find the one you want to change. Some will have names, but most will be easy-to-under-

stand numbers like -15667. You'll have to open each one to find out what menu is inside.

4. Once you've found the menu you want to change, select the menu item you want to change, tab to the Cmd text edit box, and type the Command key you want to assign to that menu item.

5. When you're through, choose Save from the File menu.

**Figure 3-1**
Adding a Command-key
shortcut with ResEdit

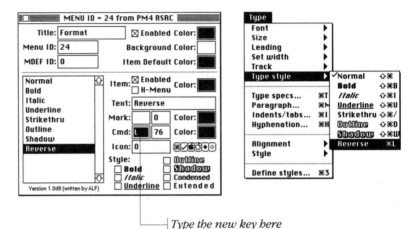

*Type the new key here*

When you restart PageMaker, the menus should show your new keys. If the key you added doesn't work, it's probably because there's some other menu item already using the same key. Alternatively, you can use one key for several things if that key becomes disabled for some reason. Ole likes to assign Command-N to "Insert pages," for instance. Think about it—if you've got a publication open, Command-N is grayed out. This key doesn't conflict with the normal operation of Command-N.

## *The Publication Window*

You've no doubt heard about Aldus marketing's oft-touted "pasteboard metaphor." It's good marketing malarkey, but it's also a good description of how PageMaker works. The Layout view is an electronic version of the good old pasteup board (Figure 3-2).

**Figure 3-2**
The publication window
in Layout view

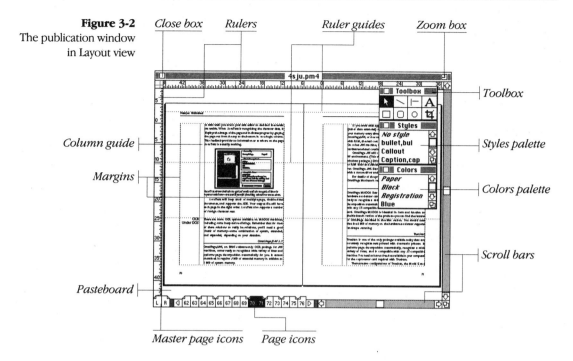

In addition to Layout view, PageMaker 4 offers a new view of your
publication—the Story view (Figure 3-3). The Story view is for text
editing, spell checking, indexing, using search and replace functions,
and other text-specific tasks.

For more information on using Story view, see "The Story Editor" in
Chapter 4, *Words*.

**Figure 3-3**
Story view

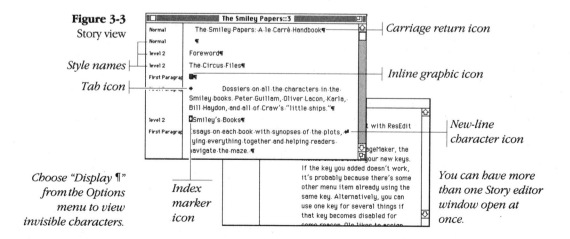

## *The Toolbox*

If the pasteboard is the palette on which you build your pages in PageMaker, the Toolbox is, well, your toolbox. It doesn't contain every tool you need (many of them are in menus and dialog boxes), but the basic tools are here for grabbing, moving, sizing, and drawing things (Figure 3-4). You want the Toolbox to be your friend. At Aldus, lines, circles, squares, and other graphics drawn in PageMaker are called LBOs (Lines, Boxes, and Ovals—pronounced "elbows").

**Figure 3-4**
PageMaker's Toolbox

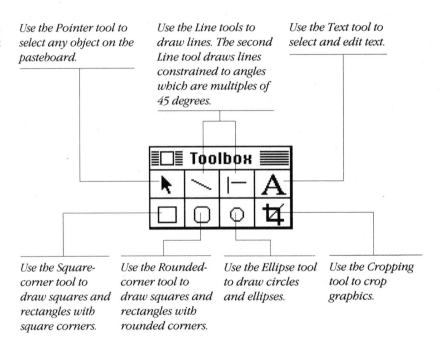

*Use the Pointer tool to select any object on the pasteboard.*

*Use the Line tools to draw lines. The second Line tool draws lines constrained to angles which are multiples of 45 degrees.*

*Use the Text tool to select and edit text.*

*Use the Square-corner tool to draw squares and rectangles with square corners.*

*Use the Rounded-corner tool to draw squares and rectangles with rounded corners.*

*Use the Ellipse tool to draw circles and ellipses.*

*Use the Cropping tool to crop graphics.*

### ▼ *Tip: Constraining Tools*

If you hold down Shift while using the Ellipse or either of the Rectangle tools, you'll draw perfect squares and circles. Hold down Shift while drawing lines with the Line tools, and you'll draw lines constrained to 45-degree angles. If you're dragging things with the Pointer tool, holding down Shift limits the movement to 90-degree angles.

▼ *Tip: Selecting Tools with Function Keys*

If you have a keyboard with function keys, you can select the tools in the Toolbox by pressing the combinations shown in Table 3-1.

**Table 3-1 Shift-key tool selection shortcuts**

| Shift+ | Selects |
|--------|---------|
| F1 | ➤ |
| F2 | ＼／ |
| F3 | ⊢⊤ |
| F4 | A |
| F5 | □ |
| F6 | ◻ |
| F7 | ○ |
| F8 | 🔳 |

▼ *Tip: Toggling the Pointer Tool*

You can also switch to the Pointer tool—no matter what tool you're currently using—by pressing Command-Spacebar. Press it again to toggle back to the tool you were using.

## *Getting from Place to Place*

The most obvious tools for getting around your publication—which you can think of either as moving your publication in the window or changing your window's view of the publication—are the scroll bars on the right and bottom of the publication window and the page icons at the lower-left.

Don't use them. It's just like driving—the tourists and the bewildered and the damned clog the obvious routes, while the cabbies and old hands scream through the back streets, reaching their destinations faster and with fewer headaches.

### ▼ Tip: Use the Grabber Hand

A good way to make adjustments in your view of the publication—particularly after you've zoomed to a point—is to use the Grabber hand. Hold down Option and drag. The cursor changes into the Grabber hand regardless of the tool you have selected, and your view of the publication moves in the direction you're dragging (Figure 3-5). Use the Grabber hand to push and pull the publication around in the publication window.

**Figure 3-5**
The Grabber hand

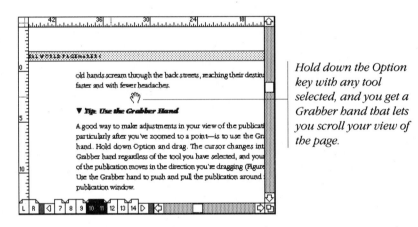

*Hold down the Option key with any tool selected, and you get a Grabber hand that lets you scroll your view of the page.*

**Zooming**

The fastest way to get from point to point on a page is by zooming (why do you think they call it zooming?). While you can use the various commands in the Page menu, the best ways to zoom combine mouse-clicks with the Command, Option, and Shift keys. You just point to the place you want to zoom to, and with the right key combination, click. See the key-click combinations in Table 3-2.

These shortcuts are generally better than pressing Command-1 and Command-2 (as shown on the Page menu) because the key-click combinations zoom in on the area you point at in the window, so they take you right where you want to go. The keyboard menu shortcuts, on the other hand, do one of three things depending on what you're doing when you invoke them.

- Take you to the center of the page (at whatever size you specify).
- Take you to the last view of the same magnification you used.
- Center any currently selected object in the window.

**Table 3-2 Key-click zoom combinations**

| *Current View* | *Key-click Combination* | *Resulting View* |
|---|---|---|
| Fit in window | Command-Option | Actual size |
| Fit in window | Command-Option-Shift | 200% |
| Actual size | Command-Option | Fit in window |
| Actual size | Command-Option-Shift | 200% |
| 200% | Command-Option-Shift | Fit in window |
| 200% | Command-Option | Actual size |

Mix and match the zooming techniques until you find combinations you like. We always use key-clicks to move to Actual size and 200% views, and Command-W to return to Fit in window view from Actual size and 200% views.

▼ *Tip: Fit in World*

A great "hidden" page view is available: "Fit in world." To see the entire pasteboard, hold down Shift and choose "Fit in window" from the Page menu. ("Fit in world" doesn't actually make sense; this should be called "Fit pasteboard in window," but we like "Fit in world" because it imparts a sense of power.)

**Turning Pages**

The quickest way to get to the next page isn't clicking on the icon for the next page. Instead, press Command-Tab. To go to the previous page, press Command-Shift-Tab. If you hit these keys several times in a row, you'll jump several pages without stopping to display each one. So even if you're moving forward ten pages, you may find it easier to hit Command-Tab ten times (or five times with a facing-pages layout).

To move to other pages, use the Go to page dialog box. Typically you'll press Command-G, type a page number, and hit Return to reach another page. If you're fast enough, the dialog box will never even appear on the screen.

### ▼ Tip: Changing to Fit in Window View as You Change Pages

You can view any page at "Fit in window"—regardless of its current page view setting—by holding down Shift as you click the page icon.

### ▼ Tip: Changing Page View for All Pages

To change the page view for every page in the document, hold down Option as you choose the page view from the Page menu.

### ▼ Tip: Viewing Your Pages One After Another

Can't remember what page you want to go to? Hold down Shift and choose "Go to page," and PageMaker will jump to the first page of the document and start displaying pages (or spreads) one after another. When it gets to the end it goes back to the first page and starts over. Click the mouse to stop at any time. This is also a great way to review a document one last time before you print it or take it to a service bureau. You might want to change the page view for all pages to "Fit in window" first (see the previous tip).

## Working with Pages

The first step in building a publication is setting up the pages—setting margins and columns, building a grid, putting running items on master pages, and moving things between pages. To begin with, define the size and orientation of the pages (42 picas wide by 57 picas tall, for instance), and the shape of the "live area" within the page. The live area is the part of the page within which the bulk of your publication will fall. Running heads and page numbers, and perhaps some special graphic elements, will lie outside the live area, but PageMaker works best if your body copy, captions, and illustrations fall inside the margins that you define in the Page setup dialog box (Figure 3-6).

**Figure 3-6**
Page setup
dialog box

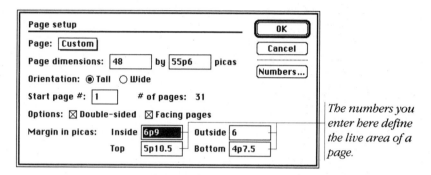

*The numbers you enter here define the live area of a page.*

You can set up multiple columns within the live area, for instance, using "Column guides" on the Options menu. When you click-place text, it automatically fills those columns. If you do not define columns using the Column guides dialog box, PageMaker defaults to one column, with column guides running down the outside of the live area. Remember: column guides and margins are different. You can move column guides with the mouse.

Complex publications may require some thought in defining the live area (what elements should and shouldn't fall inside the margins?), but for most publications it's straightforward. Body copy—the stuff that's different on every page—is inside the margins, running elements are outside.

**Working with Master Pages**

Use PageMaker's master pages for items (such as headers, footers, and page numbers) and guides (ruler guides and column guides) that repeat on most pages of your publication. There are no hard-and-fast rules for what goes on the master pages and what doesn't; the only rule is to set things up to save as much time as possible.

A new feature in PageMaker 4 is the ability to automatically wrap text around master items. This lets you customize text flow in some interesting ways. For more on using this very useful new feature, see "Wrapping Around Master Items" in Chapter 5, *Pictures.*

## Displaying Master Items

If you do not want to display the elements from the master pages on a given page or spread, uncheck "Display master items" rather than covering the elements over with no-line, white-filled boxes. This is a habit that seems to be left over from earlier versions of PageMaker. Every time we've used the "cover it up" technique, we've tripped over it when the time came to reuse the file. And every time we've tripped over it in someone else's files, we've made nasty comments about their ancestors' relations with herbivores.

If you want some items from the master pages but not others, turn off "Display master items" and copy the items you want from the master pages to the current page. (Use the Option-paste technique described in "Using Paste," later in this chapter.) If you are copying page numbers, use the page number token (Command-Option-P) rather than typing in the number of the page. You never know when you'll be adding or deleting pages before the current page.

## Adding Page Numbers

You determine the starting page number for your publication by entering it in the Start page # text edit box in the Page setup dialog box. You can return to this dialog box and change the page number at any time.

PageMaker 4 adds new page numbering features through the Page numbering dialog box, which you reach by pressing the Numbers button in the Page setup dialog box. In the Page numbering dialog box, as shown in Figure 3-7, you can specify Roman (in both upper- and lowercase), alphabetic (also in upper- and lowercase), and standard Arabic numerals. Roman page numbers revert to Arabic page numbers above IMMMM (3999), and alphabetic page numbers revert to Arabic above ZZ (52). Feel constrained? If you have a use for Roman or

**Figure 3-7**
Page numbering
dialog box

*Choose a page
numbering style.*

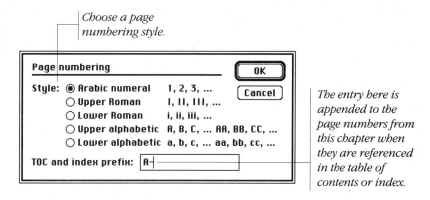

*The entry here is
appended to the
page numbers from
this chapter when
they are referenced
in the table of
contents or index.*

alphabetic page numbers above those limits, please let us know and we'll develop some kind of workaround.

If you number sections of a document separately rather than continuously (1-23, 5-18, A-33, etc.), you can enter a page number prefix in the TOC and index prefix text edit box. PageMaker inserts that prefix prior to page numbers from this pub when creating tables of contents and indices.

You enter a page number marker in a text block by pressing Command-Option-P. You can type anything you like before or after the page number marker (in this book, for example, the running heads for the left pages are entered by pressing Command-Option-P, Tab, and then typing "Real World PageMaker 4"). When you enter a page number marker on the master pages, the marker displays as "RM" if you're on the right master page, or "LM" if you're on the left master page. Otherwise, in Layout view, the marker displays the current page number. If you're in the Story view, the page number marker displays as an icon.

You can enter a page number marker on any page, anywhere on the page, and you can always override the page number on the master pages for specific pages by turning off the Display master items option on the Page menu, just as you can with all other master items.

## Adding and Deleting Pages

Adding and deleting pages is pretty straightforward. Just do it. If you're using irregular columns and facing pages, though, be prepared to have weird things happen if you add or delete an odd number of pages.

▼ *Tip: Adding Pages with a Loaded Gun*

You can add pages when you have a loaded place gun. We're always clicking the bottom windowshade handle of a text block to get a loaded text gun, then realizing that we need a new page to place the text.

---

When you delete pages, make sure that you've rolled up or pulled off the page any text blocks you don't want to lose when you delete the page. Threaded text blocks (see "Stories and Text Blocks" in Chapter 4, *Words*) on preceding and succeeding pages remain threaded to each other, but you lose the text on the deleted page.

## Selecting Objects

The standard technique for doing things with the Macintosh is to select something, then act on the selection. There are several ways to select things (text, text blocks, and graphics) with PageMaker, and the better you are at selecting things the faster you can work your will on those selections (Figure 3-8).

**Figure 3-8**
Selecting things

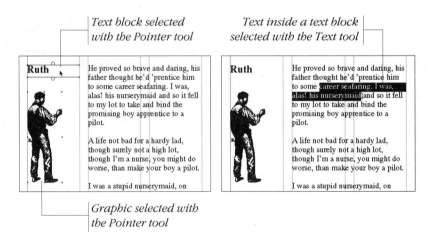

*Text block selected with the Pointer tool*

*Text inside a text block selected with the Text tool*

*Graphic selected with the Pointer tool*

You can use "Select all" (Command-A) with the Pointer tool to select all the objects, including text blocks as objects, on the current page (or facing pages). This is a great way to see "invisible" things that can trip you up, like graphics that have been set to the color Paper, reversed type, and lines that have been reversed or set to a line width of None.

Similarly, with the text cursor placed in a story, you can select all of the text in the story (including parts of the story that aren't placed yet) by pressing Command-A. This is a good way to see whether the story actually is threaded into that mysterious text block you can't figure out (Figure 3-9). There'll be more about text selection shortcuts in Chapter 4, *Words*.

**Figure 3-9**
Finding the thread

*To determine whether text blocks are threaded to other text blocks, click an insertion point in one of the text blocks and press Command-A.*

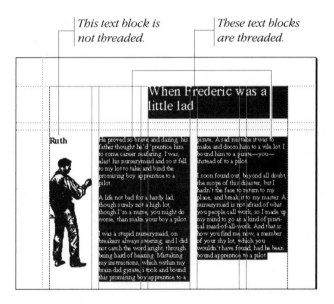

You can select several objects by holding down the Shift key while clicking on them with the Pointer tool (Figure 3-10). If you select an object you didn't want to select, just click on it again while holding down the Shift key to deselect the object.

You can also select several items by dragging a selection marquee over them with the Pointer tool (Figure 3-11). The marquee must contain the entire object, or that object won't be selected. Selecting the entire object can get tricky—text blocks, for example, can be far wider

**Figure 3-10**
Selecting a
series of objects

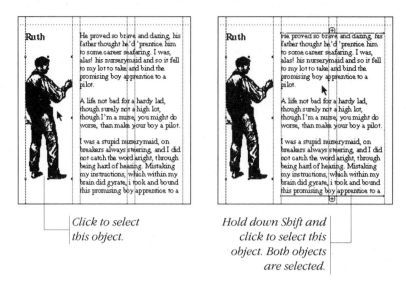

Click to select
this object.

Hold down Shift and
click to select this
object. Both objects
are selected.

**Figure 3-11**
Dragging out a
selection marquee

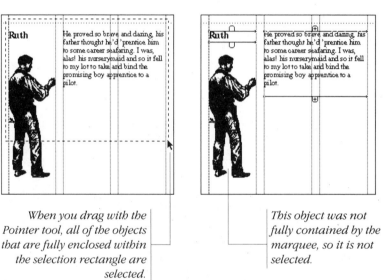

When you drag with the
Pointer tool, all of the objects
that are fully enclosed within
the selection rectangle are
selected.

This object was not
fully contained by the
marquee, so it is not
selected.

than they appear, so if you're having trouble selecting an object, press
Command-A to select everything and note the selection handles
around the problem object.

Obviously, you can use combinations of these selection techniques
to select exactly the objects you want. To select all of the objects on a
page but one, press Command-A for "Select all," then deselect the
object you don't want by holding down Shift and clicking on it.

### ▼ *Tip: Selecting the Unselectable*

You can see the items on the page but can't select them. Ever been there? Check the master pages. People sometimes accidentally compose whole pages on the master pages. We know this never happens to you, but we see it all the time, even in publications created by experienced users.

### ▼ *Tip: Selecting Through Layers*

If you have several objects on top of each other, you can select specific layers by holding down the Command key and clicking on the objects. The first click selects the object on top of the stack, the second selects the next object down, and so on. Use "Send to back" (Command-B) and "Bring to front" (Command-F) in conjunction with this technique to change the stacking order of the objects or to bring an object out of the stack (Figure 3-12).

**Figure 3-12**
Selecting
through layers

*Command-click to select
the object in front.*

*Command-click again to
select the object behind it.*

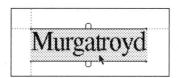 

*The text block is selected.*

*The gray box is selected.*

## *Moving Objects*

Once you've selected the objects (graphics or text blocks) that you want to act on, it's time to act. Moving is the simplest action, but PageMaker has some nifty ways of moving things that you can take advantage of if you know about them.

If you grab an item and move it quickly, PageMaker displays only a box showing the outline of the object. This is preferable if you just want to align the object to a ruler guide or to the ruler. It's fast, and you don't have the object itself cluttering up your view.

If you wait a moment before moving the item, PageMaker displays the item itself and lets you move that. This is handy if you want to align the graphic or text itself to some other graphic or text—as with dropped initial capitals that you want in perfect relationship to their surrounding text, or graphics that you want to position perfectly.

**Moving Groups of Objects**

Once you've selected a group of items, you can move them as a group. Place the Pointer tool over one of the selected items, press the mouse button, and drag the selected objects to where you want them.

The only trick to this is that you have to pick the point at which you grab the objects fairly carefully, or you may end up sizing graphics or pulling windowshade handles when what you really wanted to do was move things. We usually aim for the middle of a graphic or text block—points with few windowshade handles or selection handles nearby.

This points out another ability that you may find useful—you *can* size graphics and text blocks within a group of objects that are multi-selected. Just size the objects as you normally would, and you still have your multiple-selected group of objects (Figure 3-13).

**Figure 3-13**
Sizing selected objects

*Even though several objects are selected, you can size individual objects within the group. Try this technique for top-aligning text blocks.*

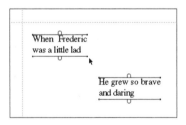

*Select two text blocks.*

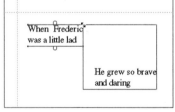

*Drag the top windowshade handle of the lower text block up as shown.*

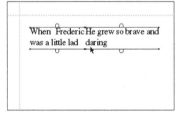

*The tops of the text blocks align.*

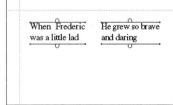

*Adjust the horizontal position of the blocks.*

**Constraining
Movement**

You can limit the movement of objects to vertical and horizontal by pressing the Shift key before you drag the objects. This comes in handy when you're aligning objects, or want a straight line to stay straight as you move one endpoint. It's also great when you're duplicating an object multiple times for placement across or down a page.

▼ *Tip: Moving Before Constraining Movement*

You can press the Shift key to constrain movement at any time while you're dragging an item. So you could move it over to a given point, then press Shift to constrain your movement to straight up and down.

▼ *Tip: Positioning Identical Objects
   Directly on Top of Each Other*

To place identical objects exactly on top of each other, position one object, then drag the other one over the top of it until both objects disappear. Even better, copy the item and use Option-paste (Command-Option-V, discussed in "Using Paste," below) to duplicate the item directly on top of itself.

What use is this? It's especially useful when you want a PageMaker-created box to have a fill of a different color from the border (a red fill and a green border, for instance). It's also great for precisely controlling how objects overprint and/or knock out when you're printing spot color overlays. See the color pages in this book for an explanation of the benefits of selectively knocking out items.

▼ *Tip: To Move an Item One Pixel at a Time*

If you have Easy Access in your system folder, and have a numeric keypad, you can use the keypad in place of your mouse for moving and selecting items. It lets you move items precisely, and in tiny increments. Press Command-Shift-Clear (on the numeric keypad) to activate Easy Access. Once you've turned it on, your keypad works as shown in "Easy

Access" in Chapter 2, *Building a PageMaker System*. Select an item, lock the selection down by pressing 0 on the numeric keypad, and press the cursor movement keys to move the locked selection. Press the period (on the numeric keypad) to unlock the selection.

Use this technique when you need to move an item one pixel at a time. At the 400% page view, you can move objects one-quarter of a point at a time. When you're through, press Command-Shift-Clear (on the numeric keypad) to turn off Easy Access.

## Rulers, Ruler Guides, and Measuring

PageMaker's rulers and ruler guides are two of the keys to using the product well. They provide real positioning accuracy and speed when you're moving objects. The rulers run along the top and left sides of the publication window.

**Rulers**

To begin with, turn the rulers on. Command-R displays (or hides) the rulers. The only time to turn these off is when you want to get an overall look at a page (though you're generally better off printing the page if that's what you want). You can adjust the increments of the vertical and horizontal rulers independently from the Preferences dialog box.

### ▼ Tip: Use Custom for Vertical Rulers

If you set the vertical ruler increment to equal your body copy leading, you can measure in lines of type, which is more than handy for many situations. For more on using custom-increment vertical rulers and leading grids, see "Leading Grids" in Chapter 4, *Words*.

As you move the Pointer tool in the publication window, notice how marks in the rulers (shadow cursors) show its position. When you drag an object, the shadow cursors try to show its left, right, top, and bottom edges—but their accuracy depends on the type of object you're dragging. With text blocks, TIFFs, and LBOs, the shadow cursors represent the object's position fairly well, but EPS graphics seem to throw them off (mainly because the screen representations of EPS graphics often have a small amount of space around them; the rulers continue to measure the size of the object by its selection handles, but the image is actually smaller than that area).

**Ruler Guides**

You can drag guides out of the rulers onto the page to function much like bluelines on grid paper in traditional pasteup. Command-J displays (or hides) the ruler guides. You can use either rulers or ruler guides or both to get things exactly where you want them. To position a ruler guide, move the cursor over one of the rulers and drag the new ruler guide onto the page. If no ruler guide appears, you've exceeded PageMaker's limit of 40 ruler guides. Drag some ruler guides off the page and try positioning the new ruler guide again.

Not only do pages snap together quickly using the rulers and ruler guides, but you can attain positioning accuracy of a quarter point. So much for the misguided idea that PageMaker doesn't provide accuracy. To get that quarter-point accuracy, though, you'll need to zoom in to the 400% view (Command-4). In 400% view, each pixel is equal to a quarter point (Figure 3-14).

**Figure 3-14**
Ruler guides at
400% view

*At 400%, each pixel on
the screen equals a
quarter point.*

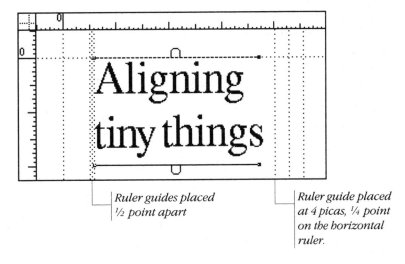

*Ruler guides placed
½ point apart*

*Ruler guide placed
at 4 picas, ¼ point
on the horizontal
ruler.*

### ▼ *Tip: Copying Master Guides*

If you've run out of ruler guides (that is, you've used more than 40 guides on a spread), select "Copy master guides" to clean up the page (assuming that you've used fewer than 40 guides on the master pages).

---

**Measurement Increments**

You change PageMaker's measurement increments via the Preferences dialog box (Figure 3-15). You can set the vertical and horizontal ruler increments independently.

**Figure 3-15**

Changing measurement increments

*These change the default measurement increment for dialog boxes, and for the vertical and horizontal rulers.*

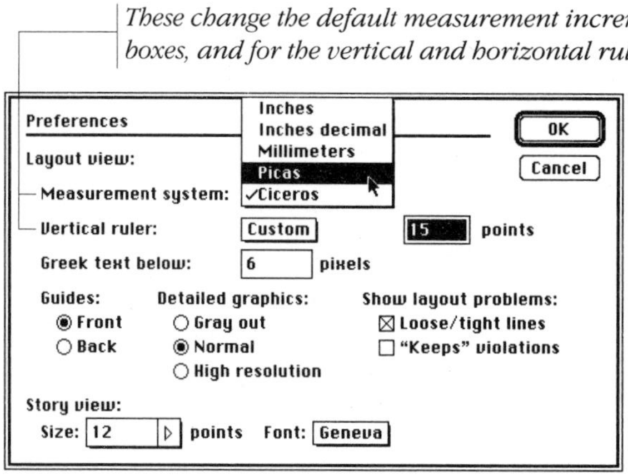

### ▼ *Tip: Graphic Design's Native Measurement System*

Use picas and points, not inches, for your measurement, because type, the backbone of your page designs, is measured in picas and points. Basing your measurement system on the type gives your page designs an underlying order that leads the reader's eye through the page, and makes your page-makeup task easier and more consistent.

---

### ▼ *Tip: To Enter Values in Inches When the Default is Set to Picas*

You can override the publication's default measurement system (which you specified in the Preferences dialog box) by typing the following characters after the value you type in PageMaker's dialog boxes (see Table 3-3).

**Table 3-3  Overriding the Default Unit of Measurement**

| *To enter the value as* | *Type (immediately after the number)* |
| --- | --- |
| inches | i |
| millimeters | m |
| picas | p |
| ciceros | c |

▼ *Tip: Typing Picas and Points*

Now that you're sold on picas and points, you should know that you can type them like this in most dialog boxes: 1p3 (that comes to 15 points: 1p3 means 1 pica + 3 points, or 12 points + 3 points = 15 points), 4p6 (that's 54 points), or 0p23 (that's 23 points).

Usually, you'll want to position the zero point at the upper-left corner of the image area (the live area inside the margins) so that you can use the vertical ruler to get everything aligned, but you'll often want to move the zero point when you want to measure from one point to another (measuring the width of a graphic, for instance, as in Figure 3-16).

**Figure 3-16**
Measuring with
the zero point

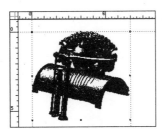

*If you set the zero point to the upper-left corner of an object, it's easy to measure the object's height and width.*

You can lock the zero point in a particular position by choosing "Zero lock" on the Options menu. An odd thing: if you choose "Page setup" from the File menu and click OK, the zero point will move to the upper-left edge of the page even if it's locked.

**Snap to Guides and Snap to Rulers**

With rulers turned on and some guides dragged out, you can align objects perfectly using "Snap to guides" and "Snap to rulers" from the Options menu. As an object gets close to a guide or ruler increment with these options turned on, the object is pulled over to align with it. Toggle the snap options on and off from the Options menu (Command-[ for ruler snap and Command-U for guides snap). You can toggle them with any tool selected. At large magnifications (200%, 400%), you can snap to individual pixels on the rulers.

### ▼ Tip: Don't Cancel that Place

We often load a place gun and then find we need to toggle snap options on or off to place the text or graphic properly. You can turn the Snap to guides and Snap to rulers options on and off even when you have a loaded place gun, using either the menu options or the keyboard shortcuts.

### ▼ Tip: An Odd Thing About Snap to Guides

When you are working with "Snap to guides" on, graphics snap directly to ruler guides on their upper-left, yet snap one pixel inside ruler guides on their lower-right. We have no idea why. The graphics print in proper position at the proper size, even if they appear to be one pixel off on the screen.

### ▼ Tip: Evenly Spaced Objects

If you want several lines or objects equally spaced over some set distance (for instance four lines dividing an 11-pica distance), you can save yourself the arithmetic (see Figure 3-17).

1. Create a "ladder" of evenly spaced lines using a draw program (or use the place-the-Scrapbook technique in Chapter 5, *Pictures,* to create and group the graphic).

2. Place the ladder on your page, and size it to fit the area you want to divide.

3. Align ruler guides with the lines in the ladder. Remove the ladder.

4. Turn on "Snap to guides" (if it's not on already), and place, paste, or draw your graphics, aligning them with the ruler guides.

**Figure 3-17**
Dividing space equally

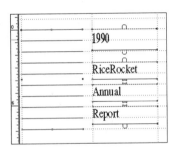

*Resize the "ladder" graphic to subdivide any area.*

*Drag ruler guides to align with the ladder rungs.*

*Align objects to the ruler guides.*

## Using Paste

Usually, there's no need to document how the Paste command works in a Macintosh program. You just press Command-V (or select Paste from the Edit menu), and whatever's on the Clipboard is pasted to the center of your screen. In PageMaker 4, though, you have a lot more control. If you just paste (Command-V), the object pastes in the center of the screen, just as it does in most apps. If you cut or copy an item and immediately paste it, it lands slightly offset from the point it was copied from.

If you hold down Option as you choose Paste, however (Command-Option-V), the object pastes into exactly the position it was cut or copied from. If the position you cut/copied from is not visible in the publication window, the contents of the Clipboard are pasted to the center of your screen, just as with a normal paste. Figure 3-18 shows how the two different pasting methods work.

**Figure 3-18**
Normal paste and
Option-paste

*Copy an object and paste normally, and it pastes into the middle or the screen (or offset slightly from the original object).*

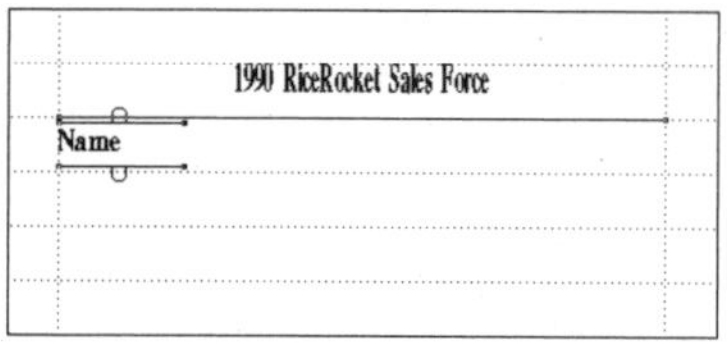

*Copy...* 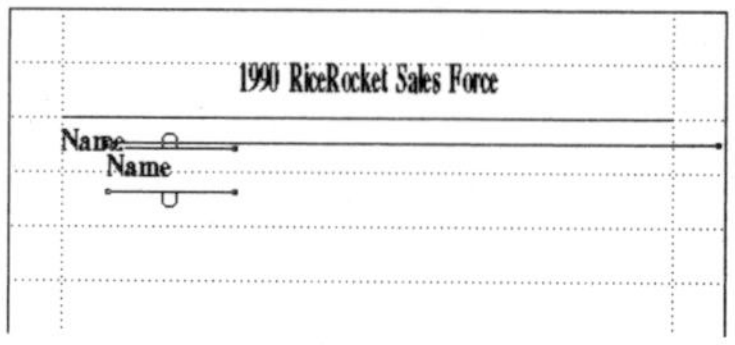                    *...and paste.*

*Copy an object and Option-paste, and it pastes directly on top of the original.*

*Copy...* 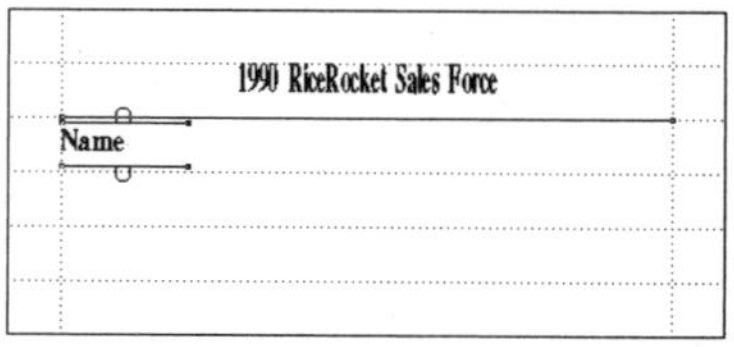                    *...and Option-paste.*

You can even turn pages and paste to the same location on a different page using this technique (even if you open a different publication). And there's more. If you copy an item, Option-paste the copy on top, drag the copy a given distance, and Option-paste again, the third copy is pasted that same distance from the second copy (see Figure 3-19).

**Figure 3-19**
Step-and-repeat
duplication with
Option-paste

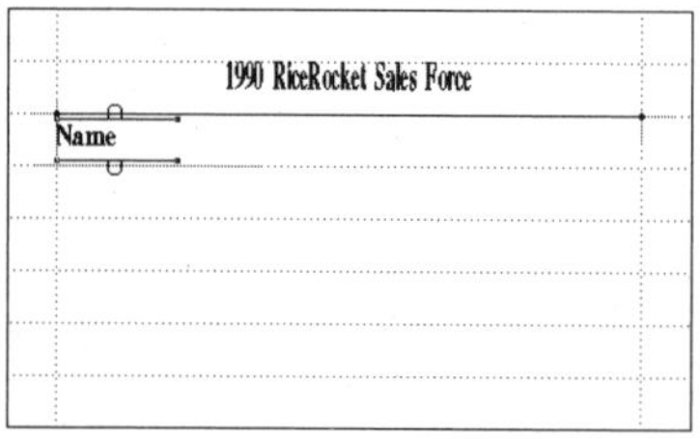

*Select an object, copy it, and Option-paste the copy directly on top.*

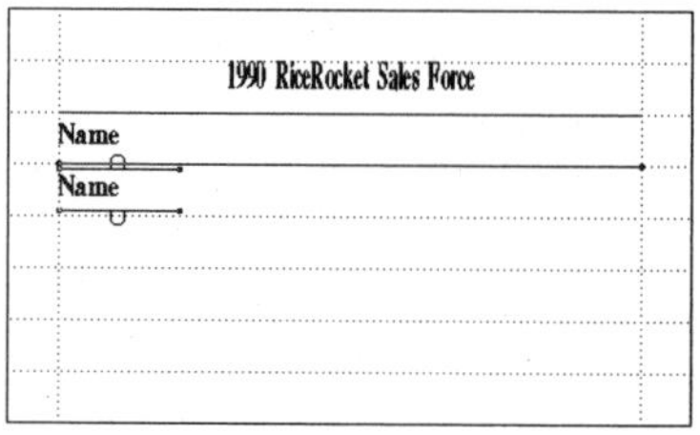

*Then move the copy.*

*Option-paste again, and a third copy is pasted the same distance from the second object as the second object is from the first.*

▼ *Tip: Copying Master Items*

When you want some master items on a page but not all, use the following technique.

1. Change to Fit in window page view.
2. Turn off "Display master items" on the Page menu.
3. Go to the master page, select and copy the items you want.
4. Go back to the page you were working on (Command-Tab is the easy way), and Option-paste the items (Command-Option-V).

The master items will land perfectly on your page. If you want most of the master items, it's generally easiest to select all the master items (Command-A), copy and Option-paste them, and delete the ones you don't need.

## *Using the Place Command*

Desktop publishing is all about bringing together material from many different sources, so PageMaker's Place command (as a pro, you'll use Command-D) is probably its most important command. You use Place to import text and graphics files into PageMaker. The Place dialog box displays only files having file types that PageMaker can import—TEXT, PICT, EPSF, TIFF, WDBN, PNTG, and so on.

If the file you want to place doesn't show up in the Place dialog box, odds are that it's a type of file that PageMaker doesn't know how to place. See the tip "When You Can't See a File You Know is There" in Chapter 5, *Pictures.*

**Place Guns**

When you choose a file from the Place dialog box, the cursor changes into a loaded place gun (they're not particularly warlike at Aldus, but that's what they call it—probably because it describes it so well). The place guns look different depending on what type of file you have loaded (Table 3-4).

**Table 3-4  Place guns**

| Icon | Place Method and File Type |
|------|---------------------------|
| | Manual flow text gun |
| | Autoflow text gun |
| | Semi-autoflow text gun |
| | PICT-type gun |
| | Paint-type gun |
| | Scrapbook gun |
| | EPS gun |
| | TIFF gun |

Once you've got a loaded place gun, you can either click to simply place the file, or drag a selection rectangle that defines the area in which the file is placed. The results vary depending on whether you're placing text or a graphic (Figure 3-20).

**Figure 3-20**
Firing place guns

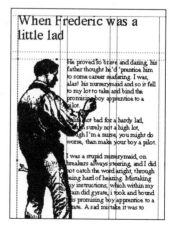

*Click-placed text fills the column.*

*Click-placed graphics place at original size.*

**Figure 3-20**
Firing place guns,
continued

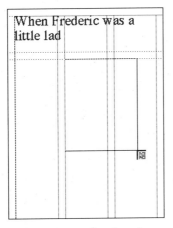

*Define an area for placed text
by dragging the place gun.*

*Placed text fills the area
you defined.*

With graphics, if you simply click (fire) the place gun, the graphic lands on the page at its original size, with the upper-left corner at the point you clicked. If you drag out a place rectangle, the graphic fills that rectangle. It ignores proper height/width proportions, though, and will probably distort the graphic. You can restore the graphic's proportions by Shift-sizing it using a corner handle.

With text, dragging a rectangle while placing is a great way to define columns for the text to occupy—especially if you have guides set up with snaps turned on.

### ▼ Tip: Placing from Right to Left and Bottom to Top

Note that you can drag the place rectangle for text or graphics in any direction. The graphics don't come in reversed or upside down, and the text doesn't come in in reverse order, as you might think. It's funny how often we get stuck thinking we have to drag from the upper-left to the lower-right, when dragging from the lower-right to the upper-left works equally well.

### ▼ Tip: Cancelling a Place

If you decide you don't want to place a file that's loaded in the place gun, you can cancel by clicking on the Pointer tool in the Toolbox (or press Command-Spacebar, or Shift-F1).

**Using Replace**

If you've selected a graphic or have a text cursor placed in a story when you choose Place, the Place dialog box offers you options for replacing the selected text or graphic. You can use graphics or text blocks as placeholders, then replace them with the material you want to use. You can build placeholders into a publication template and replace them with the final words or pictures when they're ready, or (this is where it's really useful) replace existing stories and graphics with their latest versions. For more on using Replace, see Chapters 4, *Words,* 5, *Pictures,* and 8, *Workgroup Publishing.*

## *PageMaker 4's Book Command*

Yes, it's true PageMaker 4 can handle a publication that's up to 999 pages long in a single pub file, but that doesn't mean you should create pubs that big. They get huge and unwieldy, and if the file goes south on you and you haven't backed up recently, you lose an immense amount of work. You'll find long documents to be much more manageable if you break them up into chunks—usually chapters—and build each chapter in its own publication file.

The only real problem arises when you want to print all the chapters in a row, or use PageMaker 4's new indexing and table of contents features to compile those elements from the whole book. How does PageMaker know which files are included in book, and what order they're in? That's where the new Book feature comes in. It lets you build a list of pub files in their proper order. After you choose "Book" from the File menu, the Book publication list dialog box appears (Figure 3-21).

Where's the best place to keep a book list? Should you keep the book list up to date in all of the publications in the book? We think the best place to keep the book list for a multi-publication book is in a separate publication containing just the table of contents and index for

**Figure 3-21**
Book publication
list dialog box

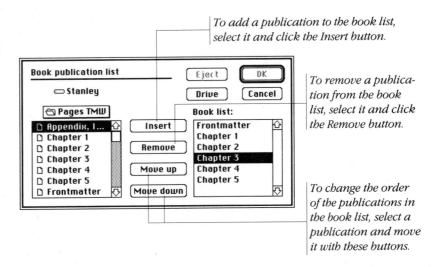

*To add a publication to the book list, select it and click the Insert button.*

*To remove a publication from the book list, select it and click the Remove button.*

*To change the order of the publications in the book list, select a publication and move it with these buttons.*

the book. That way, you don't have to worry about which file contains your book list. Even if your book list contains only one publication, you should consider creating a separate publication for the index and table of contents so that you won't have to make room for those elements in your publication.

If you need to print a draft copy of the entire book, open the master publication and choose "Print entire book" in the Print dialog box. Bear in mind, however, that there are several printing limitations associated with the Print entire book option (see "The Print Dialog Box" in Chapter 6, *Printing*).

### ▼ *Tip: No Continuous Page Numbering*

PageMaker does not update the pagination for individual publications based on their order of appearance in the book list. This is fine if you want each publication numbered independently, but if you want continuous pagination you'll have to open each publication and update the starting page number in the Page setup dialog box once you've finalized your page breaks and page count. There *should* be an option button in either the Page setup dialog box, the Page numbering dialog box, or the Book publication list dialog box to turn consecutive page numbering on or off. Maybe next time.

Note that because you can include a publication in any number of book lists, you could easily generate separate tables of contents for individual publications and groups of publications by simply creating a master publication for that section of your book. Suppose you have several chapters making up part 1 of a book, for instance, and you need an index or table of contents for just that part. Simply call up your "Part 1 book list" pub, and build the index.

If PageMaker can't find a publication in the book list when you use any of the Book-related commands (printing, table of contents, or index generation), it displays the Find pub dialog box so that you can locate the missing publication. Simply navigate through your files and folders until you find it.

## *Saving Your Work*

While PageMaker crashes infrequently these days, Macintoshes do crash (and nothing crashes like a Mac—sometimes they'll start popping and buzzing and flashing). Building and city power fluctuates or fails altogether, your Mac dies, and you start to sweat. Hours of your work might be lost.

You've heard it before and we'll say it again: save often (Command-S is all it takes). To be really safe, save under a different file name every so often so you have the old version as backup if your current version is lost somehow. Steve uses version numbers for his pub files—1.1, 1.5, 2.0, etc. That way he knows which is the latest version, and which to go back to if necessary.

PageMaker does a very good job of saving your file for you as you work on it—saving, in fact, every time you turn pages (these saves are called "mini-saves"). So in theory you'll never lose more than two pages worth of work.

### ▼ *Tip: Recovering from Crashes*

When you reopen a pub after a crash, you should find that all of the work done before the last time you turned pages has been saved. If not, or if you were working on an untitled file, you'll find a temporary version of the file stored in your system folder. The temporary files are named "PM" plus four digits—most likely your file will be named "PMF000." Open the file, save and name it, and get back to work.

PageMaker always stores a copy of the last-saved version of your file in the publication, so you can always use "Revert" on the File menu to go back to the earlier version if you've made some changes you don't want to keep. This means that you can experiment as much as you want—as long as you don't save—and still return to your starting point.

▼ *Tip: Using Save as to Compress Your File*

PageMaker files tend to grow as you work with them because PageMaker is saving the last-saved version of the file, the current mini-saved version of the file, as well as currently active information that doesn't fit in available memory.

To compress your file so it takes up less disk space, choose Save as from the File menu, then just click OK or press Return to save under the same file name. Click Yes when you're prompted "OK to replace file?" PageMaker saves the current version of the file and deletes the internal backup version, compressing the file.

## Other People's Pages

A lot of times you end up working on PageMaker pubs that other people have created. The first thing to do when you're given someone else's publication to work on is to look at each page or spread with all items selected. Select the Pointer tool and choose "Select all" from the Edit menu (Command-A).

Notice where each text block falls, and be on the lookout for reversed type or white boxes or lines. Watch for text blocks that have been rolled up but are still full of copy. Try to understand why your predecessors did what they did, based on the evidence on the pages.

We call this "PageMaker archaeology," and it's saved us enormous amounts of time.

See that you have all of the fonts used in the publication. Pull down the Font h-menu, or the Font pop-up menu in the Type specifications dialog box, and look for any fonts that are grayed out. Those fonts were used in the publication, but aren't currently present on your system. Install them, or use one of the font-juggling programs (see "Font/DA Mover, Suitcase II, and MasterJuggler" in Chapter 2, *Building a PageMaker System*, for a discussion of these handy beasts).

Bear in mind that sometimes there's just one character some-where—even a space character—formatted in some font that isn't used anywhere else. You can find it with the Story editor's Find command, even if you don't have that font installed.

## PageMaker Help

PageMaker 4 has a built-in, context-sensitive help system. To use help, press the Help key, or Command-?. The cursor turns into a question mark. Point at the item you're curious about and click (you can pull down menus to choose menu items). A screen full of information on the selected command or dialog box appears. Alternatively, you can choose "Help," from the Windows menu to go to the main listing of help topics. Or choose "About PageMaker" from the Apple menu and click the Help button.

If you're really at a loss, check out the Troubleshooting help topic. It encapsulates the first ten questions that you would be asked by an Aldus tech support rep if you called Aldus. By going through those questions, you go through a process of elimination that goes a long way toward pinpointing difficulties.

▼ *Tip: Meet Your Makers*

Hold down Shift as you select "About PageMaker," and you'll see a list of the people who created PageMaker 4.

# *Words*

Words are the backbone of PageMaker publications. Though we suppose there are people who use PageMaker for drawing pictures, we feel pretty confident in saying that words are central to most publications. If you know how type works, how PageMaker handles type, and the difference between text and type, you'll be a long way down the road toward mastering PageMaker.

## *PageMaker, Text, and Type*

PageMaker has been characterized as a good, serviceable product hampered by a lack of usable text editing or fine typesetting controls. PageMaker 4 goes a considerable distance toward correcting this perception, adding a complete word-processing environment—the Story editor—and beefed-up typographics.

The Story editor has basic word-processing tools, improves text-editing speed considerably, and adds some really slick search-and-replace functions. PageMaker 4 also adds spell-checking and index and table of contents generation to its list of publishing tools.

On the formatting side, PageMaker 4 adds the ability to specify type and leading in tenths of a point, and increases the maximum point size to 650 points. It brings word- and letter-spacing control (that pesky Spacing dialog box) down to the paragraph level (rather than being a story-level attribute), and adds type expansion and condensation. Kerning accuracy has been improved to $\frac{1}{100}$ of an em, you can now apply kerning changes to a selected range of text, and tracking has been added.

In this chapter we're going to start with the big picture—stories and text blocks—and work our way down through paragraphs and characters. Then we'll talk about using styles to automate your formatting, and finally move on to text editing—including the Story editor and text tools like indexing, searching, and replacing. In the course of the chapter, we'll cover some special situations like drop caps and fractions that lots of people have trouble with.

We've had a hard time making distinctions between type and graphics in many parts of this book. Is a piece of type placed from a draw program a graphic? It acts just like a graphic, after all—you can crop it, resize it, and apply text wrap to it (but you can't rotate it). And are paragraph rules type? You can't select them with the Pointer tool, resize them, crop them, or apply text wrap to them. Where should we draw the lines (so to speak)?

We've tried to group items functionally—by the way you act on them in PageMaker. If a piece of text acts like a graphic, we talk about it in the chapter on graphics. Of course, we've broken this rule all over the place. That's what makes life so much fun.

## Taking Measure

During the 1970s, Ole worked as a graphic designer, specifying type and sending copy to typesetting shops to have it set. Somehow it never seemed to come back quite the way he thought it should. He blamed the typesetters for misunderstanding his specifications, though he had a sneaking suspicion that something else was wrong.

One day, quite out of the blue, the manager of a typesetting shop asked Ole if he'd like to learn to set type. Ole jumped at the chance, and, for the next year, he set type for many of the best graphic designers in Seattle using a Compugraphic 7500 EditWriter.

Ole learned, to his horror, that not only had his type specifications been bad, but that very few graphic designers wrote good type specs. He found himself explaining, over and over, that leading was a vertical, rather than a horizontal, measurement.

**What's an Em?**

Understanding what units of measure to use for different situations is one key to using PageMaker effectively. We generally recommend that you use picas and points, but there are exceptions, primarily when you need to work with relative units—ems and ens—rather than absolute units. You already know what inches are, but ems and ens manage to confuse most of the people most of the time. If you've got a handle on these, feel free to skip this section.

You have to understand ems and ens if you want to use PageMaker's horizontal spacing controls and special characters. So here it is right up front. Ems and ens are *relative* units of horizontal measure—relative to the type size—unlike inches, picas, and points, which are absolute. An em is as wide as the type size—10 points wide with 10-point type, 24 points wide with 24-point type. Ens are half as wide as ems. So if you type an em space with 10-point type, you'll get a 10-point-wide space. Change the type size to 24 points, and the width of the space changes to 24 points. It doesn't matter what typeface you're using.

Relative units of measure are especially useful for specifying horizontal measurements within text, such as kerning (see "Kerning Text" later in this chapter). Since kerning is specified in fractions of an em (a relative unit), if you change the type size, the kerning changes appropriately. You'll see ems and ens used throughout this chapter (and throughout PageMaker).

## *Stories and Text Blocks*

In the legend of Theseus and the Minotaur, King Minos' daughter Ariadne gives Theseus a ball of thread to trail behind him as he explores the Labyrinth. The idea is that he can follow the trail of thread to find his way out—and, she hopes, into her arms. Remember this tale—and the idea of following a thread—when you're working with text in PageMaker.

An important concept to understand in PageMaker is that of threaded text—text that proceeds through a maze of text blocks (if you meet a guy with a bull's head, call us). Threaded text—usually one placed file—is called a story. A story may consist of one text block all by itself, or it may be made up of many threaded blocks scattered throughout a pub (Figure 4-1).

A story may even include text that hasn't been placed yet. It's still threaded with the rest of the story, but isn't on a page yet. You can tell if a text block is threaded to any other text blocks by the symbols that appear in the block's windowshade handles.

**Figure 4-1**
Text blocks, stories, and windowshade handles

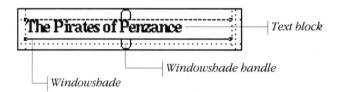

Text block

Windowshade handle

Windowshade

A single text block which is also an entire story. The blank top and bottom windowshade handle indicate there's no more text to place in this story, either preceding or following this text.

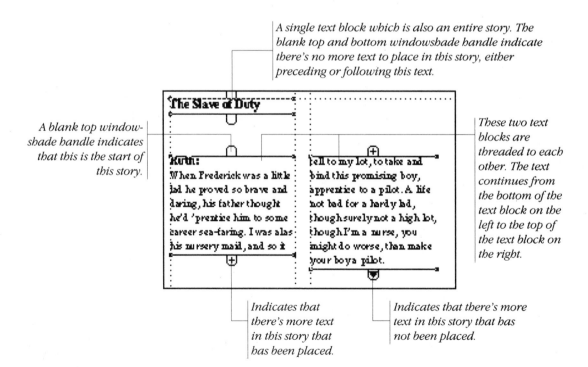

A blank top window-shade handle indicates that this is the start of this story.

These two text blocks are threaded to each other. The text continues from the bottom of the text block on the left to the top of the text block on the right.

Indicates that there's more text in this story that has been placed.

Indicates that there's more text in this story that has not been placed.

Suppose you have two threaded text blocks, with the text from the first block flowing into the next one. If you move the bottom windowshade handle of the first text block up, the text you displace flows into the second one. It's that simple. The same is true if you adjust any of the corner points of the text block. The text reflows to fill the new text block (Figure 4-2).

**Figure 4-2**
Resizing text blocks

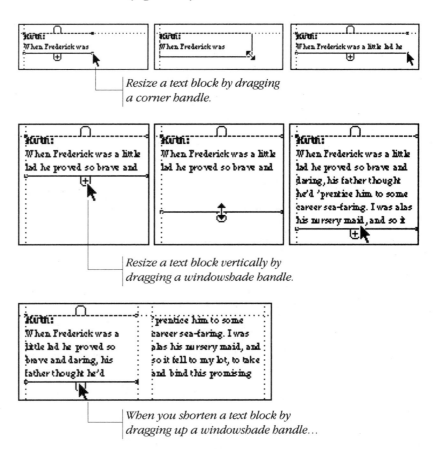

*Resize a text block by dragging a corner handle.*

*Resize a text block vertically by dragging a windowshade handle.*

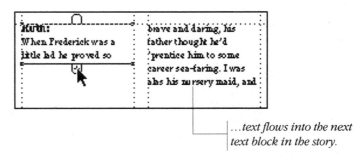

*When you shorten a text block by dragging up a windowshade handle...*

*...text flows into the next text block in the story.*

You can also interpolate another text block between two threaded blocks. Click on the bottom windowshade handle of the first block (it will have a plus sign in it) and you'll get a loaded text place gun. Click or drag out a new text block, and the new block fills with text sucked back from the second text block (Figure 4-3).

**Figure 4-3**
Adding a text block
between two text blocks

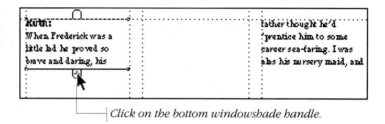

*Click on the bottom windowshade handle.*

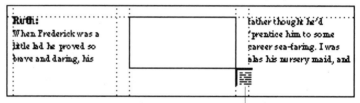

*The cursor turns into a loaded text place
gun. Drag-place a new text block.*

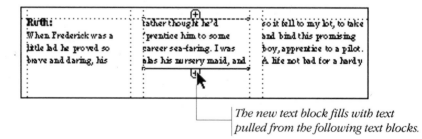

*The new text block fills with text
pulled from the following text blocks.*

### ▼ *Tip: Deleting Threaded Text Blocks*

If you delete a text block that's part of a threaded story, the thread still flows from the preceding to the succeeding text block. You just lose the text in the block you've deleted. The same is true when you delete pages that have threaded text blocks on them.

## ▼ *Tip: Moving Items from Page to Page*

If you cut items to the Clipboard, text blocks within the cut group remain threaded to each other, but lose their threads to other text blocks. If you drag the text blocks to the pasteboard, change pages, then drag them onto the new page, text blocks will retain any existing links to other text blocks in the publication.

---

You can combine unthreaded text blocks into a threaded story using any of several methods, described in the following tips.

## ▼ *Tip: Careful Method for Combining Unlinked Text Blocks*

When you have several unlinked text blocks that you want to combine into one story, and you have the time to do it right (if you're impatient or desperate, see the techniques below), use the Text tool to cut and paste the text between stories (Figure 4-4).

**Figure 4-4**
Threading stories
(safe method)

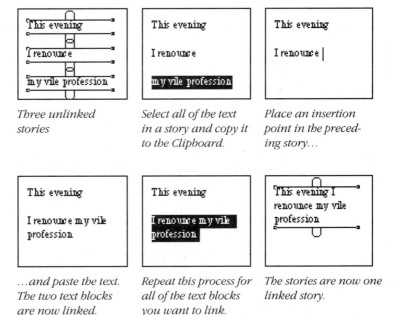

*Three unlinked stories*

*Select all of the text in a story and copy it to the Clipboard.*

*Place an insertion point in the preceding story…*

*…and paste the text. The two text blocks are now linked.*

*Repeat this process for all of the text blocks you want to link.*

*The stories are now one linked story.*

1. Place the text insertion point in one of the stories.

2. Choose "Select all" from the Edit menu, or press Command-A.

3. Copy (or cut) the text to the Clipboard.

4. Place the text insertion point in the next story at the point you want the text on the Clipboard to enter the thread of the story (generally at the start or end of the story).

5. Paste in the text from the Clipboard (Command-V).

6. Repeat steps 1 through 5 until you've threaded all the text you want.

---

▼ *Tip: Alternative Rather Dashing Method for Combining Text Blocks*

When you have several text blocks you want to combine and you want to do it the cool way, the hip way, the way they do it downtown, use a combination of the Pointer tool and the Text tool to cut and paste the type between text blocks (Figure 4-5).

**Figure 4-5**
Threading stories
(dashing method)

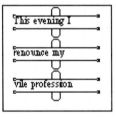

*Three unthreaded stories*

*Select a text block with the Pointer tool and copy it to the Clipboard.*

*Place an insertion point in the preceding story and paste.*

*The text blocks are now threaded together.*

*Repeat the process.*

*All three text stories are threaded together.*

1. Select a text block with the Pointer tool.

2. Choose Copy from the Edit menu, or press Command-C (or, if you're in a swashbuckling mood, choose Cut—Command-X).

3. Place the text insertion point in the next story (next, in this case, can mean either preceding or following) at the point you want the text on the Clipboard to enter the thread of the story (generally at the start or end of the story).

4. Choose Paste from the Edit menu, or press Command-V.

5. Repeat steps 1 through 4 until you've linked up all the text you want.

---

▼ *Tip: Emergency Method for Combining Unthreaded Text Blocks*

When you have several unthreaded text blocks that you want to combine into one story, and you're desperate enough to try something that has some rough spots, try this (Figure 4-6).

**Figure 4-6**
Threading stories
(insane method)

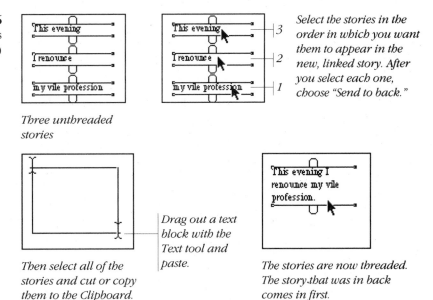

*Three unthreaded stories*

*Select the stories in the order in which you want them to appear in the new, linked story. After you select each one, choose "Send to back."*

*Then select all of the stories and cut or copy them to the Clipboard.*

*Drag out a text block with the Text tool and paste.*

*The stories are now threaded. The story that was in back comes in first.*

1. First put the text blocks in order. Select the story you want to appear last in your new story and send it to the back (Command-B). Then select the next to the last story and send it to the back. Continue this way until you've sent the story you want to appear first to the back.

2. Select the stories with the Pointer tool.

3. Copy or cut the stories to the Clipboard (Command-C or -X).

4. Select the Text tool, click or drag and insertion point, and choose Paste from the Edit menu (Command-V).

The text block that was in the back comes in first, and the text block in front comes in last.

The combined stories flow into the column you've defined for them. You will sometimes need to add or remove carriage returns where the previously uncombined stories meet. Nevertheless, this is the quickest way to join text blocks into a single, threaded story.

## Column Guides

Many people are confused about the relationship between PageMaker's column guides and text blocks. It's actually quite simple: the column guides are exactly that—guides—that make it easy to create text blocks in the sizes and shapes you want. It's important to remember that you can make the text blocks any width or height you want—regardless of the position of the column guides. Use the Column guides dialog box to set up the number of columns you want, turn on "Snap to guides," then use one of the techniques below for creating text blocks that snap to those column guides.

▼ *Tip: Using More Column Guides*
   *than You Have Columns*

If you're working with a two- or three-column design, you don't necessarily have to set up two or three columns. It's often useful to set up four columns for a design that will feature two columns of text, or six columns for a three-column design. Using more column guides than you have columns makes it easy for you to place illustrations, pullquotes, or other items at regular half- or quarter-column intervals. When you're flowing the text into a columnar grid you've created using this method, you'll have to drag-place the text. Otherwise, you'll end up flowing text into half- or quarter-columns. (See "Creating Text Blocks" later in this chapter.)

---

### ▼ Tip: Using Odd Numbers of Columns for Asymmetrical Layouts

If you are working with a page design that features two main columns of text and a narrow side (or "companion" column)—also known as "Swiss grids"—try using a five-column layout as shown in Figure 4-7.

**Figure 4-7**
Swiss grid

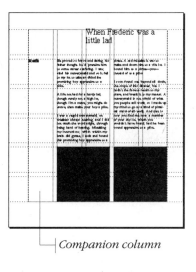
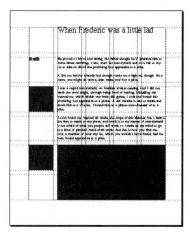

Companion column

Swiss grids are very versatile design tools.

---

### ▼ Tip: To Create Different Inside and Outside Margins on Facing Pages

Everyone tends to think of column guides for one-column layouts as automatically starting at the edges of the live area, but you can drag the column guides anywhere you want. Suppose you need a double-sided, facing-pages design, but also need an irregular inside measure.

Simple. Set the inside measure to zero, then drag the inside column guide to the measure needed for each page (Figure 4-8). Text flow, including autoflow, respects the column guides, not the margin guides, so text will autoflow into different-sized columns on each page.

**Figure 4-8**
Column guide being moved independently of margin guide

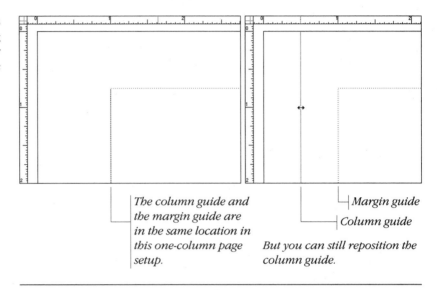

*The column guide and the margin guide are in the same location in this one-column page setup.*

*Margin guide*

*Column guide*

*But you can still reposition the column guide.*

---

▼ *Tip: Finding the Horizontal Center of a Column*

Here's a way (Figure 4-9) to find the middle of a column with an odd, difficult-to-divide measure (otherwise, you'd be able to determine the center of the column by measuring on the rulers, right?).

**Figure 4-9**
Determining the center of the column using an LBO

 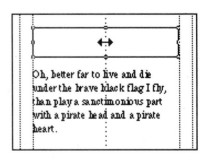

*Draw a box across the width of the column.*

*Drag out a vertical ruler guide so that it precisely bisects the center of the selection handles.*

1. Choose "Column guides" from the Options menu

2. Draw a rectangle (LBO) that is as wide as the column.

3. Place a vertical ruler guide over one of the horizontally centered selection handles. You'll need to do this at 200% or 400% view. The vertical ruler guides mark the center of each column .

---

▼ *Tip: Finding the Horizontal Center of a Column (Alternate Method)*

Here's another method for finding the center of a column.

1. Drag out a text block across the column.

2. Press Command-Shift-C for centered text. Make sure that the left, right, and first-line indents for the paragraph are set to zero. A text insertion point appears at the center of the column.

3. Though the insertion point is flashing, you should be able to drag a vertical ruler guide over from the vertical ruler so that it lines up with the insertion point. (You can slow down the blinking from the Control Panel on the Apple menu.) Since the insertion point is at the center of the column, you've just placed a vertical ruler guide at the center of the column (Figure 4-10).

**Figure 4-10**
Determining the center of the column using a text block

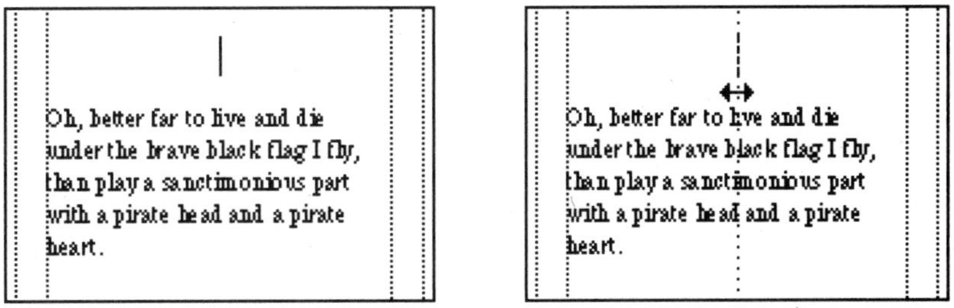

Create a text block that is the width of the column, change the paragraph's alignment to "Center" and make sure that it has no indents.

Drag out a vertical ruler guide so that it precisely aligns with the text insertion point.

**Creating Text Blocks**

People often get confused in PageMaker by the width of text blocks. They don't know why they ended up with a text block of a certain width, or what to do about it once it's there. Let's simplify things: there are four basic ways to create text blocks, with just a variation or two here and there.

***Click-creating.*** The first method of creating a text block is clicking the Text tool anywhere in the layout window, and typing. This is one of the best reasons to use PageMaker; none of the other Mac page-makeup programs make it this easy to create a text block.

- If you click within column guides and start typing, you'll get a text block as wide as those guides (unless there's another text block or a graphic with a text wrap applied inside the column, in which case you'll get a text block that's as wide as the column, minus the width of the object's intrusion into the column).

- Click on the pasteboard and type, and you'll get a text block as wide as your page margins (defined in the Page setup dialog box), with the following exception.

- Click on the pasteboard to the left of the page, and you'll get a text block that runs from where you clicked to the left edge of the page (unless that distance is greater than the width of the page margins).

Try these three techniques. Click somewhere with the Text tool, type a few characters, then select the text block with the Pointer tool to see what you've got. Figure 4-11 shows a screen shot of the PageMaker

**Figure 4-11**
Click-creating text blocks

*The text block is the width of the column guides, even if you clicked outside the page area.*

*The text block is the width from the insertion point to the edge of the page.*

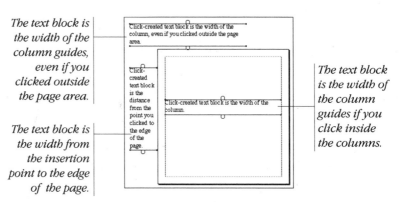

Click-created text block is the width of the column, even if you clicked outside the page area.

Click-created text block is the distance from the point you clicked to the edge of the page.

Click-created text block is the width of the column.

*The text block is the width of the column guides if you click inside the columns.*

pasteboard to use this view hold down Shift and select "Fit in window"), with several text blocks generated by clicking in various places and then typing some text.

### ▼ *Tip: Small Text Blocks*

If you want a very narrow text block, for instance to contain a single character like a drop cap, click the Text tool on the pasteboard close to the left side of the page, and type the character. Or just drag-create a narrow text block, as described below.

---

***Drag-creating.*** The second method of creating a text block is basically the same, but instead of just clicking with the Text tool, you hold down the mouse button and drag out a rectangle (Figure 4-12). You won't actually get a rectangular text block (PageMaker doesn't work with "text frames" the way other programs do), but you will get a text block as wide as you dragged. Start typing and you'll see the text wrap at the end of the line. Or type a couple of characters and then select the block with the Pointer tool to see its width.

This is actually the best method for creating small text blocks, or any text block that's not column-width—drag it out to the width you want. Ole likes to drag-create every text block, even when it's within a column and click-creating would work.

**Figure 4-12**
Drag-creating a text block

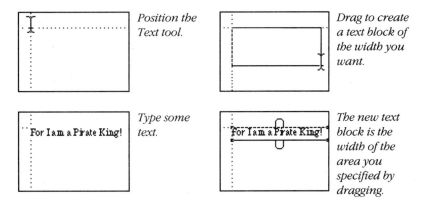

Position the Text tool.

Drag to create a text block of the width you want.

Type some text.

The new text block is the width of the area you specified by dragging.

***Place-creating.*** The third and fourth methods of creating text blocks are basically the same as the first two, but you use a loaded text gun. (You can load the text gun by placing a text file, or by clicking on the plus sign in a windowshade handle.) The only difference from the techniques we outlined above is that when you click-place text, the block flows down until it hits something that stops it (like the bottom of a column or the bottom of the pasteboard). If you drag-Place a text file, it actually fills the rectangular area you define. The column widths that result are the same as when creating text blocks from scratch.

▼ *Tip: Text Import Filters*

PageMaker comes with several text import filters—external files that it uses to place different types of text files. There are filters for Microsoft Word, WriteNow, WordPerfect, XyWrite, and Rich Text Format (RTF), among others. To see what text filters you have installed, hold down Option while selecting "About PageMaker" from the Apple menu. For more on the two most important text filters—Word and RTF—see "Our Favorite Word Tips and Tricks" later in this chapter.

**Vanishing Text Blocks**

PageMaker doesn't bother with empty text blocks. If you create a text block then don't type anything and click somewhere else, the first text block you "created" simply vanishes. This also happens if you delete all of the type inside a text block, or close up a text block completely, squeezing all the text into ensuing blocks.

This was not true in early versions, as any PageMaker veteran will tell you. Pubs from version 1.2 always ended up with dangerous phantom text blocks floating around on the page, ready to trip you up or crash the program at the slightest opportunity.

Ole once received a set of files from a very well-known, well-respected desktop publishing design and production agency. He needed to complete their work (they were months late and thousands of dollars over their budget) and take the book to press. When he opened the files, he found amazing things: Drop shadows that had been created using six boxes, rather than two; PageMaker page shots that had been saved and placed as EPS files, rather than being placed from the Scrapbook; and the rolled-up windowshades of stories that had been placed several times—increasing the size of the files by several hundred K. Many of the pages wouldn't print.

Included in the publication (with its windowshade handles rolled up) was an agency internal memo that was very critical—to the point of being very insulting—of their client. Because he understood well the particular pressures of desktop publishing projects, Ole deleted the offensive memo without bringing it to the client's attention. You cannot always count on such discretion, however, so try not to leave anything in a file calling your client/boss/whatever a "#!@&head" or "bimbo."

### ▼ Tip: Text Blocks that Don't Vanish

In the interest of completeness, we point out that there are a couple of cases where empty text blocks don't vanish.

- If all of the text is forced out of a text block by a graphic's wrap boundary.
- If text is forced out of a text block due to the Page break before or Column break before options in the Paragraph specifications dialog box.

PageMaker remembers the size and shape of these text blocks, and fills them with text if the graphic is moved or the break options are changed. This can come as quite a surprise, which is why we class autowrap as one of those things that can be invisible and trip you up.

## Replacing Text

If you have a story selected with either the Pointer tool or the Text tool when you choose Place, you can replace the entire story with the file. If you have a section of text selected, you can replace that selection with the file. If you have your cursor in the middle of a story, you can insert the file into the story at the text cursor's position. PageMaker flows the new text through the story, jumping from text block to text block.

Theoretically. The Replacing selected text and Inserting text options work quite well. But the one that everyone needs is "Replacing entire story." That option doesn't work very well. If you have a very (very!) simple publication—with one text block per page—"Replacing entire story" works as advertised. If your file is more complex, you can expect "Replacing entire story" to flow the text through about the first page or two. Plan to reflow the story for the rest of the file, even if the new file has exactly the same number of lines as the file it's replacing.

If you've clicked a text insertion point on the page or in a text block and choose a graphic file in the Place dialog box, PageMaker 4 presents you with a new option, "As inline graphic," which places the graphic file into the current story at the insertion point as an inline graphic (Figure 4-13). For more on working with inline graphics, see "Inline Graphics" in Chapter 5, *Pictures*.

**Figure 4-13**
Replace options in the
Place dialog box

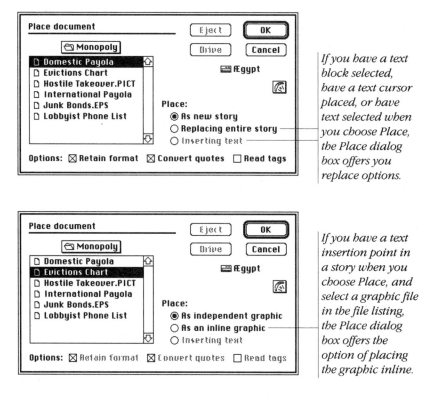

*If you have a text block selected, have a text cursor placed, or have text selected when you choose Place, the Place dialog box offers you replace options.*

*If you have a text insertion point in a story when you choose Place, and select a graphic file in the file listing, the Place dialog box offers the option of placing the graphic inline.*

**Moving and Resizing Text Blocks**

Once you've got a text block on a page, you can move it around by grabbing it with the Pointer tool and dragging. If you drag quickly, you'll see a rectangle representing the size and shape of the text block; if you drag slowly, you'll see the text inside the text block. Or you can reshape the text block, reflowing the text inside it. You can't create irregularly-shaped text blocks (we'll show you how to fake it later on), but you can create any rectangular shape you want.

To resize a text block in any direction, grab any corner handle with the Pointer tool and drag. You can constrain the motion of the corner handles to horizontal and vertical in normal Macintosh manner by holding down Shift. To resize a text block vertically, drag the top or bottom windowshade handles up or down.

▼ *Tip: Resizing with Multiple Objects Selected*

You can resize text blocks (or graphics for that matter) even when you have several other page elements selected. Just grab a corner handle or windowshade handle and resize as you normally would. This is especially useful when you're working with automatic text wraps, because you can see the wrap boundaries of the selected graphic and resize the text block at the same time.

**Rotating Text Blocks**

Using PageMaker 4, you can rotate unthreaded text blocks in 90-degree increments. The rotated type is treated as a graphic (sort of) and cannot be edited with the Text tool—though you can edit it with the Story editor (triple-click on the rotated text, or select it and press Command-E). It's not like other graphics, because you can't size it, crop it, apply a text wrap to it, or make it an inline graphic. Still, it moves like a graphic, not a text block. To get it to act like a text block again, rotate it back to horizontal (the first icon in the Text rotation dialog box), where you will once again be able to edit it.

If you've been trying to rotate a selected text block and the Text rotation command remains grayed out on the Element menu, make sure of the following.

- All of the text in the story has been placed.
- The text block is not threaded to any other text block.
- You have no more than one text block selected.
- The text block does not contain any inline graphics.
- The story is not open in the Story editor.

Rotated text printed to non-PostScript printers will be printed using rotated screen bitmaps (yuck), though the bitmaps do benefit from the smoothing presence of Adobe Type Manager, if it's installed.

▼ *Tip: The Apple Driver, Set Width, and Rotated Type*

Because the Apple PostScript driver does set-width scaling calculations after it does the character rotation, you can run into problems when you're rotating condensed or expanded type. Use the Aldus driver (for more on this, see Chapter 6, *Printing*).

If for some reason you have to use the Apple driver (like you've got to give your publication to Uncle Mort, who always uses the Apple driver), you'll probably get more consistent results by copying the rotated type to the Scrapbook, then placing the Scrapbook file and nonproportionally stretching the placed graphic (see "Placing the Scrapbook" in Chapter 5, *Pictures*).

## Inside Text Blocks

Once you've clicked an insertion point in a text block, you're ready to enter and edit text. PageMaker has lots of techniques for getting around in, selecting, and entering text, with or without the mouse.

**Moving Through and Selecting Text**

There are many different ways to move through and select text in PageMaker, besides using the mouse. It's pretty obvious that the arrow keys will move you right a character, left a character, up a line, and down a line, but by pressing Command as you press the arrow keys, you can move one paragraph at a time. Press Command-Up arrow to move to the start of the paragraph previous to the one the cursor's in, and press Command-Down arrow to move to the next paragraph.

You'd think that Command-Left arrow and Command-Right arrow would take you one word left or right, like they do in most Macintosh text editing applications. They don't. Instead, they enter fine-kern-together and fine-kern-apart increments.

If you have an extended keyboard or an add-on numeric keypad, you can use the keypad to really move around on pages (Figure 4-14). These keyboard shortcuts are very similar to Word's.

**Figure 4-14**
Using the numeric keypad to move the text cursor

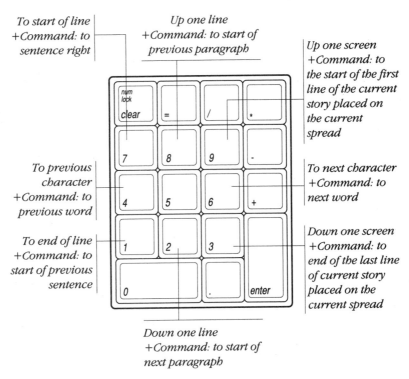

*To start of line*
*+Command: to*
*sentence right*

*Up one line*
*+Command: to start of*
*previous paragraph*

*Up one screen*
*+Command: to*
*the start of the first*
*line of the current*
*story placed on*
*the current*
*spread*

*To previous*
*character*
*+Command: to*
*previous word*

*To next character*
*+Command: to*
*next word*

*To end of line*
*+Command: to*
*start of previous*
*sentence*

*Down one screen*
*+Command: to*
*end of the last line*
*of current story*
*placed on the*
*current spread*

*Down one line*
*+Command: to start of*
*next paragraph*

*In Story view, some of the keys change your view of the text without moving the cursor:*

| | |
|---|---|
| *9* | *Up one screen without moving the insertion point* |
| *3* | *Down one screen without moving the insertion point* |
| *Command-9* | *To top of story, without moving the insertion* |
| *Command-3* | *To end of story, without moving the insertion point* |

*Pressing Shift before you press any of these keys, still does extend the selection in the direction you're moving, however.*

### ▼ *Tip: Move and Select*

Remember that you can turn any keyboard movement of the text cursor into a selection by pressing Shift as you move the cursor. Shift-right arrow, for instance, selects the character to the right.

### ▼ *Tip: Select All*

With the Text tool, click an insertion point in a text block. Then use "Select all" on the Edit menu (Command-A) to select all of the text in the story—even text that's in PageMaker's netherland and hasn't been threaded into text blocks yet.

### ▼ *Tip: Select a Paragraph or a Word*

Triple-click with the Text tool to select a paragraph. This is the fastest way to cut, copy, or delete a paragraph—triple-click and hit the killer backspace (Delete).

Double-click to select a word (including the space after the word). Note that (unlike Word) if you type over the word you've selected, you have to type a space after it so it doesn't run right into the next word.

In spite of all of these cool ways to select text, never forget that you can select text by simply clicking a text insertion point and dragging the cursor with the mouse. Sometimes it's the best way.

## Formatting Text

Moving around in text blocks and selecting text is all very well and good, but it's about time we got to the thing everyone buys PageMaker for: formatting text. We'll start with a few definitions, then get into PageMaker's leading methods, leading grids, and character formatting.

▼ *Tip: Use the Text Tool*

You cannot apply any text formatting—paragraph *or* character—by selecting a text block with the Pointer tool. You have to select the paragraph or characters with the Text tool. We know you already know this, it's just that we recently watched a person getting really frustrated trying to center a text block that was selected with the Pointer tool. To format text, use the text tool.

**Paragraphs and Characters**

One of the first things to understand about PageMaker is the difference between character and paragraph formatting. There are two completely separate menu items and dialog boxes for these two functions, but people still seem to get them confused—possibly because styles apply to paragraphs, but contain character formatting information.

Press Command-T, and the Type specifications dialog box appears (Figure 4-15).

**Figure 4-15**
Type specifications
dialog box

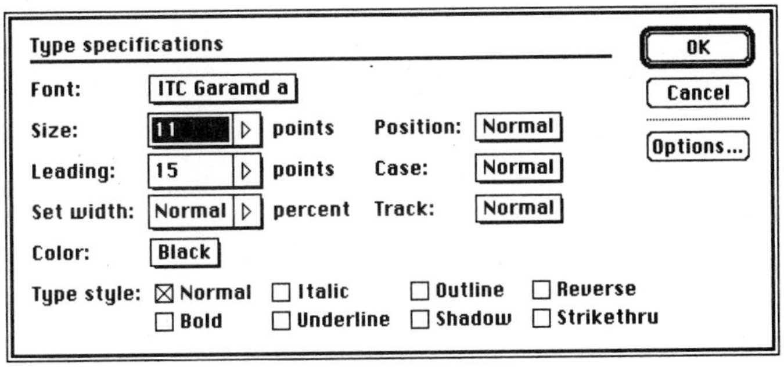

Character formatting controls the font, size, style, and all the stuff within a line of text. Paragraph formatting controls the left, right, and first-line indents, the space before and after the paragraph, automatic rules before and after—anything that affects the paragraph as a whole.

Command-M (same as Word) gives you the Paragraph specifications dialog box (Figure 4-16). A paragraph might be a single line, or even a single character—as long as it ends with a hard return (what you get when you press Return).

```
┌─────────────────────────────────────────────────────────────┐
│ Paragraph specifications                          ┌───────┐   │
│                                                   │  OK   │   │
│ Indents:                  Paragraph space:        └───────┘   │
│   Left  [9p3    ] picas     Before [0   ] picas  ┌─────────┐  │
│                                                   │ Cancel  │  │
│   First [0p11   ] picas     After  [0   ] picas  └─────────┘  │
│                                                   ┌─────────┐  │
│   Right [0      ] picas                           │ Rules...│  │
│                                                   └─────────┘  │
│ Alignment: [Justify]      Dictionary: [US English] ┌────────┐ │
│                                                    │Spacing..│ │
│ Options:                                           └────────┘ │
│   ☐ Keep lines together    ☐ Keep with next [0 ] lines        │
│   ☐ Column break before    ☐ Widow control  [0 ] lines        │
│   ☐ Page break before      ☐ Orphan control [0 ] lines        │
│   ☐ Include in table of contents                              │
└─────────────────────────────────────────────────────────────┘
```

### ▼ Tip: Selecting Paragraphs and Characters

You don't have to select all of the text in a paragraph (by drag-selecting or triple-clicking) to apply paragraph formatting to it. Just use the Text tool to click an insertion point in the paragraph, or swipe over some part of the paragraph, and you can change its indents, space before, space after, rules, justification, or any other paragraph-level control. As long as your selection is touching the paragraph, you can apply paragraph formatting to it.

You can apply character formatting to all the *characters* in a paragraph, on the other hand, by selecting them all with a quick triple-click using the Text tool.

## Vertical Spacing

In this section, we'll talk about leading—the vertical distance between the baselines of type—and setting vertical space around paragraphs.

**Leading**

There is one hazy area in the paragraph/character distinction, and unfortunately it's one of the most important specifications: leading. Leading in PageMaker can apply to any character, so two characters right next to each other might have totally different leading values. The larger value dominates, displacing the preceding and ensuing lines.

Steve thinks it's stupid that PageMaker has the leading control in the Type Specifications dialog box, because leading is a paragraph-level control. He thinks it's better the way it works in Word—with type size in the type dialog box and leading in the paragraph dialog box.

Ole disagrees with Steve. He thinks that leading is a character-level attribute, and that the leading is right where it belongs in the Type Specs dialog box. He says that you always think "10 on 12," and you should be able to spec type that way. He says all the typographers in the world agree with him, but Steve says all the typographers are wrong. Luckily (we guess), you can have it both ways—Steve's way in Word, and Ole's way in PageMaker. If there's enough demand, we'll establish a call-in hotline to debate the issue.

### ▼ *Tip: Taking Advantage of Leading Being in the Type Specs Dialog Box*

Here's one place that character-level leading can be useful. Suppose you want to use a Zapf Dingbat character as a bullet, but it's too low on the line. Just reduce the leading for that one character. To understand why this works, read the discussion of slugs and proportional leading later in this chapter.

This was actually a workaround technique for PageMaker 3. You can achieve the same effect in PageMaker 4 by superscripting the Zapf Dingbat and adjusting the superscript position. See "Fun with Type options" later in this chapter.

---

**PageMaker Leading**

If you're new to type, you need to understand leading. If you're not new to type, you still need to understand leading according to PageMaker. Traditional typographers and typesetters might have some trouble understanding PageMaker's two leading methods, Top of caps and Proportional, as neither one provides the true, baseline-to-baseline leading that they're used to. Whatever your background, unless you know how PageMaker thinks about leading, you won't really know what's going on with your type.

PageMaker uses the metaphor of the *slug*—a line of type as cast in hot metal, encompassing the space above and below the characters. To see PageMaker's slugs, select a piece of text with the Text tool (Figure 4-17). The area that turns black is the slug. Paragraph slugs show the paragraph's line slugs, plus the paragraph's Space after setting, plus any Space before setting for the following paragraph.

**Figure 4-17**
Text slugs

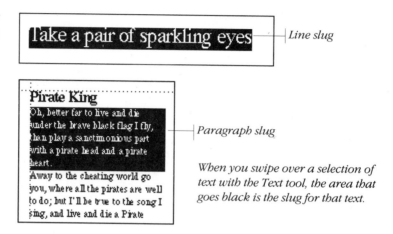

Line slug

Paragraph slug

*When you swipe over a selection of text with the Text tool, the area that goes black is the slug for that text.*

Think of a text block as a stack of slugs filling a hole.

Aldus probably chose to use slugs as the metaphor for lines of type because slugs are never far from the minds of anyone living in the Pacific Northwest. Large, 5- to 7-inch banana slugs—some with racing stripes—can be found hanging from the doorknobs of most houses on most of our rainy, cold, dark mornings. You wouldn't want to live here unless you really liked slugs. We live in Seattle because we like slugs. Steve is also partial to mildew. And yes, we're being paid by local slow-growth organizations to say these things.

## Space Before and Space After

There are two other paragraph-level controls that work very closely with leading—"Space before" and "Space after" (in the Paragraph specifications dialog box). Oddly, any added space before a paragraph appears as part of the slug of the paragraph above. This is the one area where the metaphor of the slug in PageMaker sort of breaks down.

### ▼ *Tip: Use Space Before and After Instead of Carriage Returns*

If you specify space before a paragraph, PageMaker ignores it if that paragraph lands at the top of a text block. Specify space after, and PageMaker ignores it if the paragraph lands at the bottom of a text block. This is much nicer than putting extra carriage returns between paragraphs; they're always getting in your way at one column break or another. It works especially well if you automate it with style sheets.

### ▼ *Tip: Retaining Space Before*

To retain space before a paragraph even when it falls at the top of a text block, add a paragraph rule above the paragraph and set its line width to None. To retain a Space before setting for a paragraph that has a paragraph rule above, create a spacer paragraph above it that has a "Keep with next" setting that glues it to the following paragraph.

## Leading Methods

What is this Leading method button in the Spacing attributes dialog box? Proportional? Top of caps? Which should you use?

It's simple. Use the Proportional leading method. If you use Top of caps, you won't be able to tell where the baseline of the type will fall in the slug. Even worse, PageMaker will distort the slug based on the height of the largest character in the line (Figure 4-18). If you use the Top of caps leading method, PageMaker sets the distance between the top of the slug and the baseline to the height of the tallest font ascent encountered within the line. This is not necessarily the same as the height of the tallest character in the line: a lowercase character from a large font can have a larger font ascent than an uppercase character from a smaller font. This can throw everything off. Nothing is more obvious, and looks less professional, than uneven leading within a paragraph.

And what about this "Auto" setting in the Leading pop-up menu in the Type specifications dialog box (or on the Leading h-menu)? Does

**Figure 4-18**
Top of caps versus
Proportional leading
methods

*If you use the Top of caps leading method, PageMaker distorts leading based on the height of the largest character in the line.*

*If you use the Proportional leading method, PageMaker uses the leading you specified, regardless of the characters in the line.*

*Top of Caps leading method*

*Proportional leading method*

Oh, better far to live and die under the brave black flag I fly, than play a sanctimonious part with a pirate head and a pirate heart.

Oh, better far to live and die under the brave black flag I fly, than play a sanctimonious part with a pirate head and a pirate heart.

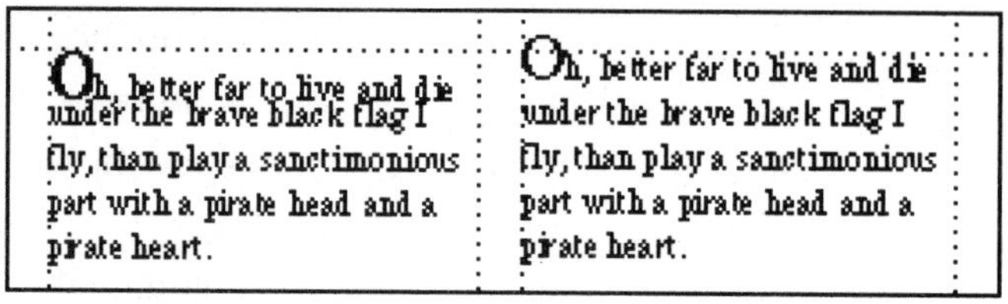

choosing "Auto" ensure good leading every time?

It's simple. Use "fixed" leading, specifying the leading you want. If you use "Auto," PageMaker will distort the slug based on the height of the largest character in the line. *Don't use Auto,* because the leading of your lines should have nothing to do with what characters or fonts they contain. Autoleading is intended to protect the innocent; Aldus doesn't want naïve users calling to complain that their type is colliding. If your type overprints on the line above, you've done something wrong (like specifying 36-point type on an 18-point lead). Fix it. You know more about what you want than PageMaker does. Furthermore, there are lots of times when you need to set 36-point type on an 18-point lead (Figure 4-19).

**Figure 4-19**
Fixed versus autoleading

*If you use autoleading, Page-Maker distorts leading based on the height of the largest point-size character in the line.*

*If you specify a fixed amount of leading, PageMaker uses the leading you specified, regardless of the characters in the line.*

Oh, better far to live and die under the brave black flag I fly, than play a sanctimonious

Oh, better far to live and die under the brave black flag I fly, than play a sanctimonious

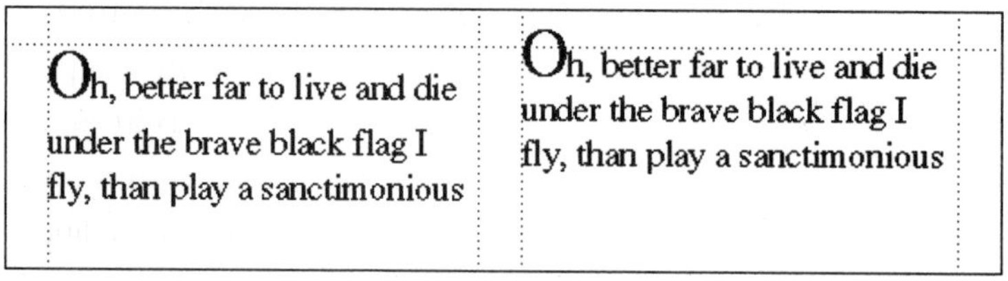

*Auto leading (10 point type with a large initial cap)*

*Fixed leading (10-point type with a 12-point lead with a large initial cap)*

Autoleading and Top of caps leading are intended for "general business users" who don't want to worry about getting the leading right. The result is type that doesn't collide, doesn't require much thought, and doesn't look professional.

We think that even if you can't consciously perceive a difference between these leading methods, you still *feel* a difference that translates into an impression of a publication's quality—or lack of quality. More significantly, as far as this book is concerned, it's easier to work with type when you know where the baseline of each line of type will fall.

If you use the Proportional leading method and fixed leading, the baseline of your copy always falls two-thirds of the way from the top of the slug (and the slug is equal to the leading setting), regardless of the height of the characters in the line (Figure 4-20). This way you at least know what's happening, which is not the case with Top of caps and autoleading. The effect with proportional, fixed leading is very similar to—but not, unfortunately, exactly the same as—baseline-to-baseline leading. You *can*, at least, always determine where the baseline will fall, which is more than we can say for "Top of caps."

**Figure 4-20**
Baseline with
proportional leading

# Doctor of Divinity

— Top of slug
— Baseline

*With proportional leading, the baseline of the type*
*falls two-thirds the way down from the top of the slug.*

Since PageMaker breaks the leading up, two-thirds above the baseline and one third below, it's easy to figure the results when you add leading. If you go from 10/12 to 10/24, for instance (adding 12 points of leading), you'll get 8 additional points at the top of the slug (above the baseline), and 4 at the bottom. Add 36 points of leading, and you get 24 above, 12 below. Therefore, the distance from the baseline of one line to the baseline of the line below is equal to ⅓ of the lead of the line above, plus ⅔ of the lead of the line below. To use a different leading for a single line in a paragraph, make sure you've selected the entire line.

**Leading Grids**

This is not a book on design, and we're not going to try and tell you how to design a newsletter, like most of the other PageMaker books do. There is one area, though, where your design interacts very closely with the way you use PageMaker—leading grids. PageMaker offers several tools that support leading grid-based design, and that let you build tight, consistent pages very quickly.

The trick here is to set up your design with all vertical measurements based on the leading of your body copy. If your leading is 13 points, you design the whole page so elements work in 13-point increments. Your captions will line up with the body copy, as will your graphics, and when you get to the bottom of the page, you'll find the baselines all nicely aligned. When you're setting up your top and bottom margins, set them so that the height of the live area is an integral multiple of your base leading, and you'll see the bottom of the slug of the last line of text land perfectly on the bottom margin—very pretty.

**Custom Rulers and Leading Grids**

One of PageMaker's best features is the ability to set custom increments for the vertical ruler. If you're using 15-point leading for your body copy, for instance, you can set the vertical ruler to 15-point increments (from the Preferences dialog box), turn on "Snap to Rulers," and everything—text blocks, graphics, captions, etc.—will line up on the 15-point grid.

At Fit in world and Fit in window page views, you'll see vertical ruler increments exactly as you specified in the Preferences dialog box. At the other page views, however, you'll see that the major increments have been divided into thirds. If that sounds familiar, it should. The baseline of type set with the Proportional leading method falls two-thirds of the way down the slug. You can align baselines perfectly using the minor tick marks on the vertical ruler. PageMaker's Proportional leading method and the Custom vertical ruler setting were made for each other—literally.

If you set up your design and your master pages with a leading grid and custom vertical rulers, you can make incredibly tight pages very quickly. And we guarantee that you'll start producing better-looking pages. Remember—when deadlines loom, consistency and accuracy make your life less—not more—difficult. If you set it up your styles and leading grid properly, pages seem to fly together of their own accord. You'll also avoid one of the hallmarks of amateur design, "leading creep" (Figure 4-21). Like mildew, once it starts, it's almost impossible to get rid of.

**Figure 4-21**
Leading creep

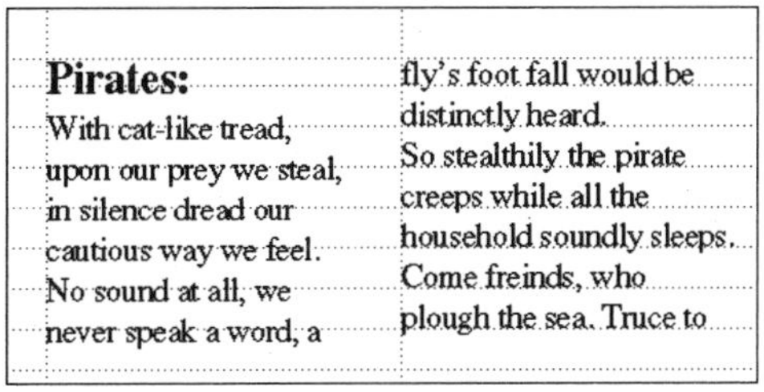

| | |
|---|---|
| **Pirates:** | fly's foot fall would be |
| With cat-like tread, | distinctly heard. |
| upon our prey we steal, | So stealthily the pirate |
| in silence dread our | creeps while all the |
| cautious way we feel. | household soundly sleeps. |
| No sound at all, we | Come freinds, who |
| never speak a word, a | plough the sea. Truce to |

*When the baselines of two adjacent columns
don't align, you've got leading creep.*

▼ *Tip: Designing for Leading Grids*

To design a publication using a leading grid, follow these steps.

1. Decide on a leading grid size—the leading for your body copy (for example, 12 points).

2. Decide how many lines you want on a page.

You can either decide on your margin measurements and choose the number of lines that's closest to the measurements you want, or you can choose a number of lines and pick the margin measurements that seem appropriate—whichever seems most natural to you.

**Dealing with
Anomalies**

Not every paragraph in your publication will have the same leading, of course. The goal is to design elements so that the space they take up equals some integral multiple of your body copy leading. Try the setup below, for instance.

Body copy    12/15
Subheads      14/15, 15 points before
Main heads   24/24, 6 points before (30 points total)

It looks tight and professional. Lines in adjacent columns line up, and the last line of a column always aligns with its neighbor. Notice that the main heads aren't specced 24/30, because that would put two points extra space below (⅓ of the six extra points), and four above. We wanted all six points above.

A leading grid has limitations, of course. If you're working with a 15-point grid, for instance, you may have to set your subheads 16 on 30 to keep things aligned, which may be more space than you want around subheads. It gets even trickier to set up styles if your subheads sometimes run two or three lines. Here are tips for handling several common situations.

### ▼ Tip: More Type than Leading

If you want subheads of a slightly larger type size than your body-copy leading, you can do it, and stay on the leading grid, without going to double leading. Try this, for instance (Figure 4-22).

Body copy:   10 on 14
Subheads:    18 on 14, 14 points before

**Figure 4-22**
Type larger than the
leading grid

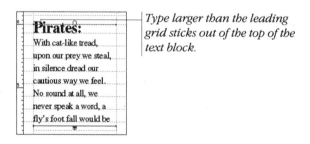

Type larger than the leading grid sticks out of the top of the text block.

The top windowshade of this text block shows how the 18-point type exceeds the 14-point leading. The line isn't there on the printed page, though, so it's much less obvious to the eye. Notice also how PageMaker ignores the Space before value when the paragraph is at the top of the column. If you want to maintain a certain amount of space before the paragraph even if the paragraph falls at the top of a text block, see the tip "Retaining Space Before" earlier in this chapter.

With this technique you'll have a top-of-page subhead every so often that hangs a point or two above the live area, but we think that looks better (it's less noticeable) than most of your pages running ragged bottom because your subheads have knocked you off the leading grid. Many, subheads will only be a point or two larger than the body copy.

---

This last tip is a good example of how you can break design rules and get away with it—how you have to sometimes. Not every line on the page has to land on the 15-point grid. Pullquotes, for instance, often work better if they're off the leading grid, because they stand out better from the surrounding text. The idea, though, is to have everything line up, especially at the bottom, without having to jimmy it around.

### ▼ *Tip: Multiple Styles for Multiple-line Heads*

If your subheads sometimes run one line, sometimes two, sometimes three, a single style doesn't cut it if you want to stay on the leading grid. Set up multiple styles with different space before, space after, and leading values. You'll need a style for the one-line subhead, two for the two-liner, and three for the three-liner—six total. You might also need to correct for those situations where the subhead's at the top of the column and there's no space before.

This is a mind bender to figure out sometimes, but it's just a matter of adding and subtracting until it looks right and the numbers add up. Then build the styles and lock them up someplace. Note that you could also solve this problem using the Align to grid option in the Paragraph rule options dialog box (discussed in "Understanding Align to Grid" later in this chapter).

---

### ▼ *Tip: Bullet List Leading*

With bulleted and numbered lists, you often want half a line or so of extra leading between the items in the list. You can spec a half line space after for each bullet (7 points with 14-point leading), but that only works when you have an even number of bullet items. With an odd number, you'll end up half a line off your grid. You also have to consider space before and after the first and last bullet items—you'll usually want it set off a bit from the surrounding copy. And don't forget the list heading, if you use one.

The following table details some sample styles that handle bullets with 14-point leading.

| | *Leading* | *Space Before* | *Space After* |
|---|---|---|---|
| **List with odd number of bullets** | | | |
| First bullet | 14 | 7 | 7 |
| Normal bullets | 14 | 0 | 7 |
| Last bullet | 14 | 0 | 7 |
| **List with even number of bullets** | | | |
| First bullet | 14 | 10.5 | 7 |
| Normal Bullets | 14 | 0 | 7 |
| Last bullet | 14 | 0 | 10.5 |

This setup means you have to count the items in the list and format accordingly, and it also means you're a little inconsistent in the space before and after bullet lists. But it keeps you on the leading grid, and people probably won't notice the 3.5-point difference between pages. As they say in the auto body business, you can't see both sides at once.

Note that you could also apply the Align to grid option in the Paragraph rule options dialog box to the last paragraph to accomplish the same effect (see below)—though you can end up with different amounts of space above and below the list.

## Understanding Align to Grid

The methods above work very well, but there are a couple of other techniques for automating your design and layout work. To begin with, PageMaker 4 adds a very powerful Align to grid feature for working with leading grids. Because it's a late-breaking feature (this happens sometimes in software development), it's hidden away in the Paragraph rule options dialog box (Figure 4-23; it's about a mile deep in dialog boxes). Even though it's hidden down there, you can use "Align to grid" even if the paragraph has no paragraph rules.

**Figure 4-23**
Rule options dialog box

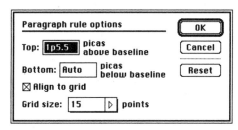

*The Align to grid option works even if paragraph rules are turned off. It should be called "Align top of next paragraph to grid."*

The other tricky thing about the Align to grid option is its name, which doesn't really describe its function. Think of it as "Align top of next paragraph to grid." It's a better description of how the option works (Figure 4-24).

**Figure 4-24**
Align to grid option

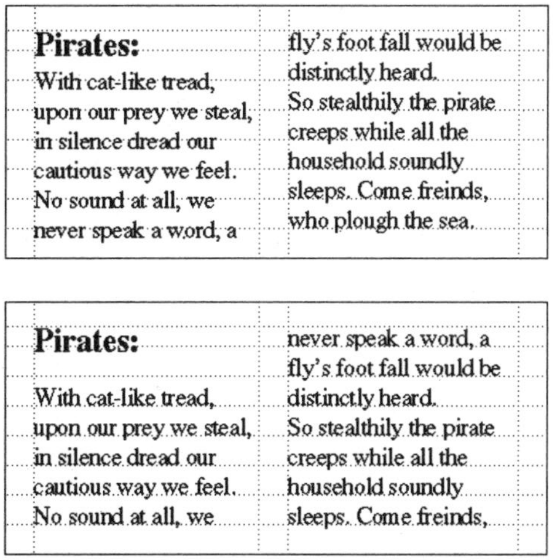

Pirates:
With cat-like tread,
upon our prey we steal,
in silence dread our
cautious way we feel.
No sound at all, we
never speak a word, a

fly's foot fall would be
distinctly heard.
So stealthily the pirate
creeps while all the
household soundly
sleeps. Come freinds,
who plough the sea.

*Without "Align to grid," baselines of adjacent columns don't align because of the heading at the start of the first text block.*

Pirates:
With cat-like tread,
upon our prey we steal,
in silence dread our
cautious way we feel.
No sound at all, we

never speak a word, a
fly's foot fall would be
distinctly heard.
So stealthily the pirate
creeps while all the
household soundly
sleeps. Come freinds,

*With "Align to grid" turned on, PageMaker adds space after the heading to make the following paragraph fall on the grid.*

When the Align to grid option is turned on for a paragraph, Page-Maker calculates where the top of the next paragraph falls relative to a leading grid measured down from the top of the current text block. PageMaker includes any Space after setting for the current paragraph in this calculation, and considers the top of the next paragraph to start at the top of that paragraph's Space before setting (if one is present). It's very easy for a Space before setting to throw a paragraph—and possibly succeeding paragraphs—off the leading grid, so be careful when you're setting paragraph space before/after attributes and using "Align to grid" in the same text block. Figure 4-25 illustrates the effect of paragraph spacing on the Align to grid option.

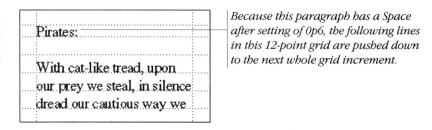

*Because this paragraph has a Space after setting of 0p6, the following lines in this 12-point grid are pushed down to the next whole grid increment.*

In practice, "Align to grid" does not align the baseline of every text element to the leading grid—only those with the same leading as that entered for "Grid size." PageMaker handles all other elements—headings and inline graphics—as they're specified, then adds space below to make the next occurrence of the specified leading fall on the grid (Figure 4-26).

**Figure 4-26**
Adding space with the Align to grid option

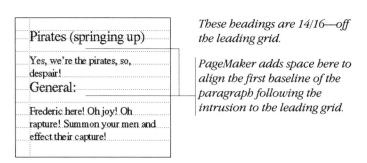

*These headings are 14/16—off the leading grid.*

*PageMaker adds space here to align the first baseline of the paragraph following the intrusion to the leading grid.*

Usually, in designing for a leading grid, it's acceptable to specify a leading for multiple-line headings that is off the leading grid. It's very limiting to constrain your choices of point sizes and leadings for headings to those that are completely compatible with the body text. With "Align to grid," it's easy to keep the body text following such a heading on the grid. (You can also create different heading styles with Space before and Space after settings that compensate for the different height of the headings. See the tip "Multiple Styles for Multiple-line Heads" earlier in this chapter.)

**Custom Vertical Rulers**

To help you align objects on the leading grid, set the vertical ruler increments to the leading value of your body copy (15 points, for instance). The Custom setting of the vertical ruler works perfectly with the Proportional leading method, because it displays the value you enter divided into thirds (Figure 4-27). Then set the ruler origin (the 0, 0 point) to the top of the text area, turn "Snap to rulers" on, and your moves will snap to the leading grid (Figure 4-28).

**Figure 4-27**
Custom vertical rulers with the Proportional leading method

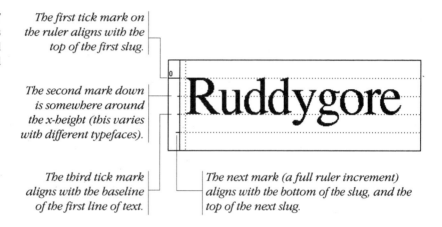

*The first tick mark on the ruler aligns with the top of the first slug.*

*The second mark down is somewhere around the x-height (this varies with different typefaces).*

*The third tick mark aligns with the baseline of the first line of text.*

*The next mark (a full ruler increment) aligns with the bottom of the slug, and the top of the next slug.*

**Figure 4-28**
Aligning text blocks using custom rulers and the Snap to rulers option

*Combined with "Snap to rulers," the custom vertical ruler makes it easy to get things lined up—try to design your pieces so you snap everything to a grid, to ruler guides, or to both.*

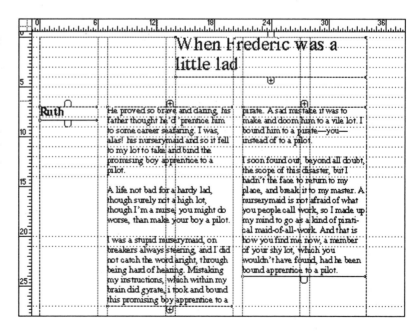

### ▼ *Tip: Placing Illustrations*

Positioning illustrations consistently between text blocks can be tricky. When you're measuring the distance from a text block down to a graphic, you should generally measure from the baseline down. When measuring from a graphic down to a text block, measure down to the top of the slug. In any case, be consistent. If you're using a leading grid, place and size the graphic so that it fits on the grid (Figure 4-29).

**Figure 4-29**
Aligning graphics to a leading grid

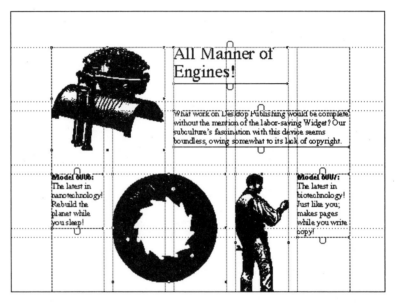

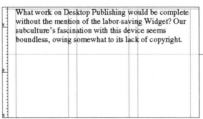

*To place a graphic on the leading grid below a block of copy, drag a horizontal ruler guide down to the next even grid increment…*

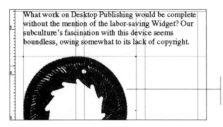

*…and place the graphic so that it snaps to the horizontal ruler guide.*

## *Horizontal Spacing and Alignment*

So much for all the details of vertical spacing. PageMaker also offers a lot of control over horizontal spacing—type alignment; left, right, and first-line paragraph indents; tabs; and letter and word spacing.

### ▼ *Tip: Keyboard Shortcuts for Type Alignment*

Don't use the Alignment h-menu to set horizontal type alignment. It's too much work. Use the keyboard shortcuts instead. Select one or more paragraphs and press one of key combinations shown in Table 4-1 for fast alignment changes.

**Table 4-1  Keyboard shortcuts for paragraph alignment**

| *Alignment* | *Keyboard Shortcut* |
| --- | --- |
| Align right | Command-Shift-R |
| Align left | Command-Shift-L |
| Center | Command-Shift-C |
| Justify | Command-Shift-J |
| Force justify | Command-Shift-F |

PageMaker 4's new Force justify option forces the last line of a paragraph to be fully justified to the width of the text block. This is handy when you want a headline spread out across a given distance (Figure 4-30), or when you want to force a line break in the middle of a justified paragraph. Just press return, creating two paragraphs, and change the alignment of the first paragraph to "Force justify."

**Figure 4-30**
Force justifying paragraphs

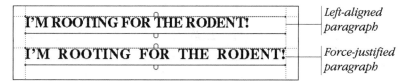

I'M ROOTING FOR THE RODENT! — Left-aligned paragraph

I'M ROOTING FOR THE RODENT! — Force-justified paragraph

### ▼ *Tip: Use the New-line Character*

There's an even better way to force a line break in justified copy. Use PageMaker 4's "new-line" character—Shift-Return. This forces a line break, but doesn't force the line flush left in fully justified paragraph, or create a new paragraph (Figure 4-31). The PageMaker manual refers to

**Figure 4-31**
Using the new-line character to break a line in a justified paragraph

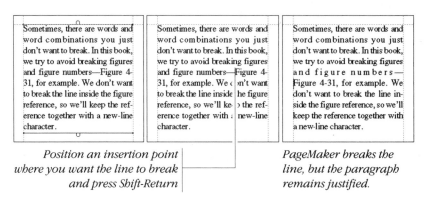

> Sometimes, there are words and word combinations you just don't want to break. In this book, we try to avoid breaking figures and figure numbers—Figure 4-31, for example. We don't want to break the line inside the figure reference, so we'll keep the reference together with a new-line character.

> Sometimes, there are words and word combinations you just don't want to break. In this book, we try to avoid breaking figures and figure numbers—Figure 4-31, for example. We don't want to break the line inside the figure reference, so we'll keep the reference together with a new-line character.

> Sometimes, there are words and word combinations you just don't want to break. In this book, we try to avoid breaking figures and figure numbers—Figure 4-31, for example. We don't want to break the line inside the figure reference, so we'll keep the reference together with a new-line character.

*Position an insertion point where you want the line to break and press Shift-Return*

*PageMaker breaks the line, but the paragraph remains justified.*

the new-line character as a soft return. This is somewhat misleading, since traditionally a soft return is entered by a word processor (like WordStar) to wrap lines within a paragraph.

## Working with Tabs

When you set tabs in PageMaker, you're setting them for the paragraph or paragraphs you have selected. You can't have different tab settings for each line in a paragraph. Tabs are measured from the left edge of the text block, and every tab you set must be at a particular point on the tab ruler—there's no way to set, say, a tab at the right edge of a text block no matter where that boundary falls on the tab ruler. We've seen lots of people expect tabs to move because the right or left indent—or the width of the text block—changed. They don't. They're determined absolutely by the positions you specify on the ruler, no matter how wide a column you're working with.

When you choose "Indents/tabs" from the Type menu (Command-I), the Indents/tabs dialog box appears, aligning its zero point with the left edge of the currently selected text block, if possible (Figure 4-32). This makes setting tabs much easier than in previous versions of PageMaker.

**Tab Selection**

In PageMaker 3, you could select a particular tab and move it around on the ruler, but, if you wanted to make it into a different type of tab, or change the leader, you were out of luck. In PageMaker 4, you can select a tab that has already been set, then change the tab to any other type of tab by clicking on the tab icon you want. You can also change the tab's dot leader by selecting the tab and making changes in the Leader text edit box, or change its position using the Position pop-up menu..

***Position.*** Type the numeric position at which you want to add, move, delete, or repeat the tab. After you enter a number in the Position text edit box, choose one of the actions on the pop-up menu. If you don't choose an action, nothing will happen.

***Add tab.*** Add a tab of the selected type at the position on the ruler specified in the Position text edit box.

***Delete tab.*** Delete the tab at the position specified in the Position text edit box.

***Move tab.*** Move the tab to the position specified in the Position text edit box.

***Repeat tab.*** Repeats the tab across the ruler in increments specified by the distance from the selected tab to the previous tab. If the selected tab is the first tab on the tab ruler, "Repeat tab" repeats the tab across the ruler in the increments shown in the Position text edit box.

▼ *Tip: Aligning Tabs Quickly*

To set up a table quickly using PageMaker's normal tabbing (as opposed to the Table Editor), first lay down some vertical ruler guides on your page. This lets you see the basic column width. You might try some type to see how it fits in the column widths at different sizes (Figure 4-32).

Once you've got the column widths set up with ruler guides, in Actual size view, call up the Indents/Tabs dialog box. Finally, set your tabs according to the ruler guides (remember that you first have to select the paragraphs to be affected). There's still trial and error involved, but this method lets you get close pretty quickly.

**Figure 4-32**
Aligning tabs
with ruler guides

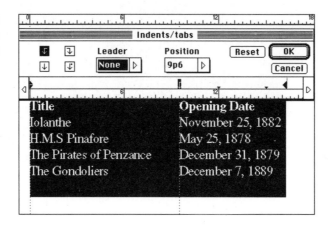

▼ *Tip: Use the New-line Character Within Tabular Matter*

Use the new line character when you want to break a line but do not want to start a new paragraph. Often, in complex tables, you need to add a second line to a table item, but don't want to start a new paragraph because you don't want a new first-line indent, space before, space after, or paragraph rule (Figure 4-33).

**Figure 4-33**
Using the new-line
character for tables

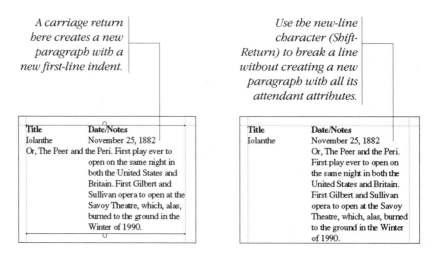

The tabs on the new line are the same as on its predecessor, because they're part of the same paragraph. If you want different tab stops on two lines, make them separate paragraphs.

---

### ▼ Tip: Use a Tab for Hanging Indents

If you want the first line of a paragraph to hang out to the left, as in a bulleted or numbered list (Ole thinks you should *always* hang bullets), make sure to use a tab after the bullet or number. Then use "Paragraph Specifications" (Command-M) or the Indents/tabs ruler (Command-I) to hang the first line. Make sure to put a left tab stop at the same position as the left indent (Figure 4-34 on the next page).

Too often, we've seen people create hanging indents using carriage returns and tabs. They'll type the first line, press a carriage return, press Tab, type the second line, press a carriage return, press Tab, and so on. Even worse, they'll keep pressing Tab until the line wraps. You don't need to work that hard to create hanging indents. If you're setting up a style for numbered lists, make sure to leave enough room in your hanging indents for those lists that go beyond 9. Adding that extra digit can blow everything. Remember, though, that no one reads numbered lists that have more than nine items.

In any case, *use tabs, not spaces* to create the indent, or things won't line up right. With tabs you can specify exact positions. Spaces are much more ephemeral.

---

### ▼ Tip: Decimal/Right Aligning Numbered Lists

When you're creating numbered lists, you sometimes want the decimals in the numbered lists to align, or the numbers to right-align. In either case, as you enter the numbered list, press Tab, then type the number and (if you're using one) the period, press Tab again, then type the body of the list item (Figure 4-35). If you're formatting copy someone else has keyed in, be lazy: remember that you can search for carriage returns and tabs in the Story editor.

**Figure 4-34**
Creating a hanging
indent

*Tab character*

*Select the paragraph
you want to format.*

Here's the right way to create a
hanging indent. It's far simpler and
easier to revise.

*First-line indent marker*

*Left indent marker*

*Drag the left indent
marker to the right, then
drag the first-line indent
marker to the left.*

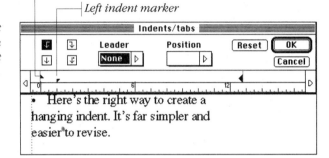

Here's the right way to create a
hanging indent. It's far simpler and
easier to revise.

*Place a tab at the left
indent marker.*

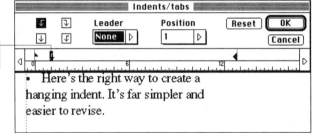

Here's the right way to create a
hanging indent. It's far simpler and
easier to revise.

*Paragraph formatted with a hanging indent*

Here's the right way to create a
hanging indent. It's far simpler and
easier to revise.

*Two bad ways to create
hanging indents*

This is the worst way to create a hanging indent.
note that the person who created this table used
tabs to force line breaks. Why is this so bad?
The paragraph below shows what happens if you
edit the paragraph.

This is the worst way to create a hanging indent.
note that the insane jerk who created this
table used tabs                    to force line breaks.

Note that this paragraph has carriage returns
at the end of each line, and tabs at the start of
each line succeeding the first. This is not the
best way to do hanging indents.

*Story view shows extra tabs and
returns.*

Set up your paragraph with a hanging indent that's greater than the width of the largest number you intend to use, then place a decimal or right tab some distance from the left indent, then place a left tab at the same point as the hanging indent.

**Figure 4-35**
Aligning numbered list items

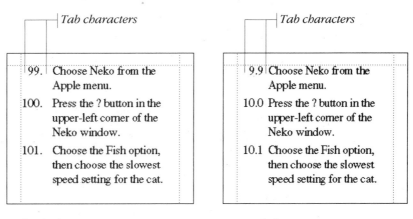

*Right alignment*

*Decimal alignment*

▼ *Tip: Flush Right/Flush Left*

If you have a single-line paragraph and want the words at the beginning of a line to be flush left, and the words at the end flush right, just hit a tab in between and spec the paragraph as flush right. PageMaker pushes the stuff after the tab flush right, and leaves the words before the tab flush left (Figure 4-36). This technique is better than setting a flush-right tab at the right edge of the text block, because a flush-right tab doesn't move when you change column widths.

**Figure 4-36**
Flush right/flush left tabs

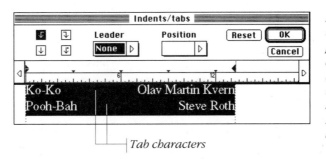

*Tab characters*

*Note that, because of the paragraph's right alignment, the tabs seem to ignore the tab settings in the Indents/tabs dialog box.*

You can also use this technique with text centered between the stuff at the right and left. Just put a center tab stop in the middle of the text block, and use tabs between the center, left, and right text (Figure 4-37). Remember, the center tab won't move if you change the width of the column.

**Figure 4-37**
Left, right, and centered
tabs on the same line

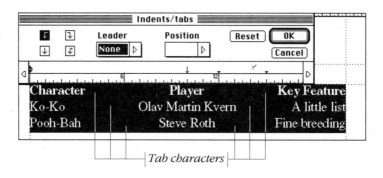

### ▼ *Tip: Aligning Financial Tabular Matter*

Aligning columns of figures is easy if you use decimal tabs, and PageMaker 4 is even smart enough to align decimal-tabbed figures contained in parentheses properly (unlike version 3). You don't even need decimal points to make this work, as you can see below.

```
   1200
   (900)
 20,000
 15,199³
```

As you can see, though, it gets a bit trickier if some of the figures are followed by footnotes, which push those figures to the left and out of alignment. We've found three solutions, but none of them is pretty.

***Method 1.*** Adjust the tab stops for each line containing a footnoted figure so the figures line up. Take note of how much you have to move the tab, so after you've done one you can just do the arithmetic and type the new position numerically, rather than dragging approximately.

***Method 2.*** Use right rather than decimal tabs. Put a thin space

(Command-Shift-T) after every figure that isn't followed by a parenthesis or footnote, select the thin space, and change its type size (changing its width) until the figure lines up properly. Once you've got a thin space sized so it works correctly, copy and paste it where you need it. Remember to plan ahead for double-digit footnotes.

***Method 3.*** Create an extra left tab for the footnote references to align to, just to the right of each column.

---

**Take Me to Your (Tab) Leader**

Tab leaders are strings of characters that run for the length of a tab. They're typically used in tables of contents (between the name of an article and its page number), or in price lists between a description of a product and its price. Their purpose is to lead the eye from one text item to another, much the same as horizontal rules or shaded bars are used in tables.

In PageMaker 4, you can use three default tab leaders (underline, dot, and dotted line), or make up your own leader from any character or two-character combination. To make up your own tab leader, choose "Custom" in the Leader pop-up menu in the Indents/tabs dialog box, and type the character(s) you want to use for the leader.

▼ *Tip: Changing The Font of Tab Leader Characters*

PageMaker formats leader characters using the font used for the character immediately preceding the tab, but will ignore normal spaces. If you want to use fancy characters for the leader dots in tabular matter, or if you just want to use tab leaders for some weird effect, you can use fonts like Symbol, Zapf Dingbats, or one of Steve's favorites, Bullets and Boxes.

1. Place the text insertion point immediately before the tab whose format you want to change.

2. Without moving the insertion point or selecting any text, choose the typeface, size and style you want to use for the tab leader (use the Type specifications dialog box—Command-T).

3. Type a fixed space—a nonbreaking space (Option-Spacebar), an em space (Command-Shift-M), an en space (Command-Shift-N), or a thin space (Command-Shift-T). The tab leader changes to the typeface, size, and style you specified (Figure 4-38).

**Figure 4-38**
Changing the format of tab leaders

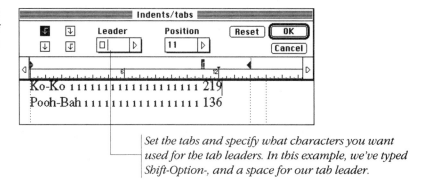

Set the tabs and specify what characters you want used for the tab leaders. In this example, we've typed Shift-Option-, and a space for our tab leader.

Place the insertion point just before the tab, then (without moving the insertion point), choose a type style for the leader characters, and type a non-breaking space character.

Non-breaking space character. In this example, we've used a thin space—Command-Option-T, and changed the font from Times to Zapf Dingbats.

After you enter or format the character, the tab leader takes on the formatting attributes you specified.

Choose the font you use for dot leaders carefully. Some fonts' FOND resources return a different value for the width of a period from the value actually in use in the printer font, and you can end up with dot leaders that cover dramatically more or less of the distance they should on printing. Make sure, in particular, that the fonts you have (both printer and screen) match the fonts your imagesetting service bureau has. Using the fonts from the font package you just bought is no guarantee, because font vendors have little control over the vintage of the packages resellers can sell, and because some font vendors—even the best-known—sometimes make mistakes.

---

### ▼ *Tip: Make These Tabs Like Those*

PageMaker fills in the tabs in the Indents/tabs dialog box based on the tab specifications of the first paragraph in a selected range.

1. Work out the tab settings for the first paragraph of a group of paragraphs you want to format.
2. Drag a selection through that paragraph and any number of following paragraphs.
3. Press Command-I to bring up the Indents/tabs dialog box. The dialog box fills in with the tab values of the paragraph you selected *first*—it doesn't matter whether you extended the selection dragging up or down.
4. Press Return (or click OK).

The indent and tab settings of the first paragraph in the selected range are applied to the other selected paragraphs.

---

**Using Table Editor**

PageMaker 4 comes with a separate application—Table Editor—for creating tables. We haven't used Table Editor much, because its development schedule has not kept pace with PageMaker's, and because the table editing features in Microsoft Word are in many ways better. Still, Table Editor's a handy application, and it might be easier to learn than Word's table features. It does ship with PageMaker, and we have a few tips we'd like to pass on. First, look at the Table Editor screen, as shown in Figure 4-39.

**Figure 4-39**
Table Editor

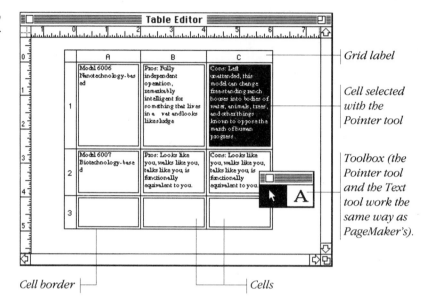

Grid label

Cell selected with the Pointer tool

Toolbox (the Pointer tool and the Text tool work the same way as PageMaker's).

Cell border | | | Cells

### ▼ *Tip: Changing Borders*

Changing the lines around cells is very confusing in Table Editor, at least at first. You can't simply point at a specific edge of a cell and choose a new line style for that specific border.

If you need to change specific borders of table cells in Table Editor, as opposed to changing all the borders, follow these steps (as shown in Figure 4-40).

1. Choose "Borders" from the Cell menu. The Borders dialog box appears.

2. Choose the lines you want to change and click OK.

3. Select the cells you want to change, and choose a new line style from the Lines menu.

Table Editor applies the line style to the lines you chose in Borders dialog box, for all the selected cells.

**Figure 4-40**
Changing borders
in Table Editor

*In this example, we want to remove all of the vertical rules in the table without removing the horizontal rules.*

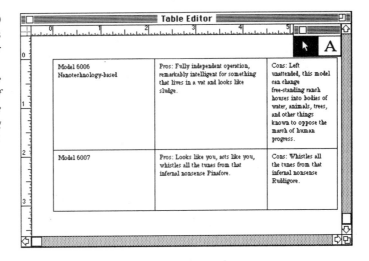

*Choose "Borders" from the Cell menu. The Borders dialog box appears. Select the borders you want to change.*

*Think backwards—in this case, we want to keep the horizontals and the top and bottom rules, so we choose everything else.*

*Select the cells you want to change, and choose a new line style from the Lines menu. In this example, we choose "None." The vertical rules at the left and right of the table and all of the internal vertical rules disappear.*

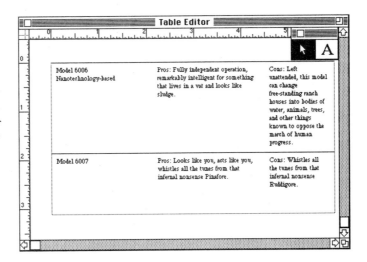

Table Editor can export tables as PICT files (just like pressing Command-Option-D to copy a Word table to the Clipboard) that you can then place in PageMaker, or as tab-delimited text (which is what you get when you place a Word file containing a table). You can export an entire table or a selected range of text (cells, columns, or rows). We prefer placing tables as text, because tables always seem to involve last-minute text changes. If it's a PICT, you can't edit the text.

Another problem with PICT files exported from Table Editor is that the ends of horizontal rules do not precisely line up if you've removed the vertical rules between columns; there's a slight gap. This gap is especially obvious if you've selected fills for adjacent columns where the rule between the columns has been removed. Depending on the resolution of your printer, you might see a fine (or not-so-fine) white line between the cells.

Because of these problems, and because PICTs can take forever to print, we recommend exporting Table Editor tables as tab-delimited text, then formatting the text in PageMaker, rather than exporting the table as a PICT.

### ▼ *Tip: Export Columnar Text from Table Editor*

When you're exporting text from Table Editor, you might want to select columns, export the columns as text, then place the text columns as separate text blocks in PageMaker. Tables are sometimes easier to set up as separate columns of text, rather than as one wider text block. You end up cutting and pasting a lot less.

### ▼ *Tip: Zooming in Table Editor*

PageMaker's zooming shortcuts work in Table Editor—holding down Command-Option-Shift and clicking on an area centers that area in your screen at 200% view. Holding down Command-Option and clicking takes you to the 100% size view if you're in Fit in window or 200% size view. And so on.

▼ *Tip: New Lines in Table Editor*

When you press Return when you're in a Table Editor cell, you move to the next cell. If you want to break lines inside the current cell without moving to the next cell, press Shift-Return to enter a new line, just as in PageMaker and Word.

**That Pesky Spacing Dialog Box**

One of the most complex and powerful dialog boxes in PageMaker is the Spacing dialog box, which you reach by pressing the Spacing button in the Paragraph specifications dialog box. The Spacing dialog box controls the amount of letter and word spacing in your type. In PageMaker 3.x, spacing settings applied to an entire story; in PageMaker 4, you can have different settings for each paragraph. At first glance, though, the Spacing dialog box is incomprehensible (Figure 4-41). Percentages of what? An em? A space character? The distance from here to Milwaukee?

**Figure 4-41**
Spacing dialog box

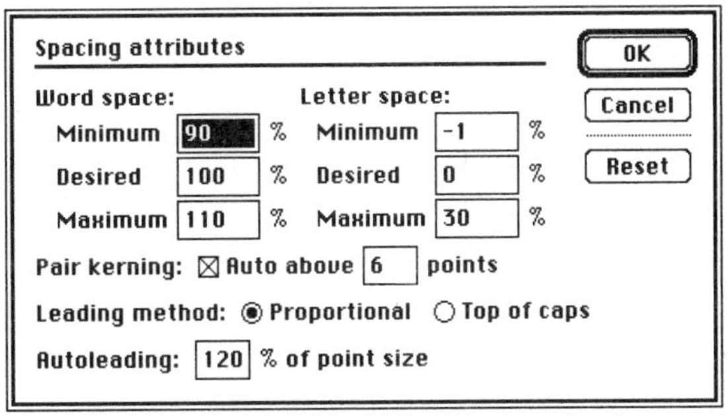

The key thing to understand is that each font has, built into it, values for the width of a space (the thing you get when you hit the Spacebar), and for every letter in the font. The percentages given in the Spacing dialog box are percentages of those values. If you type 75 for the desired word spacing value, for instance, PageMaker will do its best to compress the spaces in each line to 75 percent of their normal size. The same is true with desired letter spacing.

If the text being affected is set flush left, PageMaker won't have any problem. It will just set the text with 75 percent word spacing or letter spacing (pretty tight). If the text is justified, though, it may not be so easy. It's trying to make every line fill the column width, after all, which is no easy task. If you've ever had to manually hyphenate a column of justified text (remember version 1.2?), you'll know that words *never* break in the right places.

With justified copy, the maximum and minimum values come into play. When PageMaker encounters a point on a line where the line should break, it goes through the following steps.

- It applies word spacing within the range defined by the maximum and minimum word-space settings in the Spacing dialog box. If the line will fill the current line width before the word spaces in the line exceed that range, PageMaker composes the line and goes on to the next line.

- If PageMaker can't compose the line within the maximum or minimum word-space settings, it applies letter spacing within the maximum and minimum letter-space settings (while also looking at the word following the tentative line break to see if the word could be brought back to the current line while still respecting the minimum letter-space settings). If the line will fill the current line width before the letter spacing in the line exceeds the specified range, PageMaker composes the line and goes on to the next line.

- If PageMaker has compressed or expanded the word or letter spacing within the ranges specified in the Spacing dialog box and still cannot compose the line, it applies space to the word spaces in the line until it can compose the line to the required line width and, disgusted, moves on to the next line. If you have turned on the Show loose/tight lines option in the Preferences dialog box, PageMaker highlights the line.

### ▼ *Tip: See Loose and Tight Lines*

You can see the lines that PageMaker had to set too loose or too tight by checking the Show loose/tight lines box in the Preferences dialog box. We have this on by default, and never turn it off. PageMaker highlights lines that it can't justify within the specified parameters. On a color Mac, it highlights them in yellow; on a gray-scale Mac, in gray; on a black-and-white Mac, in a patterned gray.

---

The only sure way to discover what spacing settings look best is to experiment and see what happens. And remember that the results will vary from font to font and for different line measures. By the time we get done with this book, we'll have a good idea of what spacing settings work best for Bitstream's ITC Garamond Light, set at 11 points on a 26-pica measure. It always seems to take about 400 pages before you've run into all the possible spacing problems for any particular font. Once you have good numbers figured out for a given font and measure, write them down and put them in a safe.

In PageMaker 3, the Spacing dialog box was almost useless, because it applied to a whole story. Spacing that worked well for Times (a well-spaced font), for example, produced widely spaced text in Adobe's Condensed Bold Helvetica (a very poorly spaced font). If you tried to space the Helvetica well, the Times text would start to collide. The only way out was to either break all of the Helvetica out into a separate story, or to manually kern all of the Helvetica text. Both solutions are ugly.

PageMaker 4 lets you apply different Spacing settings to each paragraph, so you can build them into your styles for fast, automatic, good-looking type—once you've figured out the numbers.

## Tracking

When you set type in larger sizes, the apparent space between letters seems to increase. Larger type that's not adjusted tends to look loose. The solution is tracking. This function sets type progressively tighter at progressively larger sizes. How much tracking you need at different sizes depends entirely on the typeface, so in the best of all possible worlds tracking values are built into each typeface.

Unfortunately, there's no facility for designers to specify tracking values in Macintosh fonts. That's why programs generally don't offer tracking; they don't have the information they need.

PageMaker 4 reads its tracking information for specific fonts from the file "Kern Tracks" (hey! we didn't name it). The default file shipped with

PageMaker includes tracking values for the standard PostScript "Plus" font set, plus a few others. If you apply tracking to a font that PageMaker cannot find in Kern Tracks, PageMaker applies a default tracking setting. To edit the Kerning Tracks file to add your own tracking settings for fonts you use most often, you'll need PM Tracker, the tracking editor for PageMaker being developed by Edco Systems. We've just received an early version as this book goes to press, so we don't have much to say about it except that it exists.

Tracking happens before all the calculations related to the Spacing dialog box. So if the tracking value says that a character's width should be 9 points rather than 10 (to use a crude example), PageMaker uses the 9-point width as the basis of its letter-space calculations. Word spaces are also scaled by tracking.

Note also that tracking values are cumulative with manual kerning and automatic kerning (discussed later in this chapter). If the tracking tables specify tighter spacing, the kern pairs in the font specify a tighter kern for automatic kerning, and you've kerned the type manually, all those adjustments are added together to produce some very tight type.

## Paragraph Rules

Being able to specify a rule preceding or following a paragraph as an attribute of that paragraph is one of our favorite new features in PageMaker 4. No more laboriously moving rules when editorial changes force text recomposition! No more careful measuring down from character baselines in 400% view! Paragraph rules make us happy, happy, happy.

***Creating, selecting and changing paragraph rules.*** You can't select paragraph rules with the Pointer tool, or can't alter their attributes through the Lines h-menu, the Define colors dialog box, or the Colors palette. Paragraph rules are linked to their associated paragraph, and can be edited only through the Paragraph rules dialog box and the Rule options dialog box for that paragraph or style (Figure 4-42).

***Vertical positioning of paragraph rules.*** The position for rules above paragraphs is measured up from the baseline of the first line of

**Figure 4-42**
Paragraph rules
dialog boxes

```
┌─────────────────────────────────────────────────────┐
│ Paragraph rules                          ┌────────┐   │
│ ─────────────────────────────────────    │   OK   │   │
│ ☐ Rule above paragraph                    └────────┘   │
│     Line style:   │1 pt ─────────│                     │
│                                           ┌────────┐   │
│     Line color:   │Black│                 │ Cancel │   │
│                                           └────────┘   │
│     Line width:  ○ Width of text  ◉ Width of column   │
│                                           ┌─────────┐  │
│     Indent: Left │0    │ picas   Right │0  │ picas│Options...│ │
│                                                        │
│ ☐ Rule below paragraph                                 │
│     Line style:   │1 pt ─────────│                     │
│     Line color:   │Black│                              │
│     Line width:  ○ Width of text  ◉ Width of column   │
│     Indent: Left │0    │ picas   Right │0  │ picas     │
└─────────────────────────────────────────────────────┘
```

```
┌─────────────────────────────────────────┐
│ Paragraph rule options        ┌────────┐ │
│ ─────────────────────────     │   OK   │ │
│                               └────────┘ │
│ Top: │Auto│ picas                        │
│             above baseline    ┌────────┐ │
│                               │ Cancel │ │
│ Bottom: │Auto│ picas          └────────┘ │
│               below baseline  ┌────────┐ │
│ ⊠ Align to grid               │ Reset  │ │
│                               └────────┘ │
│ Grid size: │15   │ ▷│ points             │
└─────────────────────────────────────────┘
```

text, and the position for rules below paragraphs is measured down from the baseline of the last line of text in the paragraph. Make sure to use fixed, proportional leading, so you know where the baselines are (Figure 4-43).

When you set a rule above a paragraph, entering "Auto" in the Position text edit box sets the rule at the top of the line slug (not the paragraph slug—for a discussion of slugs, see "PageMaker Leading" earlier in this chapter). A paragraph rule above specified for Auto

**Figure 4-43**
Paragraph rule placement

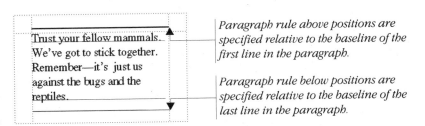

*Paragraph rule above positions are specified relative to the baseline of the first line in the paragraph.*

*Paragraph rule below positions are specified relative to the baseline of the last line in the paragraph.*

position, in a line with a lead of 24 points, will appear 16 points above the baseline of the first line of the paragraph (16 points = ⅔ of 24 points). In this case, if your characters have ascenders of 14 points and you've set the rule width to 4 points, the rule will print over the type (Figure 4-44).

When you set a rule below a paragraph, Auto position sets the rule at the bottom of the slug. In a line with a lead of 24 points, the rule will appear 8 points below the baseline of the last line of text in the paragraph. Watch out for descenders (Figure 4-45).

**Figure 4-44**
Paragraph rules
above set to Auto

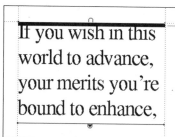

*Rules above with Position set to Auto appear at the top of the slug of the first line of the paragraph, and may print over the tops of the characters.*

**Figure 4-45**
Paragraph rule
below set to Auto

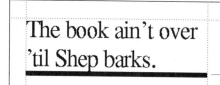

*Rules below with Position set to Auto appear at the bottom of the slug of the last line of the paragraph.*

***Horizontal positioning of paragraph rules.*** You can position paragraph rules relative to the width of the column, or relative to the width of the text. Click "Width of column," and the rule will be the width of the text block. It will increase and decrease in width as you resize the text block. Click "Width of text," and the rule will be the width of the widest line of text in the paragraph. It will increase and decrease in width as you lengthen or shorten that line.

Specifying indents based on the width of the column is pretty easy to understand—like paragraph indents, you enter a positive number for the amount the rule is indented from either side of the text block. You can even specify a negative number to force the rule beyond the borders of the text block.

Specifying indents based on the width of the text is a little trickier: you enter a negative value when you want the rule to be wider than the text, and you enter a positive value when you want the rule to be narrower than the text. These simple settings open the door to some powerful formatting capabilities, as shown in Figures 4-46 and 4-49.

**Figure 4-46**
Setting the width of
paragraph rules

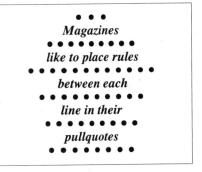

*If you enter positive values in the Indent text edit boxes, the rules are indented from the edges of the text.*

*If you enter negative values in the Indent text edit boxes, the rules extend beyond the edges of the text.*

***Rules and how they grow.*** Line weights for rules above are measured *down* from the point you specify in the Rule options dialog box. Line weights for rules below are measured *up* from the point you specify, as shown in Figure 4-47

**Figure 4-47**
Line weights for
paragraph rules

*Rules below grow from their position setting up*

*Rules above grow from their position setting down*

Rule below=1 point, position 1p

Rule above=1 point, position 2p

Rule below=4 points, position 1p

Rule above=4 points, position 2p

Rule below=12 points, position 1p

Rule above= 12 points, position 2p

***Rules and paragraph spacing.*** Rules extend the slug of the paragraph. We're sorry, but it's true. Paragraph space before is added above and in addition to a rule before. Space after is added below and in addition to a rule after (Figure 4-48).

**Figure 4-48**
Paragraph spacing and
paragraph rules

| This paragraph has a rule set to fall 0p8 from the baseline of the last line in the paragraph, and has a 1 pica space after setting. | This is what the same paragraph looks like without the rule. The 1 pica space after setting has been retained. |
| --- | --- |
| This is the first line of the next paragraph. | This is the first line of the next paragraph. |

***Paragraph rules are drawn behind text.*** This lets you put paragraph rules behind type for some wild special effects, as shown in Figure 4-49.

**Figure 4-49**
Special rule effects

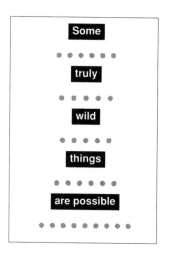

*All of these effects were created entirely with paragraph rules. No LBOs were drawn.*

***Paragraph rules and text wrap.*** Paragraph rules act like text when it comes to text wraps. If a paragraph rule encounters a graphic wrap boundary, it obeys the boundary just as text would, altering its width to be either the width of the column outside of the graphic's boundary, or the width of the text in the line, depending on the option you've specified in the Paragraph rules dialog box (Figure 4-50).

**Figure 4-50**
Paragraph rules
and text wrap

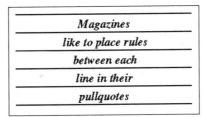
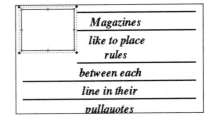

### ▼ Tip: Slaves to Fashion

These days, you often see headings with two rules above (and sometimes below) them—one that extends to the width of the column (or page, or whatever), another that runs the width of the heading text (Figure 4-51). To create those very fashionable double rules, follow these steps.

**Figure 4-51**
Double rules for
headings

## Headline

Marketing and technical comunications documents often use rules above that track to the width of a headline, while a thinner rule fills the width of the column.

## Headline

Marketing and technical comunications documents also often use rules below that track to the width of a headline, while a thinner rule fills the width of the column.

1. Create a paragraph with a paragraph rule below that falls to the bottom of its slug. You can get away with a pretty tiny leading increment (like 1 point). Set it to "Keep with next" paragraph.

2. Define your heading style as having a rule above (thicker than the rule below in the step above), with a Top setting that pushes the rule to the top of the slug (or beyond).

Now, if you use the two paragraphs together, the paragraph rule above in the heading style should touch the paragraph rule of the paragraph above, creating just the effect you're looking for.

**Playing for Keeps**

PageMaker 4 improves on the paragraph formatting features offered in PageMaker 3 by adding new controls in the Paragraph specifications dialog box over the way your paragraphs relate to each other. "Keep lines together" behaves just as you'd expect it would—keeping the lines of a paragraph from breaking across text blocks. "Keep with next" glues the paragraph to the next 1, 2, or 3 lines of text (whatever you've entered in the text edit box), and is great for keeping heads on the same page or column with following body text.

The controls for widows and orphans, however, are a little different from what you might expect. We always learned that a widow was two or fewer lines of a paragraph isolated at the top or bottom of a column, while orphans referred to single words ending paragraphs. In PageMaker terminology (based, tragically, on Microsoft Word's definitions), a widow is some number of lines at the beginning of a text block, while an orphan is some number of lines at the end of a text block. You can enter only 1, 2, or 3 in the widow/orphan control text edit boxes.

▼ *Tip: Orphan Killer*

Since PageMaker 4 has no way of preventing one word from appearing on the last line of a paragraph, we thought we'd add one with QuicKeys. Create a Sequence QuicKey containing the "Literal" key-strokes shown in Table 4-2. They go to the end of a paragraph and insert a nonbreaking space before the last word.

The nonbreaking space guarantees that the last line in the paragraph contains at least two words. Note that this key doesn't work if the last word in the paragraph is a compound number, such as "4.0," or a manually-hyphenated pair of words, such as "thought-provoking."

**Table 4-2  Orphan-killing QuicKey**

| Literal Keystroke | What it Does |
| --- | --- |
| Command-2 | Moves the cursor to the start of the next paragraph. |
| Command-4 (three times) | Moves the cursor to the beginning of the last word |
| Delete | Deletes the space between the last two words in the paragraph |
| Option-Spacebar | Adds a nonbreaking space between the last two words in the paragraph |

▼ *Tip: Setting Widow/Orphan Controls*

The widow and orphan controls don't work quite the way you'd expect at first glance. PageMaker always seems to add one line to the number you specify in the text edit box. In this case, PageMaker's right: when you enter 1 in the text edit box, you really mean that you want PageMaker to break the text block rather than allowing a 1-line widow/ orphan, so the smallest widow/orphan you'll see will be 2 lines. When you enter 2, you're really asking PageMaker to outlaw 2-line widows/ orphans, and the smallest widow/orphan you'll see will be 3 lines long. And so on.

We refer to all of these paragraph-level controls as "keeps." PageMaker tries to obey the specific keeps settings for each paragraph, but will, in some cases, be forced to break your rules. You can keep an eye on this bad behavior by turning on the Show keeps violations option in the Preferences dialog box. PageMaker highlights places where it's broken your rules using a yellow or gray screen over the paragraph, depending on whether you're using a color or monochrome Mac (just as it shows loose and tight lines).

Note that there are certain combinations of keep settings and widow and orphan settings that don't make a whole lot of sense. Why would you choose to use both "Keep lines together" and the widow or orphan controls, for instance?

### ▼ Tip: Keeping Heads with Text

As we mentioned above, you can use the "Keep with next" setting to keep heads and subheads with their accompanying text. If you're using styles—and we urge you to use styles so you get more free time away from the computer—you can set the paragraph formatting for heads to "Keep with next" so that they'll follow their body text across page and column breaks. If you've ever cursed PageMaker 3 for placing your headlines at the bottoms of text blocks, this feature is for you.

## Column and Page Breaks

PageMaker 4 also adds two paragraph-control features that are the opposite of the "keeps" discussed above—"Column break before" and "Page break before." When you're autoflowing text, PageMaker will jump to the next column or page when it encounters paragraphs that have these attributes set. With manual or semi-autoflow, it will stop when it reaches one of these items and wait for you to place the next text block.

Note that if you have "Page break before" set for paragraph, Page-Maker won't let you place that paragraph on the same page as the preceding paragraph. You just get a closed-up text block, and you can't open it unless you move it to another page or place it on the pasteboard.

### ▼ Tip: Use Column break before for Heads in a Companion Column

If you use heads hanging out in a companion column, as in this book, specify "Column break before" for those heads. PageMaker will stop when it gets to a head, and let you place the head in the companion column. Unfortunately there's no Column break after option, so you end up mucking around with the bottom windowshade handles a bit.

---

### ▼ *PageMaker 3 Tip: Forcing Column Breaks*

If you're still working with PageMaker 3, you can force column breaks by specifying a very large space (the height of the column, for instance) before a paragraph. This forces the heads to fall at the top of the next column. Remember, PageMaker doesn't apply the space before when the paragraph falls at the top of a text block.

## *Character Formatting*

Before we get heavily into character formatting, let's get our terminology straight. Apple and Adobe did a very confusing thing when they first released the Macintosh/LaserWriter combination. They mixed up fonts with faces, so you never know quite what anyone means anymore. We're stuck with it now, but for those who want to discuss and understand these things, here are some definitions.

***Font.*** A set of characters in a given typeface and size. Ten-point Futura Extra Black is a font.

***Typeface.*** In this day and age, a scalable outline from which many sizes of fonts can be made. Janson Text is a typeface. So is Times Italic.

***Typeface family.*** A collection of typefaces. Some families contain a dozen or more typefaces (Futura and Helvetica are examples); others only include four variations (roman, italic, bold, and bold italic).

It gets confusing with groups of typefaces like Stone, which actually includes three typeface families—Stone Serif, Stone Sans, and Stone Informal—each containing several typefaces.

Now that we have that out of the way, let's get on to character formatting, which is probably why you bought this book for in the first place.

## Type Specs

When you choose "Type specs" from the Type menu (Command-T) or press the Type button in the Edit styles dialog box, the Type specifications dialog box appears. The usual things one associates with specifying type are here—font, size, leading, position relative to the baseline (super- and subscripting), capitalization options, and, in Macintosh jargon, "Type styles"—bold, italic, shadow, underline, and so on. PageMaker 4 adds commands for expanding and condensing type and setting tracking values, and gives you control over small caps size and super- and subscript size and position through a new Type options dialog box

## Keyboard Shortcuts for Character Formatting

You can select type and change character formatting quickly with a number of keyboard shortcuts, as shown in Table 4-3.

Keyboard shortcuts are the most direct and immediate method of specifying type in PageMaker. Using the Type specifications dialog box (Command-T) is the next step. It lets you adjust several attributes at once. The results are all local, however; they only apply to the currently selected text. For more global changes, you'll want to adjust the paragraph styles (see "Working with Styles" later in this chapter).

## Set Width

One of the most useful new features in PageMaker 4 is the Set width option. It lets you condense or expand selected type from .1 to 250 percent, in .1 percent increments. It applies those values to all the characters in the selected text, including word space characters. In previous versions, the only way to condense or expand type was to place type created in a draw program (or place the Scrapbook, as described in "Placing the Scrapbook" in Chapter 5, *Pictures*), and stretch the graphic type with the Pointer tool.

That technique worked fine for headlines, but if you wanted some condensed or expanded type within a line, or wanted all your subheads

**Table 4-3 Keyboard shortcuts for character formatting**

| *Character Formatting* | *Keyboard Shortcut* |
| --- | --- |
| Italic | Command-Shift-I |
| Bold | Command-Shift-B |
| Plain text | Command-Shift-Spacebar |
| Underline | Command-Shift-U |
| Strike-through | Command-Shift-/ |
| Outline | Command-Shift-D |
| Shadow | Command-Shift-W |
| One point size larger | Option-Command-Shift-. (>) |
| Larger | Command-Shift-. (>) (using these sizes: 8, 9, 10, 12, 14, 18, 24, 36) |
| One point size smaller | Option-Command-Shift-, (<) |
| Smaller | Command-Shift -, (<) (using these sizes: 8, 9, 10, 12, 14, 18, 24, 36) |
| Small caps | Command-Shift-H |
| All caps | Command-Shift-K |
| Subscript | Command-Shift-- |
| Superscript | Command-Shift-+ |
| Square (Set width) | Command-Shift-X |
| Eliminate track kerning | Command-Shift-Q |
| Reverse type | ? You're right! There's no keyboard shortcut for "Reverse," and it's far more important and useful than almost every other type style command (except italic). We suggest adding one with ResEdit or QuicKeys. (See "Modifying PageMaker's Menus with ResEdit," in Chapter 3, *Making PageMaker Mind*, or "QuicKeys" in Chapter 2, *Building a PageMaker System*.) |

condensed by some percentage, there was no good solution. With "Set Width," you can specify a percentage for any selection, or build the percentage into the style for any paragraph.

Note that the percentage you specify for "Set width" works as a multiplier with the settings in the Spacing dialog box. So if you specify 90 for "Set width" and 90 for "Desired Word spacing," word spaces will be 81 percent of normal width (in nonjustified text).

**Fun with Type options**

At first glance, the Type options dialog box (press the Options button in the Type specifications dialog box) doesn't seem to offer much—control over the size of your small capitals and super- and subscript type, and the position of your super- and subscripts. Ho hum. Great if you need footnote references in the right place, but pretty mundane. On further examination, however, this dialog box can be fun, fun, fun.

Before we start, though, we have to say that this dialog box is almost as confusing, at first glance, as the Spacing dialog box. But you don't have to be a rocket scientist to understand this dialog box: the values in the dialog box are in percentages of the normal height of the characters, and are accurate to one-tenth of a percent. If, for example, you specify 90 for "Small caps size," and the type size of the selected text or paragraph is 24, the small caps will be 21.6 points.

Similarly, if you specify that superscripted type in a line with a leading of 24 is offset from the baseline by 60 percent, the baseline of the superscripted type will appear 14.4 points above the baseline of the

**Figure 4-52**
Superscript and subscript

| Superscript 20%: Ruddigore | Subscript 20%: Ruddigore |
| Superscript 40%: Ruddigore | Subscript 40%: Ruddigore |
| Superscript 60%: Ruddigore | Subscript 60%: Ruddigore |
| Superscript 80%: Ruddigore | Subscript 80%: Ruddigore |

rest of the line. With subscripted type, the baseline of the subscripted type would appear 14.4 points *below* the baseline.

What does all of this mean? Bigger percentages shift super- and subscripts away from the normal baseline by a greater amount, as shown in Figure 4-52.

### ▼ Tip: Type Within Type

We can't think of what this type effect is called, but we've seen it everywhere—particularly in corporate logos and advertising.

1. Create a text block and type a word—words starting with C, S, T, L, or other characters that are open on the right side will work better for this effect than M or N. As usual, make sure you're working with fixed, proportional leading.
2. Select the first character in the word.
3. Bring up the Type specifications dialog box (Command-T) and enlarge the selected character to three or four times the size of the rest of the text in the line.

**Figure 4-53**
Snazzy type

4. Choose Subscript from the Position pop-up menu.
5. Click the Options button to bring up the Type options dialog box. Type 100 in the Super/Subscript size text edit box, and 25 in the Subscript position box. Press Return twice to close the dialog boxes.
6. Place the insertion point to the right of the enlarged, subscripted character and kern the rest of the word back until it is nested inside the initial character.

---

### ▼ Tip: More Snazzy Type

Once again, we're not sure what this effect is called, and, once again, certain letter combinations are going to work better than others.

1. Type "LoDOWN"

2. Set the type to some point size and some fixed lead (of course you're using proportional leading).

3. Select the "o" and bring up the Type specifications dialog box (Command-T). Choose "Superscript" from the Position menu tript the "o," and press the Options button to bring up the Type options dialog box.

4. Enter 95 in the Super/Subscript size text edit box, and 20 in the Superscript position text edit field. Press Return twice to close the dialog boxes.

5. Place the insertion point immediately to the left of the "o" and kern it back until it is nested above the horizontal stroke of the "L" (Figure 4-54).

**Figure 4-54**
More snazzy type

Figure 4-55 shows a few other things you can do with superscripting and subscripting combined with kerning (*lots* of kerning).

**Figure 4-55**
Yet more snazzy type

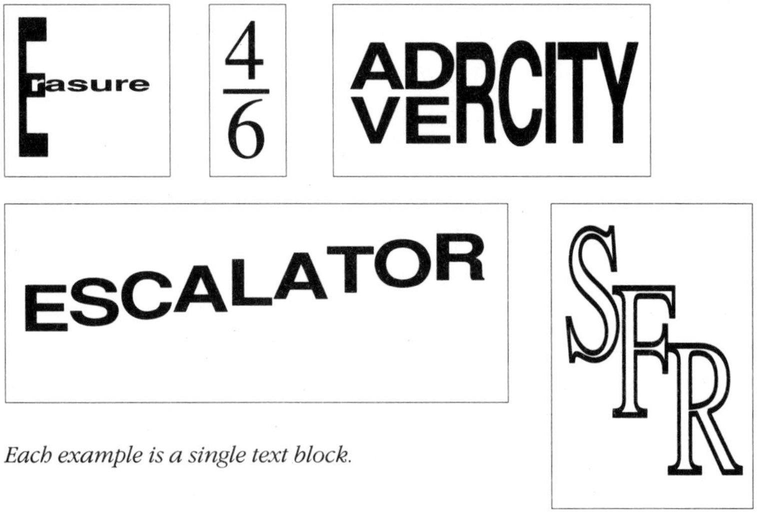

*Each example is a single text block.*

**Kerning Text**

In traditional typesetting, kerning *removes* space between characters (because *kerns*—the portions of characters on a piece of lead type that overhang the edge of the type block—make characters print closer together). In desktop publishing, there's also something called positive kerning that *adds* space between characters. Positive kerning is an oxymoron, but we're stuck with it. And since we're not using lead type, maybe it's not so bad.

There are two types of kerning in PageMaker—automatic and manual. PageMaker does the first for you. You have to do the second.

***Automatic kerning*** (which you can turn on or off in the paragraph's Spacing attributes dialog box) is based on kerning pair values built into the FOND resource of your screen fonts. PageMaker sees A and W next to each other in Times Roman, checks the FOND, and sees that a certain amount of kerning is specified. If PageMaker's automatic kerning is turned on, it nudges those two letters together by the specified amount.

Unfortunately, many of the fonts on the market have totally abysmal kerning pair tables. The Adobe Plus set of fonts are good examples. The designers and/or the developers simply didn't bother to put all the kerning pairs in. Others have quite robust kerning pair tables (like the Bitstream version of ITC Garamond used in this book, which has more than 400 kerning pairs per font). There are kerning pair editors on the market (such as LetrTuck, from Edco Systems), but we can't recommend going through all your fonts and specifying hundreds of kerning pairs each—even if you know what values to use.

There are also third-party screen fonts available for the Adobe library that include hundreds or thousands of kerning pairs each. These are wonderful, but remember that if you send the file to someone else (like a service bureau), you'll have to send them your screen fonts, as well. Otherwise, when they open the file, PageMaker will use the kerning pairs in their screen fonts. For service bureau output, you can also print the pub to disk as PostScript, so they can simply download it (see "PageMaker and Downloaded Fonts" in Chapter 6, *Printing*). We should also point out that screen redraw times increase the more kerning pairs you have in a font, and that they seem to dramatically increase when there are more than 600 kerning pairs in one of the fonts you're using.

***Manual Kerning.*** Automatic kerning is wonderful, given that there are a reasonable number of kerning pairs specified in your screen fonts. There usually aren't, though, and even if there are you always need to fine-tune large type, so you can also kern manually with PageMaker. Click with the Text tool between two letters and press the following keys to move the letters together or apart (see Table 4-4).

**Table 4-4  Kerning keys**

| *Kerning increment* | *Key Command* |
| --- | --- |
| Coarse (+/-.04 of an em) | |
| Remove space | Command-Delete<br>or Command-Left arrow |
| Add space | Command-Shift-Delete<br>or Command-Right arrow |
| Fine (+/-.01 of an em) | |
| Remove space | Option-Delete<br>or Command-Shift-Left arrow |
| Add space | Option-Shift-Delete<br>or Command-Shift-Right arrow |

In PageMaker 4, you can apply manual kerning to a range (selection) of text. (Some people call this tracking, but tracking is a more automatic and global function, nudging all letters together more as they get bigger, with tracking values based on the typeface being used.) Select the range of text you want to kern and press any combination of coarse and fine kerning keys. PageMaker applies the kerning amount between each pair of characters in the range of the text. This is really handy if you have a paragraph or block of copy that doesn't quite fit in its allotted space.

Manual and automatic kerning are cumulative in PageMaker 4 (hallelujah! at last!). PageMaker uses the kerning information from the font for automatic kerning (unless you've turned off "Pair kerning" in the paragraph's Spacing attributes dialog box), and adds your manual kerning to those values. So if the kerning pairs built into a typeface specify a -.2-em kern between A and W, and you kern the pair manually -.3 ems, you'll end up with a -.5-em kern. Kerning is also cumulative with any tracking applied to the selection.

## Kerning in PageMaker 4

The actual operation of PageMaker 4's kerning differs from Page-Maker 3's. In the earlier version, k erning increments were stored as invisible characters inserted in the line of text, between each kerned letter combination. In PageMaker 4, the kerning increments are stored as an attribute of each character, describing a *change to the space after* the character.

In PageMaker 3, you could insert kerning characters before the first character of each line that would pull the character beyond the left edge of the text block (that is, beyond the left margin). While this was useful for particular fonts and special effects (especially for drop caps), it wouldn't work well with PageMaker 4's range kerning feature. If you selected a whole paragraph and kerned it, the beginning of every line would hang to the left of the margin. If you wanted a whole paragraph of characters hanging over the left edge of the text block, wouldn't you just move the text block?

### ▼ Tip: Kerning Whole Words

If you want to kern all of the letters in a word, but don't want to apply the kerning to the space following the word, don't double-click the word to select it. Double-clicking the word also selects the space following the word. Instead, sweep the text insertion point through all but the last letter of the word. Remember, kerning is an attribute of individual characters, and is applied to the space *after* each character. Assuming your text insertion point is immediately before the first character of the word, you could also select the word by pressing Command-Shift-6, then pressing Shift-4 (both on the numeric keypad).

### ▼ *Tip: Lose that Kerning*

To clear all manual kerning increments between a pair of characters or within a kerned range, place the text insertion point between the characters or select the range, and press any of the following combinations: Command-Option-K; Option-Clear (on the numeric keypad); Command-Option-Shift-Delete.

---

When you open a PageMaker 3 document with PageMaker 4, manual kerning increments entered in PageMaker 3 will be rendered as .02 of an em. PageMaker 3's kerning increment was 1/48th (.0208) of an em, so kerning will change slightly.

### ▼ *PageMaker 3 Tip: Microscopic Kerning Increments*

PageMaker 3 stores kerning increments as invisible kerning characters between text characters, which makes this trick possible in PageMaker 3 and impossible in version 4. To get really fine kerning increments between characters in PageMaker 3, use the following technique.

1. Position the text insertion point between two characters.
2. Without moving the insertion point or selecting any text, bring up the Type specifications dialog box (Command-T).
3. In the Size text edit field, enter some type size smaller than the rest of the type in the line. If you're working in a line of 24-point type, for example, enter 12. Press Return to close the dialog box.
4. Enter kerning increments with the keyboard commands.

The difference: you are now entering spacing values based on the em size of the smaller type. Using our example values of a 12-point em in a 24-point line, you'd be kerning at twice the usual accuracy—1/86th of a 24-point em, rather than the standard 1/48th. We don't know what will happen when/if you convert publications containing this trick to PageMaker 4.

---

**Fractions and Drop Caps**

Someday, PageMaker will have some kind of run-in or character-based style that automatically creates drop caps (can you say "Ventura Publisher?"). There will also probably be a keystroke to turn 1/4 into 1/4 (can you say "Design Studio?") This parenthetical comment of Steve's so enraged Ole that he created a QuicKey to make fractions in PageMaker (see "Storing up Fractions," below). When that day comes, we'll be able to forget all of the methods for creating drop caps and fractions that we've learned over the years, and use that part of our brains for something else. We don't know what, but something else. In the meantime, here are the best methods we know.

**_Drop caps._** Gallons of ink have been spilled describing various methods for creating dropped, initial capitals in PageMaker. Here's our puddle. First, do not create drop caps by placing a character within a no-line, no-fill box and setting a text wrap for the box (this one is always turning up in tips columns). That box will trip you up in the future. Instead, use one of the techniques described below.

**▼ _Tip: The Easy Way to Create Drop Caps_**

Turn the drop cap into a graphic, and set the Autowrap boundaries for the graphic (Figure 4-56).

1. Create the drop cap in a text block all by its lonesome. Ordinarily, the drop cap should be related in size to the size and leading of the body text—two times and three times the base leading of the body text are useful sizes.

2. Select the text block with the Pointer tool, copy it to the Clipboard, and from there to the Scrapbook.

3. Choose Place (_not_ Paste), select the Scrapbook file (in the system folder), then place the first item in the Scrapbook (the drop cap _qua_ graphic). Then click on the Pointer tool in the Toolbox to unload all the other Scrapbook items from the place gun.

4. Select the drop cap and turn "Text wrap" on.

5. Use ruler guides to place the body copy on top of the drop cap.

6. Adjust the text wrap boundaries for the drop cap.

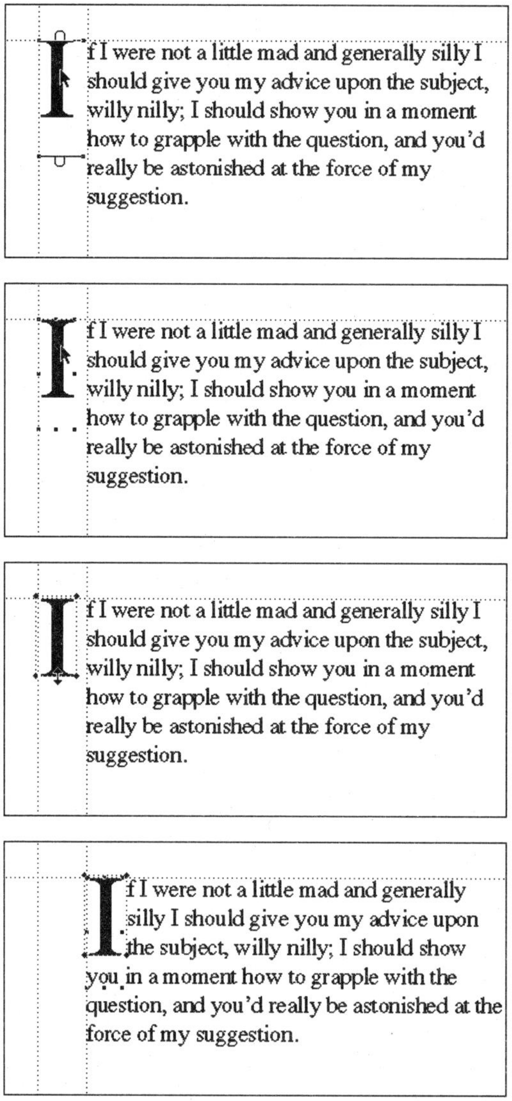

**Figure 4-56**
Creating a drop cap
using text wrap

Create a large initial
character as a separate
text block, select it with the
Pointer tool, and copy it to
the Scrapbook.

> If I were not a little mad and generally silly I should give you my advice upon the subject, willy nilly; I should show you in a moment how to grapple with the question, and you'd really be astonished at the force of my suggestion.

Place the character from
the Scrapbook. This turns
it into a graphic.

> If I were not a little mad and generally silly I should give you my advice upon the subject, willy nilly; I should show you in a moment how to grapple with the question, and you'd really be astonished at the force of my suggestion.

Apply text wrap to the
character and adjust the
wrap boundary.

> If I were not a little mad and generally silly I should give you my advice upon the subject, willy nilly; I should show you in a moment how to grapple with the question, and you'd really be astonished at the force of my suggestion.

Initial character in
position

> If I were not a little mad and generally silly I should give you my advice upon the subject, willy nilly; I should show you in a moment how to grapple with the question, and you'd really be astonished at the force of my suggestion.

## ▼ Tip: The Old, Slow Method of Creating Drop Caps

This method can still be useful. It uses two or more text blocks—one or more to the right of the drop cap, and one below it (Figure 4-57).

Ole thinks this is the best method.

**Figure 4-57**
Creating a drop cap by
breaking text blocks

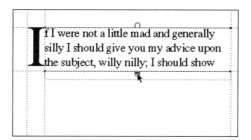

Create the large initial cap as a
single text block and drag it
into position.

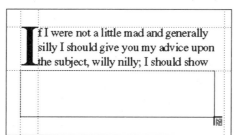

Adjust the body copy so that it's
the width you want, then click
the bottom windowshade
handle to place the rest of the
body copy.

Pull down a ruler guide from
the horizontal ruler so that it is
exactly in front of the bottom
windowshade, and then drag-
place the body copy, using the
ruler guide to align the top of
the text block.

Large initial character in
position

1. Place the column of text.

2. Create the drop cap in its own text block (make it a narrow text
   block so it doesn't get in the way).

3. Use the ruler guides to place the text block containing the drop
   cap into the column.

4. Pull the top windowshade handle of the body text block down to the next leading increment below the drop cap (you *do* have your leading grid set up, right?).

5. Click the top windowshade handle of the body copy text block. The loaded text place gun appears.

6. Drag-place the first lines of the body copy so that the copy does not touch the drop cap.

If you want to create a nonrectangular wrap—one that follows the contour of the drop cap—you'll have to drag-place each line separately, or use tabs at the beginning of each line and adjust the tab stops.

▼ *Tip: The New, Nifty Way to Create Drop Caps*

This method uses the variable subscript size and position controls available through the Type options dialog box (Figure 4-58). It works especially well because the drop cap is part of the text block, and moves with the paragraph as text reflows.

1. Select the first character in a paragraph.

2. Increase the size of the character to three times the size of the body text (two, three, and four times the size of the body text are the most common sizes for dropped initial capitals).

3. Bring up the Type specifications dialog box (Command-T). Choose "Subscript" from the Position pop-up menu.

4. Click the Options button to bring up the Type options dialog box.

5. Enter 100 in the Super/Subscript size text edit field, and 75 in the Subscript position text edit field (you'll need to adjust these values for the specific typeface and size you're using). Press Return to close the dialog boxes.

6. Place the insertion point immediately to the right of the dropped capital and press Tab.

7. Press Command-I to bring up the Indents/tabs dialog box, and adjust the tab settings to position the text following the drop cap.

**Figure 4-58**

Creating a drop cap
using the subscript
position and tabs

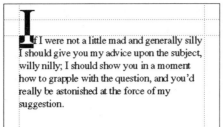

*Select the inital cap and increase
its size. In this example, we've
used 36-point (the body type
is 10/12).*

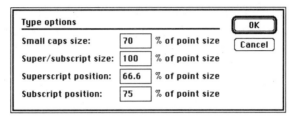

*Use the Type specifi-
cations dialog box to
make the character
subscript, then press
the Options button to
display the Type
options dialog box.*

*The baseline of the initial cap
drops to the distance you
specified.*

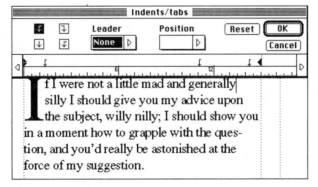

*Use tabs to align
the body copy.*

8. Press 7 on the numeric keypad to move to the end of the first line
   and add a new-line character (Shift-Enter) to break the line.

9. Press 6 on the numeric keypad to move to the start of the next
   line, and press Tab. Move to the end of the second line of the

paragraph and add another line break. Then move to the start of the third line of the paragraph and press Tab.

**_Fractions._** PageMaker doesn't offer any easy way to create good-looking fractions, and though many PostScript typefaces have a few fractions built into their character sets, there's generally no way to get at them in PageMaker (or on the Mac, for that matter, this side of PostScript programming).

You _can_ create decent fractions in PageMaker, but it's a pain. Here's the proper (if troublesome) way to create ¼—the fraction that most people grin and bear with.

1. Set the 1 as a superscript
2. Set the / (it's different from a normal slash—more upright) by pressing Option-Shift-1. No super- or subscript.
3. Set the 4 as a subscript.
4. Swipe over all three characters and adjust the values in the Type options dialog box as in Figure 4-59.

These values work pretty well with Times, Helvetica, Stone, and Janson, among others. Larger type sizes (above about 14-point) start running into the slash with these values, so you'll have to adjust with kerning as needed.

**Figure 4-59**
Creating fractions
with the Type options
dialog box

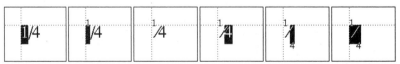

_Format the numerator as superscript, format the denominator as subscript, select the fraction, press Command-T to bring up the Type specifications dialog box, press the Options button, and then enter these values._

| Type options | | | OK |
|---|---|---|---|
| Small caps size: | 70 | % of point size | Cancel |
| Super/subscript size: | 60 | % of point size | |
| Superscript position: | 30 | % of point size | |
| Subscript position: | 0 | % of point size | |

_Here's what you get._

¼

## ▼ *Tip: Storing Up Fractions*

We strongly suggest that you build some kind of macro with QuicKeys or Tempo or the like if you plan on using fractions often. Otherwise, build yourself a library of fractions and keep them in the Scrapbook (use MultiScrap or SmartScrap if you want to have several different Scrapbook files available). A QuicKeys Sequence version of the macro would include the steps shown in Table 4-5.

**Table 4-5  Fraction-making QuicKey**

| Key | What it Does |
| --- | --- |
| Literal Command-T | Displays the Type specifications dialog box |
| Button key "Options…" | Clicks the Options button; create this key before you start building the sequence. |
| Text key <Tab>60 <Tab>30<Tab>0 | Makes the superscript/subscript size 60 percent, superscript baseline offset 30 percent, and the subscript baseline offset 0 percent. Change these values if you want your fractions to look different. Create this key before you start building the sequence. Don't type "<tab>" when you enter the key, just press a Tab. |
| Literal Return | Closes the Type options dialog box |
| Literal Return | Closes the Type specifications dialog box |
| Literal keypad 4 | Moves off the selection |
| Literal keypad 6 | Moves to the start of the fraction |
| Literal Command-Shift-keypad 6 | Selects the numerator |
| Literal Command-Shift-= | Makes numerator superscript |
| Literal Command-keypad 6 | Deselects numerator, move past slash |
| Literal Command-Shift-4 | Selects slash |
| Literal Option-Shift-1 | Makes slash proper fraction slash |

**Fraction-making QuicKey continued**

| Key | What it Does |
| --- | --- |
| Literal Command-Shift-keypad 6 | Selects denominator |
| Literal Command-Shift-- | Makes denominator subscript |
| Literal Keypad 6 | Deselects denominator, moves to right of fraction |

This assumes that there is at least one space or dash before the fraction. Assign a keystroke to this Sequence QuicKey (maybe Control-Command-Option-F), then select a simple fraction. Press your new QuicKey. Admire your new fraction.

But wait! What if you're always being handed fractions typed as 3-1/2 ($3\frac{1}{2}$) or 2002 111/345 ($2002\frac{111}{345}$)? Can't we remove the dash (or space) as we format the fraction? Sure. To the Sequence QuicKey above, add the keys shown in Table 4-6.

**Table 4-6 Additions to the fraction-making QuicKey**

| Key | What it Does |
| --- | --- |
| Literal Command-keypad 4 | Moves past denominator |
| Literal Command-keypad 4 | Moves past slash |
| Literal Command-keypad 4 | Moves past numerator |
| Literal Delete | Deletes space or slash |
| Literal Command-keypad 6 | Moves past numerator |
| Literal Command-keypad 6 | Moves past slash |
| Literal Command-keypad 6 | Moves past denominator |

All of this looks like it should take forever to execute, but (at least on our machines, a II and a IIcx), it goes by in the blink of an eye.

## *Working with Styles*

You've no doubt heard that PageMaker's styles are the key to long-document productivity—tools to automate your design and make pages come together fast. But even that's an understatement. Page-Maker styles are the most powerful text-handling tool in PageMaker, especially if you use parallel styles in your word processor to automate your copy processing. We use styles for every piece of type we place on a page. Religiously.

Many people—especially people who first learned PageMaker before version 3—have a hard time understanding styles. Somehow, they've gotten the idea that styles are esoteric, arcane things, understood and used only by gnomes pumping out ten-thousand-page government contracts for aerospace companies. They've also gotten the impression that styles are capable of only the simplest formatting. Both impressions are untrue, and lies of the vilest sort. Styles are not only easy to understand, they're an elegant way of formatting the most complex page layouts.

The main point is this: a style is a name for a collection of formatting attributes—all the specifications you choose using the commands on the Type menu. Whether you know it or not, you are already thinking in styles. When you're working with a page, you think of each kind of paragraph as having certain characteristics—font, type size, leading, indent, color, and so on. You know that subheads have one style, body copy paragraphs have another, and chapter heads have another.

**The Hard Way**

Without styles, you have to select text and manually format it by choosing commands from the menus—one piece of text at a time. The next time you use that kind of paragraph, you'll have to go through all of those menus and dialog boxes again—one at a time.

Neither of us (individually or in combination) can count the number of times we've seen people tearing out their hair because a client (or boss, or whatever) has come back to them with a flyer, newsletter, or technical manual and asked them to change every subhead in the publication to another font or point size. Because they didn't use styles, they have to go through the publication and manually swipe over each subhead (if they're smart they triple-click) and apply all the formatting changes from the menus.

With styles, you format a sample paragraph once, then create and name a style based on the formatted paragraph ("Subhead," for example). The next time you encounter a paragraph you want to format the same way, place the text cursor in the paragraph, then click on the style name in the Styles palette. The paragraph takes on the formatting characteristics you specified for the style.

Further, if you need to change the formatting for a particular kind of paragraph, you just edit the style and watch all the subheads in the document change to the new formatting.

## Styles, Tags, and Codes

Think in terms of text *elements*—body copy paragraphs, subheads, heads, bullet list paragraphs, etc.—and you're thinking in styles. You are *tagging* each paragraph, specifying what it *is*. Once it's tagged, you can make it *look like* whatever you want; you just change the style, and the tagged paragraphs change.

Those terms are worth repeating. Tagging specifies what each paragraph is. A style specifies what a tagged paragraph looks like. Tags can be in the form of actual text at the beginning of each paragraph—<subhead>, for instance—or you can tag paragraphs using Microsoft Word's style sheets (see "Our Favorite Word Tips and Tricks," later in this chapter). You can't see the tags in the Word file, but if you've applied styles then the tags are there, identifying each paragraph.

It's important to distinguish between tags, which specify what different elements are, and codes, which specify what selections of text look like. Many traditional and desktop publishing systems use embedded codes instead of or in addition to tags. You might type <it>italic<ei>, for instance, inserting codes that specify what the word should look like.

PageMaker doesn't read embedded codes in text. You can't insert a code in text to shift to italic, for instance, and expect PageMaker to understand it. It only understands tags, and formatting applied with word processors. The exception to that is importing of text in RTF

(Rich Text Format), a important new capability of PageMaker 4 which we discuss in "PageMaker and RTF," later in this chapter.

**Local Formatting**

The difference between tags and codes raises the whole issue of local formatting. We call normal text formatting without style sheets *local* or *hard* formatting. When you apply local formatting, it overrides style sheet formatting. You'll still want to use local formatting to change the type style of individual words or characters in a paragraph—*italics*, for instance. It's the one place where you can't use styles, because PageMaker styles work on the paragraph level.

PageMaker styles can contain the full complement of character formatting (except kerning), but that formatting applies to whole paragraphs. You can't apply a style just to a selection within a paragraph; it's all or nothing. We sure wish there were both paragraph *and* character styles available in PageMaker, like in the IBM version of Microsoft Word. Character styles are handy for special inline elements, like commands in a computer manual that you always put in Courier Bold, condensed to 80 percent, or run-in heads that are in a different typeface and size.

**▼ *Tip: Automate Character Styles with Change***

If you use some combination of local character formatting on a regular basis (10-point Garamond Bold, for instance), you can use PageMaker's ability to search and replace character attributes to save a lot of work (see Figure 4-60).

1. Use some weird character style in your word processor for the special text—underline, outline, or shadow, for instance—as long as you use it exclusively for the special text. You can invoke these styles in either Word or PageMaker with a keystroke.

2. Place the file in PageMaker.

3. Open the story with the Story editor (triple-click the text block, or click an insertion point with the Text tool and press Command-E),

and select "Change" from the Edit menu (Command-9).

4. Click the Attributes button and replace any text with outline formatting with 10-point Garamond Bold. Press Return to close the Attributes dialog box.

5. Click "Replace all" in the Change dialog box.

**Figure 4-60**
Attributes dialog box

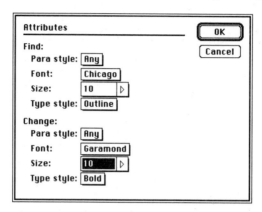

Note that you can't use this technique to change to Garamond Bold condensed to 80%, because the Set width attribute isn't there in the Attributes dialog box.

---

When you apply a style to a paragraph, the character formatting defined in the style overrides some of the local character formatting, but not all. It *does not* override any type "Style" attributes—italic, bold, underline, outline, etc. ("Reverse" is the exception; styles *will* override that attribute). All of that local formatting remains, on top of the styled formatting, so to speak. The style formatting *does* override and remove any other local character formatting—font, size, set width, tracking, kerning, etc.

▼ *Tip: Retaining Local Formatting While Changing Styles*

If you've locally formatted some text in a paragraph—made, for example, individual words a different font—and want to change styles without losing that formatting, hold down Shift as you apply the style. All of your local formatting will be retained (see Figure 4-61).

**Figure 4-61**
Applying styles with
Shift held down

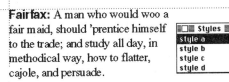

*Paragraph with local font change*

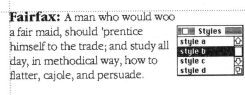

*If you change the style of the paragraph by clicking on another style name in the Styles palette, the new style's formatting overrides the local font change.*

*If you change the style of the paragraph by holding down Shift while you click on another style name in the Styles palette, the new style's formatting does not override the local font change.*

▼ *Tip: Getting Rid of Local Formatting*

If you have local formatting in a paragraph that's overriding the formatting specified in the style, you can get rid of the hard formatting.

1. Triple-click on the paragraph with the Text tool. Note that the paragraph's style name in the Styles palette has a "+" appended to it, showing that the paragraph contains local formatting.

2. Press Command-Shift-Spacebar (or choose "Normal" from the Type styles h-menu on the Type menu).

3. Reapply the style to the paragraph.

**Using the**
**Styles Palette**

The Styles palette is a shortcut; using it is much quicker than using the Define styles dialog box or the Apply styles h-menu off the Type menu. The only quicker way to apply styles is to use QuicKeys (see the tip below). To apply a style to a paragraph, follow these steps.

1. Place a text insertion point in the paragraph (or swipe over several paragraphs that you want to have the same style).

2. Click on the style name you want in the Styles palette.

Command-Y displays and hides the Styles palette. You can resize the Styles palette to display as many style names as you want, and you can drag it anywhere in the publication window. If you resize the Styles palette, put it away, and then redisplay it, it reappears at the size and position you specified before you put it away.

### ▼ Tip: Use QuicKeys to Apply Styles

We like to keep our hands on the keyboard when we're working with text, so we set up Menu/DA QuicKeys to apply styles.

Use the Styles h-menu off the Type menu to create your style keys. QuicKeys has trouble picking the style names out of the Define styles dialog box. Create keys that have some relation to the style you want to apply. In producing this book, for example, we used Control-A for our A heads, and Control-T for tip heads. Make up some mnemonic crutch that works for you. Be careful when naming styles—if you're trying to assign a QuicKey to a style named "paragraph," QuicKeys finds "Paragraph" on the Type menu first, and displays the Paragraph specifications dialog box.

### ▼ Tip: Creating Styles by Example

You can create an example paragraph that's formatted the way you want it, then build a style based on that paragraph.

1. Format a paragraph the way you want it using either the h-menus, key commands, or the dialog boxes off the Type menu.

2. Command-click on "No style" in the Styles palette. The Edit styles dialog box appears.

3. Type a style name in the Style name text edit field and click OK or press Return.

PageMaker creates a style with the attributes of your formatted paragraph. You can now apply that style to any similar paragraphs in your document. Note that creating the style this way does not apply the style to the currently selected paragraph. Usually, you'll want to scroll through the Styles palette listing and apply the style before you move on (see Figure 4-62).

**Figure 4-62**
Creating styles
by example

*Format a paragraph
using the commands
on the Type menu,
then Command-click
"No style" in the
Styles palette.*

*Type a name for
the style in the Edit
style dialog box
and click "OK." Note
that the paragraph's
formatting appears
at the bottom of the
dialog box.*

*The style name you
just created appears
in the Styles palette.
Click on the style name
to tag the paragraph
with that style.*

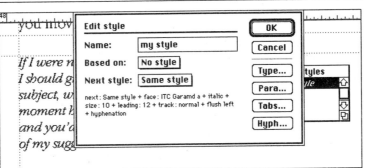

### ▼ Tip: Easy Way to Edit Styles

The quickest way to edit styles is to Command-click the style name in the Styles palette. This takes you directly to the Edit styles dialog box. Changes you make to the style are applied to all other paragraphs tagged with the edited style. Editing a style in this fashion *does not* override local formatting in paragraphs tagged with that style.

---

**Based on and Next style**

There are two options in the Edit style dialog box that many people find confusing—Based on and Next Style. Based on tells PageMaker to base the style you're editing on some other style. We like to format paragraphs that follow heads with no first-line indent, for instance. So we build a "body copy" style with a first-line indent, and a "first para" style based on "body copy," but with one difference—no first-line indent. The description of "first para" in the Edit styles dialog box reads "Body copy + first indent: 0."

Using the "Based on" feature, we really automate changes. Now if we decide that we want a different typeface for the body of the text, we can just change the "body copy" style. The font change ripples through into the "first para" style because it's based on "body copy," but the "+ first indent: 0" doesn't change. With careful planning, you can build hierarchies of styles based on other styles that let you make massive changes to a document with only a few seconds of work.

You can always break the link between styles. Just select "No Style" in the Based on pop-up menu.

### ▼ Tip: Easy Way to Base One Style on Another

If you want to create a new style based on another style:

1. Select a paragraph formatted with the base style.
2. Command-click on "No style" in the Styles palette. The Define styles dialog box appears, with the base style's name entered in the Based on pop-up menu.
3. Name the new style and make any changes you want. Those

changes define the differences between the base style and the new style. Keep clicking OK or pressing Return until you've closed all the dialog boxes.

Note that creating the style this way does not apply the style to the currently selected paragraph.

---

### ▼ *Tip: Merging Two Styles*

Sometimes, you'll need to change all of the text formatted as one style into another style (for instance if you want to change all the "Normal" paragraphs to the style "Body copy"). You could go through the entire document, clicking in the paragraphs and applying the style as you go, but there's a quicker way (Figure 4-63).

**Figure 4-63**
Merging two styles

*Paragraph tagged as first style*

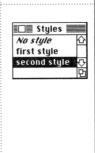

*Paragraph tagged as second style*

**Figure 4-63**
Merging two
styles continued

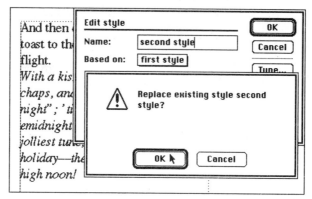

*Position a text insertion point in a paragraph tagged with the first style, then Command-click the first style's name in the Styles palette. Type the name of the second style in the Name text edit box and press Return. When the "Replace existing style" alert appears, click "OK."*

And then each ghost with his ladye-
toast to their churchyard beds take
flight.
With a kiss, perhaps, on her lantern
chaps, and a grisly grim, "good
night"; 'til the welcome knell of th
emidnight bell rings forth its
jolliest tune, and ushers in our next
holiday—the dead of the night's
high noon!

*The second style takes on the formatting characteristics of the first style. The two styles are now identical in all but name.*

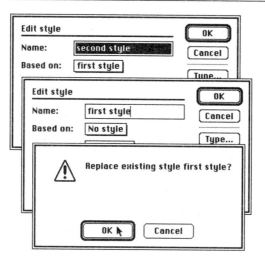

*Command-click the second style's style name in the Styles palette. In the Name text edit box, type the first style's name. Choose "No style" from the Based on pop-up menu and press Return. When the "Replace existing style" alert appears, click "OK."*

**Figure 4-63**
Merging two styles
continued

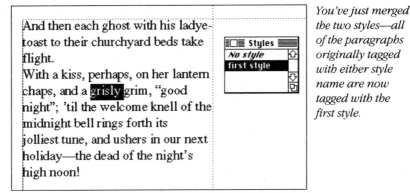

And then each ghost with his ladye-toast to their churchyard beds take flight.
With a kiss, perhaps, on her lantern chaps, and a grisly grim, "good night"; 'til the welcome knell of the midnight bell rings forth its jolliest tune, and ushers in our next holiday—the dead of the night's high noon!

*You've just merged the two styles—all of the paragraphs originally tagged with either style name are now tagged with the first style.*

In our example, we'll call the style with the correct formatting the first style, and the style we want to change the second style.

1. Click in an example paragraph of the first style.

2. Command-click "No style." The Edit styles dialog box appears.

3. In the Style name text edit field, type the name of the second style exactly as it appears in the Styles palette, and press Return. A prompt appears, asking if you want to replace the style. Click Yes. The second style now has the same formatting as the first style, and shows the first style's name in the Based on pop-up menu.

4. Command-click on the second style.

5. Type the name of the first style. Choose "No style" in the Based on pop-up menu to break the link, and press Return. A prompt appears, asking if you want to replace the style. Click Yes.

You've just merged the two styles.

▼ *Tip: Copy Styles Between Documents for Formatting Consistency*

You can use the Copy button in the Define styles dialog box to bring a style sheet from another PageMaker file into your current publication. The incoming styles will appear in the list of styles in the dialog box and will override any existing styles that have the same names. This is a great way to keep formatting consistent between publications.

Note that this is different from what happens when you place styled documents from Word with styles named identically to existing PageMaker styles. When placing text files, existing PageMaker styles override the formatting in the placed styles.

### ▼ *Tip: Build Specialized Style Sheets*

If you have a whole lot of styles that you use often, but don't want to clog up every document with two dozen unused styles, build some specialized style sheets that you can import selectively. We have several for different kinds of tabular matter, for instance.

### ▼ *Tip: Export Styles for Use in Word*

Using the Export command on the File menu, you can export styled text in Word format, with all the styles intact (at least to the extent that Word can understand PageMaker's formatting). Then you can apply the styles in Word, so the text is all styled before it ever hits the page—which is just the way you want it. You can also edit the styles in Word, so they're easier to work with during writing and editing. PageMaker's identically named styles will override Word's style formatting when you place the files.

If you're clever, you can get the writers or editors you work with to do a lot of the styling for you. That's actually the way it should work, because the writers and editors know what the different elements are—first-, second-, and third-level heads, bullet lists, etc. When you get to pages, you only have to worry about what the elements look like.

### ▼ *Tip: Printing Your Styles*

To print a copy of your styles, export them to Word then print them from there. Many of PageMaker's formatting attributes won't be reflected in the printout, but it's better than nothing.

1. Export the formatted text to Microsoft Word. If you want a record of every style, make sure that every style is used in some part of the text you're exporting. PageMaker doesn't export styles that are not used in the exported text.

2. Open the file in Word.

3. Choose "Define styles" (Command-T) from the Format menu (if you don't see it, choose "Long menus" from the Edit menu). While the dialog box is open, choose Print from the File menu.

Word prints a listing of your styles. Every style with a Based on setting of "No style" will be listed as being based on Word's default style "Normal." Ignore it. Also, PageMaker attributes that have no counterpart in Word will not appear, but the formatting information that is there will be correct.

## Editing Text

So far in this chapter, we've been talking about formatting and laying out type. PageMaker also has some impressive features, though, for editing text. You can simply click, swipe, and edit, of course, but there are sophisticated tools for search and replace, for spell-checking, and for creating indices and tables of contents.

### Using Special Characters

Beyond the normal alphanumeric characters that are so familiar from typing and word processing, there are dozens of special characters available for typesetting and desktop publishing (Table 4-7). Some of these are inherent in Macintosh fonts, so you can type them in your word processor and they import straight into PageMaker, and export back out again. Others are only available through special keystroke combinations in PageMaker; you can't type them in your word processor, and when you export a text file, they'll be lost.

These special characters can make all the difference between a publication that looks really professional and an obviously amateurish or slapdash job. Remember, this isn't typewriting, it's typesetting.

Here's a list of some common special characters, how to get at them, and whether you can get at them from programs other than PageMaker. For the characters that are *not* PageMaker-specific, you can find out which keys to hit using the Key Caps DA and selecting the current font from the Key Caps menu.

***Quotes.*** The best way to scream "desktop published!" with your publications is to use straight quotes and apostrophes (" and ') rather than open and close quotes (", ', ', and "). The straight ones are great for feet and inches (or minutes and seconds, if you're a cartographer), but you should use the curved ones everywhere else.

PageMaker converts straight quotes to open and close quotes automatically when you place or import a text file (as long as you've clicked the Convert quotes option in the Place document dialog box). When you're typing on the page, however, be careful to type the true quotes explicitly, and proof carefully for them. We're always seeing these little suckers in captions and headlines.

You can also use QuicKeys or Quote Init (see Chapter 2, *Building a PageMaker System*) to do your curly quotes automatically, as you type (though you have to watch them, also; they'll sometimes give you an open quote when you want a close quote). In any case, a quick search for straight quotes in the Story editor can save you from looking foolish.

***Em dashes.*** When you type two hyphens on a typewriter, you're approximating an em dash--like this. Double hyphens are almost as sure a sign as straight quotes for telling people that you're a desktop publisher. Use em dashes instead. An em dash is one em wide—12 points wide in 12-point type.

If you ask it to by clicking "Convert quotes" in the Place document dialog box, PageMaker converts double hyphens to em dashes as you place or import a text file. As with quotes, however, you have to be careful when you're typing copy right on the page, and vigilant when you're proofing.

***En dashes.*** These characters are half as wide as an em dash, and a

**Table 4-7  Special characters**

| For | Type | PageMaker-specific? |
| --- | --- | --- |
| Open single quote (‘) | Option-] | N |
| Close single quote (’) | Option-Shift-] | N |
| Open double quote (“) | Option-[ | N |
| Close double quote (”) | Option-Shift-[ | N |
| Em space | Command-Shift-M | Y |
| En space | Command-Shift-N | Y |
| Thin space | Command-Shift-T | Y |
| Fixed space | Option-Spacebar | Y (will import from Word) |
| Discretionary hyphen | Command-- (Command-hyphen) | Y (will import from Word) |
| Page number marker | Command-Option-P | Y |
| Em dash (—) | Option-Shift-- (Option-Shift-hyphen) | N |
| En dash (–) | Option-- (Option-hyphen) | N |
| Ellipsis (…) | Option-; | N |
| Bullet (•) | Option-8 | N |
| ¶ | Option-7 | N |
| § | Option-6 | N |
| ® | Option-r | N |
| © | Option-g | N |
| TM | Option-2 | N |
| é | Option-e, then type e (or any other vowel but y) | N |
| è | Option-\`, then type e (or any other vowel but y) | N |
| ö | Option-u, then type o (or any other vowel but y) | N |
| ô | Option-i, then type o | N |
| ñ | Option-n, then type n | N |
| ç | Option-c | N |

little wider than a hyphen. You use them in place of "to," for example in "9 AM–5 PM" or "the New York–Chicago Express." You can get away with a hyphen here, but, if you want to do it right, use an en dash.

***Discretionary hyphens.*** These are fondly referred to as "dischys" (pronounced dishies). PageMaker will use them "at its discretion" to break a word at the end of a line (unless hyphenation is turned off for that paragraph), but otherwise they remain invisible and don't do anything. Put one of these just before the first character of a word if you *don't* want PageMaker to hyphenate it.

***Em spaces.*** A lot of designers specify a one-em indent (as wide as the type size) for the first line of a paragraph. In the old days these were called em quads. You can get a one-em indent by typing an em space at the beginning of the line (though we prefer just formatting the paragraph with a first-line indent). There's no way to type em spaces in a word processor, so you're best off typing some weird character instead, then replacing it in PageMaker.

***En spaces.*** These are half the width of em spaces—half the point size.

***Thin spaces.*** These are half as wide as an en space—one-quarter the point size. They can be useful in aligning tabular matter, or for separating the dots in an ellipsis.

***Fixed spaces.*** The size of these spaces varies from typeface to typeface. A fixed space is generally the width of a normal space, but it doesn't expand or contract within a line of justified type.

***Ellipses.*** The three little dots that designate continuation are called ellipses. You can type three periods (perhaps separating them by thin spaces), or you can use a hard ellipsis. This is a judgment call; you have to decide if you like the spacing of the dots in a given typeface's ellipsis. We like using a hard ellipsis to designate a hiatus in a list (1, 2, 3…7, 8, 9), but dots and thin spaces often look better when you're trailing off into infinity. . . .

***Foreign and special-purpose characters.*** There are dozens of special characters built into the Macintosh character set. Call up your Key Caps DA, choose a typeface like Times from the Key Caps menu, and hold down the Option and Shift keys alone and in combination to see what's available. Many of these characters are "borrowed" from the Symbol typeface.

***Symbols and dingbats.*** There are quite a few typefaces that don't use the standard Mac character set. Instead they're full of strange and wonderful beasts. The most familiar are Symbol and Zapf Dingbats, but another of our favorites is Bullets & Boxes. To figure out which keystrokes to hit for all those strange characters, use the Key Caps DA.

## *The Story Editor*

The largest single new feature in PageMaker 4 is the Story editor (Figure 4-64), which provides a second view—the Story view—of the text in your publication. The Story editor is a full-featured word processor you can invoke from Layout view using one of several methods.

- Select a text block with the Pointer tool or click an insertion point with the Text tool, and Press Command-E or choose "Edit story" from the Edit menu.
- Triple-click on the text block with the Pointer tool.
- Choose the name of the story you want to edit from the Windows menu (if the story is already open in the Story editor).

To return to Layout view, click the close box in the upper-left of the story window, press Command-E (note that Command-E toggles you between Story view and Layout view), or choose "Edit layout" from the Edit menu.

When you open the Story editor, think "text." Paragraph formatting isn't visible in the Story editor, and only some character formatting is shown. The Story editor doesn't show the column widths, tab

**Figure 4-64**
Story view

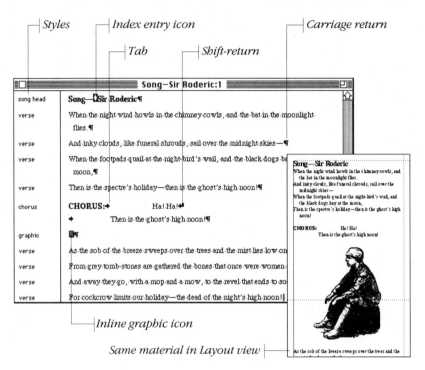

Styles | Index entry icon | Carriage return
Tab | Shift-return

Inline graphic icon

Same material in Layout view

positions, or first-line indents; it just wraps to the width of the window. This is another reason to use styles instead of local paragraph formatting—you can tell what paragraph formatting is applied to the paragraph from the style bar on the left of the Story editor window. Try to keep from worrying about the way the text looks until you return to the Layout view. You can, however, change the font and type size used by the Story editor to display your text through the Story editor settings in the Preferences dialog box.

When you're in the Story editor, PageMaker's menus change. A new menu, Story, appears in place of the Page menu, and several other menus have commands added to them or deleted from them (Figure 4-65).

While each Story editor window contains a single story, you can have several Story editor windows open at the same time. Only one Story editor window can be active at a time, but you can switch between open stories by clicking on the stories' windows to make them active, or by choosing between the names of different open stories on the Windows menu.

**Figure 4-65**
Story view menus

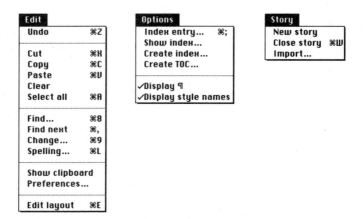

When you are working on a Story editor view of a story, the text of the story in the Layout view is grayed out (Figure 4-66). PageMaker will not recompose it until you close the Story editor and return to Layout view.

#### ▼ *Tip: Delete Next Character Right*

Use Option-Delete to delete the character to the right of the cursor. This only works in the Story editor.

The Import command on the Story menu provides a way of loading text directly into the open Story editor. "Import" is basically the same as Place, except that you won't see a loaded place gun until you leave the Story editor.

**Figure 4-66**
Story view
and Layout view

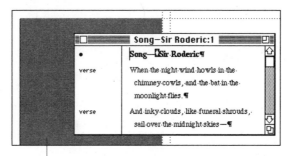

*When you open a text block in the Story editor, the Layout view of the text grays out.*

**Finding and Changing Text**

PageMaker 4's Story editor includes powerful features for finding and changing text and text attributes hitherto found only in word processors and PageMaker's competitors (Figure 4-67). You can use "Find" and "Change" to search through selected text, the current story, or all of the stories in the publication.

You can find either a string of characters or formatting attributes, or both. Likewise, you can replace either a string of characters or formatting attributes, or both. In other words, you don't have to specify any string of characters to search for; you can just search for attributes. Nor do you have to specify any characters in the Change to text edit box; you can just change formatting attributes.

**Figure 4-67**
Find, Change, and Attributes dialog boxes

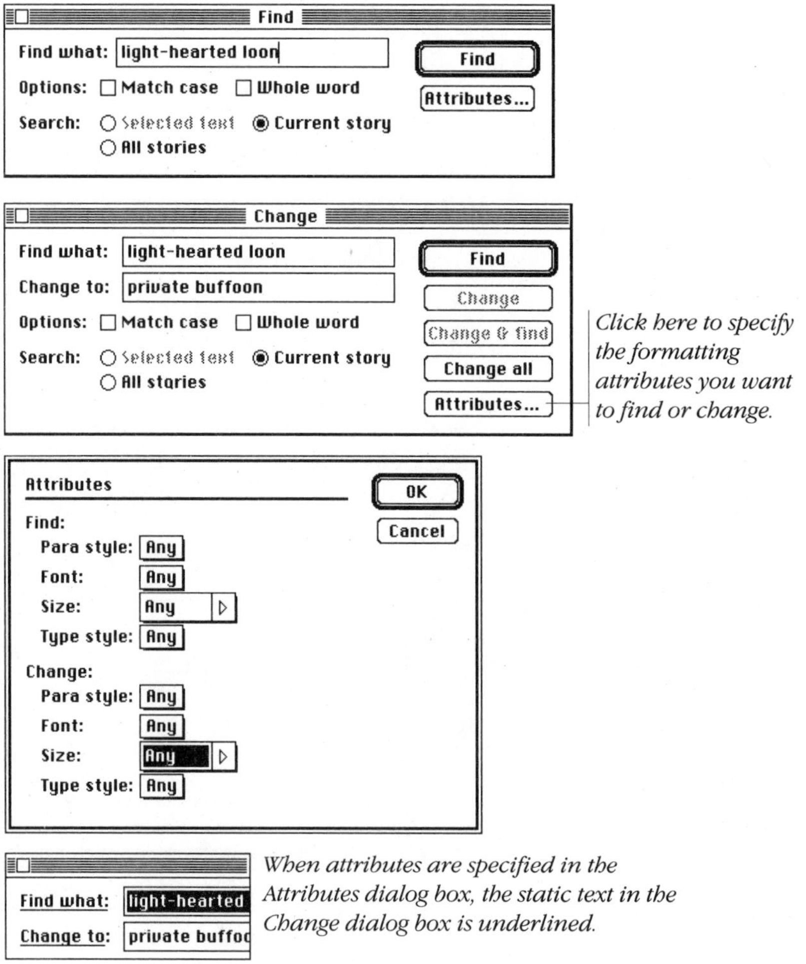

*Click here to specify the formatting attributes you want to find or change.*

*When attributes are specified in the Attributes dialog box, the static text in the Change dialog box is underlined.*

▼ *Tip: Reverting all Change Attributes to Any*

Option-click on the Attributes button in the Find or Change dialog box to return all the Attribute settings to "Any." This is useful if you've just finished an attribute search, want to start a normal text search, and don't want to go through all the pop-up menus.

---

▼ *Tip: Special Characters Used in*
*the Find and Change Dialog Boxes*

PageMaker has taken some search-and-replace lessons from Word, and it's gone farther; Word could learn a thing or two from these. To search and replace special characters, enter the codes shown in Table 4-8 in the Change dialog box. Other characters are entered in dialog boxes by typing them as you ordinarily would.

PageMaker also searches for any specific character designated by $^\wedge nnn$, where *nnn* is the ASCII decimal code number of the character. This was included for former PC users who have never figured out how to use Key Caps. Actually, it's useful when there are characters hidden away in the files that don't have keyboard equivalents on the Mac—like the linefeeds (ASCII 10) in IBM text files.

---

**Checking Spelling**

To spell check a story, triple-click on the story to open the Story editor, and choose "Spelling" from the Edit menu (Command-L). The Spelling dialog box appears (Figure 4-68). To check the entire publication, you can triple-click on any story, and then select "All stories" in the Spelling dialog box.

If the dictionary folder for at least one language cannot be found in the Aldus folder in your system folder, PageMaker displays the "Error accessing dictionary" message. Copy a dictionary folder into your Aldus folder, and try again.

Once you've started a spelling check, PageMaker scans through the range of text you've specified. If PageMaker can't find a word in the user dictionary or selected language dictionary, PageMaker displays the

**Table 4-8  Finding and changing special characters**

| Character | What You Enter in the Dialog Box |
| --- | --- |
| Paragraph end (Return) | ^p |
| New-line (Shift-Return) | ^n |
| Tab | ^t |
| Discretionary hyphen | ^- |
| Nonbreaking space | ^s |
| Caret | ^^ |
| An unspecified (wildcard) character | ^? (This only works in the Find what field; putting it in the Change to field replaces the search string with a question mark, not the wildcard character.) |
| White space | ^w or ^W |
| Thin space | ^< |
| En space | ^> |
| Em space | ^m or ^M |
| En dash | ^= |
| Em dash | ^_ |
| Nonbreaking hyphen | ^~ |
| Computer-inserted hyphen | ^c or ^C |
| Nonbreaking slash | ^/ |
| Page number token | ^# or ^3 |

**Figure 4-68**
Spelling dialog box

*Words PageMaker thinks are misspelled...*

*...are highlighted in Story view...*

*...and are displayed in this text edit box.*

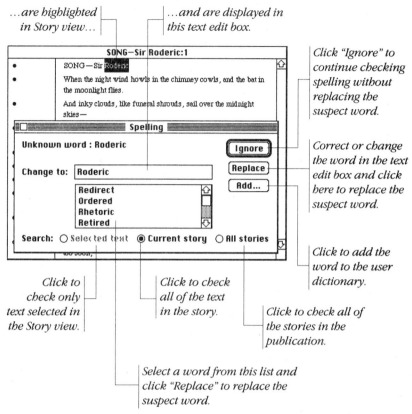

*Click "Ignore" to continue checking spelling without replacing the suspect word.*

*Correct or change the word in the text edit box and click here to replace the suspect word.*

*Click to add the word to the user dictionary.*

*Click to check only text selected in the Story view.*

*Click to check all of the text in the story.*

*Click to check all of the stories in the publication.*

*Select a word from this list and click "Replace" to replace the suspect word.*

word in the Change to text edit box and selects the word in the Story view, always scrolling to make the word visible above the Spelling dialog box.

Note that the Spelling dialog box isn't a modal dialog box; you can reach outside of it to activate DAs, change to other programs, and so on. This can be very handy if you need to sprint to a HyperCard stack to get the correct spelling of someone's name or street address to add to the user dictionary.

Note also that PageMaker checks for more than spelling. A set of grammar-checking rules is applied to the text in your story—checking for things like "the the," and other common typos. While it seems odd to have the suspect word appear in a text edit box titled "Change to," the point is that whatever is displayed in that text edit box replaces the text selected in the Story view when you click "Replace."

To retain the suspect word as-is, click "Ignore." PageMaker returns to the hunt. If you want to change the word to one of the words in the suggestion list, select the word in the selection list. It will appear in the Change to text edit box and replace the text that's selected in the Story view when you click "Replace."

And of course, if all of these automated tools don't correct the problem, you can simply type the correct word in the Change to text edit box and click "Replace."

## Adding to the Dictionary

You can add the word in the Change to text edit box to the user dictionary by clicking "Add." The Add word to dictionary dialog box appears with the suspect word entered in the Word text edit box (Figure 4-69). Most words appear with hyphenation points (PageMaker's best guess) inserted. Edit the hyphenation points as you like: delete them, change their rank (one tilde is the best hyphenation point, three tildes is the worst), or enter new points by entering tildes. Then press Return to enter the word into the user dictionary. (See "Hyphenation in PageMaker" later in this chapter for more on hyphenation points.)

If the word is already in the user dictionary, PageMaker displays "Word is already in user dictionary!" which means you'll have to remove the current version of the word from the user dictionary before you enter your new, improved version.

You can also type a new word in the Change to text edit field and click "Add" to add the word to the user dictionary, then click "Replace" when you return to the Spelling dialog box to replace the suspect word in the text file with the word you just added.

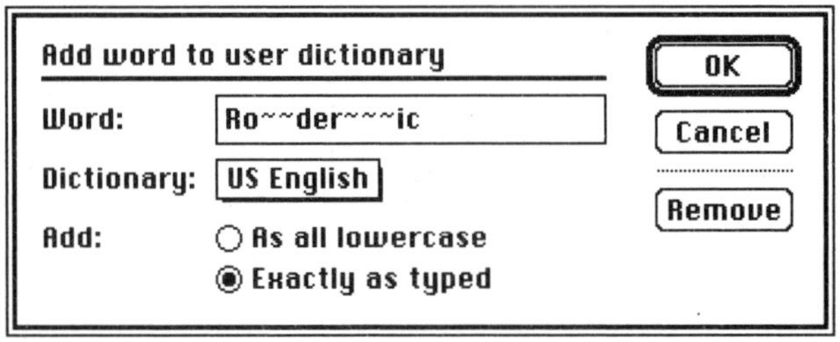

**Figure 4-69**
Add word to user
dictionary dialog box

Add word to user dictionary | OK
Word: Ro~~der~~~ic | Cancel
Dictionary: US English
Add: ○ As all lowercase ◉ Exactly as typed | Remove

## *Knockouts and Overprinting*

The illustrations on these pages demonstrate the use of both spot and process color. To save our publisher money, we're using solid tints of the process colors as spot colors.

**The Color
Paper and the
Fill Paper**

When you're printing spot color overlays, Paper-colored objects knock out of everything behind them, whether you have "Knockouts" (in the Print options dialog box) turned on or not. Paper-*filled* objects only knock out of items that are the same color. With "Knockouts" on, everything knocks out of every other color behind it.

**What You See**

All the colored items you see here are Solid-filled, and colored Cyan, Magenta, or Yellow. The white boxes are a little trickier.

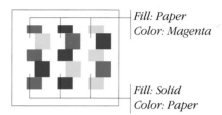

*Fill: Paper
Color: Magenta*

*Fill: Solid
Color: Paper*

**What You Get**

**Knockouts off.** When you print this illustration with the Knockouts option in the Print dialog box turned off, the overlays look like this (though of course all the overlays would come out of the imagesetter in black). Notice how the colored inks overprint on each other.

*Cyan overlay*

*Magenta overlay*

*Yellow overlay*

*When printed*

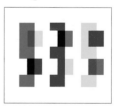

**Knockouts on.** Every object knocks out of every different-colored object behind it. None of the colored objects overprints.

*Cyan overlay*

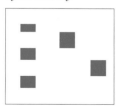

*Magenta overlay*

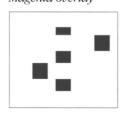

*Yellow overlay*

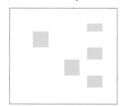

*When printed*

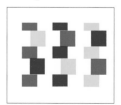

**Selective
Knockouts**

In this example, we want to knock the colored type out of the background, so it doesn't overprint. The black type, on the other hand, should overprint on the cyan background.

**Creating the
Knockouts**

Copy the text block to the Clipboard, then Option-paste (Command-Option-V) into exactly the same position you copied from. Color the type in the first line "Paper," (or reverse the type—it's the same thing), and then delete the type in the second line.

Send the new text block to the back (Command-B), and then send the black box to the back. The white type beneath the colored type creates a knockout.

**What You Get**

When you print the overlays, here's what you get (in black, of course).

*Cyan overlay*

*Magenta overlay*

*Black overlay*

*If you printed without selective knock-outs, it would look like this.*

## *PageMaker and Process Color*

You can process separate scanned color images, placed EPS color graphics, and CMYK-specified PageMaker LBOs by printing pages to disk as PostScript, and separating that with a separation utility, such as Aldus PrePrint. We used Adobe PhotoShop to separate the scanned image, then stacked up the separated TIFFs in PageMaker and printed spot color overlays one at a time.

**Scanned Images, EPS Graphics, and LBOs**

*Cyan separation*          *Magenta separation*

*Yellow separation*          *Black separation*

**Consistent Blacks**

If you add a bit of cyan, magenta, and yellow to your blacks, they'll look more consistent where they overprint other colors.

*100% Black*

*100% Black*
*20% Cyan*
*20% Magenta*
*20% Yellow*

## Building Traps

You can build traps to correct for press misregistration using either spot or process colors. The techniques vary slightly, however, depending on whether you're printing process seps or spot color overlays.

**Traps for Spot Colors**

To create traps for spot colors, we use selective knockouts, but make the knockouts slightly smaller (a "choke") and the overlapping objects slightly larger (a "spread"). In this example, the cyan and magenta overlays overlap slightly.

**Traps for Process Colors**

Traps are easier with process colors because you can mix percentages and you don't need traps if abutting colors share some percentage of a process color. The colors here don't have any process color in common, so we had to trap them.

*Layer 1*
*80M/60Y*

*Layer 2*
*80C/30K*

*Layer 3*
*80M/40C/20Y*

*As printed*

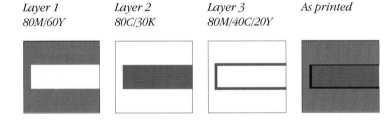

## PageMaker Color Tricks

*These samples were created entirely in PageMaker and were separated (as spot color overlays) from PageMaker.*

9  0
SOUNDWORK

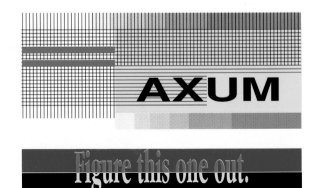

AXUM

Figure this one out.

### ▼ *Tip: Adding Without Replacing*

Sometimes, you want to add words to the user dictionary without replacing any suspect words in your file. Bring up the Spelling dialog box and click "Add." You can add words, one after another, by clicking "Add" over and over again. You can click "Add" while a suspect word is displayed in the Change to text edit box without replacing the suspect word. Just type over it in the Add word to user dictionary dialog box.

### ▼ *Tip: Removing Words*

If you add a word to the user dictionary and then find you've made an error (there's no better time for typos than when you're entering words in a spelling dictionary), you can remove the word from the user dictionary by bringing up the Add word to dictionary dialog box, typing the word (exactly as you typed it when you added it), then clicking the Remove button.

PageMaker displays a Word removed alert if you've typed the word correctly. If, instead, PageMaker displays "Word not found in user dictionary," you'll have to try typing the word again. It's kind of like playing Battleship.

### ▼ *Tip: Wraparound Spell Checking*

When PageMaker's spelling checker reaches the end of the story (or the end of the selected text if you've chosen "Selected text only," or the last story in the publication if you've chosen "All stories"), the message "Spelling check complete" appears in the Spelling dialog box.

If you think you've missed something, or you started the spelling check from somewhere in the middle of the selected range and still need to check the start of the file, or if you just want to re-experience the thrill of whizzing through the text blocks, click "Start" and PageMaker will check the spelling in the selected range again.

### ▼ Tip: Check Selected Word

One of Word's nicer features is that you can select a word you're not sure is spelled correctly, press Command-L to summon the spelling checker (same key combination as PageMaker—what a coincidence!), and Word will tell you if the selected word is correctly or incorrectly spelled. This is very reassuring at the end of a long production edit when everything—including "the," "it," and "dog"—looks misspelled.

In PageMaker, on the other hand, you have to select the word in the Story editor, press Command-L, click "Selected text," and then press "Start." It's really a bore. Instead, why not make a QuicKey that does it for you?

1. Create a Button QuicKey for "Selected text."
2. Open a Sequence QuicKey and enter the Literal Command-L (to start the spell checker), the "Selected text" Button QuicKey, and the Literal Return.

Now, each time you press the key you've assigned for this Sequence key, PageMaker checks the word you've selected in the Story view.

### PageMaker's Dictionaries

The dictionaries that make all of this spell checking work (and the hyphenation discussed below) are stored in the Aldus folder in your system folder. When you installed PageMaker, the Installer asked you which language dictionaries you wanted to install. Most likely, you chose English, and you'll find the dictionaries in your Aldus folder inside a folder named English. That's also where you'll find your user dictionary—the one you change when you add or delete words. It's called AldEng.UDC (the .UDC is what counts—the beginning of the file name depends on what language you're using).

### ▼ Tip: Swapping User Dictionaries

You can have more than one user dictionary, but you won't be able to use both user dictionaries at once. To create and use a new user dictionary, follow these steps.

1. Move your current user dictionary to another folder.

2. Add entries through the Spelling dialog box to create a new user dictionary.

PageMaker will use the new dictionary as long as it's in the current language folder.

3. When you need to use your original user dictionary, move the new user dictionary to another folder, then move your original dictionary into the dictionary folder.

The next time you open a publication, you'll be working with your original user dictionary.

---

### ▼ Tip: Using Multiple Language Dictionaries

You can use more than one language dictionary in a publication, and the number of language dictionaries you can use at one time seems limited only by the amount of RAM you have available. Additional dictionaries are available from Aldus.

## Hyphenation in PageMaker

Hyphenation controls in PageMaker 3 were pretty simple. If you wanted to use PageMaker's automatic hyphenation, you checked "Auto hyphenation" in the Paragraph specifications dialog box. If you wanted to hyphenate manually, you entered discretionary hyphens (dischys—entered with Command-hyphen). If you wanted PageMaker to show you the likely hyphenation points in a selected range of text, you checked "Prompted" in the Paragraph specifications dialog box. You controlled the hyphenation zone with an entry in the Spacing dialog box. That was it.

The good news is that PageMaker 4 offers more control over hyphenation. The bad news is that the way you interact with this control is a little tough to learn, at first. There are several hyphenation controls that interact in interesting ways.

**Hyphenation Methods**

There are three types of hyphenation in PageMaker—manual, and two automatic methods—dictionary-based and algorithmic.

- Manual hyphenation relies on discretionary hyphens that you enter manually, and that PageMaker uses at its discretion to break lines. If a dischy lands in the middle of a line, PageMaker ignores it. Dischys are visible only when they land at the ends of lines (unlike normal hyphens, which appear no matter what).

- Dictionary-based hyphenation relies on PageMaker's ranked hyphenation dictionaries. The words in these dictionaries contain hyphenation points, ranked according to the quality of hyphenation that results. Hyphenation points are designated with tildes (~); better hyphenation points have fewer tildes (Figure 4-70). You can control which ranks PageMaker uses.

- Algorithmic hyphenation relies on computer logic, which attempts to understand the way words are built in English (or whatever language you're using). By applying rules about prefixes, suffixes, and word construction, PageMaker inserts hyphens even in words not included in its dictionaries.

Manual hyphenation is the most reliable, assuming that you enter dischys properly. Dictionary hyphenation is also reliable, depending which ranks of hyphens you choose to employ. Algorithmic hyphenation is not very reliable. PageMaker will make mistakes using this method. The more reliable methods result in fewer hyphens, and less consistently justified copy (word and letter spacing will vary more from line to line). The less reliable methods result in more hyphens, and more consistently justified copy.

**Figure 4-70**
Ranked hyphenation

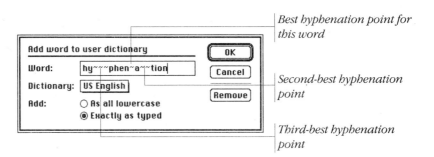

*Best hyphenation point for this word*

*Second-best hyphenation point*

*Third-best hyphenation point*

**Hyphenation Control**

The key to PageMaker 4's hyphenation power is the Hyphenation dialog box (Figure 4-71), which is a paragraph-level control (so hyphenation settings can be built into paragraph styles). Display the Hyphenation dialog box by choosing "Hyphenation" from the Type menu (Command-H).

The first odd thing to get used to is that if hyphenation is turned off, even manual hyphenation won't work. PageMaker will break words containing hard hyphens (as in "face-melting"), but it will not use manually inserted dischys. We cannot think of any reason you'd want to disallow manual hyphenation (if you don't want manual hyphenation, don't enter any dischys), but that's how it works. We strongly feel that dischys should always override settings you've made in the Hyphenation dialog box, including turning hyphenation on and off and number of consecutive hyphens. PageMaker just doesn't work that way, though.

**Figure 4-71**
Hyphenation dialog box

*Click to use manual hyphenation (dischys) in the selected range of text.*

*Click to turn all hyphenation (including dischys) off for the selected range of text.*

*Click to use the first and second rank of hyphenation points found in PageMaker's dictionaries (as well as dischys).*

*Click to use the first, second, and third rank of hyphenation points in PageMaker's dictionaries, and the hyphenation algorithm (as well as dischys).*

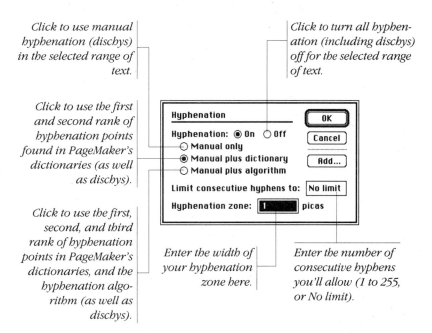

*Enter the width of your hyphenation zone here.*

*Enter the number of consecutive hyphens you'll allow (1 to 255, or No limit).*

A great new hyphenation control is "Limit consecutive hyphens to," which lets you control how many consecutive lines can be hyphenated. Stacked hyphens (or "ladders"—three or more consecutive, hyphenated lines) are another of the hallmarks of amateur page layout. Ole doesn't like to hyphenate even two lines in a row, though that's another rule that everyone has to break, sooner or later. Keep yourself looking like a pro by entering 1 in the Limit consecutive hyphens to text edit box. Entering 0 for "Limit consecutive hyphens to" does not prevent hyphenation; it allows ladders of unlimited length. Unless you're seeking a route to Nirvana or have hyphenation set to Manual, don't use this setting.

Ole still feels that the best hyphenation method is Manual with a Limit consecutive hyphens to setting of No limit. Enter dischys where you want the lines to break. Take charge. If you're serious about getting line breaks right, you'll often spend more time fixing PageMaker-entered hyphens (dictionary or—shudder—algorithmic) than you will entering your own hyphenation points. Lots of the entries in the dictionary allow two-character hyphenations, another of those tell-tale signs of the inept.

## In the Hyphenation Zone

The Hyphenation zone text edit box came from PageMaker 3's Spacing dialog box, but, as with spacing, it now applies on the paragraph level. The hyphenation zone might more accurately be called the line-break zone. It's the area where PageMaker looks for a possible line break—be it a word space, hyphen, slash, dischy, or PageMaker-generated hyphenation point.

The best way to understand the hyphenation zone is to think in terms of flexibility. If you specify a large hyphenation (read: line-break) zone, PageMaker has more flexibility in choosing where it should break the line. It's likely to find a space or some other convenient break point within the zone, so it won't have to hyphenate. The result is a looser rag (with more variation between line lengths), or less consistent, more variable justification from line to line. With a small hyphenation zone, PageMaker doesn't have much flexibility. It's less likely to find a break point, so it has to hyphenate more (Figure 4-72). The result is a tighter rag, or more consistent justification.

You're thinking that there's a loophole, right? Using small hyphenation zone settings with tight hyphenation controls? It doesn't quite work that way. PageMaker will just break your rules more often to com-

**Figure 4-72**
Small and large
hyphenation zones

If I were not a little mad and generally silly I would give you my advice upon the subject, willy nilly, I should show you in a moment how to grapple with the question and you'd really be astonished at the force of my suggestion. On the subject I shall write you a most valuable letter, full of excellent suggestions when I feel a little better, but at present I'm afraid I am as mad as any hatter, so I'll keep 'em to myself, for my opinion doesn't matter!

If I were not a little mad and generally silly I would give you my advice upon the subject, willy nilly, I should show you in a moment how to grapple with the question and you'd really be astonished at the force of my suggestion. On the subject I shall write you a most valuable letter, full of excellent suggestions when I feel a little better, but at present I'm afraid I am as mad as any hatter, so I'll keep 'em to myself, for my opinion doesn't matter!

*Hyphenation zone set to 6 picas. A large hyphenation zone results in a looser rag, or more variable justification, with fewer hyphens.*

*Hyphenation zone set to 0 picas. A small hyphenation zone results in a tighter rag, or more consistent justification, with more hyphens.*

pose the line, so you'll see more loose/tight lines highlighted on your screen. Experiment with the hyphenation zone to see what settings work best with your copy and format. To start with, try settings in the 1 pica to 2 pica range.

**Dictionary Hyphenation**

The Add button in the Hyphenation dialog box works exactly like the Add button in the Spelling dialog box, so refer to "Checking Spelling," above, for a description of working with the Add word to dictionary dialog box. PageMaker uses the same dictionaries for spelling and hyphenation, so you update both at the same time.

▼ *Tip: Keeping Words from Breaking*

You can keep words from breaking by inserting a discretionary hyphen (Command--, or ^- in the Change dialog box) immediately before the first character of the word (Figure 4-73). This comes in handy when you're fixing tight lines that end with a hyphenated word, or have a perfume product named "Dissolute" that you don't want PageMaker to hyphenate.

**Figure 4-73**
Keeping words
from breaking

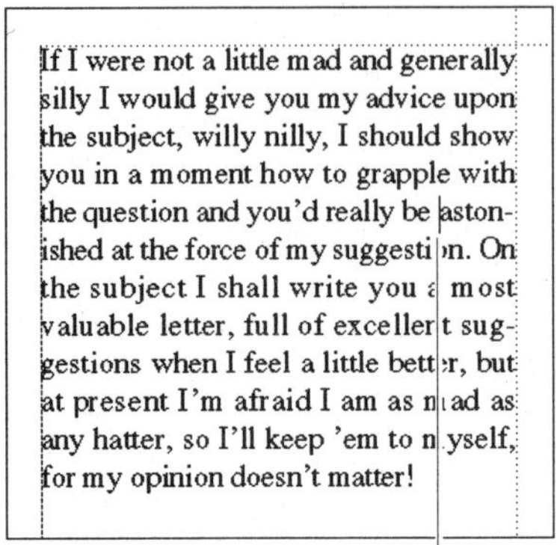

If I were not a little mad and generally silly I would give you my advice upon the subject, willy nilly, I should show you in a moment how to grapple with the question and you'd really be astonished at the force of my suggestion. On the subject I shall write you a most valuable letter, full of excellent suggestions when I feel a little better, but at present I'm afraid I am as mad as any hatter, so I'll keep 'em to myself, for my opinion doesn't matter!

If I were not a little mad and generally silly I would give you my advice upon the subject, willy nilly, I should show you in a moment how to grapple with the question and you'd really be astonished at the force of my suggestion. On the subject I shall write you a most valuable letter, full of excellent suggestions when I feel a little better, but at present I'm afraid I am as mad as any hatter, so I'll keep 'em to myself, for my opinion doesn't matter!

*Place the insertion point immediately before the word you want to keep from breaking and press Command--.*

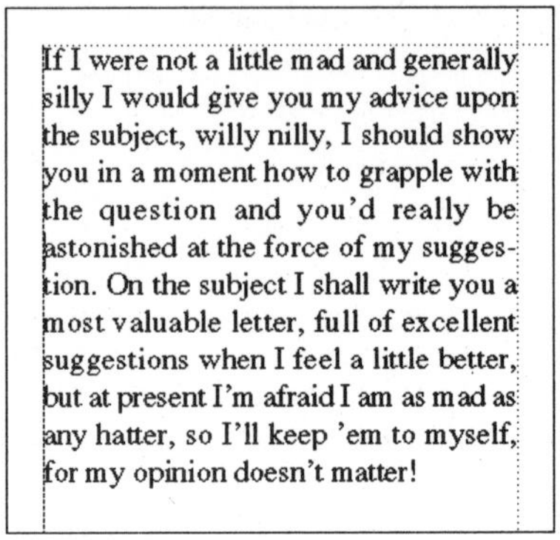

*The word moves to the next line.*

This technique also works when you're adding words to the user dictionary. Put a tilde (~) before the word to keep it from breaking.

## ▼ Tip: Keeping Words Together

You can keep words together by replacing the space between them with a nonbreaking space (Option-Spacebar, entered as ^s or ^S in dialog boxes). This is especially good for fixing the rags of ragged-right paragraphs and for repairing tight or loose lines in justified paragraphs (Figure 4-74).

**Figure 4-74**
Keeping words together

really be astonished at the force of my suggestion. On the subject I shall write you a most valuable letter, full of excellent suggestions when I feel a little better, but at present I'm afraid I am as mad as any hatter,

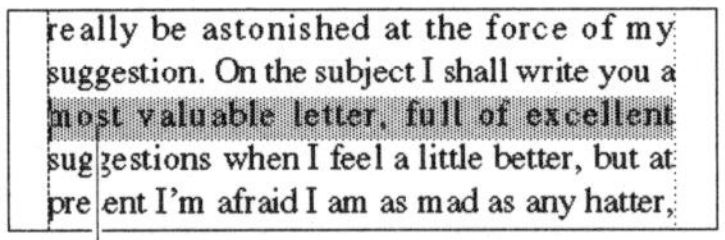

*PageMaker has highlighted this line because it is "loose," according to the current settings in the Spacing dialog box. You can correct this loose line by bringing one word—"a"—down to the next line.*

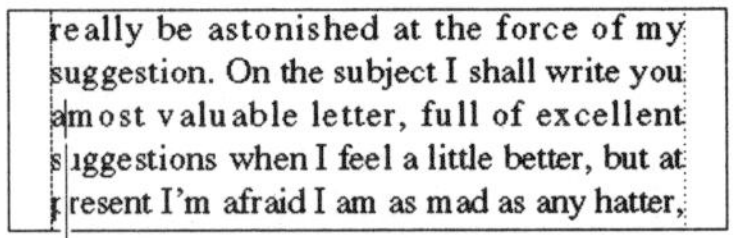

really be astonished at the force of my suggestion. On the subject I shall write you amost valuable letter, full of excellent suggestions when I feel a little better, but at present I'm afraid I am as mad as any hatter,

*Place the insertion point before "most," press Delete…*

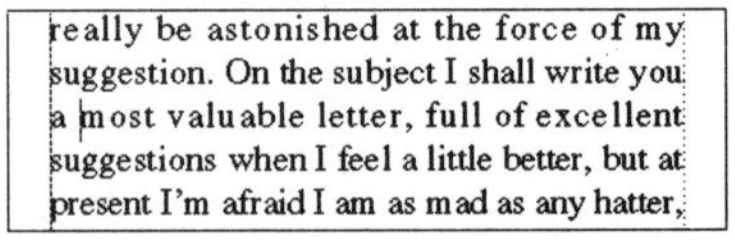

really be astonished at the force of my suggestion. On the subject I shall write you a most valuable letter, full of excellent suggestions when I feel a little better, but at present I'm afraid I am as mad as any hatter,

*…and then type Option-Spacebar.*

▼ *Tip: Keeping Compound Words from Breaking*

PageMaker 4 has a true nonbreaking hyphen—gone are the days of using en dashes (though we never did) for compound words you don't want to break. Press Command-Option-hyphen ( ^ ~ in dialog boxes) to enter the nonbreaking hyphen.

▼ *Tip: Other Nonbreaking Characters*

All of the typographic spaces—em (Command-Shift-m), en (Command-Shift-n), and thin (Command-Shift-t) are nonbreaking. The en dash (Option-hyphen) is also a nonbreaking character.

## Book Tools

There's one other text-related area where PageMaker 4 has made big improvements—book-related tools for creating indices and tables of contents. By building a "book list" that tells PageMaker what files are in the book and their order (see "PageMaker 4's Book Command" in Chapter 3, *Making PageMaker Mind*), you allow it to build tables of contents and indices based on all those files at once.

Remember, though, that the book list does not do anything for your page numbering. You still need to open each file individually, and type the starting page number in the Page setup dialog box.

**Let's TOC**

In PageMaker 4 you can tag any paragraph, specifying that the words in that paragraph should appear in a table of contents, by checking "Include in table of contents" in the Paragraph specifications dialog box. Usually, you'll want to set up styles for headings that make each heading an entry in the table of contents.

You can create a table of contents at any time by choosing "Create TOC" from the Options menu, though you'll probably want to wait until your publication's page breaks are final. After you assign a title to the table of contents and select options in the Create table of contents dialog box (Figure 4-75), PageMaker displays a progress indicator, then a loaded text gun.

When you place the text, you'll see that PageMaker has generated your table of contents, and has assigned TOC styles to each of the paragraphs you specified. The TOC styles are usually the same text format as the paragraph they're derived from. A TOC style derived from a paragraph styled "heading 1," for example, is named "TOC heading 1." You can edit the TOC styles just as you'd edit any other styles, so it's easy to format the table of contents.

**Figure 4-75**
Create table of
contents dialog box

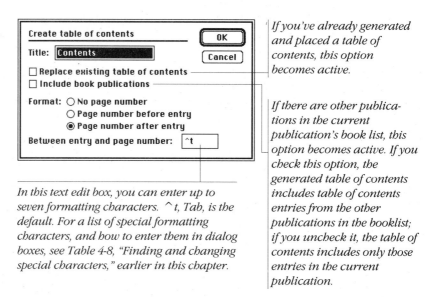

*If you've already generated and placed a table of contents, this option becomes active.*

*If there are other publications in the current publication's book list, this option becomes active. If you check this option, the generated table of contents includes table of contents entries from the other publications in the booklist; if you uncheck it, the table of contents includes only those entries in the current publication.*

*In this text edit box, you can enter up to seven formatting characters. ^ t, Tab, is the default. For a list of special formatting characters, and how to enter them in dialog boxes, see Table 4-8, "Finding and changing special characters," earlier in this chapter.*

Once you've generated and placed a table of contents, subsequent Create table of contents dialog boxes offer you the Replace existing table of contents option. If you choose that option, PageMaker replaces the table of contents you previously placed.

### ▼ Tip: Where You Can Put Your Table of Contents

For books with three or more chapter files, we recommend that you create a separate publication file just for the table of contents and index, as described in "Books" in Chapter 3, *Making PageMaker Mind*.

That way you don't need to keep track of which file the book list is in, and you only need to keep one book list up to date.

If you keep the table of contents in the publication, place it at the end of the file, rather than trying to leave pages for it at the beginning. If the addition of the table of contents story causes pages to tumble, your table of contents is inaccurate as soon as you place it.

If you're working with a publication that must have the table of contents on the first page, autoflow the text, then generate a table of contents and make room for it on the first page of the publication, then lay out the publication as you normally would. Once you're through with that, you can regenerate the table of contents—the page numbers will change, but the space the table of contents takes up will remain about the same and you won't have to reflow pages.

## Generating an Index

Many people have gotten the idea that products like PageMaker and Word generate indices *automatically*, without any assistance from a sentient being. If these programs were intelligent enough to understand the meaning and context of the words we typed into them, do you think they'd sit still and let us crank out another memo regarding corporate culture? No way. They'd be running for public office, kissing babies, and shaking hands (and writing books). Luckily (for us) they're not that smart. They can only do what we tell them, and exactly what we tell them.

The problem with almost every computer indexing system we've seen is that they create concordances—word lists with page numbers—not indices. A good index is conceptually based and carefully thought out, not mechanically generated. A typical computer-generated index will give you two different references to the word "format," even though one page is talking about text formatting, and the other is talking about disk formatting. This type of index is almost worthless.

PageMaker just provides tools that help *you* create an index. You need to do the thinking, and PageMaker does all of the record-keeping. It can't even control capitalization for you, much less the more heady matters of deciding which topics should be indexed under which index headings, and which should be cross-referenced to others.

Given that, we can say that PageMaker 4 provides the best tools we've seen for creating an index on a computer. First and foremost, you can see the existing topics in your index at any time, and add a page reference or cross reference to an topic. You don't have to worry about typing the topic exactly as you typed it before, or trying to remember what topics you've already made in that subject area, because the index topic list is constantly updated. You can simply choose an existing topic from a list. That feature alone—we might call it interactive indexing—puts PageMaker's indexing well beyond any other system we've seen.

## Creating Index Entries

To create an index entry, select a range of text and choose "Create index" on the Options menu (Command-;) to bring up the Create index entry dialog box (Figure 4-76). The selected range is automatically entered as the first-level topic under which that range will be indexed.

If you've just selected one word, that might be your topic. You will probably need to change the capitalization (first-level entries are generally capitalized), and maybe the suffix (changing automotive to Automobiles, for instance). If you're indexing a range of text larger than a single word, you'll definitely need to edit the index topic, entering some conceptual wording that describes the material in the selected range of text.

Alternatively, press the Topics button to see a list of topics already in the index, and select one. Press Return to choose the selected topic. Once you've got the proper topic entered, and all the other options (discussed below) set as you want them, press Return to add the entry to the index.

▼ *Tip: The Fast Way to Build a Topic List*

To build up a list of topics quickly without spending hours jumping in and out of the Create index entry dialog box, build the list first in Word. An entry (formatted as hidden text) might look like this:

.i.Louis XIV;

**Figure 4-76**
Create index entry
dialog box

Enter the main index topic here.
If you have a word selected, it
will appear in this field.

Promote/demote
icon. Change the
level of the selected
word by clicking on
this icon.

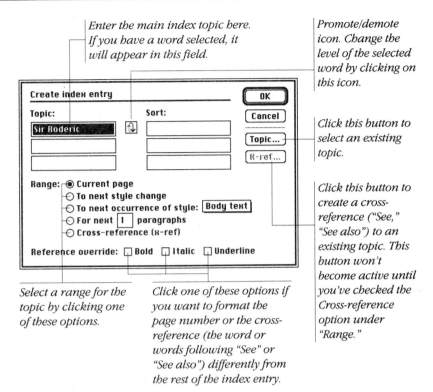

Click this button to
select an existing
topic.

Click this button to
create a cross-
reference ("See,"
"See also") to an
existing topic. This
button won't
become active until
you've checked the
Cross-reference
option under
"Range."

Select a range for the
topic by clicking one
of these options.

Click one of these options if
you want to format the
page number or the cross-
reference (the word or
words following "See" or
"See also") differently from
the rest of the index entry.

When you place a file filled with such index entries, PageMaker adds
them all to its Topic list. Then you can use those topics for specific
index entries, rather than having to create every topic as you go.

---

▼ *Tip: Multiple Topics for a Single Range*

You can index a selection under several different topics. Once you have
the text selected, just keep pressing Command-;, enter or select topics,
and press Return.

---

▼ *Tip: Quick Index Entries*

When you've found a word that should go into your index as a first level entry, select the word, press Command-;, and press Return. The word is entered into the publication's index.

When you're ready to add the index to a publication, choose "Create index" from the Options menu. The Create index dialog box appears (Figure 4-77). Type a title for the index and press Return. PageMaker generates the index and either replaces the existing index, or loads the new index into a text place gun, depending on what options you've chosen.

**Figure 4-77**
Create index dialog box

*If you've already generated and placed an index, this option becomes active.*

*If there are other publications in the current publication's booklist, this option becomes active. If you check this option, the generated index includes index entries from the other publications in the booklist; if you uncheck it, the generated index includes only those index entries in the current publication.*

**Create index**

Title: [Index]

☐ Replace existing index
☐ Include book publications
☒ Remove unreferenced topics

OK

Cancel

Format...

*If you've created index topics, but haven't linked them to any index entries, this option removes the topics from the generated index. Note that this does not remove the topics from the index list in the publication.*

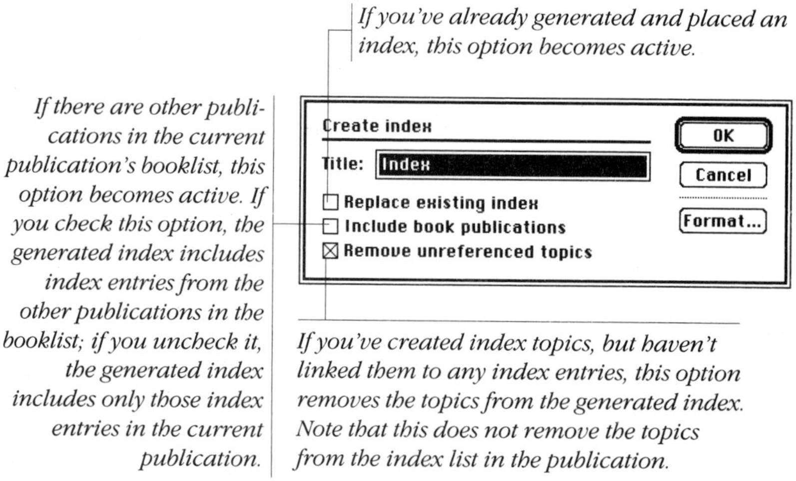

**Formatting the Index**

The Index format dialog box (Figure 4-78) is one of the most terrifying new dialog boxes in PageMaker. It's large, kind of incomprehensible, and features text edit boxes filled with Cuneiform characters. Don't be scared. The bottom third of the dialog box displays the current index format. If you like it, just click OK.

Otherwise, you'll need to know that "^ >" is how you enter an en space in a dialog box, and that "^ =" is how you enter an en dash (–) in a dialog box (see "Using Special Characters" earlier in this chapter). To see the difference between a "Nested" and a "Run-in" index format, click the different option buttons and watch how the index format example at the bottom of the dialog box changes.

Once you've generated and placed an index, you'll see that

**Figure 4-78**
Index format dialog box

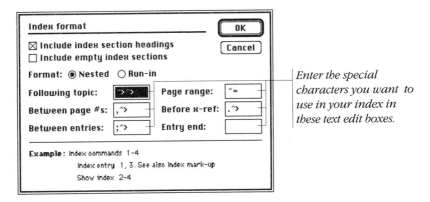

*Enter the special characters you want to use in your index in these text edit boxes.*

*For a list of special formatting characters, and how to enter them in dialog boxes, see Table 4-8, "Finding and changing special characters," earlier in this chapter.*

PageMaker has assigned index styles to the entries in your index. You can edit these styles as you would any other styles.

### ▼ *Tip: Viewing Your Index Entries*

One of the hardest parts of creating an index is remembering what entries you've already made. Suppose you come across a brontosaurus in your text, for instance. Should that go under prehistoric reptile, dinosaur, wading animal, or family pet? What entry did you create when you ran across a triceratops 40 pages back?

Click the Topic button in the Create index entry dialog box, and you can scroll through your already created topics, and add this page reference to any topic.

You can also view your index at any point by choosing "Show index" from the Options menu. You can edit the index that's displayed in the Show index dialog box by clicking the Edit, Add, or Remove buttons. Clicking the Edit button brings up the Edit index entry dialog box for the currently selected index entry, or you can double-click the index entry. The Edit index entry dialog box is functionally identical to the Create index entry dialog box.

**Index Levels**

Entries in an index are usually grouped under some topic. The brontosaurus and triceratops we mentioned earlier could be indexed as "Plant-eating dinosaurs, brontosaurus" and "Plant-eating dinosaurs, triceratops," though brontosaurus might also be entered under the "Big dinosaurs" topic and triceratops under the "Horny dinosaurs" topic. You decide; you're creating the index. PageMaker can help, though, by taking care of some of the drudge-work.

If you've created index entries for the two dinosaurs using the quick index entry method we outlined earlier in this chapter, your publication's index will contain two first-level index entries—one for brontosaurus, and one for triceratops. If you want to retain these first-level index entries, you can add their second-level references by selecting the word, pressing Command-; to open the Create index entry dialog box, demoting the entry to the second level by clicking the promote/demote icon (see Figure 4-79), and typing "Plant-eating dinosaurs" in the first-level text edit box.

**Sort Entries**

Many alphabetical sorting systems have conventional variances. For example, names in the phone book starting with "Mc" usually precede names starting with "Ma." It's not strictly alphabetical order, but many people believe it's the correct way to arrange the entries. In PageMaker, you'd enter a sort key of "M" for "Mc" entries to make them appear before "Ma" in the index. Similarly, PageMaker's ASCII sort order would put the number 10 before the number 9, so you'd enter the sort key for 9 as 09 (Figure 4-80).

**See and See also**

When you're organizing information, you need to keep in mind that not everyone thinks exactly as you do. Often, you need to create cross-references inside an index to help people think the way you do. If, for example, you've placed all of your index entries for the author of *Alice in Wonderland* under Dodgson, Charles Lutwidge, you should anticipate that people will search the index for an entry for Lewis Carroll, and enter a cross-reference under Carroll, Lewis.

In this case, we'd open the Create index entry dialog box for Carroll,

*Click the Promote/demote icon.*

**Edit index entry**               **OK**

Topic:                  Sort:              **Cancel**

Brontosaurus     ⬍                     **Topic...**

                                        **K-ref...**

Ran

**Edit index entry**               **OK**

Topic:                  Sort:              **Cancel**

Plant-eating dinos  ⬍                   **Topic...**

Brontosaurus                           **K-ref...**

Refe

Range: ⦿ Current page
        ○ To next style change
        ○ To next occurrence of style: **Body text**
        ○ For next [1] paragraphs
        ○ Cross-reference (x-ref)

Reference override: ☐ Bold  ☐ Italic  ☐ Underline

*Type the new index topic in the first-level text edit box.*

**Create index entry**               **OK**

Topic:                  Sort:              **Cancel**

McCashey, Eric    ⬍     M              **Topic...**

and Karo Syrup                         **K-ref...**

Range: ⦿ Current page
        ○ To next style change
        ○ To next occurrence of style: **Body text**
        ○ For next [1] paragraphs
        ○ Cross-reference (x-ref)

Reference override: ☐ Bold  ☐ Italic  ☐ Underline

*Type characters or words here to change the sort order. These characters are used instead of the characters in the Topic text edit boxes when PageMaker sorts the index.*

Lewis, and click the Cross reference option. Once you've done that, the X-ref button becomes active. Press the X-ref button and choose the Dodgson, Charles Lutwidge topic, and press Return. When you generate an index, the entry for Carroll, Lewis will read "Carroll, Lewis, See Dodgson, Charles Lutwidge." The formatting for the word "See," in this case, is controlled by the mysterious Reference override options: click the Bold check box, and the word "See" will appear in bold in your index. "Reference override," no matter how dramatic and drastic it sounds, only controls the text format of the page number reference and the words following "See" and "See also" (Figure 4-81).

"See also" entries are produced in cases where the entry has a page number, but you'd also like to direct people to some other topic. If you wanted to cross-reference an entry for "Liddell, Alice," to "Alice in Wonderland," you could select the entry you'd created for Liddell, Alice, then press Command-; to bring up the Edit index entry dialog box. Then choose the Cross-reference option, click the X-ref button, and choose "Alice in Wonderland." When you create your index, the

**Figure 4-81**
Creating a
cross-reference

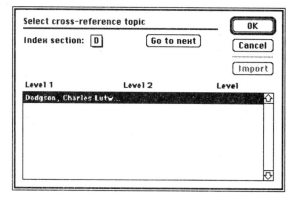

*Under "Range," select "Cross-reference (x-ref)." Click the X-ref button to display the Select cross-reference topic dialog box.*

*Specify the cross-reference's formatting (how "See" will appear).*

*Choose a section from the Index section pop-up menu, then select a topic in the topic listing under that section.*

Carroll, Lewis. *See* Dodgson, Charles Lutwidge

*Cross-reference as it appears in the generated index*

entry for "Liddell, Alice," will read "Liddell, Alice, 1, See also Alice in Wonderland" (Figure 4-82).

**Figure 4-82**
See also reference

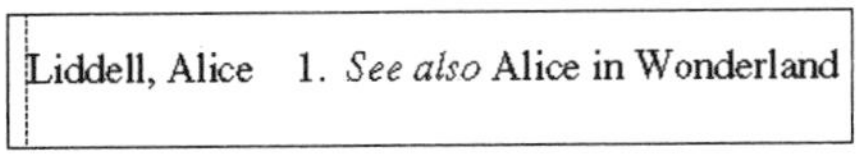

Liddell, Alice    1. *See also* Alice in Wonderland

**Index Ranges**

When you're creating an index, you indicate that the discussion of a particular topic runs for several pages by setting the index Range option in the Create/Edit index entry dialog box. If the topic continues no further than the current paragraph, choose the Current page option. If the topic will continue to the next time you change styles, choose the To next style change option. If the topic will continue to the next occurrence of some style (notably some heading or subhead style) choose that style in the pop-up menu. You can also enter an explicit number of paragraphs that pertain to the index entry by entering a number in the For next *x* paragraphs text edit box. When you generate the index, the entry shows where the range of text you specified starts and ends in the publication (Figure 4-83).

**Figure 4-83**
Specifying an index
entry's range

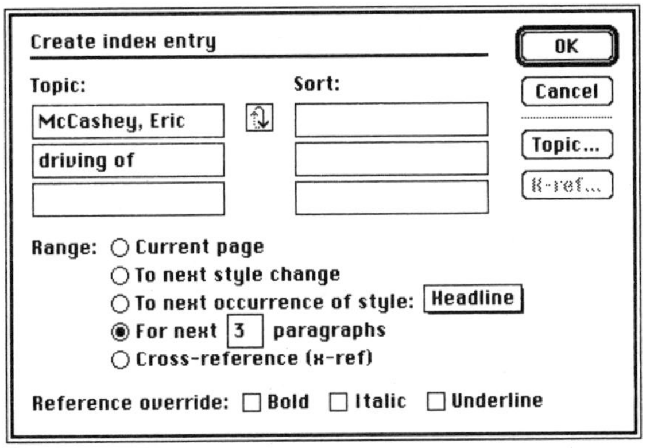

Create index entry                                    OK

Topic:                        Sort:                   Cancel

McCashey, Eric      ⬆                                 Topic...

driving of                                            x-ref...

Range:  ○ Current page
        ○ To next style change
        ○ To next occurrence of style: Headline
        ◉ For next  3  paragraphs
        ○ Cross-reference (x-ref)

Reference override: ☐ Bold  ☐ Italic  ☐ Underline

*Select one of the range options to specify the range an index entry will cover.*

## *Our Favorite Word Tips and Tricks*

While PageMaker 4's Story editor covers quite a few word-processing needs, like it or not, Microsoft Word is still an important part of a PageMaker publishing system. You can use other word processors—

notably Nisus from Paragon (*great* for sophisticated copy processing—search and replace, etc. If you know what grep is, you need Nisus), Claris' MacWrite II, and WriteNow from TMaker. But PageMaker's closest ties are with Word. The formatting tools and dialog boxes are similar, so you can move formatted text between the two programs without worrying too much about what's getting lost in between.

**Word's Own Import Dialog Box**

As we've said, PageMaker has very close ties to Microsoft Word. The formatting and styling of the two programs are very similar, so they move back and forth relatively transparently. They are not identical, though, so you need to give some thought to importing and exporting Word files—considering what elements and attributes will move over, and what won't.

PageMaker 4 gives you much more explicit control over that movement than previous versions provided. When you select a Word 4 file in the Place dialog box, hold down Shift, and click OK, the Microsoft Word 4.0 import filter dialog box appears (Figure 4-84). In this dialog box, you can choose from a variety of options that control the way PageMaker formats and places the file. PageMaker does not import any Word page-format settings (i.e., page numbering, headers/footers, columns, etc.).

**Figure 4-84**
Microsoft Word 4.0
import filter dialog box

```
┌─────────────────────────────────────────────┐
│ Microsoft Word 4.0 import filter    ┌──────┐ │
│ ─────────────────────────────────  │  OK  │ │
│ ⊠ Import table of contents entries  └──────┘ │
│    ◉ From .c. paragraphs           ┌────────┐│
│    ○ From outline                  │ Cancel ││
│                                    └────────┘│
│ ⊠ Import index entries                       │
│                                              │
│ Import condensed/expanded spacing as         │
│    ◉ Set width                               │
│    ○ Manual kerning                          │
│    ○ Track kerning                           │
│                                              │
│ ⊠ Import page break before paragraph         │
│    ◉ As page break before                    │
│    ○ As column break before                  │
└─────────────────────────────────────────────┘
```

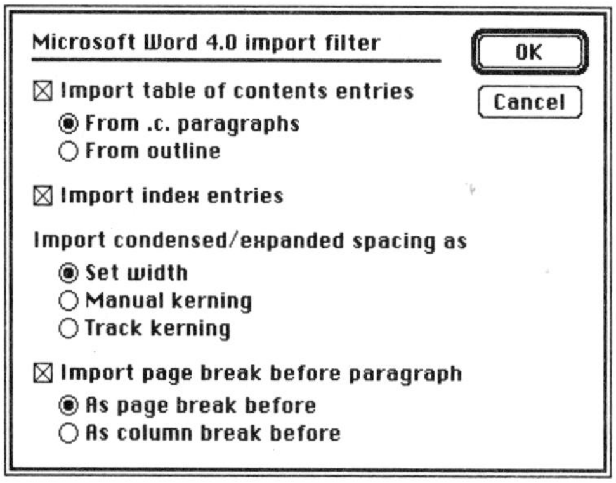

***Text formatting.*** PageMaker imports Word's local text formatting (typefaces, styles, and subscripting, etc.), with the exceptions below.

- Word's expanded and condensed settings (which don't really condense or expand type; they adjust letter spacing to be tighter or looser) are interpreted according to the settings you choose in the Word import filter dialog box. The Set width option changes the appearance of the imported characters, actually condensing and expanding the type. "Manual kerning" provides the most accurate simulation of Word's letter spacing by applying kerning to the range of text. "Track kerning" applies tracks to the expanded/condensed text. The effect is usually somewhat subtler than Word's expanded/condensed settings.

- Hidden text is stripped out of the file on import. PageMaker does import table of contents and index entries, however, which are usually hidden text in Word.

**Paragraph formatting.** PageMaker also imports all of Word's paragraph formatting features, with the exceptions below.

- Boxes around and vertical bars beside paragraphs are not imported. Paragraph rules above and below *are* imported.

- Word widow and orphan control settings are not imported.

**Style sheets.** PageMaker imports all of Word's style sheet attributes, excluding those text and paragraph-level attributes noted above. Some style sheet attributes which PageMaker cannot import (vertical bar paragraph borders, for example) are retained for export and will appear again in exported Word documents.

Remember that if there's an identically named style in the PageMaker publication when you place or import the word file, that style's formatting overrides the formatting in the Word style sheet. PageMaker just uses the Word tag specifying what the paragraph is, and ignores the formatting information.

**Footnotes.** PageMaker also imports footnotes, complete with their numbering, and puts all of the footnotes at the end of the placed story. And unlike version 3, PageMaker 4 imports the footnote references in the text.

**Index entries.** PageMaker imports Word index entries and index levels (up to two subordinate index levels) directly. Because PageMaker does not import Word's page numbers, index ranges specified in Word are imported as two individual page references, separated by a comma—not as a single entry with a page range specified.

For example, if a Word index reference for "Dogs, Nova Scotia Duck Tolling Retriever" begins on PageMaker page 255 and ends on page 258, the index entry would read "Dogs, Nova Scotia Duck Tolling Retriever 255, 258." If the range in our example were to end on page 255, you'd see "Dogs, Nova Scotia Duck Tolling Retriever, 255, 255."

It's probably easiest to delete the second index markers (in PageMaker) and re-enter the range using PageMaker's index range options. If you're making index entries in a Word file that's destined for PageMaker, don't use Word's index ranges.

**Tables of contents.** PageMaker imports Word's table of contents tags (entered in Word's outline mode or coded with ".c") as a paragraph attribute. If you enter a hidden table of contents entry followed by a semicolon, however (which works in Word), PageMaker ignores it and uses the following text, through to the end of the paragraph, as shown in Figure 4-85.

**Figure 4-85**
Hidden table of contents entries

*PageMaker ignores hidden table of contents entries imported from Word. This entry in Word...*

.c.Nova Scotia Duck Tolling Retriever;          Little River Duck Dog

*...results in this entry in the PageMaker table of contents*

Little River Duck Dog

**Inline graphics.** PageMaker imports graphics pasted into Word files as inline graphics, which appear in the same position (relative to the text stream) in the PageMaker story as they do in the Word file. Any graphics that come in from Word this way—be they bitmaps, EPS files, TIFFs, or whatever—are treated as PICTs, because that's all Word can handle. You can't magic stretch bitmaps, for instance, that are imported this way.

***Tables.*** To import tables created with Word's table features, add a paragraph before the table containing one character—a "t" formatted as hidden text. With this addition, Word's tables will be imported as tab-delimited text. You can also copy a Word table to the Clipboard in PICT format by selecting the table (with "Show ¶" turned off) and pressing Command-Option-D. Then paste it into PageMaker.

***Equations.*** PageMaker strips equations out of imported Word files. You can copy Word equations to the Clipboard in PICT format by selecting the equation and pressing Command-Option-D. Then paste it into PageMaker.

***Page breaks.*** Word only has a Page break before attribute for paragraphs. PageMaker has that, and a Column break before setting as well. Depending on your choice in the Word import filter dialog box, PageMaker converts Word's Page break before attribute to either a Page break before or Column break before setting in PageMaker.

### ▼ *Tip: Fast Styles*

Give all your style names in Word key equivalents by following the name with a comma and the equivalent: "Subhead,sh" or "Heading 1,1." To apply the style, select a paragraphs, press Command-Shift-S, then the equivalent (sh, or 1, or whatever), then Return. It's even faster than using PageMaker's Styles palette.

### ▼ *Tip: Lose Those Styles*

Is the Style menu in your Word documents clogged up with dozens of styles that you don't ever remember seeing, much less creating? Are you tired of arduously Command-Xing them in every single document? Just copy your whole document into a clean, empty document. You'll just get the styles that are actually used.

## ▼ *Tip: Word's Margins and PageMaker's Paragraph Indents*

PageMaker ignores document page margin settings specified in Word, but uses the paragraph indents. When you place the Word file in PageMaker, the paragraph indents push the paragraph in from the edges of the text block (Figure 4-86), just like PageMaker's paragraph

**Figure 4-86**

Importing Word's paragraph indents

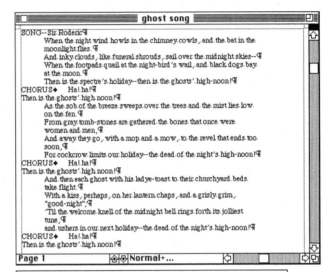

*Paragraph and page margins and indents set up in Word*

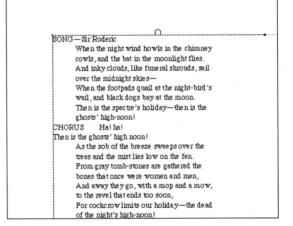

*Word document placed in PageMaker. The paragraph specifications are retained; the page margins are ignored.*

indents. In general, PageMaker ignores Word's document, page, and section formatting specifications when you place the Word file.

## ▼ *Tip: Do It Again*

If you're doing the same thing over and over (like applying subhead styles), do it once, then hit Command-A to do it again. PageMaker could learn something from this.

---

## ▼ *Tip: Find It Again*

If you're searching for something repeatedly, Press Command-Option-A to find it again. This works great with the last tip if you want to do something like finding all the uses of *Arms and the Man* in a document and changing them to italic. (Though PageMaker 4's Change dialog box is even better. Word could learn something here.)

---

**Rich Text Format**

Microsoft's Rich Text Format (RTF—also known as Interchange format) is an ASCII (or, in Macintosh-ese, text-only) coding scheme capable of describing everything in a Microsoft Word file, including graphics, style sheets, and local font changes. RTF is also the Clipboard format that PageMaker uses when you cut or copy text with the Text tool.

Being able to specify the entire content of a file in ASCII is important because it opens the door to formatting automation. Documents could be written and specified with the text-editing applications found on mainframe computers or workstations, then imported into PageMaker as fully-formatted, styled text. Most database management software, including HyperCard, can create ASCII versions of their files, inserting codes and tags for formatting as they go.

RTF files must start with the code {\rtf. This lets PageMaker or Word know that this is an RTF file. Immediately following is the font table. If you create your RTF file with PageMaker or Word, the font table and numbering match the fonts on your system. If you create the file with a text editor or by other means, you need only include the fonts you want to use in the document. The application opening the RTF file compares the font names in the font list with the fonts on the current system and reconciles the document's font numbering with the system's font list. This makes RTF a great format for transferring text between different installations.

Following the font table are tables for colors, and style sheets. Take a look at the example RTF document (Figure 4-87) to see how styles are specified. Note that some of the numbers used to specify type size, leading, and space after look a little different than you'd expect. Type size ("fs"), for example, is the size you want multiplied by two. Most space settings look like they've been multiplied by 20, because they're in *twips*—twentieths of a point.

Note that the ASCII codes for bold and italic make it easy to change character formatting. If you wanted to change all of the bold Times in a document to Helvetica Oblique, you could search for "\b" and replace with "\f21\i" (using the font number from the example above). When you interpret the RTF text, the text that had been formatted as bold Times will appear as Helvetica Oblique.

Further, since RTF includes a complete coding scheme for graphics, you can direct a searching/replacing program to insert a certain graphic every time it locates the string <icon> in the text. In case you're curious, PageMaker items placed from the Scrapbook, copied to the Clipboard, and pasted into Word convert to RTF very nicely.

We've only begun to scratch the surface of RTF. With everything in ASCII format, so mere mortals can view and edit it, the possibilities are limitless. Almost any program can generate ASCII, so any program can generate RTF-formatted copy—including inline graphics—for import into PageMaker.

### Getting Text Out of PageMaker

To get text out of PageMaker and into a format readable by a word processor, place a text insertion point in a story, select a range of text, or select a text block with the Pointer tool, and choose "Export" from the File menu (Figure 4-88). PageMaker can only export the text in the currently selected story; there's no Export all stories option. If you need to export text from several stories (unthreaded text blocks), you have to export each story separately (or thread the stories together

**Figure 4-87**
How RTF works

```
{\rtf1\mac\deff2
```
*This line identifies the file as RTF and must be the first text in the file.*

```
{\fonttbl
{\f20\froman Times;}
{\f21\fswiss Helvetica;}
{\f15250\fnil ITC Garamd a;}
{\f15252\fnil ITC Garamd b;}
{\f15253\fnil ITC Garamd d;}
{\f15979\fnil ITC Garamd c;}}
```
*Font table*

```
{\colortbl\red0\green0\blue0;
\red0\green0\blue255;
\red0\green255\blue255;
\red0\green255\blue0;
\red255\green0\blue255;
\red255\green0\blue0;
\red255\green255\blue0;
\red255\green255\blue255;}
```
*Color table*

```
{\stylesheet
{\f20 \sbasedon222\snext0 Normal;}
{\s1\fi-240\li240\sl240\tx2660\tx3420 \f20\fs20
\sbasedon222\snext1 verse;}
{\s2\sb240\sa240\sl240\tqc\tx2160 \f20\fs20
\sbasedon222\snext2 chorus;}
{\s3\qc\tqc\tx2160 \f20\fs20 \sbasedon222
\snext3 graphic;}}
```
*Style sheet*

*This style ("verse") is Times 10/12, with a negative first line indent of 1 pica*

```
\enddoc\sectd\linemod\cols1
```
*End of definitions*

```
\pard\plain \sl240\tx2660\tx3420 \f20
```
*Start of text*

*Bold on*    *Bold off (back to plain)*

```
{\b\fs28 Song--Sir Roderic}{\fs20 \par }
```
*End of paragraph*

*verse style tag—defined as s1 in header*

```
\pard\plain \s1\fi-240\li240\sl240\tx2660\tx3420 \f20\fs20 When the
night wind howls in the chimney cowls, and the bat in the moonlight
flies.\par
\pard\plain \sl240 \f20 {\fs20 And inky clouds, like funeral shrouds, sail
over the midnight skies--\par
```

**Figure 4-87**
How RTF works
continued

When the footpads quail at the night-bird\'05s wail, and the black dogs bay at the moon,\par

*Special character*

Then is the spectre\'05s holiday--then is the ghost\'05s high noon!\par
}\pard\plain \s3\qc\tqc\tx2160 \f20\fs20

*Start of a graphic*

{{\pict\macpict\picw146\pich181
0a390000000000b50092110101000a0000000000b5009

- We've omitted the body of the graphic. It's about twenty
- pages more of this sort of thing. You get the idea.
-

e00023ffff8f30007fe00010ffff20002ed0002ed
0002ed0002ed0002ed0002ed0002ed00ff}}\par

\pard\plain \s2\sb240\sl240\tqc\tx2160
\f20\fs20 {\b CHORUS\:}\tab Ha!
Ha!\line \tab Then is the ghost\'05s high
noon!\par
\pard\plain \s3\qc\tqc\tx2160 \f20\fs20
\par
\pard\plain \s1\fi-
240\li240\sl240\tx2660\tx3420 \f20\fs20
As the sob of the breeze sweeps over the
trees and the mist lies low on the fen,\par
\pard\plain \s1\fi-
240\li240\sl240\tx2660\tx3420 \f20\fs20
From grey tomb-stones are gathered the
bones that once were women and men,\par
\pard\plain \s1\fi-
240\li240\sl240\tx2660\tx3420 \f20\fs20
And away they go, with a mop and a mow,
to the revel that ends to soon,\par
\pard\plain \s1\fi-
240\li240\sl240\tx2660\tx3420 \f20\fs20
For cockcrow limits our holiday--the dead
of the night\'05s high noon!\par }

**Song—Sir Roderic**
When the night wind howls in the chimney cowls, and
the bat in the moonlight flies.
And inky clouds, like funeral shrouds, sail over the
midnight skies—
When the footpads quail at the night-bird's wail, and
the black dogs bay at the moon,
Then is the spectre's holiday—then is the ghost's high
noon!

CHORUS:        Ha! Ha!
        Then is the ghost's high noon!

As the sob of the breeze sweeps over the trees and the
mist lies low on the fen,
From grey tomb-stones are gathered the bones that
once were women and men,
And away they go, with a mop and a mow, to the revel
that ends to soon,
For cockcrow limits our holiday—the dead of the
night's high noon!

*Interpreted RTF file*

**Figure 4-88**
Export dialog box

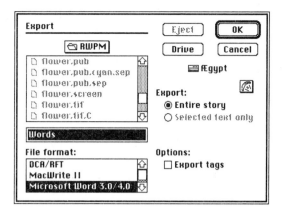

before exporting). This is another great reason to keep text threaded in your publications.

You can export text in the file formats of several leading word processors—Microsoft Word (3 and 4), Word Perfect (1.02), and MacWrite (5.0 and II). You can also export text in "Text-only" (that's ASCII to everyone outside of the Macintosh world, more or less), DCA, and RTF formats. You can export style name tags to any of these formats.

### ▼ Tip: Text and Tags

If you need to export text for someone else to work on, and don't know what word processor they use, choose the Text only and Export tags options. Virtually every word processor in the world can read this format—from Nisus to emacs, from Word to vi. And, since you've chosen "Export tags," you've got a reasonable chance of still having a styled document when you get the file back to place in PageMaker.

You lose all your local formatting with this method, however, because PageMaker only knows about embedded style tags. It doesn't know from formatting codes—<I> for italics, for instance.

## Fixing Bad RIX

"Bad record index." RIX for short. It's the touch of Death. It's Matthew Hopkins, Witchefinder General, come to ask you about your two black cats. It's the last thing you want to see two hours before a deadline. It's what PageMaker displays when your publication is hosed, has passed on, is pushing up the daisies.

We know that you'll never see a "Bad record index" error, because Aldus engineering will have tracked down all of the imponderabilities in the baroque (and beautiful—tell us about another desktop publishing program that keeps from losing work when the dog chews through the power cord) maze of PageMaker's file system by the time you get this book. For every possible installation. For every possible file. Well, we're from Missouri (or Steve is, anyway). We'll believe it when we see it. In the meantime, we'll pass on a some tricks we've used to fix bad RIX in PageMaker 3.x and in ßeta versions of PageMaker 4.

Every "Bad record index" error we've ever seen has resulted from PageMaker's style definitions becoming confused. This doesn't mean that every bad RIX error has to do with styles—theoretically, it could mean anything. Still, if you've imported several files from a word processor that supports style sheets, you should probably do a little clean-up work.

When PageMaker imports a document that has styles attached, it first looks to see if the style names match styles already defined in PageMaker. If it finds any such styles, it overrides any style definitions created in the word processor with the PageMaker styles. If it doesn't find a matching PageMaker style name, it imports the style definitions from the word-processing file and displays an asterisk (*) after the imported style's name in the Styles palette and the Define styles dialog box. If you edit the style in PageMaker (even if you just Command-click the style name in the Styles palette and press Return), the style becomes a PageMaker style and the asterisk disappears.

What happens, though, when you import a word-processing document containing styles that have no match in PageMaker, then import another word-processing file containing styles with the same style names? Who's on first? Sometimes, in the confusion, duplicate word-processor styles become corrupt—especially the Microsoft Word style "Normal," which you always get when you import a Word file. At this point, you'll start seeing "Bad record index" messages. Bad RIX masquerade as several error messages—notably "Cannot turn the page" when you choose "Define styles" from the Type menu. To get rid of bad RIX, try the following technique.

1. Locate the afflicted style, if possible, by Command-clicking on suspect style names in the Styles palette to bring up the Edit styles dialog box, then hitting Return (or pressing OK). Suspect styles with asterisks first. Once you get the bad RIX message, you've found at least one of the sick styles.

2. Command-click on "No style" and type the name of the bad style. Make sure you type the name exactly as it appears in the Styles palette (you don't type the asterisks or plus signs). This replaces the style with a new PageMaker style.

3. Use Save as to compress and clean up your publication.

At this point you're probably safe, but we usually move to exterminate the offending style. You can't trust them once they've turned to evil. Bear in mind, however, that removing the style removes the tagging from the styled paragraphs. They'll be styled "No style."

1. Sprint to the Define styles dialog box (Command-3).

2. Select the bad style name and click "Remove."

3. Use Save as to compress and clean up your publication.

Continue through the all styles in the Styles palette until you can open each one and click OK in the Edit style dialog box without encountering the "Bad record index" message.

You can take steps toward preventing bad RIX by making sure that every style is a PageMaker style before you import a new text file. Command-click each style name followed by an asterisk in the Styles palette and press Return to close the Edit styles dialog box. The asterisk disappears, indicating that the styles are now PageMaker styles and will, therefore, override any incoming style with the same style names.

▼ *Tip: Recompose World*

One last tip for words: You can recompose all the text in a pub by holding down Option as you choose "Hyphenation" from the Type menu. PageMaker will recompose all the text in the publication before bringing up the Hyphenation dialog box. This is especially useful for users of PC PageMaker who are switching between different printers and font sets, but it's a nice clean-up technique on the Mac, as well.

Better than that, if you hold down Command-Option-Shift as you choose "Hyphenation" from the Type menu, PageMaker will check the publication's file structure and make an attempt to fix any errors it finds. If your publication is clean (or if PageMaker can't find the error), you'll hear one beep. If PageMaker finds and fixes any file structure errors, you'll hear two beeps. If PageMaker finds errors and can't fix them, you'll hear three beeps—and you'll need to start trying some of the other remedies in this book.

# Pictures

In contrast to the volume of new features, enhancements, bells, and whistles on the text and type side of PageMaker 4, there are only two significant changes when it comes to graphics—inline graphics, and the ability to automatically wrap text around master items. Those two features, though, do more to affect and improve the way PageMaker works than half a dozen typographic niceties.

The ability to wrap text around master items—items that appear on your pages because they're on the master pages—means that you can customize your text flow behavior in ways you never could before. You can arrange things so PageMaker does much of your page layout for you as the text lands on the page.

Inline graphics work just like graphics in a Mac word processor. An inline graphic is like a character in the text (in most ways), so it moves when the text reflows. That may seem trivial, but PageMaker is the first Mac page-makeup program to offer inline graphics, and it completely changes the way you make pages, especially for longer documents.

Both of these new features draw on capabilities that have been present in PageMaker for some time. This chapter starts by covering the way PageMaker works with graphics in general—pasting, placing, sizing, cropping, etc. At the end, we cover inline graphics and auto text wrap, drawing on the conceptual underpinnings developed throughout the chapter.

## *Graphics in PageMaker*

To begin with, it's important to understand that there are three ways to get graphics into a PageMaker pub.

- Create them with PageMaker's drawing tools.
- Paste them in from the Clipboard.
- Place them from an external graphics file.

That seems pretty straightforward, but in fact there are a variety of combinations and permutations to these three methods that provide a lot of flexibility.

**Working with Layers**

Every object on a PageMaker page, wherever it comes from, is on a layer—either in front of or behind other objects. This may not matter if objects don't touch, but when they overlap, it definitely does matter. Depending on the type of graphics you're using, underlying objects (graphics or type) may or may not be visible through a graphic that's on top of them. You need to get understand what's transparent and what's opaque if you want to build pages without doing a lot of layer shuffling.

Type is easy: the white space around characters is always transparent. You're not working with text "frames" as in some other programs, that can have a fill or color applied to them. If you want that effect in PageMaker, you can draw and fill a box behind the type. The inside of outlined type, on the other hand, is opaque, even though it appears transparent on a Mac II screen.

PageMaker-created boxes and ovals can be either transparent or opaque. Choose a fill of None to create a transparent graphic, any other fill for opaque. Remember that since PostScript uses what's called a "nontransparent ink principle," any fill is opaque. Even if you use only a 10 percent fill or one of the more open patterns, anything behind it will be completely obscured. What you see on screen is what you get on paper (except when you're printing to non-PostScript printers with improperly written driver).

PageMaker-drawn lines are always opaque. Even if you choose a dashed or multiline line, the white areas within the line are opaque—even if you reverse the line. This can cause problems—what if you have a colored, patterned line running over a colored area? You don't want to knock out the whole line, just the patterned part. We've developed a few workarounds, which we cover in the color pages in this book.

### ▼ Tip: White-out Boxes

We hesitate to even include this tip because we've been screwed up by it so many times. But sometimes you need it. You can create a paper-colored, no-line box to cover up little glitches on the page or to hide master items.

It works, but as we've said twice already, don't do it. These little monsters hide on the page, waiting to bite your ankles and bury your face in toner. It also slows down display and printing because PageMaker has to draw the underlying items anyway, then draw the box over them.

---

You control the layer relationships between objects using the Bring to front and Send to back commands on the Element menu (Command-F and Command-B). You can't move items forward or back one layer at a time, however; it's all or nothing.

### ▼ Tip: Bringing Multiple Objects to Front

You can select several objects using the selection techniques described later in this chapter, and bring them all to the front (Command-F). Their layer relationships to each other remain the same.

---

For the ultimate in layer control, check out the color pages in this book, which demonstrate ways to get around the nontransparent ink principle—using white boxes to selectively knock out and overprint layers for spot color overlays.

Aside from basic layer control, and the Snap to rulers and Snap to guides features, we have to say that PageMaker does not offer very robust tools for manipulating objects. There's no elegant way to move an object by a specified amount, for instance, group objects together into a combined object, or align objects automatically. Still, PageMaker provides the basics. And for more than the basics, people have invented some very usable—often brilliant—workarounds.

## Placing the Scrapbook

The most usable and brilliant workaround we know of—one that we use constantly—was invented by Aldus engineering and incorporated in PageMaker 3. You can convert any item or group of items on your page into a single graphic (a PageMaker-written EPS graphic) by copying them to the Scrapbook and then placing the Scrapbook. This arche-tip is a key component of many of the other tips in this book.

1. Select and copy the item(s) you want to convert to a graphic, copy them, and paste them into the Scrapbook (you'll find Scrapbook on the Apple menu).

2. Choose Place from the File menu (Command-D).

3. Choose the Scrapbook file (you'll find it in the system folder) and click OK (or double-click on Scrapbook). PageMaker displays a loaded place gun that looks very much like the PICT-type (draw-type) place gun, but it has a number displayed in it. The number shows the number of images in the Scrapbook.

4. Click the place gun to place a graphic from the Scrapbook.

5. You can click again to place another graphic from the Scrapbook, or you can unload the place gun by selecting the Pointer tool in the Toolbox (Command-Spacebar, or Shift-F1).

If you don't see Scrapbook or some equivalent (like SmartScrap) on your Apple menu, you'll need to install it with Font/DA Mover (or load it with MasterJuggler or Suitcase II). Scrapbook comes on the Apple

System disks. Even if you prefer one of the third-party Scrapbook-substitutes, we urge you to use the Apple Scrapbook as well—it's that important to working with PageMaker.

Some items copied to and placed from the Scrapbook may not print, or may print as screen-resolution bitmaps—notably EPS graphics, but also rotated type, TIFFs, and other Scrapbook-placed PICTs. This tip works very well for most PageMaker-drawn graphics, though fine reversed lines sometimes won't print even though they appear on the screen. Also, PageMaker sometimes clips off the right edge of the graphic, and won't let you pull out a wider bounding box with the Cropping tool. In that case, draw a line (or box, or whatever) slightly off to the right, and apply a line style of None, so it's invisible. With one-line text blocks, add a few spaces at the end of the line, or drag the text block slightly wider. Then copy the item(s) to the Scrapbook, and place the graphic from the Scrapbook again.

### ▼ *Tip: Grouping Objects*

Placing the Scrapbook is a great way to group objects. Select the objects you want to group, copy them to the Scrapbook, and place the combined graphic from the Scrapbook. It places as a single graphic that you can resize, move, or crop as a unit. If you find you need to edit the graphic, paste from the Scrapbook (rather than placing), make your changes, copy the objects back to the Scrapbook, then place the Scrapbook again. You could easily create keyboard macros to do this for you. You can back up your grouped objects by copying the Scrapbook to another disk.

### ▼ *Tip: Making Text into a Graphic*

By turning text into a graphic, you can stretch, crop, or group it with other graphics (you can no longer edit it as text, however). Again, copy it to and place it from the Scrapbook to turn it into a graphic, as shown in Figure 5-1 on the next page.

**Figure 5-1**
Stretching text

*The text you place from the Scrapbook becomes a graphic and can be resized. These examples were created entirely with PageMaker.*

You can combine these place-the-Scrapbook techniques in a number of ways. For example, you could convert some text to a graphic, stretch it, copy the stretched text and some graphics to the Scrapbook, and then place the Scrapbook to create a grouped logo.

## PageMaker's Drawing Tools

The simplest way to add graphics to a PageMaker pub is to draw them with the tools in the Toolbox. At Aldus, these objects are called LBOs (again, it's pronounced "elbows")—lines, boxes, and ovals. We've seen some amazing logos and graphics that have been created with nothing but LBOs. If you want to see some face-melting examples, check out the images that Ole created for the color pages in this book.

**Lines and Fills**

You can assign various attributes to PageMaker's LBOs. Lines can have various line weights, patterns, and colors, while boxes and ovals can have both line attributes and fills (None, Paper, Solid, several tint percentages, and some weird fill patterns that some people like, for some reason). LBOs can have any color you've defined applied to them. We do the whole rundown on colors, fills, and patterns in Chapter 7, *Color*. (Remember: grays are colors, too, so that chapter is worth reading even if you're creating black-and-white pubs.)

Bear in mind that you can't control the line style and line weight independently in PageMaker. Either you use a dashed line or a one-point line; you can't specify a one-point dashed line. Also, you're limited to the line weights and fills that are on the menu. You can't get a 50 percent fill, for instance, or a 5-point line. Sorry, no workarounds this side of importing lines and fills from a drawing program.

▼ *Tip: Use QuicKeys to Select Lines and Fills*

Set up QuicKeys to choose lines and fills quickly. It's far too difficult and slow to choose a line or a fill from the h-menus off the Element menu. If you get tired of popping off the Element menu and into the Windows menu while you're trying to choose "Hairline" (or whatever), think about how nice it would be to press a key and have the selected line change to a hairline.

▼ *Tip: Custom Gray Fills*

You may have noticed that there aren't many choices of tints in PageMaker's Fill menu. It's missing some standard ones, like 25 and 50 percent, not to mention odd ones like 33. If you want to specify a gray percentage explicitly:

1. Command-click on "Registration" or "Black" in the Colors palette (use "Define colors" from the Edit menu if you feel you must), and create a new color called Gray33 or something like that.
2. Choose the CMYK color model, and specify 33 percent black, with zero in the other boxes.
3. Use this color with the Solid fill when you want 33 percent gray.

This works great as long as you're producing a one-color or process-separated pub. It doesn't work at all for spot color overlays. For more on fills, shades, and tints, see Chapter 7, *Color*.

Finally, you can't apply colors to an LBO's lines and fills independently. Nor can you specify a percentage for lines this side of applying a color. If you want a box to have a 20 percent fill and a 50 percent line, or a green fill and a blue line, you have to stack two identical objects with different attributes on top of each other (Figure 5-2).

**Figure 5-2**
Creating composite objects

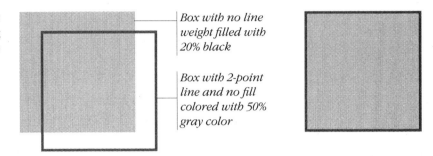

Box with no line weight filled with 20% black

Box with 2-point line and no fill colored with 50% gray color

## Precise Line Positioning

When you draw a horizontal or vertical line in PageMaker—let's say you use a 4-point line width—you may wonder whether the 4-point line goes above or below the line (or to the right or left with vertical lines). The answer? It's your choice. Change your line weight to something heavy—four points or above—and drag out some lines. Notice how you can pull the weight of the line to either side of the line you are drawing (see Figure 5-3). PageMaker doesn't "stroke" horizontal and

**Figure 5-3**
Lines positioned relative to ruler guides

*When you drag up on a horizontal line, the line weight is pulled to the top.*

*Drag down for the opposite effect.*

*Drag to the left to pull the line weight to the left of the ruler guide.*

*Drag to the right for the opposite effect.*

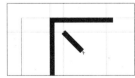

*Diagonal lines have their line weight divided equally around an imaginary centerline.*

vertical lines equally on either side as you might expect if you're familiar with PostScript or most Mac drawing programs. It puts everything on one side or the other.

The same is true for boxes and ovals. PageMaker always adds the line weight toward the inside, so your box stays the same size even when you make the line heavier. The inside of the box, naturally, gets smaller. The opposite is true with diagonal lines. PageMaker divides the line's weight equally on either side of an imaginary center line.

Line positioning is important when you're aligning objects to grids. With perpendicular lines, PageMaker will snap to either the top or the bottom (or left or right side) of the line. With diagonal lines, it snaps to the center of the line.

### ▼ *Tip: Positioning Thick Diagonal Lines*

If you want diagonal lines—especially thick ones—to end at an exact position, you need to decide what part of the line you want to end where. If you want the corner of the line to end at a given point, turn "Snap to guides" off and position the line ending visually (use the 400% page view). If you want the center of the line to end at a given point, you can use "Snap to guides."

---

**Constraining LBOs**

Using the Shift key, you can draw, move, and scale PageMaker-drawn objects within perpendicular and proportional constraints. This is basic Mac stuff: hold down the Shift key to constrain lines to 45-degree angles—whether you're drawing them or moving an end. When you're moving an object, holding down Shift constrains movement to horizontal or vertical. Shift also constrains ovals and rectangles to circles and squares.

One (admittedly minor) thing that drives us crazy in PageMaker is the way proportional scaling works (or actually, doesn't work) with ovals and rectangles. If you draw a rectangle then grab it by a corner and Shift-drag to size it, it doesn't size proportionally; it turns into a square and *then* sizes proportionally. It's because PageMaker thinks of its rectangles as nonproportional squares. We're happy to say that it does maintain the line weights you've specified; they aren't scaled with the graphic.

The only solution to the proportionally scaled rectangle problem is to create the rectangle in a draw or paint program, paste or place the rectangle, then size it proportionally. You can also use the place-the-Scrapbook technique described earlier in this chapter to convert PageMaker rectangles into rectangles that will size proportionally. Remember, though, when sizing graphics that aren't LBOs, that line weights scale along with the rest of the graphic.

## *Pasting Graphics From the Clipboard*

At first glance, pasting objects in PageMaker 4 works the same as in previous versions of the program—objects copied or cut to the Clipboard are pasted to the center of the screen. With PageMaker 4, though, you can Option-paste objects (Command-Option-V) into exactly the position they were cut or copied from (see "Paste" in Chapter 3, *Making PageMaker Mind*). You can even change page views and turn pages before you Option-paste, and the graphic will land in the same position on the page.

### ▼ *Tip: Pasting Recalcitrant FreeHand Graphics*

When you're having trouble printing pages with placed FreeHand EPS graphics on them, try this.

1. Open the original graphic (not the EPS) in FreeHand.
2. Select all of the items you want to place in PageMaker.
3. Hold down Option and choose Copy from the Edit menu. Free-Hand displays a "Converting Clipboard" alert.
4. Return to PageMaker and paste (don't place) the FreeHand graphic from the Clipboard.

Try printing the document again. This also works with Illustrator.

## *Placing Graphics*

While creating graphics with PageMaker's LBO tools may be the easiest method, more often than not you'll need graphics that surpass the awe-inspiring powers of these tools. At that point, you'll want to use Place to bring in graphics created with other graphics applications.

Placed graphics can be resized, moved, copied, and pasted, just like PageMaker-drawn LBOs. One interesting limitation: PageMaker will not allow you to size any imported graphic so that it is smaller than 3 points in any dimension. Even if you're placing an EPS line that's one-half point tall in FreeHand, it will place with two-and-one-half points of extra space around it. LBOs, on the other hand, can be sized down to one-quarter point in any dimension.

**Bitmaps and Objects**

Before we go any farther, we need to explain about the different kinds of graphics and file types that PageMaker can handle. (If you know this already, feel free to skip it.) The first important distinction is between bitmapped and object-oriented graphics.

Bitmapped graphics are collections of dots. You create them with paint programs, screen capture programs, and scanners. The dots can be black and white, they can have shades of gray, or they can be in color. The white background of black-and-white bitmaps can be either transparent or opaque, but it's usually transparent. The background of gray and color bitmaps is always opaque. Black-and-white bitmaps are sometimes called bilevel TIFFs or paint-type graphics, while people usually call gray-scale bitmaps TIFFs, scanned images, or gray-scale TIFFs. Since black-and-white bitmaps and gray-scale/color bitmaps behave differently, it's important to know what type of bitmapped graphics file you're working with.

Object-oriented graphics are collections of objects—circles, squares, complex curved paths, and blocks of type. Objects are created with PageMaker's drawing tools, or with object-oriented draw programs like Illustrator, FreeHand, and MacDraw. The objects can be black and white, shades of gray, or color. Bear in mind also that an object-oriented graphic can contain bitmapped graphics as objects. The backgrounds of object-oriented graphics can be either transparent or opaque, depending on the fill specified for the objects.

## File Types

The Macintosh does many things differently from other computers, but one of the most important is the way it keeps track of file types and creators. Among other things, the file type and creator let the Finder know what application created a file, so you can double-click on a file and it will open the file with the creating application.

Similarly, file types PageMaker knows how to place appear in the file listing in the Place dialog box, while files PageMaker doesn't know how to place don't. File types also tell PageMaker how to place the file (as text, as a graphic, and so on). You can see the file type (and change it) using a variety of programs, but our favorite is DiskTop (Figure 5-4).

**Figure 5-4**
Viewing file types and creators with DiskTop

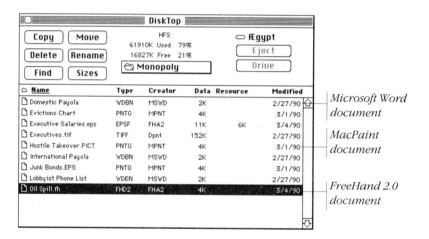

*Microsoft Word document*

*MacPaint document*

*FreeHand 2.0 document*

## Graphics Formats

The file types on the Macintosh tell programs what format the file is in, so the program can handle it properly. PageMaker handles several different graphic file formats, each of which is appropriate for different types of images.

### ▼ Tip: When You Can't See a File You Know is There

If a file that you want to place doesn't appear in the Place dialog box, it might have a file type that PageMaker doesn't recognize. RIFF files, for example (created by ImageStudio), won't be recognized as TIFF files (because they're not). SuperPaint LaserBits files and ThunderScan files won't be recognized as bitmaps. FreeHand files won't be recognized as EPS (you have to export to EPS). PageMaker doesn't know how to use any of these file types. Just changing the file type with DiskTop won't help in this case.

Luckily, all of these file types come from programs that can save the files in formats that PageMaker does recognize and can place. Simply open a RIFF file with ImageStudio, for instance, "Save as Other," and choose the TIFF format. If there's no way to save the file in another format, you can try changing the file type with DiskTop to one that PageMaker recognizes. It shouldn't work, and probably won't, but we've seen it save the day on a couple of occasions. This is called "witch-doctoring."

---

**_Paint graphics_** (type PNTG) are in the format of good old MacPaint. They're black-and-white, bitmapped, 72 dots per inch (dpi), 8 by 10 inches (576 by 720 dots)—no more and no less. That's all fixed. Paint-format graphics are nice because almost every program can read them, but at 72 dpi they're pretty jaggy, so if you're doing anything besides Mac screen shots, you should probably be working with TIFF. Even with screen shots, you'll need to use TIFF files if the screen's bigger than the standard Paint format, or if you want color or gray in your screen shots.

**_TIFF_** (type TIFF) is a standard bitmapped file format that is supposedly the same for different programs on different computers. In fact, though, there is a lot of variety in TIFF files; different programs create them slightly differently, so you can't always be sure that another program will be able to read them. PageMaker is about the best program around at reading different programs' TIFF files—not surprising, since Aldus was central to promulgating this format.

Bitmaps in TIFF format can be any size and resolution, and they can include gray scales and color (it's the format of choice for gray-scale scans). There are also compressed and uncompressed versions of the format (see "Compressing and Decompressing TIFF Images" later in this chapter).

*PICT* (type PICT) is the standard object-oriented file type on the Mac. PICT files can include just about any type of object (including bitmaps), but they have trouble with sophisticated stuff. Line widths are not reliable when you move PICTs between programs, and type spacing often goes screwy.

To get around these PICT problems, some programs attach the PostScript code that describes the graphic, hiding it away in the PICT file's resource fork (see "ResEdit" in Chapter 2, *Building a PageMaker System*). That double file (PICT and PostScript) is what you get when you Option-Copy graphics out of FreeHand or Illustrator. Programs can use the PICT rendition for screen display, but use the PostScript version for printing.

*EPS*, or Encapsulated PostScript graphics (type EPSF), come in two basic varieties—with and without screen representations. Straight EPS files are just PostScript code (straight text) which follows certain conventions defined by Adobe. You can place these on a page, but all you'll see is a gray box with filename, date, and creator, but they'll print correctly when you send them to a PostScript printer.

EPS graphics can also contain a screen representation (which is in either TIFF or—usually—PICT format). Viewable EPS files let you see a graphic on the page, while all the PostScript code is there for printing purposes (these are the opposite of the PICT-and-PostScript files described above; the PostScript is in the data fork, and the PICT is in the resource fork).

EPS is the format of choice for object-oriented graphics, as long as you don't have to edit the graphics. Once a file is in EPS format you can count on it to print reliably, but with a couple of exceptions, you can't change the contents this side of editing the PostScript code. It's a rotten format for bitmaps, as well; EPS-format bitmap files are huge. And of course, you can't print the high-resolution PostScript version unless you have a PostScript printer. You'll just get the low-resolution screen rendition.

There is one other subclass of EPS—Illustrator-format EPS. It's the format that was used by Adobe Illustrator 1.1. You could call it editable EPS, because several programs (including Illustrator and FreeHand on the Mac, and Corel Draw on the IBM) let you open and edit these files. As with normal EPS, there are viewable and nonviewable varieties.

### ▼ Tip: EPS Graphic Places as Gray Box

If an EPS graphic places as a gray box, it doesn't have a screen rendition; it's just PostScript code. The graphic will usually print correctly, regardless of the screen display (see Figure 5-5).

**Figure 5-5**
A PostScript graphic without a screen representation

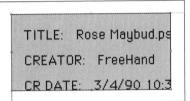

*Graphic as it appears when placed in PageMaker*

*Graphic as it appears when printed*

Several of the tips following explain how to add a screen image to a nonviewable EPS graphic.

### ▼ Tip: Creating Your Own EPS Graphics

To create your own PostScript code and place it as a graphic, you just need to add a few comment lines to the top of the file, as follows.

```
%!PS-Adobe-2.0
%%Title: My EPS Graphic
%%Creator: Me
%%CreationDate: 10-27-1989, 7:49:27
%%BoundingBox: 0 0 612 792
```

PageMaker displays the title, creator, and creation date in the gray box that shows up on the on-screen page. The bounding box defines the size of the gray box. The numbers are the lower-left x and y coordinates, and upper-right x and y, measured from the lower-left corner, in points. To figure out your bounding box coordinates, print out the image and measure it.

---

### ▼ *Tip: Extracting EPS Files*

If you need to get at an EPS graphic for some reason, but don't have the original EPS file, you can extract it from your pub by printing the page containing the EPS to disk as normal PostScript (see "PostScript Print Options" in Chapter 6, *Printing*) and extracting the EPS files from the PostScript text file with a text editor (see Figure 5-6).

**Figure 5-6**
Extracting an EPS graphic from PageMaker-written PostScript

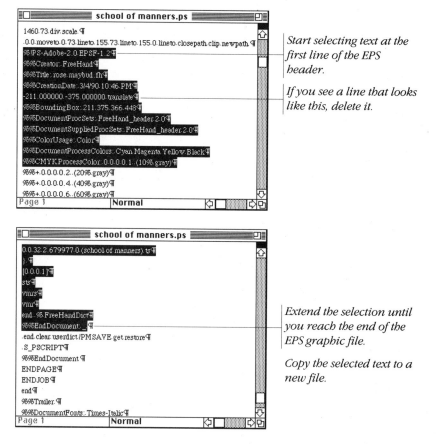

*Start selecting text at the first line of the EPS header.*

*If you see a line that looks like this, delete it.*

*Extend the selection until you reach the end of the EPS graphic file.*

*Copy the selected text to a new file.*

1. Open the PostScript file with a text editor (Microsoft Word, Write-Now, or whatever). In Word, you can open any file by pressing Shift-F6, or by holding down Shift as you choose "Open."

2. Search for "%!PS-Adobe" to find the first line of the placed EPS file. You can probably identify the graphic by looking at the "%%Title:" line.

3. Select all of the text from the start of the first line of the EPS file through the last line of that file that begins with %%. To locate the end of the EPS section, search for %%Trailer, or %%EOF, or perhaps %%EndDocument. It varies depending on what program created the EPS.

4. Copy the selection, then paste it into another file.

5. Save the file as text-only.

If you notice something like "-20.000000 145.000000 translate" immediately preceding the line beginning with "%%BoundingBox" at the start of the file, delete the whole line—the numbers and the word translate. PageMaker adds this line to EPS files when you place them. It moves the origin (the 0, 0 point) of the graphic to the lower-left corner of the graphic. It also makes it hard or impossible to open Illustrator 1.1 graphics for editing in a draw program, or to place any type of PostScript graphics on a page properly.

---

▼ *Tip: Using SmartArt to Create*
  *a Screen Rendition of a Straight EPS File*

If you have an EPS file with no screen rendition included, and it's not Illustrator-format EPS, you can still create a screen rendition with SmartArt. Just open the EPS file, click the Reimage button, then save the file as EPS. This only works if there's a %%BoundingBox comment in the file, however. If there isn't, print out the graphic, measure the bounding box, and type in your own %%BoundingBox comment before you use SmartArt.

---

▼ *Tip: Using LaserTalk and Illustrator or FreeHand to Create a Screen Rendition of a Straight EPS File*

This method is a lot more work, but if you've got LaserTalk (also from Emerald City) but not SmartArt, you can at least get the job done.

1. Use LaserTalk's Preview feature to get an image of the graphic on screen.

2. Grab a screen shot using Command-Shift-3. You'll end up with a Paint file called Screen00 in the system folder (if you're using a large screen, or color or gray-scale display, you'll need to use a screen capture utility like Capture).

3. Use the screen capture as a template to quickly trace the graphic in FreeHand or Illustrator. Save the tracing as viewable EPS.

4. Open the EPS file with LaserTalk and replace the operative Post-Script code with your own code. Save the file.

You'll end up with the PICT screen rendition created by Illustrator or FreeHand, but with your PostScript for printing.

---

▼ *Tip: Invisible EPS*

Sometimes, you want to include PostScript files in your PageMaker publication, but don't want them to appear on the screen—even as a gray box. This is particularly true for complex EPS files—it can take all day for PageMaker to display their PICTs. Since you need to place and view other graphics, you don't want to use the Gray out display option in the Preferences dialog box. Here's what you do (see Figure 5-7).

1. Make a copy of the EPS file.

2. Open the EPS file with ResEdit.

3. Open the EPS file's PICT resource.

4. Delete the PICT, then create a new PICT resource.

5. Choose "Get info" or press Command-I to display the new PICT's resource information.

**Figure 5-7**
Creating an invisible
EPS graphic

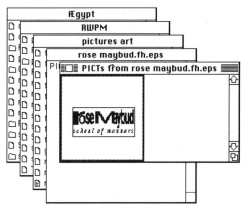

*The screen version of an EPS graphic is stored in the graphic's PICT resource. Select the PICT, choose Clear from the Edit menu, then choose New from the File menu.*

*Select PICT from the listing of resource types.*

*ResEdit creates a new PICT resource, and assigns it an ID number.*

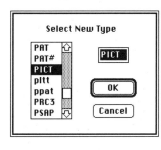

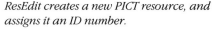
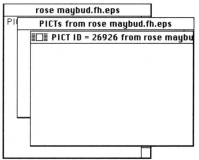

*Choose "Get info" from the File menu. Change the blank PICT resource so that it has an ID of 256.*

6. Change the PICT's resource ID number to 256.

7. Save the changes you've made to the file.

Now, return to PageMaker. Place the original EPS file and position it on the page. Then, replace the graphic with the EPS file you just edited.

You'll be able to see the selection handles on the graphic when its selected, but, otherwise, the graphic is invisible. It takes no time to redraw, but will print.

We often place invisible EPS files on our master pages when we want things like custom registration marks that we don't need to see except on the printouts.

---

### ▼ *Tip: Nonprinting PICT*

If you need to place instructions, guides, or other visible items on a page, but don't want them to print, try using the opposite of the technique above. Keep the PICT screen rendition, but kill the PostScript (see Figure 5-8).

1. Make a copy of the EPS file.

2. Open the EPS file with a text editor (change its file type to TEXT, or in Word, use Shift-F6) and delete all the operative PostScript—the information between the "%%BoundingBox" line and the "%%End Document" line (excluding those lines!). Save the file as text only.

**Figure 5-8**
Creating a
non-printing graphic

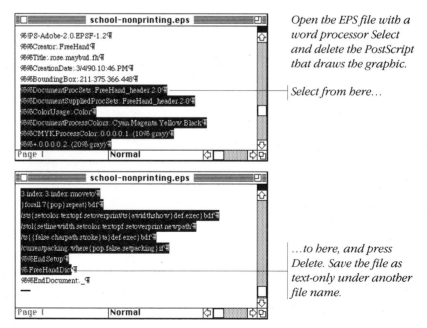

*Open the EPS file with a word processor Select and delete the PostScript that draws the graphic.*

*Select from here…*

*…to here, and press Delete. Save the file as text-only under another file name.*

**Figure 5-8**
Creating a
non-printing
graphic, continued

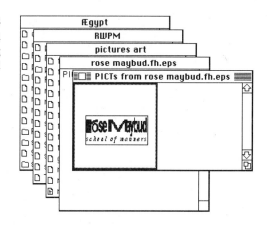

*With ResEdit, open the
original EPS graphic and
copy the graphic's screen
representation out of the
file's PICT resource.*

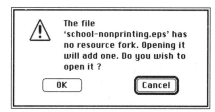

*Open the file you just edited in your
word-processor. When you open the
text-only file, this alert appears.
Click "OK."*

Select PICT.

Paste the original PICT into the file.

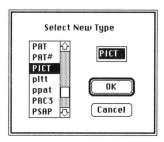

*Choose "Get info" from the
File menu. Give the new
PICT resource an ID of 256.*

3. Open the original EPS file with ResEdit, select and copy the PICT resource.

4. Open the edited EPS file. ResEdit asks if you want to add a resource fork to the file. Click Yes, and paste the PICT resource into the resource fork. Make sure that the PICT resource is ID number 256.

5. Save the changes you've made to the EPS file.

Return to PageMaker and place the edited EPS file. The PICT screen representation appears on the page, and can be resized and moved like any other graphic, but won't print on PostScript printers. This is especially useful for building templates where you want instructions and markers right on the page.

## *Back to Placing*

Once you've chosen a graphic file (clicked on it once) in the Place dialog box, the options in the dialog box change (Figure 5-9). Choose the option you want, and press Return. If you want to bypass all the

**Figure 5-9**
Place options for graphics

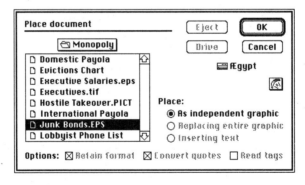

If you have the Pointer tool selected when you select a graphic file in the Place dialog box, the As independent graphic option becomes active.

If you have a graphic selected with the Pointer tool when you choose Place, you have the option of replacing the selected graphic.

With the Text tool selected and an insertion point clicked in a story, "As inline graphic" becomes active.

options and place as an independent graphic, just double-click on the file name. PageMaker loads a place gun with the graphic. Different graphic file types produce different place guns (Figure 5-10).

**Figure 5-10**
Graphic place guns

*Paint*  *EPS*  *TIFF*
*PICT*  *Scrapbook PICT*

Position the gun where you want the upper-left corner of the graphic, and click the mouse button to place the graphic on the page. You can also drag-place it—hold down the mouse button and drag the place gun to the approximate size you want the graphic.

### ▼ *Tip: When a File Places as Some Other Kind of File*

If a file you think should be a graphic places as text, it might have the wrong file type. This sometimes happens with EPSF files that have been exported to an AppleShare volume or with TIFF files that have been transferred from an IBM PC-based scanning application like the best-selling Aldus SnapShot. Use some utility program (such as the indispensable DiskTop or Apple's ResEdit) to change the file's type to one of the those that PageMaker accepts (like EPSF or TIFF). You don't need to do anything to the file's creator tag.

You'd think that holding down the Shift key while drag-placing a graphic would constrain it proportionally, but it doesn't. It doesn't do anything, in fact. Neither does the Command key when drag-placing cause a magic stretch (discussed later in this chapter). If you try to drag-place an object to a size smaller than 3 points in any dimension, the graphic places at full size.

### ▼ *Tip: Extending your Range of Fills with EPS Graphics*

We commented earlier in this chapter that PageMaker has a limited number of percentage fills on the Fill menu. Here's a workaround. You can store a set of FreeHand (or Illustrator) EPS files, each file containing only a borderless, filled box. The boxes could contain gray tints, graduated fills, radial fills, or PostScript fills. Skip FreeHand's patterned fills, which are PICTs. You can size the placed EPS graphics without distorting the fill, and set them to any PageMaker color.

If you need a box with a 25 percent blue tint (you want the 25 percent screen to print on the blue spot color overlay), place a 25 percent EPS object, size it, then apply the color blue. Use the same placed file to produce a 25 percent black box (that prints on the black spot color overlay) by copying and pasting the box and applying the color black.

## Replacing Graphics

Some people like to put graphics onto a page temporarily—in templates, for instance—then replace them with the final graphics when those are ready. If you have a graphic selected when you choose Place (Command-D), a new option appears in the Place dialog box— "Replacing entire graphic." If you have a bitmap (TIFF or PNTG) selected when you use the Replacing entire graphic option, PageMaker places the new graphic in the same position as the selected graphic, using the same text wrap as the graphic you had selected. If you have an LBO, EPS graphic, or PICT selected, PageMaker places the graphic in the same position as the selected graphic, applies the same cropping and text wrap as the selected graphic, and stretches the incoming graphic to the same size as the selected graphic.

Sometimes, you will not be able to see the new graphic. In this case, pan or uncrop the image until you see as much of it as you want. (For more information on panning and cropping, see "Cropping Placed Graphics" later in this chapter).

PageMaker-drawn squares replace perfectly, but are rarely the proportions of the art you want to place. You can, at that point, hold down Shift and drag one of the graphic's corner handles to restore the graphic to its original proportions. But if you'd wanted to do that, why would you have chosen to replace the rectangle in the first place?

The bottom line? Use "Replace" when you are replacing graphics with an updated version of the same image (you can also use "Link info"). It works very well. Don't expect it to perfectly scale and crop an imported graphic into the space held by a PageMaker-drawn placeholder, though. You'll have to hold down Shift and drag a corner handle of a replacing graphic to restore it to its original proportions, then crop as needed. Further, placeholders imported from a graphics program (or LBOs placed from the Scrapbook) will have the same problems—incoming graphics will be stretched to fit the dimensions of the placeholder.

Don't bother trying to replace circles, ovals, and diagonal lines (PageMaker-drawn or imported); you'll just get a square or a rectangle. Replacing PageMaker-drawn horizontal and vertical lines is lots of fun, but we've yet to find a use for it (remember—imported graphics are always at least three points tall—even if it's replacing a hairline rule). Any ideas?

### ▼ *Tip: Replacing LBOs with EPS Shades*

Actually, there's a bright side to PageMaker's stretching imported graphics when you're replacing LBOs. If you want a 50 percent gray box, you can just draw a box the size you want in PageMaker, then replace it with an EPS box that has a fill of 50 percent. It will come in just the size of your PageMaker-drawn box, but with the percentage fill specified in the drawing program. (See "Extending Your Range of Fills with EPS Graphics" earlier in this chapter.)

Aha, you're thinking—you could replace PageMaker-drawn lines with gray patterns and get gray lines of any percentage that will print on your Black overlay (or whatever overlay you want). Sorry. Lines replaced with EPS graphics always pop out to 3 points—PageMaker's minimum size for imported graphics.

### ▼ *Tip: Replacing Paint-type Graphics*

If you're working with lots of paint-type graphics (like the screen shots in this book), select and drag the bitmaps to the upper-left corner of the page in your paint program. This way, each graphic you place and replace will have the same upper-left point of origin, and you won't have to pan or crop graphics as often. Figure 5-11 shows how this can be a problem.

**Figure 5-11**
Replacing paint-type graphics

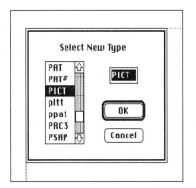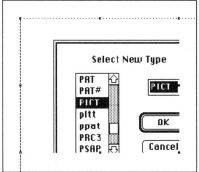

Even better, crop the image to exactly the size you want, and save it as a TIFF file. DeskPaint does a great job of this.

## Working with Bitmaps

As we explained above, there are several different kinds of bitmapped images. Bitmaps can have any resolution, and they can just have black and white dots, or include gray shades or color. There are several tools in PageMaker specifically for working with bitmaps, and the tools work in different ways depending on the type of bitmap you're working with. We've already discussed several methods for scaling bitmaps, but PageMaker also lets you control the appearance of bitmaps, both on screen and on printout.

**Image Control**

You can adjust the brightness, contrast, screen frequency, screen angle, and halftone cell shape of bitmapped images you place in PageMaker by choosing "Image control" from the Element menu. The Image control dialog box appears (Figure 5-12). Note that you can't select multiple bitmaps and then select "Image control;" you have to modify each one individually. Neither can you select "Image control" for bitmaps pasted from the Scrapbook or placed as inline graphics from a text file, because PageMaker views them as PICT images, not TIFF or Paint bitmaps.

**Figure 5-12**
Image control
dialog box

*Choose "Black and white" for a bilevel image, "Gray" if you want to adjust gray levels, or "Screened" if you want to adjust the halftoning shape, angle, or frequency.*

*Canned presets: normal, reverse, posterize, and solarize*

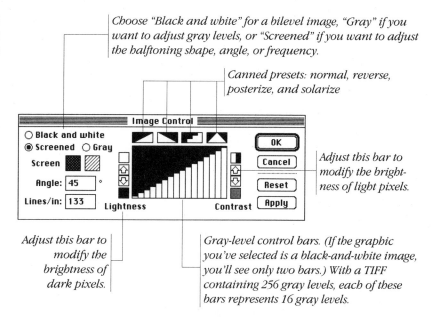

*Adjust this bar to modify the brightness of light pixels.*

*Adjust this bar to modify the brightness of dark pixels.*

*Gray-level control bars. (If the graphic you've selected is a black-and-white image, you'll see only two bars.) With a TIFF containing 256 gray levels, each of these bars represents 16 gray levels.*

### ▼ Tip: PICT or Bitmap?

One of the easiest ways to tell if a graphic is a PICT or a bitmap is to select the graphic and pull down the Element menu. If the Image control command is grayed out, the graphic is a PICT; if it becomes active, the graphic is a bitmap. You can convert a PICT bitmap to a TIFF by copying it, pasting it into a paint program or gray-scale editor, and saving it as TIFF.

With gray-scale images, the Image control dialog box lets you adjust sixteen different gray ranges spread across the range of grays available in the TIFF. If you are working with a 256-level gray-scale TIFF, for instance, each of the bars in the chart affects 16 of those gray levels.

With a 64-level TIFF, each bar represents four gray levels.

### ▼ Tip: Image Control Settings for Gray-scale Images

Gray-scale images are tricky, and it takes a good deal of experience to predict what will come off a laser printer or imagesetter based on what you see on screen. The settings of the bars in Figure 5-13 work pretty well for printing gray-scale images off imagesetters. It's a crude approximation of a logarithmic curve.

These settings brighten the dark areas considerably, so the images don't clog up and go black as they tend to do when you're printing imagesetter-output gray-scale TIFFs. The screen settings you see here are just our preferences, though they're pretty standard settings.

**Figure 5-13**
Image settings for a gray-scale image

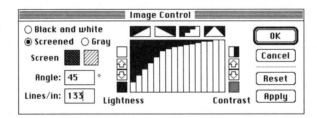

With black-and-white bitmaps, the Image control dialog box comes up with just two bars—one for black and one for white. Click either the Screened or Gray button, and you'll be able to adjust those two bars, and use the Contrast and Brightness sliders to adjust the gray levels of the black and white dots in the image (see Figure 5-14).

**Figure 5-14**
Image control dialog box with a bilevel TIFF selected

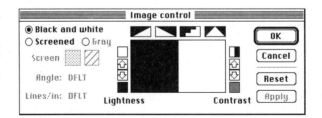

### ▼ Tip: Improving Bitmapped Clip Art

Bitmapped clip art often looks a lot better if you mute it a bit by graying it out (Figure 5-15). Select the black bar and drag it down a little.

**Figure 5-15**
Applying a gray screen
to a bilevel bitmap

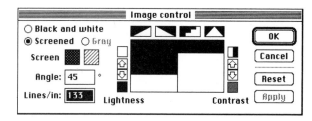

Choose "Screened," set the line frequency and screen angle you want to use, then adjust the slider bars to a gray level.

---

### ▼ Tip: Muted Backgrounds

You can use a scanned image or other bitmap as a background for a page or part of a page by dimming it to near invisibility. Then build your page on top of it.

---

### ▼ Tip: Giving Screen Shots a Classy Look

If you use many screen shots, you can make them look better by giving the white pixels a slight gray tint, and muting the black pixels a little to a dark gray. There are a couple of problems, though.

First, you must have perfectly cropped screen shots, or the gray outside the screens will show up. Secondly, there's no way to reuse image settings or apply them to multiple graphics at once, so you have to adjust each screen shot individually, setting the levels for black and white exactly the same for each one—by hand.

---

If you set a gray bitmap to "Gray," PageMaker will print the graphic using the screen frequency and screen angle settings found in the selected printer's APD file (for more on APDs, see "Those Mysterious APDs," in Chapter 6, *Printing*). To print at a different screen angle, screen frequency, or using a different screening method, choose "Screened." See "Halftone Screens" in Chapter 6, *Printing*, for recommended screen settings.

### ▼ *Tip: If PC Bitmapped Graphics Place Reversed*

We won't explain why (it doesn't matter), but a lot of TIFF files moved over from the PC place reversed (black for white) in Mac PageMaker. This is especially true with screen shots. Just select the graphic, choose "Image control" from the Elements menu, and reverse it back.

Sometimes, TIFF images print (especially to older Linotronic RIPs) as positives when you've specified "Invert" in the Print dialog box. For more on this bad thing and how to avoid it, see the tip "Negative Negatives" in Chapter 6, *Printing*.

### ▼ *Tip: Compressing and Decompressing TIFF Images*

You can use PageMaker to compress TIFF images to around one-third of their original (uncompressed) size to save space on disk. But bear in mind that some programs may not be able to read PageMaker's compressed TIFF format. To compress TIFF files, follow these steps.

1. Choose Place from the File menu (Command-D), and select the TIFF file you want to compress.

2. Hold down Command-Option-Shift and click OK for the maximum compression. (You can also hold down Command-Option and click OK for a lesser compression, but why would you opt for less than maximum compression when the two compression levels are functionally equivalent?)

PageMaker creates a new, compressed version of the TIFF file and adds "LD2" or "L" (depending on the type of file that's been compressed) to the file name. Once you've created the compressed file, you can delete the original version of the file (the careful user will back the file up first).

If, for some reason, you need to decompress a TIFF image (if you threw away the original TIFF file without backing it up, for instance, need to edit it, and find that your image-editing program cannot read the compressed TIFF), here's how to decompress it.

1. Choose Place from the File menu (Command-D).
2. Select the TIFF file you want to decompress.
3. Press Command and click OK.

PageMaker decompresses the TIFF file, and adds the letter U to the file name.

## *Displaying Graphics*

In the Preferences dialog box, you'll see several options for displaying graphics: Gray out, Normal, and High resolution. Here's what these options mean.

***Gray out.*** PageMaker displays gray boxes instead of any placed graphics. PageMaker-drawn graphics are displayed normally. Gray out is the fastest display mode.

***Normal.*** PageMaker displays LBOs, EPS files, object-oriented PICTs, and bitmaps under 50 K in normal manner. For bitmapped graphics over 50 K, PageMaker creates and displays a lower-resolution screen image, with a pointer to the high-resolution version on disk. The Normal display mode is basically the same as in previous versions of PageMaker.

***High-resolution.*** PageMaker displays bitmapped images at their full resolution. This can take a long time (especially with high-res color TIFFs), so only use it when you want to impress clients (and remember to get it set up before they come in the room, or they'll just stand there tapping their feet).

In High-resolution mode, if PageMaker cannot find the original graphic file, it displays the normal resolution screen image. If a graphic does not seem to be displayed at high resolution, check the Links dialog box to see if PageMaker has lost track of the source file. PageMaker's Detailed graphics display options have no effect on printing.

### ▼ *Tip: Switching to High Resolution*

To see a bitmapped graphic at high resolution, hold down Control as a graphic starts to display. PageMaker displays the image at its full resolution, regardless of the setting for Detailed graphics, and continues to display the graphic at full resolution until the screen is redrawn. This only works if you have a Control key on your keyboard, of course.

## *Resizing Placed Graphics*

The eight handles that appear around the edges of a selected graphic are used for resizing the graphic. The four handles that appear on the corners of the graphic resize the graphic diagonally, while the handles on the sides, top, and bottom resize it horizontally and vertically, respectively. Hold down Shift while dragging a corner handle, and PageMaker retains the graphic's original proportions. PageMaker sizes all of the elements in placed graphics uniformly, including line weights.

### ▼ *Tip: The Vanishing Point*

Sometimes, PageMaker's sizing of EPS and draw-type graphics makes very fine lines disappear. Usually this happens if the graphic is very large when imported, then sized down so it is very small. Try to get your draw and EPS graphics fairly close to the size you want them before placing them in PageMaker.

FreeHand and Illustrator, for example, have options to retain line widths while scaling, so you can scale graphics without approaching the vanishing point. If you don't have a copy of the original file, try extracting the EPS file from a PostScript version of the PageMaker publication (see the tip "Extracting EPS Files" earlier in this chapter). If it's in Illustrator 1.1 format, you'll be able to open and edit it with Illustrator or FreeHand.

If you're working with a FreeHand EPS graphic and don't have the original file, you won't be able to edit it in FreeHand. You can edit the code with a text editor, though, to thicken up the line weights.

1. Open a copy of the EPS file with a text editor.

2. Search for "setlinewidth".

3. Change the value immediately preceding "setlinewidth" to something larger. For a hairline, for example, use "0.2 setlinewidth" (the values are in points).

4. Save the EPS file as text-only. It's a good idea to give it another name.

Once you've edited the EPS file, you won't be able to see its screen image—just a gray box containing the file name and creation date. Don't worry; it will still print the way you want it. If you can't live without a screen image, try this technique.

1. Open the original file with ResEdit and copy the PICT resource.

2. Open the edited file. ResEdit asks you if you want to add a resource fork to the file. Click Yes, and paste the PICT into the resource fork.

3. Save your changes to the file.

When you place the file, you'll see the original screen image, but the file prints with the thickened line weights. You could also use SmartArt to add a screen image to the text file—see the tip "Using SmartArt to Create a Screen Rendition of a Straight EPS File" earlier in this chapter.

---

▼ *Tip: Resizing Graphics to a Mathematical Proportion of their Original Size*

While we would very much like to see a feature in PageMaker that would resize graphics to a percentage you could enter in a dialog box, the following technique works pretty well.

1. Place the graphic.

2. Choose "Preferences" from the Edit menu, and choose "Inches decimal" for your unit of horizontal measurement (you could also choose "Millimeters").

3. Move the zero point to the upper-left corner of the graphic.

4. Measure the width of the graphic.

5. Multiply the width of the graphic by the percentage reduction (or enlargement) you want. For example, if your graphic is 6 inches wide and you've specified an 80 percent reduction, you'd multiply 6 times .80.

6. Drag out a vertical ruler guide until it reaches the measure on the horizontal ruler you found in the preceding step. In our example, we would place the ruler guide at 4.8 inches.

7. Make sure that "Snap to guides" is on (Command-U toggles it on and off), then hold down Shift, select the handle on the lower-right corner of the graphic, and resize the graphic until it snaps to the ruler guide.

This technique is fairly accurate, especially if you zoom to 400% view before setting your ruler guide. In that view, the ruler increments are every point, .05 millimeters, or 100th of an inch, depending on your Measurement setting in the Preferences dialog box. In the next section, on magic stretch, we demonstrate some techniques for scaling bitmapped graphics by percentages.

**Magic Stretch**

With black-and-white bitmaps, you often have to pay attention to the image resolution vis-a-vis printer resolution to avoid ugly patterns. This is a problem with any bitmap that contains regular, repeating patterns (like the dots in Macintosh scroll bars in placed screen shots), but it's especially bad with dithered, black-and-white scanned images. Few things will make your pub look so bad as a dithered scan that's plagued by these plaid-like patterns, as shown in Figure 5-16.

**Figure 5-16**
Avoiding ugly patterns
with magic stretch

*Magic-stretched graphic. When the
printer resolution and bitmap
resolution have an integral relationship, you get good quality output.*

*Non-magic-stretched graphic. When
the printer resolution and image
resolution do not have an integral
relationship, ugly patterns result.*

The trick to avoiding these patterns is to make sure that the image
resolution is some integral multiple (or divisor) of the printer resolution. That way you end up with one, or four, or nine printer dots for
every dot in the image. If you don't have this integral relationship,
there may be 6.4 printer dots for every image dot (see Figure 5-17), and
a laser printer can't print four tenths of a dot. Something has to give,
and what gives is image quality.

Image resolution is affected, of course, by scaling. If you reduce a
72-dpi image to 50 percent, you have a 144-dpi image. There are the
same number of dots in half as much space. Since there's no percentage scaling in PageMaker, it's tough getting the integral relationship
you need—even if you *could* figure out what the reduction should be.

**Figure 5-17**
Integral and nonintegral
relationships

*An integral relationship between
graphic and printer resolution.
There's dot-for-dot equivalency.*

*When there's a nonintegral relation-
ship, image quality degrades.*

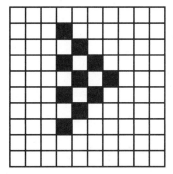 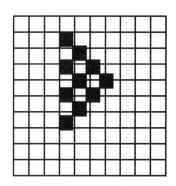

PageMaker provides an excellent solution, though, that most people call magic stretch. Hold down Command while you size a bitmapped image, and it snaps to sizes that provide an integral relationship. Magic stretch works with proportional stretching, so you can hold down Shift and Command and size graphics both proportionally and to the printer's resolution at the same time.

Since there's no problem with patterns when sizing object graphics, holding down Command has no effect when you're sizing them. Note that bitmapped images inside PICT or EPS graphics are not affected by magic stretch, even if the bitmap is the only item in the PICT or EPS, because PageMaker thinks of these as object graphics. This last point is especially important when you're placing text files containing bitmapped inline graphics. These graphics come in as PICTs, so you won't be able to magic stretch them.

### ▼ Tip: Use the Right APD

PageMaker is able to do this magic stretch arithmetic for you because it knows the printer's resolution; it's defined in the APD (see "Those Mysterious APDs" in Chapter 6, *Printing*). So if you want magic stretch to work right, you have to use the right APD. Graphics that you've magic stretched based on 300-dpi resolution will give you patterns if you print them at 1270 dpi (they'll work fine at 1200, though). So before you magic stretch, choose your final target printer (or one with the same resolution) from the Printer type pop-up menu in the Print dialog box.

Note that you have many more choices of magic stretch sizes when you're printing to a high-res device. That factor alone may make it worth printing your final output to an imagesetter.

### ▼ Tip: Lazywriter.apd

Suppose you usually proof your work with an Apple LaserWriter II NT (after owning one for a while, Ole decided that "NT" stood for "No Toner") and print your final copies on a Linotronic 300. You could easily go crazy changing to the Linotronic 300 APD every time you want to magic stretch a graphic, and back to the LaserWriter II NT APD every time you want to print. To avoid this problem:

1. Open the LaserWriter II NT APD with a text editor.

2. Search for a line starting with @Resolution (in our example, the line will read @Resolution: "300 300").

3. Change the resolution to the resolution of the printer you'll use for final output (in this case, we'd change the line to @Resolution "1270 1270").

4. Save the file as text-only under another file name, making sure that the file name ends with .apd. We call ours Lazywriter.apd.

5. Open your publication and choose the new APD in the Print dialog box.

Now you can magic stretch to your final printer's resolution and print to your proof printer without having to change APDs. The 300-dpi proofs will have patterns, but the final, high-resolution output won't.

---

We've been told, by supposedly authoritative sources, that magic stretching has no effect on gray-scale TIFFs. It really shouldn't, because they don't pose the pattern problems that black-and-white bitmaps do. Try it, though: place a gray-scale TIFF in your publication, hold down Command-Shift, and resize the TIFF. Does it size smoothly, or does it pop to various sizes?

Right. It pops to various sizes, just like a black-and-white graphic. While you won't see the plaid patterns in gray-scale TIFFs, and they'll look fine whether you hold down Command while you resize them or not, we're glad it works because there are some cool things you can do, described in the following tips.

▼ *Tip: Sizing Scanned Images*

If you know the resolution of a scanned image (or any bitmapped image, for that matter), you can use magic stretch and custom APDs to size the image by percentages. With a 300-dpi scan, for instance, use an APD with resolution set to "3000 3000". Magic stretching will size the image in 10 percent increments. Set it to "6000 6000", and you size in five percent increments. You can even use "30000 30000" if you want, for sizing in one percent increments. When you get that fine, though, you have to use the rulers and do the arithmetic anyway; it's almost impossible to count how many percentage stops you've moved, so it's not really worth it.

To determine the resolution of a bitmap, see the tip "Determining and Changing Resolution with DeskPaint" in Chapter 2, *Building a PageMaker System.*

---

### ▼ *Tip: Extracting Paint-type Graphics*

If you try to copy a resized paint-type graphic out of PageMaker and into a paint program, you're probably in for a shock. The image you paste into your paint file will be identical to the image of the sized graphic in PageMaker, rather than popping back out to its original 72-dpi splendor. In other words, information has been lost. You could try to proportionally stretch the graphic back out to its original size in PageMaker before you copy it to the Clipboard, but it's a pretty painful procedure. It always seems you're just one pixel off this way or that.

Once again, a combination of the magic stretch technique and judicious APD-rewriting saves the day.

1. Open the LaserWriter II NT APD with a text editor.

2. Search for a line starting with @Resolution (in our example, the line will read @Resolution: "300 300").

3. Change the resolution to the resolution of the Macintosh screen: @Resolution "72 72").

4. Save the file as text-only under another file name (maybe Paint.apd), making sure that the file name ends with .apd.

5. Open your publication and choose the new APD in the Print dialog box.

Now hold down Shift-Command and stretch the paint-type graphic you want to extract. It pops back out to 72 dpi. Copy the graphic to the Clipboard, paste it into your paint program, and edit away.

### ▼ *Tip: Correcting Aspect Ratio for IBM Screen Shots*

You can use magic stretch with a custom APD to convert distorted IBM screen shots that came from EGA- or CGA-equipped IBM PCs. Just use the particular graphic adapter's resolution in the APD @Resolution line. Note that most of the PC resolutions are asymmetrical. "72 96" works well for EGA screen shots, although you may have to fine-tune it for your particular flavor of EGA. VGA (and MCGA, the graphics card in the IBM PS/2 Model 30) screen shots have square pixels, so you don't need to undistort them. "72 72" works just fine. For CGA correction, use "48 96". It's fun to resize Macintosh screen shots to EGA and CGA resolutions just to see what you're not missing.

## *Cropping Placed Graphics*

Cropping is pretty straightforward, and we don't have much to say about it that you don't probably already know. You probably already know, for instance, that you can't crop PageMaker LBOs—only placed graphics. To crop placed graphics, select the cropping tool, click on the graphic to select it, grab one of the handles (center the handle inside the cropping tool before you press the mouse button), and crop, as shown in Figure 5-18.

Once you've cropped a graphic to the size you want, you can move—or pan—the graphic inside the cropped area. To pan a cropped graphic, put the cropping tool right on top of the graphic, press down and drag. The cropping tool turns into a grabber hand. Push the grabber hand around without releasing the mouse button, and you'll see that the crop works sort of like a window, and you can move the graphic around behind that window (Figure 5-19). The whole graphic's still there; it's just masked out.

**Figure 5-18**
Cropping a graphic

*Center the graphic's selection handle in the Cropping tool, press the mouse button...*

*...and drag to crop the image.*

**Figure 5-19**
Panning an image

*Position the Cropping tool over the image and hold down the mouse button. The Cropping tool changes into a Grabber hand.*

*Drag to change your view of the cropped image.*

### ▼ *Tip: Cut, Don't Crop*

Ordinarily, avoid cropping graphics. In particular, don't use the cropping tool to pull out just a tiny part of a large scanned image—for example, isolating one face from an enormous class reunion photo. Instead, use an image manipulation or paint program to save just the part of the scanned graphic you want. Or just scan the section you need to begin with, and save the disk space.

We've seen people place a 300-dpi, 256-gray-level TIFF image a dozen times on a page, crop it down and use little parts of it, and then look surprised when it wouldn't print. Those files are huge, and the world of PostScript is imperfect. When you crop, you don't remove any part of the image. That's why you can uncrop it and move the image within the crop. The whole image remains in the publication (or linked to it, at least), and must be processed by the printer, whether you can see it or not.

### ▼ *Tip: Colorizing Placed Graphics*

Placed graphics can have PageMaker colors applied to them. If you're printing spot color separations, the graphic prints on the spot color overlay of the color that's been applied to it in PageMaker. If you're separating the publication with a process separation program (like Aldus PrePrint or Adobe Separator), the graphic prints using the colors specified in its originating graphics application (and/or according to any changes you make in the separation program).

## *Inline Graphics*

The ability to place a graphic into a text block—to make an inline graphic—is one of PageMaker 4's most powerful new features. You may think it's pretty mundane, since you've been able to do it ever since the days when there was only MacPaint and MacWrite (pasting MacPaint images into MacWrite), but PageMaker is the first Macintosh page-makeup program to let you do it, and it's very nicely implemented.

Using inline graphics, you can anchor a graphic to a particular position in text so that the graphic moves with the text as the text reflows. The inline graphic acts just like another character in the text (with a few exceptions). The result? No more laborious reflowing text blocks and repositioning graphics to keep your graphics in the same position relative to text. (If you want to keep your graphics in the same position on the page, you'll want to place or paste them as independent, or non-inline, graphics.)

There are a few of ways to insert inline graphics into a story.

- Paste a graphic into the text just as you would paste a text character.
- Place a text file that contains inline graphics (a Word or MacWrite file, for instance).
- Place a graphic as inline at a text insertion point (using the option in the Place dialog box). This works in either Layout or Story view (in Story view you use Import instead of Place).

Inline graphics are different from normal text characters in several ways. For one thing, they can hang out of the text block on the right or left. If a graphic is larger than the column in which it has been placed, it sticks out of the column as follows.

- Left-aligned graphics stick out to the right of the column.
- Right-aligned graphics stick out to the left of the column.
- Centered, justified, and force-justified graphics stick out equally on either side of the column.

Likewise, if a graphic is bigger than the leading of the line, it may hang off the top of the text block. We'll get to the leading issue below.

### ▼ *Tip: Redraw Your Screen*

Any time you're working with elements in a text block that extend beyond the edge of the text block, you need to redraw your screen fairly often. The easiest way to force PageMaker to redraw your screen is to choose the current page view (use the Page menu, or, better, use the keyboard shortcut for the page view—Command-2 if you're at 200%, and so on).

**Selecting and Modifying Inline Graphics**

You can select inline graphics with either the Text tool or the Pointer tool, but the way you select them affects what you can do with them.

**Select as text.** If you select the inline graphic with the Text tool, you can cut, copy, paste, and apply text formatting commands just as if it were a character of text—with the following limitations.

- You cannot change the font, size, or type style.
- You cannot change the positioning of the graphic using the Superscript or Subscript options.

**Select as object.** If you select the graphic with the Pointer tool, the graphic behaves as any other, non-inline graphic—you can change line styles, corner styles, and color for LBOs; you can crop, resize, cut, copy, paste, and replace the inline graphic—with the following limitations.

- You cannot drag-select or Shift-select an inline graphic. If you have other objects selected when you select an inline graphic with the Pointer tool, those objects are deselected and the inline graphic is selected. Choosing Select all from the Edit menu (Command-A) while the Pointer tool is selected will select the text block containing the inline graphic, not the inline graphic individually. Choosing Select all with the Text tool selected selects all of the text in the story—including the inline graphic.
- You cannot apply text wrap to an inline graphic.
- You cannot use the Bring to front or Send to back commands on an inline graphic independent of the text block containing it.
- If you click on an inline graphic with the Pointer tool, you select only the inline graphic, not the text block containing the graphic. To select the text block (including the inline graphic), click on the text block or Command-click through the inline graphic.

Commands that affect the entire text block affect any inline graphics contained in the text block. If you cut, copy, or delete a text block, the inline graphics in the text block are cut, copied, or deleted. If you replace an entire story containing inline graphics, the inline graphics are replaced along with the rest of the text in the story. Resizing a text block will not resize the graphic, but may change the position of the graphic on the page; it depends on how the text reflows.

You can apply various text formatting commands to inline graphics—leading, leading method, kerning, tracking, word and letter spacing, and color. All the paragraph-level attributes (indents, spacing before and after, alignment, Keep with next, Column break before, etc.) work with inline graphics.

In Story view, inline graphics appear as icons embedded in the text (see Figure 5-20). You can cut, copy, paste, and delete these icons, and you'll see the repositioned graphics when you return to Layout view.

**Figure 5-20**
Inline graphic icons
in Story view

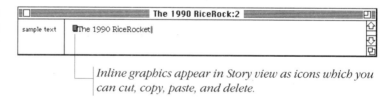

*Inline graphics appear in Story view as icons which you can cut, copy, paste, and delete.*

*Layout view*

**Horizontal Positioning for Inline Graphics**

Since inline graphics act like text characters, you can use most of the horizontal text adjustments to position them. You can center them in a text block, position them flush right, kern them to the left or the right relative to other characters, and use tabs to position them exactly.

### ▼ *Tip: Make Graphics Inline to Center Them*

It can be tough getting an independent graphic centered on a page or across a particular part of the page using the rulers and ruler guides. You measure and measure, and do all sorts of arithmetic, and still seem to come out just a little short on one side or another. If you make the graphic inline, on the other hand, PageMaker centers it for you.

1. Place or paste the graphic inline in a paragraph of its own.

2. Press Command-Shift-C to choose centered alignment for the paragraph (make sure that there's no paragraph indent in effect).

3. Drag the text block out so that it stretches across the area in which you want to center the graphic.

The graphic is perfectly centered.

### ▼ *Tip: Incredible Horizontal Positioning Accuracy with Inline Graphics*

We've said that one-quarter point accuracy is the best you can expect using the ruler guides, but there's a way to get very fine horizontal positioning accuracy for graphics using tabs.

1. Make a graphic inline. Make sure that the edges of the text block containing the graphic snap to the horizontal point you want to measure from.

2. Insert a tab in front of the graphic.

3. Press Command-I to bring up the Indents/tabs dialog box.

4. Place a left tab on the ruler and, with the tab selected, type something like 0p6.1 in the Position text edit box.

5. Choose Move tab from the Position pop-up menu. The tab moves to 6.1 points on the tab ruler. Press Return to close the dialog box.

The left edge of the graphic is now exactly 6.1 points from the left edge of the text block.

▼ *Tip: Precise Repeating Graphics*

To position repeating graphics at exact positions, choose "Repeat tab" from the Indents/tabs Position pop-up menu to repeat tabs along the ruler in precise increments (up to PageMaker's limit of 40 tabs). Do not touch any of the tabs with the mouse cursor, or they will snap to the nearest full ruler increment. This trick comes in very handy if you're designing for measurement-intensive work such as instrument panel silk-screens, and need centering marks every 1.001 mm (though you might consider investing in FreeHand or a CAD program).

By the way, we wouldn't trust either of the last two tips for increments under 1/1440 of an inch.

**Leading for Inline Graphics**

While you can place graphics inside a line of text—for symbols, complex dingbats, or company logos—probably the most common use of inline graphics will be to create single paragraphs containing only the inline graphic (see Figure 5-21). In either case, it's important to understand how the leading works; it's a little tricky.

**Figure 5-21**
Positioning inline graphics relative to text

*Inline graphic within a paragraph*

*Inline graphic as its own paragraph*

We cover leading in detail in Chapter 4, *Words*, but we'll reiterate here that if you want to know what's going on with the leading, you need to use the Proportional leading method, and specify the leading you want rather than relying on autoleading.

That said, here's how leading works with inline graphics: it's basically the same as leading for any text character, except that you can change the position of the baseline. Just grab the graphic with the Pointer tool and drag the graphic up and down. It may feel like you're moving the graphic, and that's essentially the result, but what you're really doing is shifting the position of the graphic's baseline, hence its position relative to the rest of the line (Figure 5-22).

**Figure 5-22**
Adjusting the baseline of
an inline graphic

*When you drag an inline graphic, you're actually changing its position relative to the text baseline.*

*Old baseline position*          *Drag to change the baseline.*          *New baseline position*

You cannot drag the baseline of a graphic above the top of the graphic's bounding box. It takes quite a bit of experimentation to get the hang of how this adjustment works—sometimes the graphic appears to pop back to its original position while the text around it reflows. Try moving the baseline of a few graphics until you develop a feel for what's going on.

Since you're using proportional leading, the baseline starts out two-thirds of the way down the graphic. Just as with any text character, one-third of the graphic falls below the baseline; two-thirds of the graphic fall above. When you drag the graphic down, you're actually moving the baseline up. This makes it easy to get small graphics inside a line of text looking right on the line. (You can't do that with text characters; you have to use sub- and superscript.)

### ▼ *Tip: Using Autoleading with Inline Graphics*

We know we told you never to use autoleading. It seems that every time we make a hard-and-fast rule, we end up having to present an exception, which is illustrated in Figure 5-23.

**Figure 5-23**
Autoleading with
inline graphics

*When you place an inline graphic in a paragraph by itself, make the leading for that paragraph "Auto," and PageMaker will make the paragraph slug larger than the graphic. If "Autoleading" is set to the default 120% of type size, though, you'll get an indeterminate amount of space above and below the graphic.*

Here's the exception: if you have a paragraph style that will contain only inline graphics, using autoleading is the best way to keep the graphic from hitting lines of text above it or disappearing off the top of the page. PageMaker pushes preceding and ensuing lines out of the way as needed, and, since the paragraph contains only the graphic, you don't have to worry about having one oddly-leaded line.

Whoa, you're saying—isn't this going to throw us off our leading grid? How can we know where the baselines of text following the graphic are going to fall if we don't know the height of the graphic?

Simple. In the style you create for the inline graphic paragraph, turn on "Align to grid" in the paragraph Rule options dialog box, and set the grid to your body copy leading. Add space after in even increments of your leading grid, and you can count on ensuing lines aligning to the leading grid.

If you want a paragraph containing only a graphic to be exactly the height of the graphic, use autoleading, and set the autoleading percentage to 100 for the entire paragraph (see Figure 5-24). The slug

**Figure 5-24**
Slugs around inline graphics

*Select the paragraph containing the graphic.*

*Slug of graphic is taller than the graphic.*

*Set the autoleading to 100 percent.*

*The graphic's slug is now exactly the height of the graphic.*

*You can add space before and after the paragraph to make room for the graphic.*

will be the same size as the graphic, and you can add space before and after the paragraph to make room for it. You can make this an attribute for paragraph styles that contain only graphics.

---

### ▼ *Tip: Boxed Paragraphs*

You can create boxed paragraphs in PageMaker using inline graphics, as shown in Figure 5-25.

**Figure 5-25**
Creating boxed paragraphs

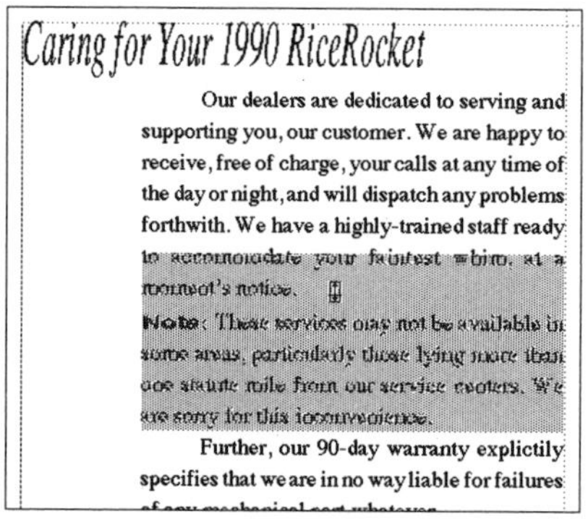

*Create a shaded box and paste it in as its own paragraph, preceding the paragraph you want to box. Set the paragraph's leading to 1 (or some other small number) in the Type specifications dialog box.*

*In the Paragraph specifications dialog box, enter 1, 2, or 3 in the Keep with next text edit box. This glues the paragraph to the following paragraph.*

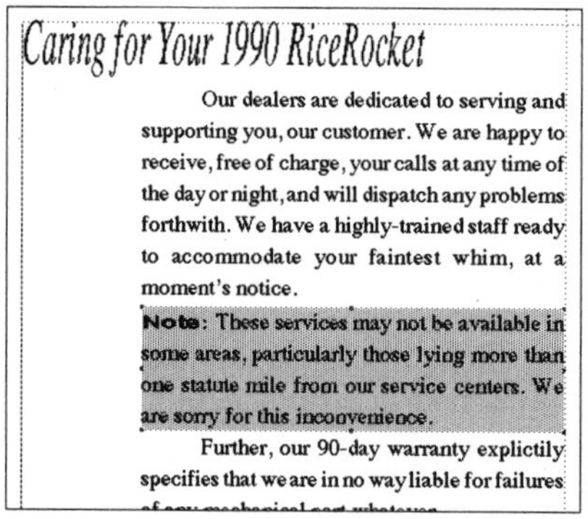

*Adjust the baseline and size of the box so that it encompasses the paragraphs you want in the box.*

*The shaded box and paragraph will now stay together if the text reflows.*

1. Create a paragraph with 1-point leading.
2. Create a shaded box and paste it into the paragraph before the paragraph you want boxed as an inline graphic.
3. Adjust the baseline and size of the box so that it covers one or more of the paragraphs following.

4. Set the paragraph's Keep with next option to 3 to glue the paragraph containing the box to the following paragraph.

The box will move with the text as the text recomposes. Build this into a paragraph style, and boxed paragraphs are easy.

You may be able to use 0-point leading (that's right—zero) for this trick, but as we went to pages, it was unclear whether it would work. If it does, you'll be able to stack up multiple paragraphs full of inline graphics, all with 0-point leading (not to mention creating hidden paragraphs, for whatever they're worth). You won't be able to specify fractional leading between 0 and 1, however.

### ▼ *Tip: Hanging Inline Graphics in the Companion Column*

Many books and magazines these days have a design featuring a narrow column to the left of the page that contains headings and small graphics—usually called a companion column. The pages in this book, for example, feature an 8-pica-wide companion column on the left. You can use inline graphics and inline graphic baseline adjustment to hang graphics in the column on the left (make sure that the graphic's leading is the same as that of the text). It works much like normal handing indents (see the tip "Use a Tab for Hanging Indents" in Chapter 4, *Words*). Once again, refresh your screens often when using techniques of this sort.

**Figure 5-25**
Hanging an inline graphic in the companion column

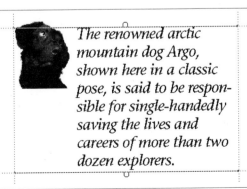

It may not look like it, but that doggie is the first character in the paragraph.

*The renowned arctic mountain dog Argo, shown here in a classic pose, is said to be responsible for single-handedly saving the lives and careers of more than two dozen explorers.*

## *Using Text Wrap*

We have serious qualms about using text wrap (it's slow and doesn't let you control the text positioning explicitly), but even we admit that there are a lot of situations when it comes in handy. There are a number of mind-boggling effects you can get with text wrap that you simply cannot get any other way. Ole still feels it shouldn't be used for rectangular wraps, though, except under threat of torture.

You add text wrap to a graphic by selecting the graphic (or graphics—you can apply text wrap to any number of selected graphics) and choosing "Text wrap" from the Element menu. The Text wrap dialog box appears (Figure 5-26).

**Figure 5-26**
Text wrap dialog box

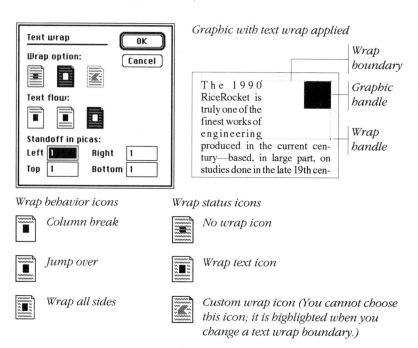

Once you've applied a wrap to a graphic, a text wrap boundary appears around the selected graphic. You can adjust the boundary by pointing at a handle and dragging the handle to a new position with Shift constraining the movement to horizontal or vertical. Or you can drag an entire boundary segment to a new position (Figure 5-27; again, Shift constrains the movement).

**Figure 5-27**
Adjusting a graphic
wrap boundary

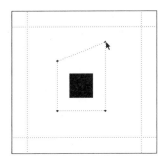

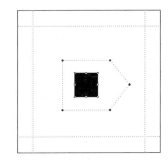

*Drag one of the wrap handles to create an irregular wrap.*

*Click on a wrap segment to add a wrap handle.*

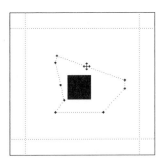

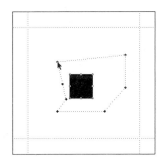

*Drag a boundary segment to adjust a wrap.*

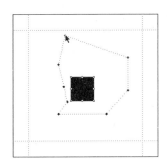

*Drag one handle over another to delete a handle.*

Finally, you can add wrap handles by clicking on the wrap boundary. This lets you create very weird irregular wraps. If you end up with too many handles, just drag one on top of another, and they combine into one handle. If the wrap gets too crazy, and you'd like to start over, you can open the Text wrap dialog box, click the Wrap text icon, and press Return to create a simple, rectangular wrap.

### ▼ *Tip: A Graphic's Wrap Boundaries Can be Anywhere*

The text wrap boundaries attached to a particular graphic can fall anywhere on a page—or even off the page, if you want, as shown in Figure 5-28.

**Figure 5-28**
Graphic wrap boundaries
can be anywhere

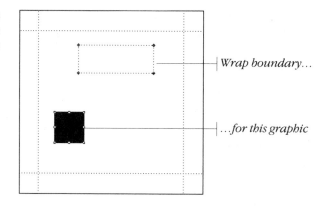

Wrap boundary...

...for this graphic

### ▼ *Tip: Delaying Text Reflow When Adjusting Wraps*

When you're adjusting a wrap boundary, waiting for the text to recompose every time you move a wrap handle gets old fast—especially if you have a lot of handles to add or adjust. Instead, hold down the Spacebar as you adjust the wrap. PageMaker does not recompose the text as long as the Spacebar is held down, so you can add and adjust as many points as you want without having to wait for the screen to redraw.

### ▼ *Tip: Angled Margins*

You can use text wrap to create columns with angled margins. We can't count the number of times we've seen ads in magazines sayingyou couldn't do this in PageMaker. It's pretty easy to do, as you can see in Figure 5-29. You can also use an inside-out wrap for this technique. See the next tip for more on inside-out wrap boundaries.

**Figure 5-29**
Creating angled
column guides

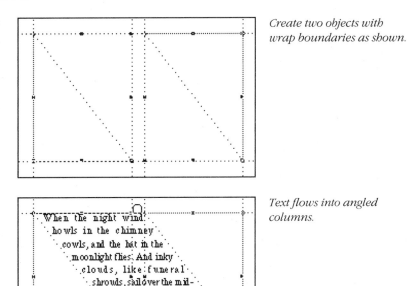

*Create two objects with
wrap boundaries as shown.*

*Text flows into angled
columns.*

▼ *Tip: Inside-out Text Wrap*

It's only appropriate that we end this section with what is probably the coolest tip in the book. It's not the most useful, but it's arguably the coolest. Just watch.

Usually, text wrap repels text outside the graphic's border. But what if you want to wrap text *inside* the border? Here's how to create inside-out text wraps (Figure 5-29).

1. Select a graphic and choose "Text wrap" from the Element menu.

2. Apply a wrap to the graphic. "Wrap all sides" seems to work best.

3. Select one wrap handle and drag it to near the other side of the wrap boundary.

4. Select the side of the wrap boundary that you have not yet moved, and drag it in the opposite direction, to near the original location of the handle you moved in step 3.

**Figure 5-30**
Creating an
inside-out wrap

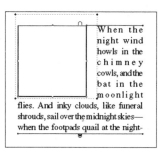

*Graphic with normal wrap
applied*

*Move the lower-right handle
across the graphic.*

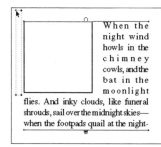

*Move the upper-right handle
across the graphic.*

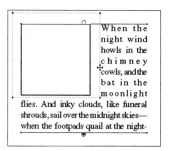

*Move the original left bound-
ary across the graphic.*

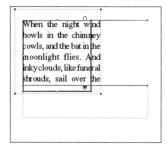

*The text now wraps to the inside
of the graphic wrap boundary.*

5. Place or paste text inside the wrap boundary.

Instead of wrapping to the outside of the boundary, the text wraps to the inside of the boundary. The upper-left corner of the text block must be inside the text wrap boundary for this to work.

Some very complex inside wraps are possible using this technique, as shown in Figure 5-31.

**Figure 5-31**
Wild inside wraps

*As long as the upper-left corner handle of a text block falls inside an inside-out text wrap, the text will wrap to the inside of the boundary.*

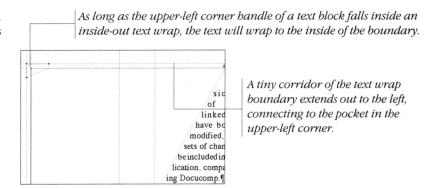

*A tiny corridor of the text wrap boundary extends out to the left, connecting to the pocket in the upper-left corner.*

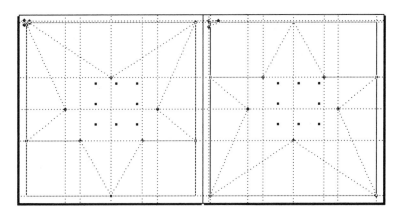

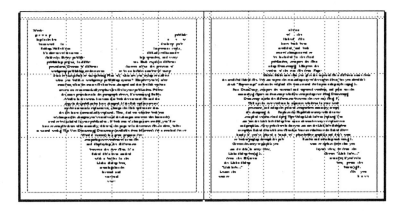

**Wrapping Around Master Items**

If you have applied a text wrap setting to graphics on the master pages, text on pages that have "Display master items" turned on will wrap around that boundary. This is especially handy when you're auto flowing text into pages (see Figure 5-32).

**Figure 5-32**
Using text wrap on
master pages to
control text flow

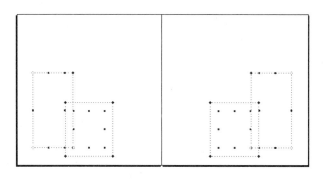

*Master page items
with text wrap
applied*

*Autoflowed text*

When the nightwind howls in the chimney cowls, and the bat in the moonlight flies. And inky clouds, like funeral shrouds, sail over the midnight skies—when the footpads quail at the night-bird's wail, and the black dogs bay at the moon, then is the spectre's holiday—then is the ghost's high noon!
As the sob of the breeze sweeps over the trees and the mist lies

low on the fen, from grey tomb-stones are gathered the bones that once were women and men, and away they go, with a mop and a mow, to the revel that ends to soon, for cockcrow limits our holi-day—the dead of the night's high noon! Rats, note nough text to finish this example, better repeat some. When the night wind howls in the chim-ney cowls,

You can easily keep text from flowing into a column during autoflow, for instance, yet keep the column open for manual text flow—a good way to produce a book that, like this one, has a companion column on the left for subheads. Just place a no-line weight line with a Text flow setting of "Column break" at the top of the companion column on the master pages (see Figure 5-33). Or you could keep text from colliding with a large page header or an ornamental border by applying text wrap to the item on the master pages.

**Figure 5-33**
Using text wrap on
master pages to
control text flow

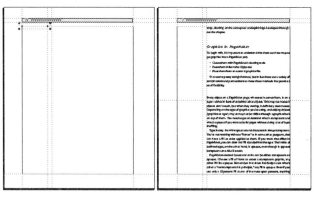

*Place a line
with text wrap
set to "Column
break" at the
top of compan-
ion columns on
master pages to
keep text from
autoflowing
into them.*

# Printing

The ultimate test of any desktop publishing program is its ability to put images on paper (or film) to produce camera-ready copy. The slickest tools and the best numerical accuracy inside the program mean nothing if the same flexibility and accuracy cannot be repeated outside the program—in printing. Most Mac desktop publishing programs use the Apple LaserWriter driver to send their pages to PostScript printers. Unfortunately, the Apple LaserWriter driver and its accompanying Laser Prep file do not let you take full advantage of the capabilities of different printers. Until recently (LaserWriter driver version 6.0), they had troubles with gray-scale images, and didn't provide any good way to control halftone screen frequency and angle. While some programs using the Apple driver got around it, it was a problem.

## The Aldus Driver, Aldus Prep, and APDs

Aldus got around the problem of working with the LaserWriter driver by writing their own PostScript printer driver into PageMaker. The Aldus driver matches PageMaker's internal positioning accuracy of 1440 dpi (.05 point) perfectly.

▼ *Tip: Using the Apple Driver*

There are times when the Apple driver is better than the Aldus driver. Steve's old version 23 LaserWriter sometimes prints PageMaker pages with multiple downloaded fonts *much* faster using the Apple driver. It's also worth trying when you can't get a page to print. To use the Apple driver, hold down Option while choosing Print from the File menu.

Along with its own PostScript printer driver, PageMaker uses its own PostScript prep file, called Aldus Prep, instead of Apple's Laser Prep. This file is just a set of PostScript routines. It's downloaded to the printer, and thereafter PageMaker can call on those routines. In this chapter we'll show you how to modify Aldus Prep to do things you can't do otherwise.

Aldus' printer driver also uses APDs (Aldus printer description files) that tailor PageMaker's printing to the specific make and model of printer. APDs are text files that contain information on the printer's resolution, default halftone screen, paper sizes, automatic and manual feed mechanism, and so on. You can rewrite APDs to add new paper sizes, change screen frequencies and angles, and do various other tricky and devious things. In this chapter we'll show you how to rewrite APDs for your own purposes.

## PageMaker and Downloaded Fonts

Before we go any farther into printing, we need to discuss PostScript printer fonts. Actually, they're typefaces, because they're scalable outlines, and that's what we'll call them here, to distinguish them from fixed-size, bitmapped screen fonts. There are two types of PostScript typefaces: resident and downloaded. Actually, they're the same, but they're located in different places. The resident typefaces are in a chip in the printer, and you can use them at any time.

Downloadable PostScript typefaces live on your Mac's hard disk. You (or PageMaker) can download them into the printer's memory, at which point you (or PageMaker) can use them just like the resident typefaces. Printers don't have unlimited memory, though, so there are

three different ways to handle downloading of typefaces—automatic/
temporary, manual/semipermanent, and manual/permanent.

***Automatic/temporary downloading.*** Simply print from Page-
Maker. When it needs to, PageMaker goes and finds the downloadable
printer typefaces on your Mac disk (usually in the system folder),
downloads them to the printer, and uses them. When printer memory
is full and it needs to download another typeface, it flushes out the
least recently used typeface to make room.

As long as you have the screen fonts installed and the printer
typefaces in the system folder (or somewhere PageMaker can find
them—see "Font/DA Mover, Suitcase, and MasterJuggler," in Chapter 2,
*Building a PageMaker System*), you don't even have to think about
what gets downloaded when. You just see the message "Downloading
Hobo Oblique."

This method lets you use many different typefaces, sizes, and
variations within your pub, because the Aldus PostScript driver is very
good at handling printer memory for downloaded typefaces. It lets you
put more typefaces in a single text block than the Apple driver lets you
put in a whole print job.

This is also the slowest method of printing with downloadable fonts,
though. Watch PageMaker download the same typeface 20 or 30 times,
and you'll agree. It's not such a big problem if you have 2 or 3 MB of
memory in your printer, but if you have 1 or 1.5, PageMaker ends up
flushing and downloading a lot. It depends on how many typefaces you
use in your pub, how often they change (3 times per page, or 20?), and
how big they are. In the worst case, every time PageMaker hits a change
in typeface (from Garamond to Garamond Italic, for instance, or from
Stone to Stone Sans), it has to download that typeface to the printer.
Then it flushes it out of the printer's RAM, only to download it again,
maybe just a few lines later. No matter what, it has to download all the
faces at the beginning of every print job, and flush them at the end.

***Manual/semipermanent downloading.*** You can minimize that
repetitive automatic downloading and flushing by manually downloading the typefaces you use most often. Manual downloading is simple;

all you need is a downloading utility like SendPS, LaserWriter Font Utility, or LaserStatus (see Chapter 2, *Building a PageMaker System*).

Once you've manually downloaded a typeface, it's there until you turn off or reset the printer. That's why it's called semipermanent. PageMaker doesn't have to keep downloading it, which speeds things up a lot. How many typefaces you download manually and how many you leave to PageMaker depends on how much printer memory you have, the size of the typefaces, and the number of different typefaces you're using. If you manually download too many and fill up the printer's memory, PageMaker won't be able to do it's typeface-shuffling magic, and you may not be able to print your pub. If you don't download enough, you're not getting all the speed you can.

### ▼ Tip: Download the Most Frequently Used Typefaces

To get the most printing speed, manually download the typefaces that are used most frequently in your pub. It's the best way to avoid repetitive downloading and flushing. Remember, even if your printer has enough memory to hold all the typefaces you're usign, with automatic downloading, PageMaker still has to download all those faces each time you print.

If your body copy's in Garamond Light, for instance, definitely download that. Then decide which you use more often—the Futura Extra Bold in the subheads, or the Garamond Light Italic that's scattered through your text for emphasis. Or you might choose to download the Futura Light you use for callouts. But you can only download so many before you constipate the printer.

If other people are using the laser printer, remember that your manually downloaded typefaces are clogging up their printer memory, too. We won't get into interoffice politics here; suffice it to say that diplomacy and compromise are necessary. If nothing else, make sure to reset the printer, flushing out the faces, when you're done (LaserStatus lets you reset the printer without ever leaving your Mac; otherwise, turn the printer off and on).

***Manual/permanent downloading.*** Yes, Candide, there is a best of all possible worlds. Some PostScript devices (the LaserWriter II NTX, for instance, and all imagesetters) let you connect a hard disk that holds downloadable typefaces. It's just as if the fonts were downloaded to memory, but they're on a disk. You have to use a special downloader to put them on disk (you can get one from the company that makes the device, or from Apple or Adobe), but once they're there, you can use them just like ROM-resident typefaces.

## *The Print Dialog Box*

The whole area of printing with PageMaker starts with the Print command on the File menu (Command-P). It brings up the Print dialog box (Figure 6-1), which varies somewhat depending on the type of printer you've selected in the Chooser. Here's what it looks like if you've chosen LaserWriter (in other words, PostScript).

Most of the discussion here applies to printing on PostScript printers, since almost all serious PageMaker users also use PostScript. Here's a rundown of the choices in the Print dialog box, and how you should use them for different situations.

**Figure 6-1**
The Print dialog box

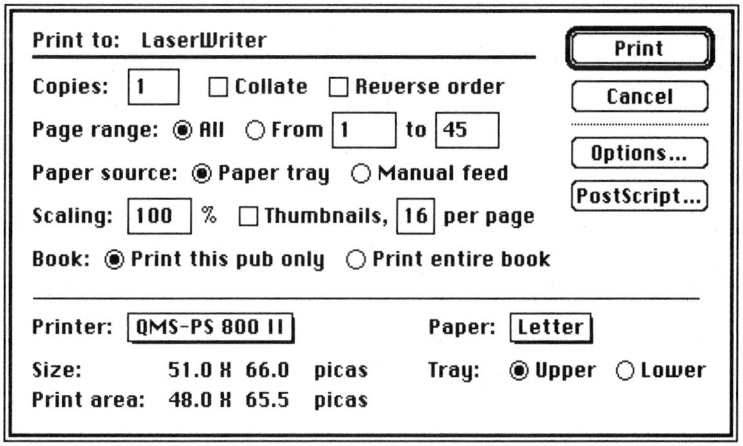

```
Print to:  LaserWriter                          [ Print ]

Copies: [1]    □ Collate  □ Reverse order       [ Cancel ]
Page range: ◉ All  ○ From [1]  to [45]
Paper source: ◉ Paper tray  ○ Manual feed       [ Options... ]
Scaling: [100] %  □ Thumbnails, [16] per page    [ PostScript... ]
Book: ◉ Print this pub only  ○ Print entire book

Printer: [QMS-PS 800 II]          Paper: [Letter]
Size:      51.0 H 66.0  picas     Tray: ◉ Upper  ○ Lower
Print area: 48.0 H 65.5  picas
```

***Copies.*** This is easy. Just type in the number of copies you want. It interacts with the following choice (Collate), however, in ways that can slow you down or speed you up a lot. Also remember that if you're printing color overlays, you'll get the number of overlays, times the number of pages, times the number of copies you specify here.

**Collate.** This option makes the pages in your document come out in the correct order, subject to the paper feed mechanism of your printer and your choice in the next option, Reverse order. If you're printing multiple copies and have "Collate" turned on, PageMaker prints the pub from beginning to end (or the reverse), then goes back and does it again. You don't have to sort pages by hand, but PageMaker and your printer have to rebuild each page from scratch for each copy, which is slow. It's like printing a single copy, then printing another, and so on.

If you have "Collate" turned off, PageMaker and your printer build each page one time, and spit out the number of copies you asked for all at once, at the full speed of the laser engine. You'll have to hand-collate the pages, but it's generally much faster than waiting for multiple, collated prints. If you're printing very many copies, just print one and have it copied on a collating photocopier.

**Reverse order.** PageMaker is smart about printing pages in the right order. The APD file for your printer tells PageMaker how the output bin works, so it can send the pages either front to back or back to front, as needed so they land in proper order. If you want to override PageMaker to get pages in reverse order, select this option.

**Page range.** This is simple, too. Just type in the range of pages you want to print (inclusive), and go. If you click the All button, PageMaker fills in the full page range for you.

### ▼ Tip: Voodoo Page Ranges

You can enter a page range by pressing Tab, first page #, Tab, last page #, and Return. Do this fairly quickly and your job will start printing without the Print dialog box appearing. It might not add up to a huge speed improvement, but boy, does it ever feel faster.

***Paper source.*** If you're printing odd-sized pages, card stock, envelopes, or other odd papers, you can tell PageMaker to use the manual feed instead of the paper tray. You'll still need to have a paper tray in the printer, though, or it won't print. We don't know why.

***Scaling.*** Scaling lets you reduce or enlarge your pages as they print. It's handy for getting large-sized pages to print on smaller sheets for proofing, or enlarging pages that will be reduced photographically to improve printed resolution. Just type in the percentage you want. You can also use this when you're printing a page to disk as EPS to size it up or down.

Bear in mind, though, that you can only type integer values here. PageMaker won't accept 100.35, for instance—the value necessary to convert PostScript 72-dpi points to traditional printer's points.

### ▼ *Tip: Fitting Tabloids on Letter and Legal Paper*

To fit a single tabloid page on a letter-size sheet, reduce it to 62 percent. If you have a legal paper tray and legal-size sheets, you can fit a tabloid page by reducing to 80 percent.

### ▼ *Tip: Improving Output Resolution*

You don't have to buy one of the fancy new high-resolution lasers to improve the look of your printed publications. Just print them enlarged, then have the printer reduce the pages photographically before they make plates. If you print your job enlarged to 125 percent, for instance, and then ask the printer to reduce the output photographically to 80 percent. You end up with an effective printed resolution of 375 dpi.

### ▼ *Tip: Have the Printer Overexpose to Smooth out Jaggies*

This doesn't have anything to do with enlargement and reduction, but it works with the previous tip. When you deliver laser-output pages to the printer for offset printing, ask them to overexpose the film negatives a little. The dark area around the type encroaches slightly, smoothing out the jaggies. Have them underexpose if they're making film positives.

---

***Thumbnails.*** Thumbnails gives you an overview of a pub by printing multiple reduced pages on a single sheet. The fewer pages per sheet, the larger the thumbnails. PageMaker prints thumbnails of all of the pages in the publication or the selected page range, even if the Print blank pages check box is not checked. Remember that this takes just as long as printing all the pages full-size.

***Book.*** If you've built a book list of multiple chapters using the Book option on the File menu, the Print entire book and Print this pub only options will be enabled in the Print dialog box. If you choose Print this pub only, the printing process proceeds exactly as in PageMaker 3.0—it prints with the options specified. If, however, you choose "Print entire book," PageMaker prints all of the publications listed in the Book publication list dialog box (see "PageMaker 4's Book Command" in Chapter 3, *Making PageMaker Mind*). If you choose Print entire book, though, "Copies" will be set to 1, and you will not be able to choose the following options in the Print dialog box.

- Print PostScript to disk
- Thumbnails
- Tiling
- Even/odd pages
- Spot color overlays
- Crop marks
- Scaling
- Substitute fonts
- Print blank pages

The book feature is mainly for index and table of contents generation. With printing, it's primarily useful for proofs (though it can speed that process tremendously). Because of these limitations, we recommend preparing your file for its final printing the old-fashioned way: print each file separately (to the printer or to a PostScript disk file), with the print options you want.

**Printer type.** This pop-up menu lists all the printers for which you have APD files in the APDs folder in the Aldus folder. If the names look confusing, it's because many of them designate the Adobe PostScript ROM version used in the printer. Use LaserStatus to check what version your printer is equipped with.

If your printer doesn't appear on the Printer type pop-up menu, make sure you have the APDs in the proper folder (the Aldus folder goes in the system folder), try "General," or call Aldus to see if they've developed an APD for your printer. Later in this chapter we show you how to modify and create APD files for different types of printers, or to do things you can't do with the standard Aldus-issue APDs.

**Paper.** This option lets you tell PageMaker the exact dimensions of your physical paper size (different from the page size you define with "Page setup"). Your choices in this pop-up menu are determined by which printer you have chosen (i.e., which APD file you're using).

Most laser printers only allow a few familiar paper sizes like letter and legal, but imagesetters and other large-format output devices offer much more flexibility, including the option to print normal or transverse (with normal lines of type across or along the roll). With imagesetters, you can create your own paper sizes by rewriting APDs (see "Custom Paper Sizes" later in this chapter). You can't add paper sizes to most laser printers because their ROMs won't accept the PostScript command "setpageparams."

### ▼ Tip: Use Letter Transverse for Imagesetters

The best paper size for most imagesetter output (assuming your pages are letter-size or smaller) is Letter Transverse. This prints the pages perpendicular to the roll of film (with lines o' type running the length of the roll). Especially if you're printing a lot of pages, this saves paper and makes it easy to cut the pages apart because they're side by side on the roll (make sure to choose "Tall" for the following option).

## *Aldus Print Options*

When you click the Options button in the Print dialog box, the Aldus print options dialog box appears (Figure 6-2). These options are available with

**Figure 6-2**
Aldus print options
dialog box

```
┌──────────────────────────────────────────────────┐
│ Aldus print options                    ┌────────┐ │
│ ──────────────────────────────────     │   OK   │ │
│ ☐ Proof print        ☐ Crop marks      └────────┘ │
│ ☐ Substitute fonts   ☐ Smooth          ┌────────┐ │
│ ☐ Spot color overlays: [All colors]    │ Cancel │ │
│ ☐ Knockouts                            └────────┘ │
│ ☐ Tile: ○ Manual    ○ Auto overlap [3p10.8] picas │
│ ☐ Print blank pages                               │
│                                                   │
│ Even/odd pages: ○ Both  ○ Even  ○ Odd             │
│                                                   │
│ Orientation: ○ Tall ○ Wide   Image: ☐ Invert ☐ Mirror │
└──────────────────────────────────────────────────┘
```

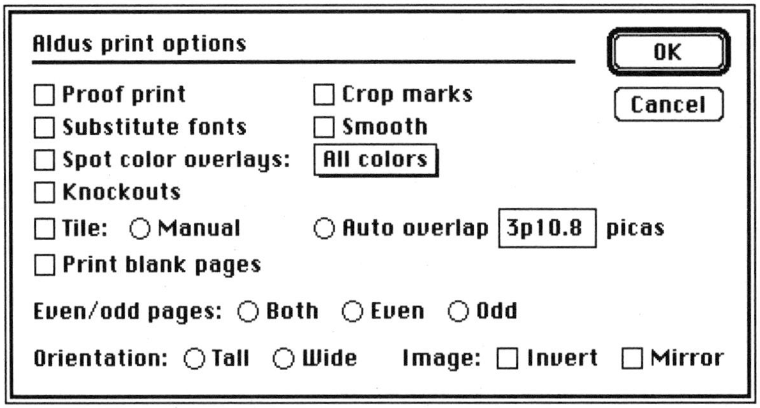

any printer, unlike the PostScript print options (from the PostScript button), which only work with PostScript output. Here's how the Aldus print options work.

***Proof print.*** If you have many complex graphics that slow printing, and you just want to see the text, check this box. PageMaker will print all the graphics as white boxes with Xs through them. This works especially well with the Print entire book option, when you want a fast proof of a big document.

***Crop marks.*** Check this box to print lines outside the page area, showing the boundaries of the page. Note that these are different from registration marks (the little target-like things you see on color separations and overlays). To define your own marks, see the tip "Printing Outside the Page Area" later in this chapter.

***Substitute fonts.*** This option takes effect if the fonts you have in your document aren't available on the printer or in downloadable form on your system. PageMaker has a table of substitutions (replacing Geneva with Helvetica, for instance) that it uses if you check this box. If it doesn't have a substitution set up in its table, you'll get Courier (Post-Script's default substitution).

We're a little unclear about the value of this option, and generally keep it off. No matter what gets substituted for your fonts (whether it's Courier or Helvetica doesn't much matter), your pub is going to print out wrong. At the very least, all the letter spacing will be screwed up. The more important option is "Download bitmapped fonts" (in the PostScript print options dialog box), which we explain more fully below. See that section for a table of what happens with these options turned on and off.

***Smooth.*** This is an option that's been with us since the dawn of desktop publishing. It smooths the edges of bitmapped images and fonts. Unless you truly love the look of smoothed bitmaps (it sometimes looks okay with coarse bitmapped clip art), make sure that "Smoothing" is off—it slows down printing.

Further, if you're doing documentation that involves captured screen images, turn "Smoothing" off. The bitmaps aren't smoothed on the screen, so you don't want them smoothed on your printout. Also, jagged bitmaps are rather fashionable right now.

***Tile.*** Use tiling if your page size is larger than your paper size. Page-Maker prints multiple sheets that you can paste together to make up the whole page.

Automatic tiling starts at the upper-left corner of your page (leaving room for crop and registration marks), and prints enough tiles to get the whole page out. You choose the overlap, based on how much unprintable area your printer has around the edges of pages. Note that if you use automatic tiling, PageMaker prints all of the tiles—even the blank ones—even if the Print blank pages check box is not checked.

With manual tiling, PageMaker starts the upper-left tile at the ruler origin (the 0, 0 point) and works down to the right. This lets you control the exact positions of the tiles by changing the origin point in the publication window.

### ▼ Tip: Double Your Pages, Double Your Funds

You can save 50 percent on Lino charges by printing two PageMaker pages side-by-side on a single piece of paper or film. You have to have room for two pages on the roll, of course, so the practical limit on a Linotronic 300 is 5-1/2-inch-wide pages—about half of the L-300's 11.7-inch width limit. (This also works with laser printers, by the way.)

The trick is to use manual tiling.

1. Set the page size you want in Page setup. Choose double-sided, facing pages.
2. Set the ruler zero point to the upper-left corner of the left page. This sets the upper-left corner of your tile.
3. In Print Options, select "Letter" and "Wide" (or build a custom paper size in your APD that will fit two of your pages).
4. In the Print dialog, select the left page to print and press Return.

PageMaker will print both the left and right pages side by side, within the size limits of the imagesetter. You have to choose each left page to print individually, and service bureaus won't want to babysit the job that much, so you might want to print each spread to disk as PostScript then send all the PostScript files to your service bureau (see "Printing PostScript to Disk" later in this chapter).

PageMaker won't print automatic crop marks for the right-hand pages using this method, so you'll want to place your own crop marks on the master pages (see the tip "Printing Outside the Page Area" later in this chapter).

### ▼ Tip: Another Way to Get Double Pages

Ole thinks the tip above is ugly, and suggests creating a page twice the size of your pages, and putting two pages on the single on-screen page.

1. Use the Page setup dialog box to set up a page that is twice the width of your page (if you use an odd page size, you'll probably need to add the page size to your APD). Set the Top, Bottom, and Outside settings as you would if you were setting up a single page, then make the Inside setting equal to the Outside setting.

2. Use the Column guides dialog box to set up two columns, then make the space between the columns equal to twice the setting you want to use for the Inside measure of your page.

Now lay out your publication, using the column on the left as your left page, the column on the right as your right page. You can place a vertical ruler guide down the middle of the column to indicate the edge of the pages (Figure 6-3).

**Figure 6-3**
Two pages on one

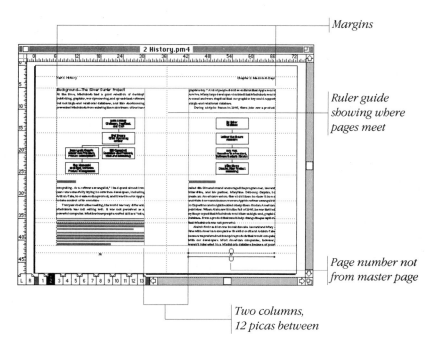

Margins

Ruler guide showing where pages meet

Page number not from master page

Two columns, 12 picas between

The most common use of this technique is laying out 5.5-by-8.5-inch pages to print on 8.5-by-11-inch sheets of paper (run "Wide"). Steve thinks this tip is ugly because you have to renumber every page manually, rather than having PageMaker do it for you.

***Print blank pages.*** If you have a lot of blank pages in your pub, you can save paper by unchecking this box. It doesn't work if you've chosen "Tile," "Print whole book," "Thumbnails," or "Even/odd pages."

***Spot color overlays.*** If you're printing a two- or three-color job (on an offset press or a photocopier, or even with multipass laser printing and color toner cartridges), you can have PageMaker print each color on a separate sheet. Check "Spot color overlays," and the pop-up menu is enabled so you can choose which color overlay to print. Unfortunately, you can't ask PageMaker to print yellow *and* blue but not black. You either choose one or all. For more on spot color overlays, see Chapter 7, *Color,* and the color pages in this book.

PageMaker prints registration marks automatically if you choose "Spot color overlays." You can even get registration marks on a one-color job if you want them for some reason, by choosing "Spot color overlays" and just printing the one color.

### ▼ *Tip: Printing Outside the Page Area*

You can print whatever you want outside the page area (within the limits of the physical paper size). If you want registration marks someplace other than where PageMaker puts them, or if you want to print a job name or date or time, here's how (Figure 6-4).

**Figure 6-4**
Placing printing
objects off the page

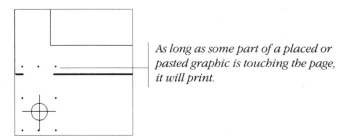

As long as some part of a placed or
pasted graphic is touching the page,
it will print.

Create a white box in a draw program, put the registration mark inside the box, and copy/paste both the box and the registration mark onto the page (with FreeHand and Illustrator, you'll have to Option-copy). As long as the white box is touching the page, the whole graphic will print.

You can also create the crop marks by copying multiple PageMaker elements to the Scrapbook and then placing the Scrapbook (see "Placing the Scrapbook" in Chapter 5, *Pictures*).

---

**Knockouts.** This option, which is only enabled when "Spot color overlays" is turned on, lets you decide whether PageMaker should "knock out" underlapping color elements (a portion of a red circle underneath a blue box, for instance). If you're using multipass printing with a laser printer or photocopier to put the color on the page, check this box so red toner doesn't print on top of blue and get all muddy. If you're printing offset, see Chapter 7, *Color*. For a graphic representation of how "Knockouts" works, see the color pages in this book.

**Even/odd pages.** This option is a real boon if you want to print on both sides of the sheet. Just print the odd pages, then put the odd pages back in your laser printer's paper tray and print the even pages. Orientation varies from printer to printer, but for LaserWriters and LaserWriter Pluses (Canon CX engines), put the paper in face up, head in. For LaserWriter IIs (and other printers using the Canon SX engine), put it in face down, head in. You can use the same kind of technique with photocopiers.

Note that if you choose "Even/odd pages," PageMaker prints all of the pages in the range—even if the Print blank pages check box is not checked. That's so you get the correct pages back to back.

### ▼ *Tip: Chill Out Those Pages Before Printing Side Two*

If you put the freshly laser-printed pages back in the laser printer immediately, you're likely to get paper jams, and you may even gum up the works with the still-soft toner. Let the pages cool and dry for a few minutes before you print the second side.

---

**Orientation.** With laser printers and letter or legal-size paper, this option is pretty simple. Choose "Tall" to print in "portrait" mode (with the short edge of the paper running horizontally), and Wide to print in "landscape" mode. In general, you should choose the same mode as you used in the Page setup dialog box.

When you start printing on imagesetters and other printers with more flexible paper sizes (technically, those that support the PostScript "setpageparams" operator), this option gets a bit more confusing. If you choose "Letter Transverse" *and* "Wide," for instance, you end up with almost (but not quite) the same thing as with "Letter" and "Tall." Again, see "Those Mysterious APDs" later in this chapter.

***Mirror and Invert.*** There's not much reason to print mirrored (left for right) or inverted (black for white) pages on a laser printer, so you'll mainly use these two options for film output, to set up the film the way your printer wants it. Most printers want to get right-reading negatives, emulsion side down. That means when you hold up the film with the emulsion side of the film away from you, you can read it, though you're reading clear type on black film. Negative is easy—if you want negs, check invert. Mirror is a little trickier. Table 6-1 lays it out for you.

**Table 6-1  Mirror settings**

|  | *Right Reading* | | *Wrong Reading* | |
|---|---|---|---|---|
| Emulsion | Up | Down | Up | Down |
| Set Mirror to | Off | On | On | Off |

Many imagesetting service bureaus prefer to use little PostScript programs or the imagesetter's front-panel controls to control these options (especially inverse) rather than having PageMaker control them, so talk to your service bureau before you set this up. We provide several of these programs later in this chapter.

▼ *Tip: Mirror and Invert for One-color Printing*

For some reason "Mirror" and "Invert" are grayed out unless you choose "Spot color overlays." If you need to print a one-color pub

mirrored or inverted, just click "Spot color overlays" and choose the
color you want to print (probably black).

---

▼ *Tip: Negative Negatives*

The main reason for not using PageMaker's inverse option is a
negative-printing bug in certain versions of the Adobe ROMs on
Linotronics. In some cases they invert TIFF images from PageMaker
even if you don't ask them to. Aldus fixed this by writing a patch that
reverses the TIFFs back again. That's fine, but Adobe fixed the bug in
later versions of its ROMs, so the double fix resulted in a double invert.
The result is a lot of confusion, so call your service bureau before you
check the Invert setting, especially if you're using TIFF images,
especially if they're gray-scale TIFFs. They may prefer to simply handle
the negatives themselves.

## PostScript Print

When you click the PostScript button in the Print dialog box, the
PostScript print dialog box appears (Figure 6-5). You can adjust these
options for any PostScript printing, but as you'll see (or as you already
know), they're mainly for printing PostScript to disk.

**Figure 6-5**
PostScript print
dialog box

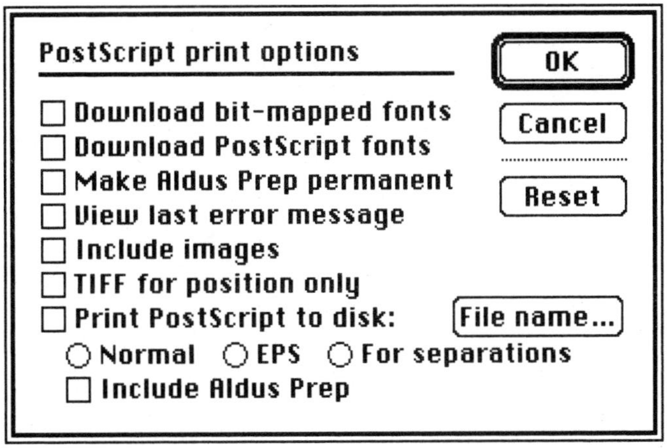

**Printing
PostScript
to Disk**

You can print PostScript to disk as normal PostScript—straight text that you can download to a printer—or as viewable EPS (encapsulated PostScript) that includes a screen representation for placing on pages. A third option includes comments in the file (in Aldus' Open Prepress Interface format) that separation software can use.

Normal PostScript is what you use when you're printing PostScript to disk to send off to a service bureau for output. Most service bureaus we work with give a discount of two or three dollars a page if you print the pages to disk rather than giving them PageMaker files. With printed-to-disk PostScript, all the service bureau has to do is download the PostScript, rather than opening your PageMaker file and worrying about what fonts you've used, whether they have the right font IDs, whether you have the same version of PageMaker, what print options you've used, or whether you have special words in your hyphenation exceptions dictionary. What you give them is what you get.

This means that you have to be careful. If your job comes back without crop marks, positive instead of negative, or without spot color overlays, it's your fault—you won't be able to pin these mistakes on your service bureau. At the same time, you have control over everything this way.

### ▼ Tip: Name Your PostScript Output Files

Always, always click the File name button and give your PostScript output file a name—preferably the same name you're using for your pub file plus a ".ps" extension or something else that makes sense to you. If you don't name your file, PageMaker writes the file to disk as PostScript*nn* (where *nn* is the number of files written since you started PageMaker). This can get confusing; was Chapter 2 in PostScript12 or PostScript13? Consider naming normal PostScript text files with a .ps extension, and viewable files with a .vps extension.

You might also print normal PostScript to disk if you want to mess with PageMaker's PostScript output before sending it to the printer (more on that later). Another reason is if you want to create process color separations with another program (Like Aldus PrePrint, SpectreSeps PM, or Adobe Separator).

## Creating EPS Files with PageMaker

EPS files are basically the same as normal PostScript files, but they also include a pretty good screen representation (a PICT image) so you can see the image when it's placed on a page, get it positioned right, wrap type around it, and generally see what's going on. You can only print a single PageMaker page to disk as EPS, but this feature is handy if you want all the objects on a page combined into one EPS graphic that you can place back on a page and scale to fit (though you're generally better off copying all the page elements to the Scrapbook and then placing the Scrapbook). Or you can place the EPS graphics in other programs.

### ▼ Tip: Making Small EPS Files

When you print a page to disk as EPS, PageMaker makes the graphic the size of the page. If you want a small graphic, define a small page size in Page setup—just big enough to hold the objects.

## PostScript Print Options

Your choices in the PostScript print dialog box will vary depending on whether you're printing straight to a PostScript printer, printing PostScript text to disk (for normal output or for separations), or printing EPS to disk to create a graphic. Here's a rundown of the right choices for different situations.

**Include Aldus prep.** This option only applies when you're printing PostScript to disk. When printing to a printer over AppleTalk, PageMaker checks to see if Aldus Prep has been downloaded, and downloads it if it hasn't. (Note how this works with the Make Aldus Prep permanent option, discussed below.)

When printing PostScript to disk (normal or EPS), check this box. That way your version of Aldus Prep will override any other version that's lodged in the printer or imagesetter.

***Download bit-mapped fonts.*** This option is only relevant if you have screen fonts in your pub that don't have corresponding PostScript versions. We won't ask why you have them there. Some people (Ole is one) like screen fonts. If you check this option, PageMaker will download the screen bitmaps and use them to print. If you don't check it, any of three things might happen, depending on whether you have "Substitute fonts" checked (see above) and whether PageMaker knows about the screen font you're using and has a substitute font in its table (see Table 6-2). You might get the bitmap, you might get PageMaker's substitution, or you might get Courier, which is PostScript's default substitution (you can change *that* default by editing your APD file. See "Those Mysterious APDs" later in this chapter).

The rules for this option are the same whether you're printing to a printer or to a PostScript disk file. Just remember that downloading bitmapped fonts makes PostScript files a lot bigger.

**Table 6-2  PageMaker's font substitution behavior**

| *Settings* | | | | |
|---|---|---|---|---|
| Font substitution | On | On | Off | Off |
| Download bitmap fonts | On | Off | On | Off |
| *Results* | | | | |
| If PageMaker has substitution pair | PM subst. | PM subst. | Bitmap | Courier |
| If PageMaker doesn't have substitution pair | Bitmap | Courier | Bitmap | Courier |

***Download PostScript fonts.*** This option tells PageMaker to download PostScript typefaces automatically (and temporarily) as needed. If you're simply printing to your printer, check this box. PageMaker will do its typeface-shuffling magic, downloading faces that aren't already available on the printer. If you don't check this box and the faces aren't available, you'll either get the bitmapped screen font version on output, PageMaker's substitute font, or Courier (depending on the settings of "Substitute fonts" and "Download bit-mapped fonts").

If you're preparing a disk file to send out to a service bureau, you should check to see if they've got the typefaces on their hard disk. If they do, uncheck this box, because all the downloaded typefaces will make the file huge, and it will take a lot longer to print. If they don't have them, check this box and they can live with the wait.

▼ *Tip: Selective Downloading of Typefaces to PostScript Files*

If you want to download some of the typefaces used in your pub but not all, edit the @Font section of the APD file you're using, so PageMaker knows which typefaces are already resident on the printer (see "Those Mysterious APDs" later in this chapter). PageMaker will only download the nonresident typefaces. This makes no difference when you're printing directly; PageMaker queries the printer to see what typefaces are available.

You can give your service bureau the PostScript typefaces to download to their hard disk in advance, and uncheck "Download PostScript fonts." If they don't own the typefaces, though, the practice is illegal (and arguably immoral), and they may not be willing to do it.

If you're preparing an EPS file, you'll have to choose whether to use this option based on the final destination of the file. You can include the PostScript typefaces, but it makes the file much bigger and may make it difficult to print when placed in other programs. If you do include the typefaces, on the other hand, you know they're there no matter what printer it goes to or what computer or program it's being printed from.

**Make Aldus Prep permanent.** If you don't check this box, Page-Maker will have to download Aldus Prep every time you print, flushing it out again at the end of the job. Check this box to make Aldus Prep "stick" in the printer's memory. The next time you print to that printer,

PageMaker will check and find that Aldus Prep is already there, so it won't have to download it again. In our terminology, this means it's downloaded semi-permanently. If you turn the printer off or reset it with something like LaserStatus, Aldus Prep will be flushed out, and it will need to be downloaded again.

If you're printing to disk (no matter what the reason) turn this option off. Service bureaus will hate you if you lodge a different version of Aldus prep in their printer, and they have to reset it. EPS files are even worse, because every time anybody prints the EPS graphic, your version of Aldus Prep will lodge itself in their printer.

**View last error message.** This option is available only when you're printing directly, not when you're printing to disk. It causes PageMaker to display the last error generated by the PostScript printer before it went down in flames. It's often useful to know what the last error message was, especially when you're mucking around with EPS files, APDs, and Aldus Prep. Unfortunately, this option is off by default, and you can't change that default.

**Include images.** This option controls whether PageMaker prints color bitmaps—color scans, color paint images, and color screen shots. Turn it on if you're printing to a color printer, or if you want PageMaker to treat the image like a gray-scale file for output to a black-and-white printer. Turn it off if you're preparing a file for separation by a program that can't handle color bitmaps (like Adobe Separator). Always turn it off when you're printing to disk, unless you have a huge hard disk.

If you have a program that can separate color images which are included in PageMaker pages, by all means feel free to include them in your output file. Color images are big (as in *lots* of data), so no matter what the output method, including color images will make the resulting files larger, and print times much longer.

If you're preparing an EPS file, you have to figure out where it's going. Some programs can handle color bitmaps within EPS files, others can't. Most can't. EPS is a lousy format for bitmapped graphics anyway, especially color graphics, so in general you should avoid including color images in EPS files.

**TIFF for position only.** If you want the linked, high-resolution TIFF files to print, uncheck this box. If you just want the low-res screen rendition, check it.

## Using PostScript Downloading Utilities

Once you've printed a file to disk as PostScript (normal, not EPS), you can send it to a printer using a PostScript downloading utility (see "PostScript Tools" in Chapter 2, *Building a PageMaker System*. If you're printing to an imagesetter (especially if you're running an imagesetting service bureau) this is the best way to print your publication. You can queue up a large number of jobs limited only by the amount of film your imagesetter can run before changing output cassettes (on a Linotronic 300 this is about 90 feet). And then you can go home for the night, start working on another machine, process film you've previously printed, and so on.

Because the spooling utilities are very small (LaserStatus and TOPSpool are desk accessories), you can run them on older Macs—Pluses or even old 512Ks—and continue using your newer Macs for other work. You can save your PostScript files to a networked file server, so the older Mac doesn't even need a hard drive.

We often send strings of jobs to an imagesetter, including PostScript housekeeping files where they're needed. A typical list of files for a batch download might look like this:

1270 SetResolution
Mirror Off
Negative Off
Aldus prep
Font file 1
Font file 2
Publication 1.ps
2540 SetResolution
Mirror/Negative On
Publication 2.ps

Both publications use Aldus prep and fonts 1 and 2, but while Publication 1.ps is run at 1270 dpi to film positive, Publication 2.ps needs to be run to film negative at 2540.

**Some Handy PostScript Programs**

We often prefer to send little PostScript programs down to the imagesetter rather than using PageMaker's print options. It's nice because we know exactly what's going on, and can batch the jobs up nicely (that's *batch*, not botch). Here are some that we find useful.

```
% L300 1270 setresolution
serverdict begin 0 exitserver
statusdict begin
1 2000 2000 assignresolution
1270 setresolution
end quit
```

```
% L300 2540 setresolution
serverdict begin 0 exitserver
statusdict begin
0 1000 1000 assignresolution
2540 setresolution
end quit
```

```
% Mirrorprint on
serverdict begin 0 exitserver
statusdict begin
/mirrorprint true def % false for normal printing
end
```

```
% Negative printing on
serverdict begin 0 exitserver
statusdict begin
/negativeprint true def % false for positive printing
% add /mirrorprint true def here for mirror and negative
end
```

```
% Turn off startup page permanently
serverdict begin 0 exitserver
statusdict begin
false setdostartuppage % true to turn startup page back on
```

```
% Change RIP name
serverdict begin 0 exitserver
statusdict begin
(Linotype) setprintername
end quit
```

# *Changing PageMaker's PostScript*

All of these little programs are handy, especially if you're running a service bureau or printing to an imagesetter a lot. There's a lot you can do with PageMaker's PostScript, though, that you can't do by downloading files in advance. There are basically three ways to get at the PostScript.

- Modify PageMaker's printed-to-disk PostScript output.
- Modify the APD files.
- Modify Aldus Prep.

The most direct method of tweaking PageMaker's PostScript is to print normal PostScript to disk, then edit it with your word processor (remember to save the edited file as text-only—unformatted—or the printer will choke on it). This method is more work than adjusting APD or Aldus Prep files, but it lets you make changes both globally and locally—changing the screen frequency for a single page element, for instance. Or you might cut out an EPS graphic that won't print from a PostScript file that someone's sent you.

Don't expect complete discussions of the PostScript we show you here. We are not PostScript programmers, and don't understand a lot of it ourselves. We are, however, very good at trial and error. Most of the knowledge we've acquired in this area is the result of trying things until they worked. We suggest you use similar tactics. As we said in the Preface, the most important technique is to poke at it until it works.

If you want to figure out how reversed lines work in PageMaker's PostScript, for instance, try drawing one reversed line on top of a black box, on a page all by themselves. Print the page to disk as PostScript, open the PostScript file, and look at the results. By isolating objects in this manner, you can figure out how more complex PostScript assemblages are built.

If you want to learn PostScript the easy way, as opposed to flailing around in the code the way we did, we recommend *Learning Post-Script: A Visual Approach* by Ross Smith (Peachpit Press), which Steve edited and produced. Also consider the three Adobe books (Red, Green, and Blue).

**Modifying
PageMaker's
PostScript Output**

Here's some sample PostScript output from PageMaker. This was a simple two-page file with a single gray box on each page. We did not include Aldus Prep, assuming that it was already lodged in the printer. Besides, we're going to talk about Aldus Prep later.

The file starts with a bunch of comments (preceded by %) that satisfy the Adobe requirements for EPS files. PostScript printers ignore anything preceded by a %, so changing these has no effect on output.

```
%!PS-Adobe-2.0
%%Title: Untitled
%%Creator: PageMaker 4 rocky
%%CreationDate: 10-27-1989, 7:49:27
%%For: Steven
%%BoundingBox: 0 0 612 792
%%Pages: 2 0
%%DocumentPrinterRequired: "" ""
%%DocumentFonts: (atend)
%%DocumentSuppliedFonts: (atend)
%%DocumentNeededFonts: (atend)
%%DocumentNeededProcSets: AldusDict2 209   44
%%DocumentSuppliedProcSets:
%%DocumentPaperSizes: Letter
%%EndComments
```

The most important comment in this output is BoundingBox. PageMaker and other programs use this information to create the gray box representing the position of the graphic if you place this file on a page. Most programs will also display the Creator and CreationDate information in the gray box.

Next, PageMaker inserts any PatchFile that's defined in the APD you're using. This stuff is mainly for job control, and doesn't usually affect actual output.

```
%%BeginFile: PatchFile
statusdict begin userdict begin /a4f {
0 setblink
statusdict /jobstate (printing) put
margins exch 141 add exch 256 add 8 div round cvi frametoroket
statusdict /jobstate (busy) put
1 setblink
```

```
} bind def end end
%%EndFile
```

This PatchFile is for a LaserWriter with version 23 ROMs. It does some housekeeping of how the printer will blink and what process messages it will send back to your Mac, and adjusts the margins.

The job setup section is next. It opens AldusDict2 (a.k.a. Aldus Prep), so it can call on all those routines. Then it sets up assorted variables, most of them based on values in the APD file you're using.

```
%%IncludeProcSet: AldusDict2 209   44
%%EndProlog
AldusDict2 begin
%%BeginSetup
letter
/#copies 1 def
 (Steven; document: Untitled)
 statusdict /jobname 3 -1 roll put
 statusdict /waittimeout 300 put
3300 2550 false false false BEGJOB
300 SETRES
true SETOVERPRINT
25000 S_WORKING
save /SUsv exch def
userdict /AldusDict known {(A previous version PageMaker header is
loaded.) = flush} if
%%EndSetup
```

If you want to enter any commands that affect the whole job, enter them here. You could enter PostScript to adjust the halftone screen, for instance, or to skew all the pages. If you want all the pages to print reduced 50 percent, for instance, type ".5 .5 scale" right before "save / SUsv exch def."

Unfortunately, this technique doesn't scale EPS graphics, because PageMaker builds scaling right into those graphics when it places them (see the tip "Extracting EPS Files" in Chapter 5, *Pictures*). As a result, if you try to insert a PostScript scaling instruction for the whole page, the EPS graphics stay right where they are, while the rest of the page is scaled. If you figure out how to scale everything without editing every placed EPS file, please call us.

▼ *Tip: Scaling to Match True Printer's Points*

PostScript uses 72 points to the inch, which seems sensible and useful until you consider that traditional printer's points come to a little more than 72 to the inch. If you are set up for traditional printer's points, and don't want to change, scale your pages up to 100.35 percent ("1.0035 1.0035 scale"). With laser printers, for some reason, we've had better luck using 100.6 or 100.7 percent. In any case, you can't type decimal values in the Scaling text edit box; you have to do it here. And again, this doesn't scale EPS graphics.

---

This is also the place where PageMaker places the AldusPatchFile value from the APD—just before %%EndSetup. So you can put some PostScript in the APD, and it will show up here. Remember that commands you enter here affect all the pages.

Finally, we get into the pages themselves. By flailing around in here, you can make changes to individual page elements. This code describes a couple of PageMaker boxes. They're defined by PRRECT and the four values preceding it, colored by PCOLOR, filled by PPAINT, and outlined by PFRAME.

```
%%Page: 3 1
BEGPAGE
0. 0. 2550. 3300. true PBEGIN
0. 0. LW 80. PTINT 176. 176. 304. 229. 2321. 3071. PRRECT 0.00 0.00
0.00 1.00 (Black) PCOLOR PPAINT PRESETTINT
4. 4. LW 188. 188. 300. 225. 2325. 3075. PRRECT 0.00 0.00 0.00 1.00
(Black) PCOLOR PFRAME PRESETTINT
PEND
ENDPAGE
%%Page: 2 2
BEGPAGE
0. 0. 2550. 3300. true PBEGIN
0. 0. LW 80. PTINT 229. 229. 2246. 3071. PRECT 0.00 0.00 0.00 1.00
(Black) PCOLOR PPAINT PRESETTINT
4. 4. LW 225. 225. 2250. 3075. PRECT 0.00 0.00 0.00 1.00 (Black)
PCOLOR PFRAME PRESETTINT
PEND
```

```
ENDPAGE
ENDJOB
end
%%Trailer
%%DocumentFonts:
%%DocumentSuppliedFonts:
%%DocumentNeededFonts:
%%EOF
```

The file ends with more comments (preceded by %%) as required by the document structuring conventions published by Adobe.

## Changing PageMaker-drawn Objects in PostScript

It's pretty easy to find PageMaker objects in a printed-to-disk PostScript file, and once you've found them you can make changes that are impossible from within PageMaker. You can also make emergency changes to files when all you have is the PostScript output. If you want to change the halftone screen values for just one rectangle, for instance, edit the code above so it reads as follows.

```
gsave
20 0 {pop} setscreen
 0. 0. LW 80. PTINT 229. 229. 2246. 3071. PRECT 0.00 0.00 0.00 1.00
(Black) PCOLOR PPAINT PRESETTINT
grestore
```

This little snippet saves, or "remembers," the graphics state, specifies a 20-line, 0-degree linescreen, fills the rectangle (the fill), then restores the graphics state so ensuing graphics aren't affected. For more on modifying halftone screens with PageMaker and PostScript, see "Halftone Screens" later in this chapter.

If you just want to change the angle or frequency and leave the rest of the values intact, use the following instructions, substituting the values you want for the Xs here. The first specifies the angle (in degres), the second specifies the screen frequency (in lines per inch).

```
currentscreen 3 1 roll pop X 3 -1 roll setscreen
currentscreen 3 2 roll pop X 3 -2 roll setscreen
```

Note that in this example the line surrounding the rectangle isn't affected. That's "PFRAME" in the ensuing line, not "PPAINT." You can change that, as well, though, by just moving the "grestore" down. For more on setting PostScript screens, see "Halftone Screens" later in this chapter, and get *Real World PostScript* (Addison-Wesley). (Yes, Steve was the editor, and he wrote the chapter on halftoning.)

Editing PageMaker's PostScript output lets you get right into the trenches and modify anything, but you can modify PostScript parameters for the whole job more easily by modifying the APDs or Aldus Prep, which are auxiliary files PageMaker uses when it prints PostScript. Change these files, and you change the output.

## *Those Mysterious APDs*

If you've been working with PageMaker for more than a week or so, you've probably wondered what those APD files are and why you need them. APDs are just text files, with a name that ends with .apd, that PageMaker (and FreeHand) can read. You can too, using a text editor or word processor. You can also modify them to your own ends. Once you've modified them (and saved them under a different name), you can select them from the Print dialog box's Printer type pop-up menu.

### ▼ *Tip: Where You Can Put Your APDs*

Put your APDs in the APDs folder in the Aldus folder in the system folder (or just leave them there; that's where the Aldus Installer puts them). That way FreeHand and PrePrint can get at them, as well, and you won't have folders full of APDs proliferating all over your hard disk like we do.

**What's Where in an APD**

Before you go any farther, open an APD or two with your word processor to see what they look like. Remember to copy the file or use Save as with a new file name before you make any changes.

APDs are made up of comments, keywords, and values. Every line starts with an @ and ends with a carriage return. (If you want to see the carriage returns, open the file in Word and press Command-Y to Show ¶s.) Comments are labeled as such.

@Comment: Adobe Printer Description (APD) file for Linotronic 100/300.
@Comment: This APD produced for use with Aldus PageMaker 2.0.
@Comment: 6/17/87
@Comment: keyword values are limited to 255 characters in length.

Anything that's not a comment is either a keyword or a value for that keyword. Here are four keywords with their associated values:

@FormatVersion: "1.0"
@Product: "(Linotype)"
@PSVersion: "(38.0)"
@PSRevision: "1"

Notice that keywords are followed by a colon and a space, and the values are surrounded by quotes.

### ▼ Tip: Programmers are not Typographers

Remember to use regular quotes within APD files—"the straight ones"—rather than open and close quotes.

---

You won't have much reason to change most of the values, or to modify most sections of APD files. The ones you will probably be interested in are summarized in Table 6-3. The two main reasons to modify an APD file are to adjust halftone screen settings, and to create custom paper sizes for imagesetter output. You can mess around with the other settings, but these two areas are the most widely used. Remember to make copies of your APD files before modifying them.

**Custom Paper Sizes**

PageMaker has gotten to the point that you can create ridiculously large pages (up to 17 by 22 inches), even in facing pages mode (34 by 22 inches total). But let's face it: you still have to print them. And

**Table 6-3 APD file modifications**

| Keyword | Typical Value | Why You Care |
|---|---|---|
| @Product | "(Linotype)" | Change to avoid irritating error messages if your printer has a different product name (check it with LaserStatus). |
| @PSVersion | "(38.0)" | If your printer's PostScript version is different from the one specified in the APD (check it with LaserStatus). |
| @Resolution | "1270 1270" | Affects magic stretch for bitmaps, can affect EPS placement (see "Magic Stretch" in Chapter 5, *Pictures*). |
| @FreeVM | "170000" | Change if you have more or less memory in your printer, or are taking up memory with pre-downloaded fonts (check it with LaserStatus). |
| @WorkingMem: | "25000" | Same as FreeVM |
| @PatchFile | "statusdict begin 0 setjobtimeout end userdict /AldusDict known {(A previous version PageMaker header is loaded.) = flush} if" | Use for device- and job-control code. |
| @AldusPatchFile | "statusdict /waittimeout 2500 put" | Use for special PostScript you want to apply to the whole job-- scaling, etc. |
| @Password | "0" | Change if someone's set a password on your printer. |
| @ScreenFreq | "" | Adjust the halftone screen for LBOs and type. |
| @ScreenAngle | "" | Same as previous |
| @ScreenProc | "" | Same as previous |

## APD file modifications continued

| | | |
|---|---|---|
| @Transfer | "" | PostScript code that adjusts the gray curve for your printer |
| @InvertTransfer | "{1 exch sub}" | InvertTransfer causes inverted printing (black for white). |
| @NormalizedTransfer | "{<br>mark<br>1.0 1.0 .92 .76 .64 .54<br>.44 .36 .28 .2 .1 .0<br>counttomark dup<br>3 add -1 roll exch<br>2 sub mul dup floor cvi<br>dup 3 1 roll sub<br>exch dup<br>3 add index exch<br>2 add index dup<br>4 1 roll<br>sub mul add<br>counttomark<br>1 add 1 roll<br>cleartomark<br>} bind" | PageMaker always uses NormalizedTransfer unless you change it or delete it here (read *Real World PostScript* to learn how to write transfer functions). |
| @DefaultPageSize | "Letter" | What the printer uses if it isn't told otherwise |
| @PageSize A4 | "statusdict begin 596 842 0 1 setpageparams end" | Add page sizes here. |
| @PageRegion A4 | "0 0 595.28 841.89" | Add page sizes here. |
| @PaperDimension A4 | "595.28 841.89" | Add page sizes here. |
| @ManualFeed | "none" | Change if your printer has manual feed and APD says it doesn't. |
| @DefaultFont | "Courier" | What the printer uses if it can't find the requested font |
| @Font | "Times-Roman" "Standard" "(001.000)" | Tells PageMaker which typefaces are resident in the printer; several in each APD. |

PostScript output devices can only print so large a page without tiling. (If you must. As far as we're concerned, hot wax is for skis).

You can determine the limits for your printer by creating a PageMaker page that you know is larger than you can print, covering the whole thing with a black box, and printing it. Then measure how much prints, and you have your maximum image area. That trick may not work so will with imagesetters, though, because the new ones (Linotronics after version 49.3 ROMs, for instance) can print the full width of the roll for as long as the roll (or memory) holds out.

When you get to working with imagesetters, you really have to get into PageMaker's APDs. If you're creating anything other than standard letter- and legal-size pages, or if you want things hanging outside the crop marks (or simply want to make room for the crop marks), it's probably to your advantage to modify PageMaker's APD files for custom paper sizes. Remember that we're talking about paper sizes here—the device's imageable area—distinct from the document's page size, which you specify in the Page setup dialog box. There are several reasons for building custom paper sizes.

- To print standard sizes like letter and legal and still have room for bleeds, crop marks, registration marks, and other goodies hanging off the page.
- To save a lot of film or paper.
- To print pages side-by-side so it's easy to cut them apart with a paper cutter.
- To print big, odd-sized pages (like 3-by-19 inches) that you couldn't print otherwise without tiling.
- Pages will often print faster if you use the exact page size you need, because there's a smaller area to image.
- Pages that won't print due to printer memory limitations may work if you use a page size that's just big enough. Less image area requires less memory in the imagesetter.

You can only build custom paper sizes with certain PostScript devices—those that recognize the PostScript "setpageparams" command, which generally means high-res imagesetters. Custom paper sizes just don't work with most PostScript laser printers. With imagesetters, though, it's easy. All it requires is a plodding, meticulous approach to life.

Make a copy of the Linotronic 100/300.apd (or the appropriate file for the imagesetter you're using), and open the copy with a text editor or word processor. Scroll to the part that looks like what you see below, and edit it.

```
@Comment: PageSize options appear in the
@Comment: Paper pop-up menu in the Print dialog box.
@DefaultPageSize: "Letter"
@PageSize Letter: "letter"
@PageSize A4: "statusdict begin 596 842 0 1 setpageparams end"
@PageSize Legal: "legal"
@PageSize A3: "statusdict begin 842 1191 0 1 setpageparams end"
@PageSize Tabloid: "statusdict begin 792 1224 0 1 setpageparams end"
@PageSize BookTrans: "statusdict begin 666 432 0 0 setpageparams end"

@Comment: PageRegion gives the printable area of each paper option.
@PageRegion Letter:        "0 0 612 792"
@PageRegion A4:            "0 0 595.28 841.89"
@PageRegion Legal:         "0 0 612 1008"
@PageRegion A3:            "0 0 841.89 1190.55"
@PageRegion Tabloid:       "0 0 792 1224"
@PageRegion BookTrans:     "0 0 432 666"

@Comment: PaperDimension gives the total paper size of each option.
@PaperDimension Letter:    "612 792"
@PaperDimension A4:        "595.28 841.89"
@PaperDimension Legal:     "612 1008"
@PaperDimension A3:        "841.89 1190.55"
@PaperDimension Tabloid:   "792 1224"
@PaperDimension BookTrans: "432 666"
```

We added the lines in bold (and deleted a couple of page sizes because the lines wrapped on this page). They define a new paper size we created for a 5.5-by-8.5-inch book page (that's 396 by 612 points— 72 points to the inch). We added some extra room for items that PageMaker places automatically (crop marks, registration marks, separation names), and that we place ourselves outside the page boundaries (file name and date, etc.). You can experiment with how much space you need, but this table gives good basic guidelines for the space you need for different elements.

The best bet is to add 54 points or a little more to the height of the page, and 36 or a little more to the width. You're better off with a little extra rather than too little, unless you're hitting the limits of the paper width on the imagesetter, you're trying to print pages exactly next to each other, or you're reaching the imagesetter's memory limit and crashing it.

The comments in the APDs explain things pretty well. You have to add the new paper size in three different places, and you can see that you reverse the order of the height and width numbers for @PageRegion and @PaperDimension. What's less apparent is how "transverse" works, and how it works in relation to the Tall and Wide options in PageMaker's Page setup dialog box. It's a bit of a mind-twister, but here goes.

The size and orientation of the "paper" on the roll is defined absolutely by those two numbers in @PageSize, repeated in @PageRegion and @PaperDimension. Those numbers specify the measurement across the roll of film, and along the length of the roll. Always. Without exception.

Printing transverse means that normal, unrotated text prints parallel to the length of the film roll. Normal printing prints normal text across the roll (it's easy to remember because it's the same way as it comes out of a laser printer). The fourth (last) number in the @PageSize value specifies whether the page prints transverse or normally; 1 is normal, 0 is transverse.

The key thing to remember is that choosing transverse *does not affect* the paper size or orientation. It only affects the way your page prints on that paper size. The same is true with PageMaker's Tall and Wide options. They rotate the the page, not the imageable paper area.

The confusing thing is when you start using *both* transverse and wide printing. There are about sixteen different combinations of portrait/tabloid, Tall/Wide, Normal/Transverse, Figure 6-6 provides a visual guide to the various combinations of options, and what happens when you use them.

**Figure 6-6**
Page size and
orientation for
imagesetters

*Pages shown here alternate down the roll (gray area)—portrait, then landscape.*

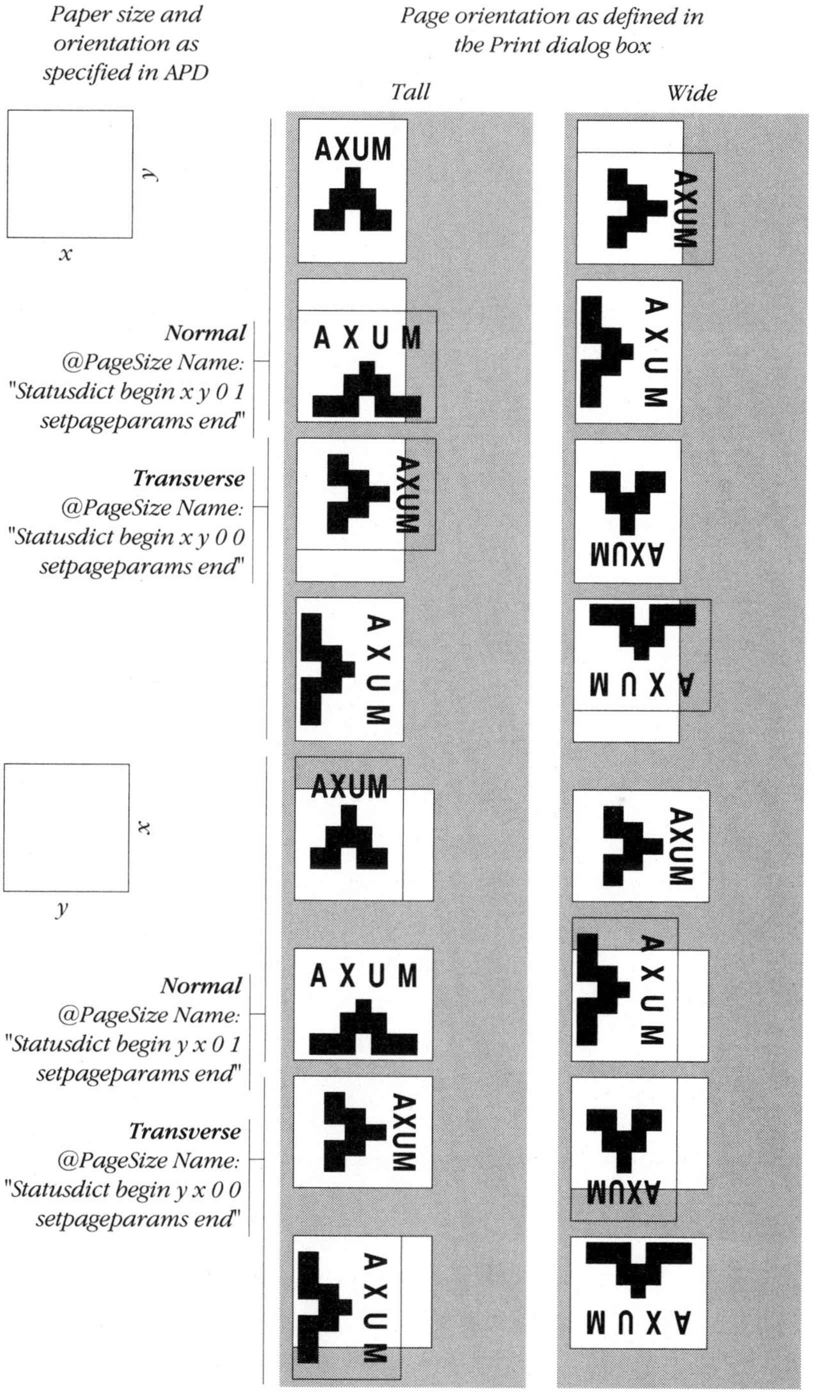

*Paper size and
orientation as
specified in APD*

*Page orientation as defined in
the Print dialog box*

*Tall*   *Wide*

*The first argument to
"setpageparams"
specifies the paper size
across the roll. The
second specifies the
size along the the roll.*

*The fourth number
specifies orientation—
1 for normal (type
printing across the
roll), 0 for transverse
(type printing the
length of the roll).*

*Note that you can
generate a transverse
page with either Wide
plus normal, or Tall
plus transverse.*

**Normal**
*@PageSize Name:
"Statusdict begin x y 0 1
setpageparams end"*

**Transverse**
*@PageSize Name:
"Statusdict begin x y 0 0
setpageparams end"*

**Normal**
*@PageSize Name:
"Statusdict begin y x 0 1
setpageparams end"*

**Transverse**
*@PageSize Name:
"Statusdict begin y x 0 0
setpageparams end"*

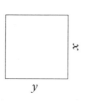

▼ *Tip: Offset Printing*

For those who are interested, the third number in the APD's @PageSize value specifies the offset of your "paper"—its distance from the edge of the imagesetter's printable area. You can use this to get pages centered on the paper. We needed it on a QMS ColorScript once, because it was so far out of adjustment that tabloid pages were bleeding off the edge of the paper (yes, the ColorScript does support the setpageparams operator).

## Halftone Screens

One thing that makes PostScript so powerful is the control it provides over halftone screens—not just for scanned images, but for everything where you use gray. Anything with a gray percentage comes out of a PostScript printer screened. That's the only way to represent gray on a black-and-white device. PostScript lets you control three aspects of the halftone screen—screen frequency (how many halftone cells per inch), screen angle (the orientation of those rows of cells), and cell shape (dots, lines, squares, ovals, etc.). Another function—"settransfer"—adjusts the gray levels for an image. It's used to create negative images, and to calibrate imagesetters for proper density at different gray levels (among other things).

Even though PostScript gives you all that control over screens, however, PageMaker doesn't—at least not from the menus. For gray-scale images, you can set the frequency and angle of the halftone screen, and choose between a dot and a line screen (use "Image control"). But you can't make any of those adjustments with the much more common screens used for LBOs, placed object graphics, and type. You have to edit PageMaker's PostScript output (see "Changing PageMaker-drawn Objects in PostScript" earlier in this chapter), or to change the screen for the whole job, get into the APDs.

The PostScript operator that provides the basic control over halftone screens is, not surprisingly, "setscreen." The setscreen operator takes three arguments, controlling the three parameters of a halftone screen:

frequency, angle, and spot function (this last controls the shape of the halftone cells). The following command, for instance, produces a 75 line-per-inch, 45-degree linescreen.

75 45 {pop} setscreen

Most people won't be too interested in writing their own spot functions, but if you can edit an APD file, it's easy to change the screen frequency and angle for the whole job. Just scroll to the keywords and put in your own values (most people will just change the frequency):

@ScreenFreq: "75"
@ScreenAngle: "45"
@ScreenProc: "{pop}"

***Screen Frequency.*** The frequency you choose depends on how you're going to produce and reproduce the publication. Also remember that the higher the frequency, especially on laser printers, the less possible gray shades you can get. So if you choose a fine screen frequency, you're less likely to get exactly the percentage you ask for. Table 6-4 gives some typical scenarios, and recommended frequencies for each.

▼ *Tip: Defaults Faults*

When Linotype released the version 49.3 ROMs for the L-300, a lot of people were surprised to find that the default screen frequencies had changed. The defaults used to be 90 lines per inch at 1270 dpi, and 120 lines per inch at 2540. For version 49.3, it's 150 for both. Linotype has a PostScript file that you can download to change defaults back to what they were. You have to download it each time you restart the machine, or put it in your "Sys/Start" file on the Lino hard disk. If your Lino service doesn't have this file, or doesn't care what screen frequency you get, make sure to make the modification in your APD file, print the pages to disk as PostScript, and send the PostScript files.

***Screen angle.*** For normal gray screens, you'll generally want to use a

**Table 6-4  Recommended screen frequencies**

| Output Device/ Resolution | Output Medium | Reproduction Method | Reproduction Medium | Screen Frequency |
|---|---|---|---|---|
| Laser/300 | Copy paper | Laser | Copy paper | 60 |
| Laser/300 | Laser paper | Photocopier | Coated paper | 60-80 |
| Laser/300 | Laser paper | Offset printing | Newsprint | 60-70 |
| Imagesetter/1200 | Paper | Photocopier | Uncoated paper | 70-80 |
| Imagesetter/1200 | Paper | Offset printing | Uncoated paper | 80-90 |
| Imagesetter/1200 | Paper | Offset printing | Coated paper | 90-100 |
| Imagesetter/1200 | Film | Offset printing | Coated paper | 100-150 |
| Imagesetter/1200 | Film or paper | Offset printing | Newsprint | 75-85 |

45-degree angle. It's the least apparent to the eye, so it gives an impression of a smooth gray fill. For special-effect screens, however (linescreens, square dots, ellipses, and the like), you may want to use a 0-degree angle.

### ▼ Tip: What You Ask for Ain't What You Get

A lot of people think that when they ask for a given screen frequency and angle on a PostScript device, that's what they're going to get. That just ain't so, although you're more likely to get close if you choose a 0-, 45-, or 90-degree screen frequency. It's just a fact of life with digital halftoning. There are only so many frequency/angle combinations available. The lower the resolution, the less available combinations, so the less likely you are to get the frequency and angle you ask for. Table 6-5 shows some standard angles and frequencies requested at 300 and 2,540 dpi, and the angles and frequencies you actually get.

This is just a sampling to demonstrate the realities. You can see that the variations aren't great with higher resolutions, but if you're doing color separations this will count. If you just want some flat gray tints, especially if you stick to 45-degree increments, you should be fine with whatever spits out.

**Table 6-5  Requested versus actual screen frequencies and angles**

| | *Requested* | | *Actual* | |
|---|---|---|---|---|
| | *Frequency* | *Angle* | *Frequency* | *Angle* |
| Apple LaserWriter | 60 | 45 | 53 | 45 |
| at 300 dpi | 50 | 45 | 53 | 45 |
| | 60 | 15 | 58.8 | 11 |
| | 70 | 45 | 67.1 | 27 |
| | 75 | 45 | 67.1 | 27 |
| | 65 | 45 | 60 | 37 |
| | 65 | 0 | 60 | 0 |
| Linotronic 300 | 100 | 0 | 101.6 | 0 |
| at 2540 dpi | 100 | 45 | 99.8 | 45 |
| | 120 | 0 | 121 | 0 |
| | 120 | 45 | 119.7 | 45 |

***Spot function.*** The main reason to modify the spot function is to create special-effect screens. You might want a vertical or horizontal linescreen, for instance, or square dots, or little Humpty-Dumpties, for all we know. You usually use special-effect spot functions with a coarse screen frequency, so the cells are readily apparent. You might also need to use special spot functions (ellipses, for instance) for process separations.

Writing spot functions is tricky. It's a lot more difficult than simply typing in a number for the screen frequency or angle. We do know of several good sources for spot functions, but we can't reprint the functions here. In lieu of that:

• Find someone with Corel Draw (yes, we know that it's a Microsoft Windows program running on IBM-PCs and compatibles), and ask them if you can look at a file called USERPROC.TXT. It's loaded with cool spot functions, from leaves to spirals, fully editable and well commented.

- Use ResEdit to open FreeHand's "scrn" resource, and check out all the spot functions in there.

- Look in *Real World PostScript.* There are a several spot functions, and good information on how to write your own.

***Transfer function.*** The PostScript settransfer operator controls the gray response curve of the output. You can write functions to invert the output, for instance, posterize it, or adjust for idiosyncrasies of your output device. PageMaker uses the @NormalizedTransfer value in the APD to adjust the output for a whole print job, so if you want to adjust the transfer function yourself, replace that value with your own code. Again, read *Real World PostScript.* If you're really interested in calibrating your imagesetter, check out Technical Publishing Services' Color Calibration Software for PostScript Imagesetters.

## *Modifying Aldus Prep*

PageMaker's Aldus Prep file is a set of PostScript procedures that PageMaker downloads into the printer's memory, then calls on as needed. PageMaker expects to find Aldus Prep in the Aldus folder in the system folder. It looks for it by name, but it will only find it if it has the file type ALDP and creator ALD4. If you want to edit Aldus Prep, use ResEdit, DiskTop or the like to change the file type to TEXT, edit it with your word processor, and save it as text-only. You'll need to change the type and creator back to ALDP and ALD4, though, so PageMaker will be able to find it.

### ▼ *Tip: Multiple Aldus Preps*

If PageMaker can't find Aldus Prep at print time (either in the printer's memory or on disk) it brings up a dialog box asking where to find it. You can specify any file that has the proper type and creator, so you can have multiple Aldus Prep files. Every time you print to an "unprepped" printer, you'll have an opportunity to choose the prep file you want.

### ▼ *Tip: Helvetica Narrow*

Most PostScript printers create a narrow version of Helvetica by scaling the normal Helvetica in their ROMs. Unfortunately, the ROMs in most imagesetting RIPs don't tell them how to generate Helvetica Narrow, so what many service bureau customers see when they ask for Helvetica Narrow is Courier (or Times, which is a common default for Linotronic RIPs). You can trick the RIPs into printing your Helvetica Narrow, though, by downloading the following program. If you're a service bureau operator, you might want to graft this file into your Aldus Prep.

```
serverdict begin 0 exitserver  % Remove if inserted in Aldus Prep.
/makenarrow{
        /newname exch def
        /basefontdict exch findfont def
        /newfont basefontdict maxlength dict def
        basefontdict
        { exch dup /FID ne
        { exch newfont 3 1 roll put }
        { pop pop }
        ifelse
        } forall
        newfont /FontName newname put
        newfont /FontMatrix basefontdict
        /FontMatrix get [0.82 0 0 1 0 0]
        [0 0 0 0 0 0] concatmatrix put
        newname newfont definefont pop
} bind def

/Helvetica /Helvetica-Narrow makenarrow
/Helvetica-Bold /Helvetica-Narrow-Bold makenarrow
/Helvetica-Oblique /Helvetica-Narrow-Oblique makenarrow
/Helvetica-BoldOblique /Helvetica-Narrow-BoldOblique makenarrow
```

## *Printing Problems*

While all these nifty tricks are fun and often useful, you probably turned to this chapter because something didn't come out of your printer the way you expected, or didn't come out of your printer at all. (Everyone's seen the sadistic dialog box, "A PostScript error has been generated by the printer. The document is OK but cannot be printed." This does nothing good for your blood pressure.) Given the great things we've said about the Aldus PostScript printer driver, there are, alas, still things that can go wrong. Here are some favorites, and some favorite solutions.

**Running Out of Memory**

Most often, PageMaker printing problems have to do with the printer running out of memory—particularly on one-megabyte printers with PostScript ROM versions earlier than 42 (see Figure 6-7).

**Figure 6-7**
Checking printer memory

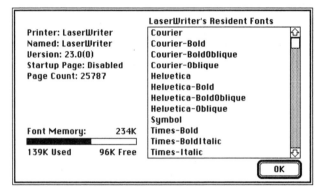

*The less-than-copious memory in Steve's old version 23 LaserWriter*

When PostScript printers run out of memory, they send back whatever their last instruction was as an error message. So you'll often see error messages citing common PostScript commands like "def" (you can't have PostScript without "def") as the offending code. Don't search through a PostScript dump of the file looking to eliminate "def!" It's just the last thing that the printer knew before it lost its mind. Instead, try these techniques.

***Print fewer pages at a time.*** Or print pages one at a time. Try to discover what pages don't print and identify what items on them might be difficult to print. RAM-consumptive items include:

- TIFF images (especially with heavy cropping)

- EPSF images (especially suspect Cricket Draw, Illustrator 1.1, and PageMaker-generated EPS)
- Complex PICTs
- Text that uses lots of different downloadable fonts

***Reset the printer to clear its memory.*** Either use LaserStatus, or turn the thing off and on. If you have been printing from other applications, you may have downloaded other PostScript user dictionaries to the printer's RAM (notably Laser Prep—the PostScript prep file that is automatically downloaded and used by 98 percent of Mac programs). Rebooting the printer flushes out the RAM.

***Try using Save as.*** PageMaker compresses the file, and sometimes it will print afterward.

***Print the troublesome pages to disk as PostScript and download them.*** Sometimes the downloading techniques require less of the printer's RAM than PageMaker's downloading processes.

***Proof print.*** This will tell you whether it's the graphics on your page that are causing your problem.

***Remove items from a page and print again.*** Eventually, you'll find the item the printer's getting stuck on. "But wait!" you're saying. "If I didn't need the item on the page, I wouldn't have put it there, and the program's worthless if I can't print the page!" Fine. We only want to establish which item is choking the printer. Then we can work on it. If the item is a graphic, think about ways you might be able to simplify it.

***Shrink the page size.*** With imagesetters, try creating a paper size in the APD file that is exactly the size of your page, and use that. Less imageable area means less memory, so this may work, especially if you're getting VM errors (that's virtual memory).

***Try the Apple driver instead of the Aldus driver.*** Hold down Option while choosing Print from the File menu. The Aldus driver is usually better than the Apple driver, but we've seen cases where the Apple driver printed pages that stopped the Aldus driver dead.

### ▼ *Tip: Fixing EPS Files that Won't Print*

If your publication contains EPS files that aren't printing, try this:

1. Print the file to disk as normal PostScript (you need only print the pages with the offending EPS graphics on them).

2. Open the PostScript file with a text editor.

3. Search for "BoundingBox".

4. The line containing the BoundingBox comments should read "%% x y Bounding Box x y 0 0". If, instead, it reads "% x y %Bounding Box x y 0 0", change it so that it reads correctly. The graphic will print properly when downloaded. This bug was fixed with PageMaker 3.02CE, but if you're converting PageMaker 3 pubs, it's something to watch for.

### ▼ *Tip: If a TIFF Image Prints as a Low-resolution Bitmap*

PageMaker stores graphic images larger than 64 K (and most TIFFs are larger than 64 K) outside of the program. If your TIFF image prints as a low-resolution bitmap, PageMaker probably couldn't find the linked file. Choose "Links" from the File menu and update the link. For more information on and linking source files, see "Link and Link options" in Chapter 8, *Workgroup Publishing*. When you take your PageMaker files to a service bureau, make sure you take all of the linked files— especially the TIFFs—with you.

### ▼ *Tip: Forever and a Day*

If your print jobs are so complex that the printer or imagesetter gets tired of waiting and times out after a while waiting for data, you need to teach it to be more patient. Open the appropriate APD file, find the

@AldusPatchFile keyword, and modify the value (or add to what's there) as follows.

@AldusPatchFile: "statusdict /waittimeout 2500 put"

This will give you 2,500 seconds before the printer gives up (PageMaker has it set to 300). Set it to zero (0), and it will never give up. This is especially useful if you are printing big bitmaps over a network, where communications can get very slow.

---

### ▼ *Tip: Nested EPS Files*

Watch out for EPS files within EPS files within EPS files. Suppose you create an EPS graphic in Illustrator, for instance, place it in FreeHand and combine it with other graphics, and then save that conglomeration as EPS and place it in PageMaker. It's quite possible that the nested EPS files won't print. If they do print, the Illustrator EPS will quite probably print as a bitmap, and it's highly unlikely that it will print the proper downloaded fonts.

---

As always, the most important trick when you run into problems is to keep poking at it until it works. We've had to go through incredible contortions at times to coax pages out of the printer, but we never (or hardly ever) have to resort to manual pasteup or stripping by the printer. Just keep telling yourself, "it will work."

# *Color*

PageMaker first ventured into the world of color with version 3.0. That version offered the ability to specify up to 256 colors, and to print spot color overlays. We always thought 256 colors was kind of overkill when all you could do was print spot colors (you couldn't even print in color on color PostScript printers). It's not often that we have a 256-color press to work with, and if we did, we'd need to rent out the Stanford linear accelerator building to house it. Of course, we could do it on a 128-color press with work-and-turn...

With the arrival of 3.02 CE (Color Extension), PageMaker gained several color-related features.

- The ability to place color bitmapped images
- Printing in color on color PostScript printers
- Printing color information to PostScript disk files for separation with other programs
- A color palette that could handle 32,767 colors

PageMaker 4 doesn't add a whole lot for color publishers that wasn't there in Color Extension. It even removes one thing—the Colors button in the Preferences dialog box, which let you adjust your monitor colors to more closely match printed output. This version lets you specify more colors than anyone will ever need, print spot color overlays directly from the program, and print PostScript to disk that can be separated with other programs like Aldus PrePrint, Adobe Separator, and high-end prepress systems. In addition, you can print selected spot color overlays, rather than printing all of them.

In this chapter, we explain the different methods of color production and reproduction (they're intimately connected), and the best ways to use PageMaker to make those methods work—defining colors, applying them to objects on the page, getting output from those pages, and reproducing that output. In addition to this chapter, refer to the color pages in this book for in-depth discussion and illustration of how PageMaker works with color for offset printing.

## Color Printing Techniques

The first thing to consider when you're working with color in PageMaker is how you're going to produce and reproduce the pages. There are basically three options, and you'll need to use different techniques in PageMaker depending on which you're using.

**Color printing.** Print on a color printer or slide recorder. This is for one-off type of work—printed comps for approval, for instance, or slides for a presentation. You might use color printers for very short runs (less than 50), but they're mainly good for getting one or two copies.

**Spot color printing.** Print using multiple passes on a laser printer or photocopier with different colored toners, or on a printing press using one, two, or three PMS inks (PMS stands for Pantone Matching System—a standard, numbered set of colors). Use PageMaker's Spot color overlay feature to print the different color elements on separate overlays, and combine the overlays using multiple passes or a multicolor press.

Multipass printing with different color toners is an easy, inexpensive way to get color on your pages for short runs, especially if you combine it with colored paper. One-, two-, and three-color offset printing is less expensive than four-color process printing (the next scenario), and you can ask your printer for PMS inks that are difficult or impossible to reproduce with the process colors—silver, copper, or gold, for instance, forest green, or a creamy, rich slate blue.

***Four-color process printing.*** Print on a printing press using percentages of the four process inks (cyan, magenta, yellow, and black—CMYK). You print the pages to disk as PostScript files, and then use a utility like Adobe Separator or Aldus PrePrint to separate the colors into four separations. The printer uses those four pieces of film to make the printing plates, and prints the job using the four process inks. You can create millions of different colors by combining the four inks (even reproducing photographs), but the printing is expensive, and you face the (formidable) problems of creating process color separations from your color pages.

You can combine the PMS and process methods if you have the budget for a five-or six-color print run. You might use the process inks for most of the work, and use PMS inks for special colors you can't get from the process inks.

**Color Models**

PageMaker lets you specify colors using any of four different color models. Depending on how you're printing the job, you'll want to use different models. You can use CMYK percentage specs, a Pantone palette, or the HSB/RGB model.

- CMYK (for cyan, magenta, yellow, and black) is the color model used for four-color process printing. You specify percentages of the four colors, and the four inks combine on press to create your colors .

- Pantone is a standard set of numbered colors that are available in many forms—pens, markers, printing inks, etc.

- RGB is Red/Green/Blue; HSB is Hue/Saturation/Brightness (also called HLS, for Hue/Lightness/Saturation). RGB and HSB are used for screen displays and most slide recorders. They're different views of the same thing, as you can see with the Apple Color Picker.

**Table 7-1 Color reproduction**

| Reproduction Method | Recommended Color Model | Number of Overlays/Separations | Separation Method |
| --- | --- | --- | --- |
| Color printer or slide recorder | RGB, HSB, or Apple Color Picker | One full-color | No separation required |
| Multipass printing or photocopying with color toner | Any method | One overlay for each color | Spot color overlays |
| Offset printing with PMS inks | PMS colors with percentages from the Fill menu | One overlay for each color | Spot color overlays |
| Four-color process | CMYK percentages with solid fills | Four separations | Process separator |
| Process plus PMS | CMYK for process colors, PMS for PMS colors | Four separations plus one overlay for each PMS color | Process separator |

### ▼ Tip: Using the Apple Color Picker

If you have a color monitor, you can use the Apple Color Picker dialog box to choose your colors. Bring up the Define colors dialog box, select a color, hold down Shift, and click the Edit button. Now you can choose a color on the color wheel in the dialog box. You can adjust the darkness and lightness of the color wheel with the scroll bar that's to the right of the wheel. Notice how the RGB and HSB numbers change in tandem.

## Overlays and Separations

Remember that process separations are different from spot color overlays. Overlays are often called mechanical separations, which adds to the confusion. We'll stick to the two distinct terms—separations and overlays—but we can't totally alleviate the confusion, because the way you specify color in PageMaker is sort of confused.

You can use CMYK specs, for instance, to define a spot color, which basically means a color that will be output on an overlay and printed with PMS inks—with no reference to the CMYK specs. That's weird and confusing (and something different happens if you're using a process separation program), but we'll do our best to comb it out.

To begin with, look at Table 7-1, which shows the different color reproduction methods and how you should spec colors for each. Note for each scenario how you separate the colors, and what you'll get out of the printer.

## Defining Colors

If you need any colors besides PageMaker's canned Red, Green, and Blue (one of the first things we do is delete those from our default palette), you'll want to define some colors. Using the Define colors menu item, you can define up to 32,767 colors, all available from the Colors palette.

### ▼ Tip: The Fast Way to Define Colors

Don't go to the Define colors dialog box just to create a new color. Turn on the Colors palette if it's not already on (Command-K), then Command-click on Black or Registration. If you have a colored object selected, the Edit color dialog box fills in with the color values of that object. The new color you define won't be applied to the selected object (just as new styles aren't applied to selected text), which means you can create any number of colors derived from the color of the selected object by Command-clicking, defining the color, and Command-clicking again.

### ▼ Tip: The Fast Way to Redefine Colors

Command-click on a color in the Colors palette to bring up the Edit color dialog box. Unfortunately, you can't change the color name from here as you can when you Command-click a style in the Styles palette. You need to go through the Define colors dialog box.

## *Applying Colors and Fills*

Applying colors in PageMaker comes down to the good old Macintosh select-then-apply approach, but you'll use different methods for creating overlays and separations. PageMaker has two controls that govern colors and tints for page elements—the Colors palette and the Fill menu—and they interact with each other. To apply a color, select an object and click on the color in the Colors palette. You can apply colors to just about anything on a page, except a graphic that has color specified internally—a color EPS or TIFF file, for instance.

When you apply a color to an object, it applies to the whole object. To create a box with a green border and a red fill, for instance, you'll need to create two boxes—one with a green border and no fill, another with a red fill and no border—and align the green-border box on top of the red-fill box. (For more on this, see "Overprinting, Knockouts, and Traps" later in this chapter.)

You apply color to text by selecting it with the Text tool and applying the color. You can also build a color specification into a paragraph style, of course. Selecting a text block with the pointer tool and applying color has no effect.

▼ *Tip: Taking Advantage of Being Unable to*
   *Apply Color to Text Blocks*

Don't worry about selecting text blocks when you're trying to color other items. If everything on a spread but the text is to be PMS 274, select everything and click on PMS 274 in the Colors palette. The color is applied to everything except the type.

The second method for controlling the color of objects is the Fill menu. Use this to control "tints" of spot colors. Just as you can assign a

20 percent fill to a box, you can assign a 20 percent fill and use PMS #286. If you're printing overlays, the box will come out on the PMS #286 overlay with a 20 percent fill.

### ▼ *Tip: Spot Color Tints for Type*

Note that you can't apply a fill to type, no matter how you select the type, so you can't have type in a percentage tint of a PMS color using PageMaker's Spot color overlays feature. You just can't.

### ▼ *Tip: Gray Type*

If you're working with a one-color publication, you can use the CMYK color model to define shades of gray as colors (50% black, for instance) and apply them to text to get gray type.

Things get more complicated when you're using CMYK specs *and* the Fill menu for process color printing. We don't recommend it, simply because it's confusing and you can do it a better way. Suppose you define a color that's 50 percent magenta, for instance, then apply that color to an object and choose the 10% fill for the same object. You'll get a 5 percent tint. You're better off just defining a color that's 5 percent magenta and using that with a Solid fill. Table 7-2 shows the results of color/fill combinations when you're creating overlays and separations.

**Table 7-2  Color/fill combinations**

| Color Name | C | M | Y | K | Fill | Results on Spot Color Overlay | Results on Process Separations |
|------------|---|---|---|---|------|-------------------------------|--------------------------------|
| C80 | 80 | 0 | 0 | 0 | 10% | 10 percent | 8C |
| C80 | 80 | 0 | 0 | 0 | Solid | 100 percent | 80C |
| PMS 188 | 0 | 79 | 65 | 47 | 10% | 10 percent | 0C/7.9M/6.5Y/4.7K |
| PMS 188 | 0 | 79 | 65 | 47 | Solid | 100 percent | 0C/79M/65Y/47K |

Notice that the color name has no effect, except that the name prints on the proper overlay when you create spot color overlays. Also notice that CMYK values don't have any effect when you're using PageMaker's Spot color overlays feature.

**The Color Paper**

There is one extremely strange color in the PageMaker Colors palette, called Paper. There's also a choice on the Fill menu by the same name. Both of them are opaque, but they work somewhat differently when you're printing spot color overlays. If that confuses you, join the club. The setup actually makes sense, though; it lets you obscure items on individual overlays selectively, rather than obscuring items of all colors.

If you apply the color Paper to an object, it prints on every color overlay, obscuring any objects that lie behind it, whatever their color. If you apply the *fill* Paper to an object, though, it only obscures objects that lie behind it if they are in the same color. A blue, Paper-filled box, for instance, will obscure a blue circle that lies behind it, but it won't obscure a red circle, despite what you see on screen. Wysiwyg is a relative thing.

Paper-colored objects and paper-filled, registration-colored objects print white on all overlays, so use them when you want to obscure something on all overlays. If this all seems confusing to you, see the color pages in this book for a graphic representation of what knocks out of what with different combinations of fills and colors.

### ▼ Tip: PageMaker-drawn Graphics Print on the Wrong Overlay

Watch the Colors palette when drawing LBOs, especially with the Paper and Registration colors, and on monochrome Macs. It's easy to draw in the wrong color so graphics end up on the wrong overlay. Usually, you'll want the Paper-filled objects to end up on the Black overlay, so make sure to choose "Black" in the Colors palette when you fill something with "Paper." Even better, use the color Paper. That way you know it obscures everything behind it, just as it does on screen.

▼ *Tip: To See What it Will Look Like on Colored Paper*

You can redefine the color Paper in PageMaker, so all your on-screen pages are the color you choose. Just Command-click on Paper in the Colors palette, and change it to whatever color you want. All your pages on screen are the color of your paper. It doesn't affect output, though; it's just so you can see what your pages will look like on colored paper.

Again, the combinations of colors and fills for separations and overlays result in exceptions to exceptions to exceptions. This is a real mind-bender, especially when you add the choice of printing overlays with or without knockouts. Take a look at the color plates in this book to see the results with various permutations.

## Color Specs and Color Correspondence

One piece of advice before we go any farther: what you see on screen, or what comes out of a color printer, will look very different from the final printed output—no matter what your output method. Some colors may be close, but others will be way off. Screen displays, color printers, and printing presses are simply too different to expect good color correspondence. And when you get into overprinting of inks, you can throw wysiwyg right out the window. The screen display is mainly useful to get a general idea of the look, and to make sure you have the correct colors assigned to different page elements.

So how do you know what the colors are going to look like? Use printed color charts, just like always. If you're printing offset, you can get a book full of color swatches printed on coated and uncoated stock. You can get charts of process color combinations (if you're printing CMYK), and charts of PMS inks printed at different percentages. You can even get charts of PMS ink combinations (what does it look like when you combine a 20 percent tint of PMS #206 with a 40 percent tint of PMS #286?). *Use these charts. Do not rely on your display.* The charts will show you much more accurately what you can expect off the printing press.

Remember, also, that you can't expect to use a color printer as a true proofing device for color printing. The colors won't be the same, whether you're using process or PMS inks. You can do a color printout to show to clients or other mucketymucks, but you'll need to get a true color proof (Matchprint, Chromalyn, or the like) from your printer based on the separated film. As they say in the printing trade, "the Chrome is the contract."

### ▼ Tip: Easier-to-Read Composites

When you print composite proofs of your publication to a black-and-white printer, PageMaker renders the colors as shades of gray, making it difficult to proofread color type. Before you print composite proofs, edit the colors you've defined so that they print as black (a K setting of 100 percent does a wonderful job of this). Now your color type prints as a readable black, but separates as a spot color. If you're using process colors, you'll need to change the color back to its original settings before you print the publication to disk for separation.

### Color Printer Output

For printing on color printers and slide recorders, you can use any color model you want; you don't need to worry about separations and overlays. You end up with one full-color page or slide. The colors still won't be exactly what you see on screen, but if you use a given output device much, you can create a swatch book for yourself. That way you know how a color you've created will actually come out.

### Spot Color Output

For spot color printing—whether on a laser printer or photocopier with color toner, or an offset press with PMS inks—it doesn't really matter what color you see on screen, except to get an idea how your pages look. All that counts is that you have the correct colors assigned to different page elements so they come out on the right overlays.

You can use any color model you want, but the PMS palette is most convenient and the least confusing. You can even modify the CMYK percentages for the PMS colors if you think it gives a better screen representation of what the colors will look like. They'll all come out black on the overlays, anyway; the CMYK percentages have no effect when printing spot color overlays.

### ▼ *Tip: Use Process Separation for Spot Color Printing*

You can get all the percentage tints you want for up to four spot colors by using a process color separation utility. Use cyan for one spot color, magenta for the second, yellow for a third, and black for the fourth. When the page is separated using a process separation program, you'll get what is effectively four overlays—one for each spot color. If your separation utility lets you do it, change the screen angle for all four process colors to 45 degrees, and make sure it's set up to create knockouts in underlying objects.

What you see on the screen with this method looks nothing like the final output, but it gets around the limitations of the Fill menu.

### ▼ *Tip: Use PMS Color Names and Numbers*

If you're printing using PMS inks, name your colors according to the actual PMS color, chosen from a PMS palette or a printed swatch book. Your printer will be happier with you if the PMS color number you want is specified on the page you give them. Printers have enough to do; they don't need to spend time figuring out color names like "Swamp." There's no reason for you to worry about exactly what CMYK (or HSB, or RGB) values produce that color on screen, except to protect your delicate aesthetic sensibilities.

### ▼ *Tip: Working with Spot Colors on a Monochrome Display*

If you're creating a spot color job using a monochrome display, the most important thing is to make sure you have the right colors assigned to the right elements. To that end, choose colors that display very differently in black and white. Don't worry about which color you choose—just make sure you can distinguish quickly between the different colors on your display. If you're doing a three-color job, for instance, choose one color that displays as black, one that displays as dark gray, and one that displays as a dithered pattern. You'll still end up with three black overlays, and you can always change the color names to conform to the previous tip.

This solution is not perfect. If you use percentage fills with the spot colors, for instance, it quickly becomes impossible to distinguish between the different colors. The only really good solution is to buy a color Macintosh.

---

### ▼ Tip: To Replace Every Instance of One Color with a Different Color

If you've ever defined more colors than you want and need to merge two colors (to end up with fewer spot color overlays, for example), here's what to do. This example shows how to change all the red objects to blue. (This technique is almost identical to the same technique for replacing one paragraph style with another. See the tip "Merging Two Styles" in Chapter 4, *Words*.)

1. Choose "Define colors" from the Element menu.
2. Select the color whose name you want to change (Red), and click the Edit button.
3. Change the name of the color to the name of the color you intend to merge it with (type "Blue") and click OK. PageMaker displays the prompt: "Change all Red items to Blue?"
4. Click OK. PageMaker merges the two colors.

At this point a peculiar thing happens (that may or may not be a bug)—the OK button goes gray and you can't leave the dialog box and keep your changes. Just select a color, and you'll be able to click OK or press Return. Every item that was either color becomes the new, merged color. In our example, for instance, all the red objects turn into blue objects.

**Four-Color Printing**

If you're creating a four-color process job, specify your colors by looking at a process color chart, and use the CMYK color model. Do not rely on the screen colors, do not use RGB/HSB or the Apple Color Picker, and do not use the Pantone palette. There is no direct relationship between RGB/HSB and CMYK, and there's no such thing as a printed RGB or HSB color chart. You're flying blind with those models. And although most Pantone inks can be simulated using process inks, specifying PMS numbers for CMYK output just puts another layer of uncertainty between you and the printed product.

You're a lot better off specifying the CMYK values yourself rather than letting some separation program do it for you based on mysterious PMS-to-process lookup tables. You may find it easier to remember one number than four numbers, but the paint-by-numbers approach went out with rubber knickers. (For some reason even some printers use PMS numbers to spec colors for four-color jobs. We hope they're reading this paragraph.) If you're printing CMYK, spec your colors using CMYK.

▼ *Tip: Blacks that are Really Black*

In process printing, you can get richer, more saturated blacks—especially in large black areas—if you add a bit of cyan to the black ink. You can't redefine Black in the PageMaker Colors palette, so create a new color with a name like BlackC or C30K100, and specify 30C/100K. Use this color wherever you have large black areas.

Some people use 20C/20M/20Y/100K, but that's kind of overkill, and it results in a lot of ink on the page, especially if you're printing on uncoated stock. It does have advantages, though; it avoids any problem with trapping (discussed below) when you have black type on top of another process color.

## *Overprinting, Knockouts, and Traps*

The previous tip—including some of the other colors in your blacks—raises the whole topic of overprinting. This is the area where what you see on the screen differs the most from what comes off the printing press. Using overprinting effectively requires a good deal of visualization, and careful planning. Take a look at the color pages in this book to get an idea of what overprinting does, and why you need to know about it.

The basic question with overprinting is whether colors on top of other colors cause the underlying areas to be "knocked out." Whether you use the Knockouts option in the Aldus print options dialog box depends on many factors: whether you're printing separations or overlays, whether you want to do the knockouts yourself or let your printer handle them photographically, and whether you want to create "traps" for abutting colors (or again, let your printer do them for you).

First, the bad news: PageMaker doesn't let you specify that a given object on a page should overprint on underlying objects. You can't put two blue circles in front of a yellow box and have one circle overprint while the other is knocked out. Without resorting to trickery, at least. If you want trickery, use the selective knockout techniques demonstrated in the color pages in this book, or print the whole page without knockouts and mark up the overlays telling the printer to knock one out, and leave the other to overprint.

By contrast, both Illustrator 88 and FreeHand let you specify overprinting for an object. They even let you specify that the outline of an object—the "stroke"—should overprint, while the fill should not (or vice versa). These controls give you the flexibility to really control your color jobs. In PageMaker, you have to make do with less.

Let's start by discussing overprinting for spot color overlays, because they're a lot simpler. The basic choice here is whether or not to check the Knockouts option in the Aldus print options dialog box. If you do check "Knockouts," you'll get a hole in overlays where an object of another color is in front. A blue circle in front of a yellow square will result in a circular hole in the yellow overlay. If you don't check "Knockouts," you'll end up with a green circle instead of a blue one off the printing press, because the blue ink will print right on top of the yellow (unless you ask your printer to create the knockouts photographically).

### ▼ *Tip: Knockouts of EPS Graphics*

PageMaker can't normally create knockouts underneath placed EPS graphics. Here's how to create knockouts for it.

1. Zoom in to actual size and grab a screen shot of the graphic (Command-Shift-3 on small-footprint Macintoshes without big screens; use something like Capture with other displays).
2. Use a paint program (DeskPaint is our choice) to save the applicable portion of the screen shot as a black-and-white paint (or bilevel TIFF) file.
3. Place the paint file (you'll notice that nonblack areas are transparent) and in 400% view, align it perfectly with the original graphic.
4. With the paint image selected, click on Paper in the Colors palette.
5. Select the original image (Command-click through the paint image), and bring it in front of the paint image.

Knockouts sound like just the ticket for printing overlays, but you may not want to use them. Instead, you may want to pass the overlays to the printer without knockouts, marking them up for them so they can create the knockouts using their magical photographic methods. The reason? Trapping.

**Getting Trapped**

Traps are slight overlaps of abutting colors that ensure the colors meet completely when the printing press is out of register. If you use the Knockouts option, PageMaker creates absolutely perfect holes in underlying areas—just the size and shape of the overlying graphics. Unfortunately, the real world is not perfect. Printing presses rarely print two colors in perfect register, so you're likely to end up with the overlying objects slightly offset from the underlying objects. This results in thin white lines where the colors should abut. It's subtle, but it makes an impression. Think about all those color direct mail pieces you get, for instance. If you look closely, you'll find that a lot of their hokey appearance results from sloppy trapping and registration.

There are a few of solutions. You can live with the misregistration; avoid abutting colors; or print with "Knockouts" turned off, mark up the overlays, and ask your printer to knock out the underlying colors, building traps at the same time.

### ▼ Tip: Trapping LBOs

You can build traps for LBOs and spot color printing by working with Option-paste and PageMaker's ruler guides.

1. Pull down ruler guides so that they're 1 point (or whatever distance you feel is appropriate for your trap) inside the selection handles of the LBO you want knocked out.

2. Copy the LBO to the Clipboard.

3. Option-paste the copy of the LBO with Command-Option-V.

4. Snap the upper-left and lower-right selection handles to the ruler guides you positioned in step 1.

5. Fill the LBO with Paper and color it the color of the underlying object.

6. Command-click through the Paper-filled LBO to select the original LBO, then press Command-F to bring it to the front.

7. Print the page with the Knockouts option turned off.

For an example of creating traps for spot colors, see the color pages in this book.

### ▼ Tip: Overprinting Thin Lines

If the only place that your second color overlaps on black is thin lines—for instance callout lines pointing to diagrams—you can just skip the knockouts and let the lines overprint on other colors. The eye fills in where they overprint, much more so than it would if the press is out of register and the lines don't land on the knockouts perfectly.

---

Building traps is a lot easier when you're working with process inks, and there's less chance that you'll need them. If the two abutting colors share any significant percentage of a color (if each of them has at least 20 percent cyan in it, for instance), you don't need a trap. If the press is out of register you won't end up with a white line between the two, but a cyan, yellow, or magenta line, which is much less noticeable.

### ▼ Tip: Traps for Process Colors

If two abutting colors don't share a common process color, you can build traps for them pretty easily. Imagine a 50 percent yellow circle on top of a 50 percent magenta square. Here's how to avoid a white line where the two colors abut.

1. Copy and Option-paste the yellow circle, so you have two duplicates directly on top of each other.
2. With the front circle selected, change the fill to none, and give it a 2-point line.
3. Define a color with 50Y/50M, and apply it to the new circle.

The line around the circle now has both process colors in it, and it overlaps on the circle, so if the press is out of register you'll get a yellow line or a magenta line between the objects, not a white one. See the color pages in this book for an example of trapping with process colors.

---

The trapping methods described here are pretty elementary and limited (and they're a pain), but for the time being, at least, they're about the only methods available for creating traps in PageMaker.

# Workgroup Publishing

Workgroup publishing is the hot new buzzword in desktop publishing. While it's an important topic, it's also one of the most difficult to discuss definitively. Every publishing operation, and every publishing project, is different. Each requires different procedures. Dozens of factors affect the process of workgroup publishing, so there seems to be an infinite number of exceptions to exceptions to exceptions.

PageMaker 4 addresses the difficulties and opportunities of workgroup publishing with a family of features for controlling links to external source files. These features let you keep track of revisions to the text and graphic files that make up your publication. In this chapter we discuss ways to use those features to achieve the goals of workgroup publishing, and to avoid the pitfalls.

## What You're Trying to Achieve

First off, what are you trying to achieve when you build a workgroup publishing system? Simple—you're after seamless, effortless revision control and file transfer. Achieving that goal, however, is not so simple. It involves a complex interplay of people, products, and procedures.

Workgroup publishing systems are not made up of just hardware and software. More than anything, seamless production management results from well thought out procedures for who does what and when. The procedures apply to you (the person making pages), your fellow page makers, and anyone who is supplying you with material—artists, writers, and editors.

On the other hand, your hardware and software system and the capabilities of different components in that system have a direct impact on your procedures. One example: Steve was working on a four-color process publication using QuarkXPress, with illustrations created in Adobe Illustrator 88. QuarkXPress will color separate placed Illustrator images along with the rest of the elements on a page, so everything looked skookum—just place the Illustrator EPS files provided by the artists, and separate the whole page into four pieces of film, ready for the printer.

Unfortunately, a tiny technical detail required a complete change in the production cycle. The artists were using Illustrator's Overprint feature to create traps for the color images (see "Getting Trapped" in Chapter 7, *Color*), and that version of QuarkXPress ignored any Illustrator overprint instructions. So the illustrations had to be separated on their own, and stripped into the page film by the printer. Steve had to use dummy versions of the illustrations (provided by the illustrators) for positioning, and type notes to the printer for each.

Four-color process may not be in your future, but this is a good example of how one little technical detail can affect the best-laid plans and publishing procedures. The goal is to set up procedures with all the technical details in mind, so you can just make pages without worrying about those details. Publishing projects have enough details to keep track of without bothering with computers.

## What You're Trying to Avoid

Managing the publication process is just as much (or maybe more so) about what you're trying to avoid. The following three scenarios, for instance, are enacted far too often.

- Two or more people making changes to separate copies of the same file, so the changes have to be compiled manually
- Using old versions of files, rather than the latest revisions
- Having your only copy of a file destroyed

Both of us have had to enter changes manually because two (or more) people made changes to copies of the same file. Both of us have had the unpleasant experience of going to imagesetter output only to find that either the pub or one of the source files contained in the pub were not the most up-to-date versions. It's infuriating, and it's well worth setting up procedures to avoid it.

## The Fascist Approach Versus the Laissez-Faire Ideal

The kind of procedures we talk about here may sound pretty compulsive. They really stress control rather than the free exchange of material that so often makes a publishing project fun and great. In fact, publishing management procedures *are* about control. Ole's version of the "who does what and when" line is "who can do what to whom and when." The corporate ideal has always been to set up your group so that they can do whatever they want to whomever they want whenever they want, so every group ends up feeling oppressed by every other group (witness the proliferation of "You want it when?!" cartoons in print shops). We hope that this is not how people want to work in the 1990s, and that networks and cooperation replace hierarchies and competition (we also look forward to Santa Claus visiting every winter).

The goal in any workgroup is to establish procedures that smooth out the normal work flow, while providing back doors that people can dash through when they need to get something done fast. It may be as simple as a writer walking over to the production department an making some changes in a PageMaker file (or looking over production person's shoulder and telling them what changes to make) Or these exceptions might be procedures in their own right.

When Steve was working for *Publishers Weekly,* everyone had terminals on a big minicomputer-based Atex editorial/production system. Each person had a password and a "queue" of files. Once you sent a file to someone else's queue, you couldn't get at it again unless you had their password.

Of course, everyone knew everyone else's passwords, so they could go into other people's queues and make changes when necessary without having to ask that person to send the file back. That didn't diminish the value of the system, though. Sending a file off to someone else was effectively saying, "I've finished with it for now." People were polite and sensible, and if they had to make some changes they would inform the person whose queue they'd invaded that they'd done so. The production department (editorial had their passwords, too) would often ask an editor to go into the production queue to cut 15 lines in a file, or whatever.

The point is that procedures are necessary, but they can't be cast in stone. People are sick, busy with other things, working on someone else's machine, or (most likely) in meetings, so you're back to the seat of your pants. A big part of workgroup publishing is walking over and talking to the person in the next cubicle, and that will never change (nor would we like it to).

So no matter how up-tight we sound here, remember that we want people to continue doing whatever needs to be done to finish the job. Procedures should help them do that, not hinder them. And once again, the most important procedures in workgroup publishing are also the most important procedures in daily office life: be courteous, thoughtful, understanding, and sensible. Remember that while they're just extras in your movie, you're just an extra in theirs.

## Link, Link info, and Link options

PageMaker 4 offers a group of features—Links—that are designed specifically for workgroup publishing. These features provide a lot of flexibility in developing procedures, but they can also open the door to disaster if used injudiciously. With Links, PageMaker keeps track of the external source files that make up your publication. You can direct it to automatically replace the stories and graphics when the source files change, and to notify you before making the replacement.

PageMaker always keeps a copy of a text file in a publication, but graphics are a more complex matter. Graphics over 50 K are generally stored outside the publication. PageMaker displays a low-resolution version of the graphic on screen, and sends the linked file to the printer when it's time to print. You can choose to store large graphics inside the publication, but you pay the price in increased file size.

To begin with, you can see where any linked page element came from—its source file—by selecting the object and choosing "Link info" from the Element menu (Figure 8-1).

**Figure 8-1**
Link info
dialog box

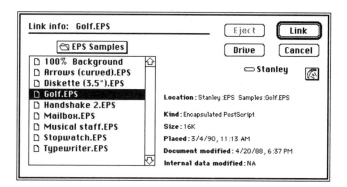

Change your default link options for a specific publication by choosing "Link options" from the Element menu with no objects selected (Figure 8-2). You can set the defaults for all publications by choosing "Link options" with no publication open.

**Figure 8-2**
Link options:
Defaults dialog box

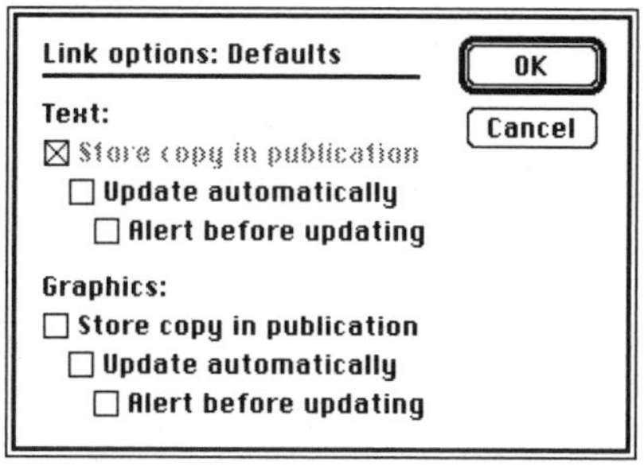

*If you check "Update automatically," be sure to check "Alert before updating," or be prepared for nasty surprises.*

You can also set link options for a specific element by selecting the element and then choosing "Link options" from the Element menu. This brings up the Link options dialog box, which varies slightly depending on whether you have a text or graphic object selected (Figure 8-3).

These options are powerful and useful, but they raise a lot of questions. All of the choices you can make regarding a publication's

**Figure 8-3**
Link options
dialog boxes
for graphic and
text objects

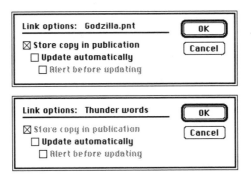

links affect in a very direct and immediate way who does what and when. If you want PageMaker to automatically replace a file with the latest version every time you open a pub, for instance, you have to make sure that the person working on that source file saves the latest version in the same folder, with the same file name. If they make changes and save the file with a different file name or in a different folder, PageMaker blithely proceeds to use the old version.

You can get an idea of how all the files in a publication are linked, and the status of the files, by choosing "Links" from the File menu (or press Command-=). The Links dialog box appears (Figure 8-4), showing the file names of all your source files, the pages on which each file appears, the type of file it is (this is not the same as its Macintosh file type), and the file's link status.

The status column (the narrow one on the left) is probably the most important part of the Links dialog box. If it's blank, be happy. That means the external files are the same as the files in the pub (if you're keeping a copy in the pub), and neither has changed since you placed the file (or the item is not linked to an external file).

***Black diamond.*** A black diamond in the status column means the external file has changed (you're not working with the most recent version), and that PageMaker is set to automatically replace the file the

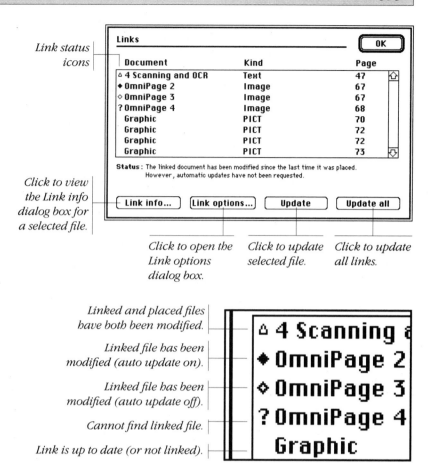

**Figure 8-4**
Links dialog box

Link status icons

Click to view the Link info dialog box for a selected file.

Click to open the Link options dialog box.

Click to update selected file.

Click to update all links.

Linked and placed files have both been modified.

Linked file has been modified (auto update on).

Linked file has been modified (auto update off).

Cannot find linked file.

Link is up to date (or not linked).

next time you open the publication. You should ask the person responsible for changing the file if their changes need to get into your publication. Sometimes, they've made the changes in error, or they're working on the file for some reason other than inclusion in your publication. If you haven't made any changes inside the pub, and you know that the external changes are intended for inclusion in your publication, select the file and click "Update" to replace the version of the file in the publication with the most current version of the source file.

***Hollow diamond.*** A hollow diamond means that the source file has been changed and that the link options are not set to automatically replace the file in your publication. Follow the same procedures as in the paragraph above, if necessary.

***Hollow triangle.*** A hollow triangle is the worst. It means that *both* the external file and the copy in the publication have changed. If the link options are set up for automatic replacement, change them so that the file is not automatically replaced. Then, find out whether both sets of changes (the changes in the pub and the external changes) need to be included in the publication. If both sets of changes are needed, you'll to have to compile those edits manually, either on the page or in the source file. In short, $\Delta$ = wasted work.

### ▼ *Tip: Use DocuComp*

DocuComp (available from Microsoft for a nominal fee to Word 4 buyers) is a great program for comparing two versions of a text file and displaying the differences between the two files. If a linked file has been marked with a hollow triangle in the Links dialog box, meaning that both the internal and external versions of the linked file have been modified, and both sets of changes need to be included in the final publication, compare the files using DocuComp. You can see the two versions on screen with changes highlighted, or save a composite version (saved in RTF, which Word or PageMaker can read; Figure 8-5).

**Figure 8-5**
A composite document
created with DocuComp

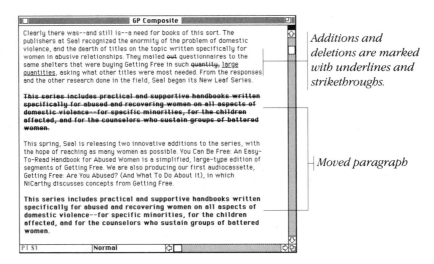

1. Export the version of the text file from PageMaker. Make sure to give the exported file a different name from the modified linked file. You

can export the text using any of the export filters, but don't check "Export tags" unless the original file was created for import using style tags.

2. Run DocuComp, compare the external and exported versions, and print the summary, or save it to disk (DocuComp saves it in Rich Text Format, which you can open with Word).

3. Call up the two versions in separate windows in your word processor, and using the printed comparison summary, merge the changes.

4. Replace the PageMaker story with the new compiled version.

---

### ▼ Tip: Using Link info as Replace

You can use the Link info dialog box as an alternate method of replacing text and graphics. The newly linked files need bear no relation to the current file—handy if you've placed a bunch of placeholder graphics and don't want to bother paging through the publication and selecting each one to replace it.

1. Choose the story or graphic you want to replace (you can do this in Story view, Layout view, or from the Links dialog box).

2. Choose "Link info" from the Element menu (or, if you're in the Links dialog box, press the Link info button).

3. Locate the file you want to replace the currently linked file.

4. Click the Link button. PageMaker replaces the selected file with the file you specified.

---

### ▼ Tip: Link Placeholders for Automatic Replacement

Because PageMaker links to a file name and file type, it doesn't matter what's actually *in* the linked file. You can create an entire dummy publication by placing and linking placeholder files for every graphic and story in the publication, then create the pub automatically once the text and graphics are checked in. This is handy for people doing database publishing of material that changes little in overall shape from publication to publication.

1. Create and name a set of placeholder files. Put them in a folder named "Placeholders" (or anything else that strikes your fancy).

2. Place the placeholder files in PageMaker. Flow the text, and size the graphics as you want. Set the link options for the placeholder files to "Replace automatically." Save the publication. You can save it as a template, so that every time you open it you get an untitled file that you can save under a new file name.

3. Once the actual files you want to use in the publication are ready, give them the same names as the placeholder files, and put them in "Placeholders."

4. Open the publication. PageMaker replaces the original placeholder files with the current files.

## Live Files and Dead Files

One important concept with revision control is that of live and dead files. The live files are the current revisions—the ones that will be changed if further revisions are necessary. Dead files are old versions, and electronic versions that you've sent out for review and comments.

The key to workgroup publishing is to make sure there is only one live file for any illustration, story, or pub. That live file might be a story or illustration that's in the pub itself, or it might be an external file that's either linked or has yet to be placed.

You'll often find that when you send out an electronic text file for review or comments, people will insist on editing that dead file with their word processor. Their edits are useless, because there's no automatic way to compile them with other edits into the live file. Talk with them about this, as politely as you can.

▼ *Tip: Name Files with Version Numbers*

Every time you make a major change to a pub, save it with the same file name, but give each revision a higher version number ("May newsletter 1.1," "May newsletter 2.3," etc.). You can key the version numbers to various milestones, like first review, final page proofs, or editorial close. The version you send out for second review might be 2.0, while 3.0 might be the final version.

This doesn't work so well in naming source files when you're using PageMaker's links, because PageMaker will still be looking for version 1.2 when the latest version is 4.3. You can use the Link options dialog box and grab the latest version, but it won't happen automatically.

You'll have the same problem if you use this naming convention for your pub files and use the Book command to index several chapters. Your book list may have old files listed, so you'll have to tell PageMaker the names of the latest files (and their order) before you create an index or table of contents.

## File Transfer Methods

There are several methods for avoiding the problem of multiple copies—making sure that everyone works on a single, master live file—while having the freedom to move files around between co-workers as needed. The method you use depends on how your workgroup is set up.

*Floppy disks.* If you're passing around floppies, set up a check-in/check-out system for the floppies, and put each file on a separate floppy. Those are the live files, and only one person can work on them at a time. Nobody can change the file unless they actually have the physical disk in their possession. Nine-tenths of the law and all that. People are free to copy the live files onto their hard disks to make changes (it's actually good practice, because it creates a backup at the same time), but they have to copy it back onto the floppy and return the floppy to get the changes into the production system. Make sure one person is responsible for the floppies, and for copying the revised files onto a hard disk when they come back to Floppy Central.

▼ *Tip: If You've Already Placed It*

If you're working with a floppy check-in system and someone wants to make changes to an already-placed source file, you can just hand them the floppy. If you're using Links, though, it's also a good idea to move the file on your hard disk into a temporary "dead files" folder. That way when you open the pub and look at the Links dialog box, you'll know that a live file is missing. Alternately, open the source file on your hard disk and make some change (any change) when you hand off the floppy. That way you'll get a black diamond in the Links dialog box, reminding you that something's not right.

---

***AppleTalk network.*** If you're using a network like Tops over Apple-Talk, so people can publish volumes from their machines and mount other people's published volumes, you need a different strategy. Since there's no single, physical object to control the file, copies start to proliferate. Every time someone sends a file to someone else, they're actually copying it. You can get in trouble fast.

One solution is for everyone to use DiskTop Move command, moving the file instead of copying it. This deletes it from their disk at the same time that it places it on someone else's. This is easy, but it's a scary approach, because the file might get corrupted en route, and there's no backup. Another approach is to copy the file to the other person's disk, then move the original into a backup "dead files" folder. That way it's backed up, but it's also in a place where no one will confuse it with the live file.

The main rule is not to publish your live files folder. If a writer or artist wants to make a change to a file you've already received, set it up so they ask you for it, and you send it to them. That way you can delete it from your live files folder at the same time, or change it so the Links dialog box shows it's been changed, or whatever. Then when they're done making changes, they can copy it into a temporary transfer folder (call it "incoming" or something) that you publish as a volume. You're responsible for moving it into the live files folder.

The incoming folder works much like the floppy check-in system. People can still make changes to dead files, but they can't get those changes into the production system without the administrator (the person who moves the files) making it happen.

***Network with server.*** If you have a file server on your network, you can have one master live files folder. Anyone can have access to the folder, so everyone works on a single master document. But a problem arises if someone makes changes to a file that you've also changed in PageMaker. The solution, again, is to create an incoming files folder, make sure people inform you when they send an update, and move the update into your live files folder.

## *Dealing with Text Files*

You'll want to use different procedures for managing text and graphics files. Here's an example of a situation where a technical detail affects your procedures: PageMaker always keeps a copy of a placed text file in the pub, and you can change its contents after it's been placed. This is the source of the dreaded hollow triangles next to your linked files in the Links dialog box: you've made some edits to a placed story, then a writer comes to you and delivers a revision of that file. You have to replace the story then make all your edits again. And if you've set up any text wraps, corrected for bad line, column, or page breaks, kerned, tracked, or adjusted spacing to make copy fit, you have to start all over.

Once you make edits in a story on the page, you have to consider it as your live file. If writers want to make further changes, you'll have to either give them the pub and let them make the changes in PageMaker, or export the file for them to edit with a word processor—with all the problems of lost formatting. It's hard to say which is worse. Once you've let someone loose in your pub ("But I had to put all those spaces in there to make the line break!"), you can expect to rework the thing quite a bit anyway.

**Using Export with Links**

When you export a text file from PageMaker with the default for "Links" turned on, that exported file becomes the linked file for the story. Any changes made to that source file will be reflected in your pub the next time you open or print it. The Export feature is a wonderful, idea, but we find it useful primarily for archiving text files. Because many of the changes you make in PageMaker (kerning, tracking, etc.) aren't included in the exported text file, you're losing a lot of your work when you export and then replace. This problem points out again the importance of getting the copy right before it hits the page. Minor changes are all right, as long as you can make the changes easily in PageMaker and don't have to export or replace the story.

The solution is to get it right in your word processor. You're a lot better off doing the bulk of your copy processing in your word processor and bringing it into PageMaker fully formatted. This is also a nice approach because you can farm a lot of work off on writers and editors. Build style sheets for them (if they're using Word), and teach them how to use them. They should be specifying what different text elements are, anyway. Styles sheets make it easy for them and you. Otherwise, you may need a production editor to do the copy processing, or if worse comes to worst, you may have to do it yourself. In any case, do your copy processing *before* the file hits the page.

## Dealing with Graphic Files

Controlling versions of graphics files can be tough. You place and link a graphic, then an artist posts a new version. But the new version is larger or smaller, so when you replace (or update the link of) the graphic, it gets resized nonproportionally. You end up having to resize the graphic and sometimes, rebuild your page around it.

The best method to deal with graphic files is to spec the size of illustrations *after* you've built the pages, and let the artists work to fit. When you can't do that, another alternative is to insist that artists make any changes within the size of the original art. Have them draw a box for the size of the graphic, and work within it.

## If at First...

If it seems like we've posed more problems in this chapter than we've suggested solutions, you're right. Neither of us has ever built a workgroup publishing system that worked flawlessly under the pressures of deadlines, last-minute changes, and workgroups that don't work as groups. We've come close, and the tips here are the best general approaches we've come up with.

When it comes right down to it, the best approaches are those that worked when publishing was done with clay tablets: set up a system for handling the flow of work through the group and adhere to it, and communicate honestly with the other people in the group regarding any problems. Don't build empires. Don't point fingers. Get the job done, figure out where improvements can be made in your process, and refine it. You'll always be refining your process.

# *How We Made This Book*

This chapter comprises a rather lengthy colophon—a bit more than you usually want to know about what went into making a book. In a book about using PageMaker 4 in the real world, though, it seemed appropriate to provide a lengthy, real-world example. Since this book is the only such example so far (aside from the manuals, which Ole also produced), it was the obvious choice.

*Real World PageMaker 4* was produced, beginning to end, using ßeta versions of Aldus PageMaker 4. Most of the production work was done using ßeta 11 (engineering build 103), a remarkably full and robust ßeta. We wrote most of the copy in Microsoft Word 4.0. Screen shots were made with Capture and Exposure, and cleaned up in MacPaint II and DeskPaint. Other art was created with Adobe Photo-shop and Aldus FreeHand. We used QuicKeys, DiskTop, and Master-Juggler extensively. And, naturally, Neko.

## *Hardware*

Steve has a Macintosh II. Ole did most of his writing on an SE, but borrowed a IIcx from friends for production (thanks again!). Steve's creaky version 23 ROM LaserWriter got a workout, but held up to steady use. Ole's LaserWriter II NT, on the other hand, pointed out the weakness of Apple's warranty by needing its motherboard replaced at around 100 days of ownership. For that much money, he could have had an NTX. (Get with it, Apple. Support your customers!)

## Design

The book was designed by Nancy Sugihara, who sent us a design specification covering most of the text elements and graphic treatments used in the book (but not all; it's almost impossible to create a spec that covers everything for a book that has not yet been finished). We created PageMaker templates and style sheets that conformed to this specification, making slight adjustments here and there to make the design work with PageMaker and conform to a leading grid.

## Fonts

We set the book using Bitstream's ITC Garamond family of typefaces (primarily Garamond Light and Bold), with the exception of program listings, which are set in Optima (code listings are generally set in monospaced fonts, but PostScript isn't space-sensitive, so it doesn't matter). Working with the Bitstream fonts was a breeze, and they're gorgeous (though we had to remove almost all the ugly screen fonts and let ATM build them for us on the fly). We do wish we'd gotten them a few weeks earlier, though; we're only now feeling that we understand their spacing—far too late for such knowledge to help this book.

The Bitstream fonts are set up in an interesting way, which we need to explain so you can understand the style sheet explanation following. In some cases, you get something very different from what you thought you specified. Who would expect to get ITC Garamond Light Condensed, for instance, when they specify ITC Garamond Light with bold applied? The configuration of the screen fonts in the Bitstream ITC Garamond set is shown in Table 9-1.

**Table 9-1  Bitstream ITC Garamond screen fonts**

| Screen font | Style | What You Get |
| --- | --- | --- |
| ITC Garamd a | Normal | ITC Garamond Light |
| | Italic | ITC Garamond Light Italic |
| | Bold | ITC Garamond Light Condensed |
| | Bold italic | ITC Garamond Light Condensed Italic |
| ITC Garamd b | Normal | ITC Garamond Book Condensed |
| | Italic | ITC Garamond Book Condensed Italic |
| | Bold | ITC Garamond Book Condensed Bold |
| | Bold italic | ITC Garamond Book Condensed Bold Italic |
| ITC Garamd c | Normal | ITC Garamond Book |
| | Italic | ITC Garamond Book Italic |
| | Bold | ITC Garamond Bold |
| | Bold italic | ITC Garamond Bold Italic |
| ITC Garamd d | Normal | ITC Garamond Ultra |
| | Italic | ITC Garamond Ultra Italic |
| | Bold | ITC Garamond Ultra Condensed |
| | Bold italic | ITC Garamond Ultra Condensed Italic |

## Styles

Creating the styles for *Real World PageMaker 4* presented a number of challenges. A-heads, for example, needed to displace an even number of text lines (4 lines, 60 points) to keep ensuing paragraphs on the leading grid—no matter where the A-heads fell on the page. It would be easy to develop separate styles—one to use when the A-head falls at the top of the page, and another for when it falls in the middle of the page—but we wanted to develop one that would work the same way in either case, to prevent problems with last-minute changes. Similarly, the rule above a B head needed to top-align with the top of caps of the body text to its right, though doing that takes the rule off the leading grid. We compensated for this with space above and by specifying invisible rules above the baseline of the paragraph, so that the paragraph would be pushed down a set amount even if it fell at the top of a text block (remember: PageMaker ignores space before settings when the paragraph is the first paragraph in a text block.) This meant we could use "Snap to grid" and "Snap to r ulers" in production.

Once we'd finished the style sheet, we exported it for use in Microsoft Word, and modified it so it was easy to read and edit on screen and on paper. The one- and two-letter abbreviations at the end of each style name helped us apply styles in Word (type Command-Shift-S, the abbreviation for the style, and press Return to apply the style). We did almost all the styling in Word, then placed the files in PageMaker, where the fully-specified PageMaker styles with the same names took over.

Table 9-2 is a listing of the styles used in this book, with notes on their use, along with the QuicKeys we created for styling paragraphs in PageMaker. This is the documentation we created at the start of the project for our own use. If you're working on a complex production project, especially with several people involved, you should consider documenting your styles in a similar fashion.

**Table 9-2  Styles used in *Real World PageMaker***

| *Style Name* | *Notes* |
| --- | --- |
| <a head,ah> | Preceded by a <rule above> and a <rule below> (paragraphs containing a carriage return only). <rule above> has a line above set to "None" width to force the <a head> down so that succeeding paragraphs align to the grid and observe the 20-point specified baseline-to-baseline from the <a head> to the following <para1>—even if the <a head> falls at the top of the page. |
| | ITC Garamd c Bold Italic, 14/13 (negative lead forces the top of caps to fall the specified 6 points below the preceding <rule above>), flush left. The <rule above> contains the space above setting (specified as 3-1/2 lines). The baseline of the first line of the <para1> following the <a head> falls 20 points below the baseline of the last line of the <a head>. |
| | **Keys:** Control-F3 adds the rules and styles the head if invoked from a text insertion point in the paragraph above; Control-1 invokes the <a head> style. |

**Table 9-2  Styles used in *Real World PageMaker*, continued**

| *Style Name* | *Notes* |
| --- | --- |
| <b head,bh> | Has a rule above, plus enough space above to force the rule to Top-of-caps-align with the text following. Procedure for working with <b head>: flow text down to break just below the <b head>, break the text block, then reflow from the grid point just above the <b head>'s rule above. |
| | ITC Garamd c Bold 11/13, flush right on an 8-pica width (the companion column), 2p9 space above. |
| | **Keys:** Control-2 invokes the <b head> style. |
| <c head> | C heads are local formatting applied to the first sentence of a <para1> (or <para1 plus>). They're preceded by a "plus" style paragraph (<para plus> or <para1 plus>, usually) so that we don't have to make a <para1> style with space above. |
| | (local only) ITC Garamd c Bold Italic 11/15 |
| | **Keys:** Control-3 formats a selected range of text; Command-F2 selects and styles the text when invoked from an insertion point in the paragraph above. |
| <chapter title,ct> | Chapter title. Top of text block aligns to the fifth grid increment. |
| | ITC Garamd a Italic 28/34 |
| <chapter #,cn> | Chapter number. Insert 10 word spaces between each letter (too much to do with the Spacing dialog box, so do it manually or make a key). 11 word spaces between the word "CHAPTER" and the chapter number. Reversed and centered in a black rectangle 1p tall x 26p wide across the text column. |
| | ITC Garamd c Bold 10/15 (leaded to center vertically in the black rectangle) All caps. |

**Table 9-2 Styles used in *Real World PageMaker*, continued**

| Style Name | Notes |
|---|---|
| \<header left,hl\> | Header left. Centered vertically in a 35p3 wide x 1p tall 10% filled, hairline-stroked rectangle. Page number is on a right tab at 2p3, followed by a tab at 2p9, then REAL WORLD PAGEMAKER 4, letterspaced out with 1 word space between each character, two word spaces between words. Spec says "indent r.h. 12pt from folio, but all of the printed samples show 6pt at most.<br><br>ITC Garamd a 7/15 (leaded to center vertically in 10% rectangle), on a left tab at 2p9. Page number in 10/15 ITC Garamd c Bold, on a right-tab at 2p3. |
| \<header right,hr\> | Header right. Centered vertically in a 35p3 wide x 1p tall 10% filled, hairline-stroked rectangle. Page number is on a left tab at 33p, chapter title (letterspaced out with 1 word space between each character, two word spaces between words) on a right tab at 32p6.<br><br>ITC Garamd a 7/15 (leaded to center vertically in 10% rectangle), on a right-tab at 32p6. Page number in 10/15 ITC Garamd c Bold, on a left tab at 33. |
| \<drop folio,df\> | Drop folio—page numbers for chapter opening pages. These fall 1 grid increment below the bottom of the live area, flush right.<br><br>ITC Garamd a 10/15, flush right. |
| \<para,p\> | Paragraph. Has a 1 em (11pt) indent.<br><br>ITC Garamd a 11/14, justified.<br><br>**Keys:** Control-Shift-p |
| \<para plus,pp\> | Same as \<para\>, plus one line space (15pt) below. Use it for paragraphs that fall before \<c head\>s, etc.<br><br>**Keys:** Control-Shift-Option-p |

**Table 9-2 Styles used in *Real World PageMaker*, continued**

| *Style Name* | *Notes* |
|---|---|
| \<para1,p1\> | First paragraph. Same as \<para\> but with no first-line indent. Follows \<a head\>s, \<b head\>s, etc.<br><br>**Keys:** Control-p |
| \<para1 plus,p1p\> | Same as \<para1\>, with a line space after. Use it for paragraphs that fall before \<c head\>s, etc.<br><br>**Keys:** Command-Control-Option-Shift-p |
| \<bullet,b\> | Hanging indent at 22pt from text left margin (which is 9p3—meaning the bullet falls at 10p2, the text at 11p1). Used for l-line bullet list entries, if all or most of the bullet list is made of 1-line entries.<br><br>ITC Garamd a 11/15, justified.<br><br>**Keys:** Control-B |
| \<bullet plus,bp\> | Bullet list plus. \<bullet\> plus 3pt space after. For use in bullet lists containing multiple-line entries, as dictated by the spec. We'll use this for most of our bullet lists.<br><br>**Keys:** Control-Shift-B |
| \<bullet1,b1\> | First entry in a bullet list. Same as \<bullet\>, with the addition of 7.5pt (½ extra line space above, as specified).<br><br>**Keys:** Control-Option-B |
| \<bullet1 plus\> | Same as \<bullet first\>, plus 3pt space after. Use to begin bullet lists containing multiple-line entries, as in the spec.<br><br>**Keys:** Control-Option-Shift-B |

**Table 9-2 Styles used in *Real World PageMaker*, continued**

| *Style Name* | *Notes* |
| --- | --- |
| &lt;bullet end,be&gt; | Bullet end. Same as &lt;bullet&gt; or &lt;bullet plus&gt;, but with "Align to grid" turned on so that the next paragraph will fall back on the grid.<br><br>**Keys:** Command-Control-Option-Shift-B |
| &lt;list,l&gt; | Numbered list. All of the &lt;list&gt; styles work the same way as the &lt;bullet&gt; styles, and the keys work the same way, too. (&lt;list plus,lp&gt;, &lt;list1,l1&gt;, &lt;list1 plus,lpl&gt;, &lt;list end,le&gt; |
| &lt;callout,c&gt; | Callout. If callouts have a callout rule, a rule goes 3pt right, left, above, or below the callout text, and the callout rule intersects this line (which we'll call a backstop). The callout rule should encounter this line near the horizontal or vertical center of the callout. Callout backstops could be paragraph rules above or below (hairlines) if the callout line comes off the callout horizontally. This is confusing, so let's illustrate: |

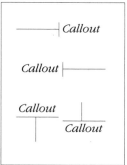 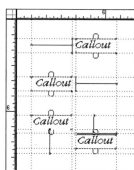

Callouts sometimes hang out in the companion column with the figure title/number, in which case they're flush right in the companion column (just like the figure number/title).

ITC Garamd a Italic 8/9, flush left

**Keys:** Control-C

**Table 9-2  Styles used in *Real World PageMaker*, continued**

| *Style Name* | *Notes* |
| --- | --- |
| \<figure number,fn\> | We do figure numbers like this: "Figure 8-4" where "8" is the chapter number and "4" is the number of the figure, counted from the first figure in the chapter. Figure numbers are always followed by the \<figure title\>, and top aligned with the illustration (1 full grid unit from the last line of text above—which is typically the last line of the paragraph containing the major text reference to the figure). |
| | ITC Garamd c Bold 9/11, flush right on 8p companion column. |
| | **Keys:** Control-F |
| \<figure title,ft\> | Figure titles are text that describes the figure. Should not be sentences or imperatives, so no period following. If the figure is the Print dialog box, the figure title should be "Print dialog box" but it's fine being creative with figure titles. Figure titles always follow a \<figure number\>. |
| | ITC Garamd a 9/11, flush right on 8p companion column. |
| | **Keys:** Control-Shift-F |
| \<rule above,ra\> | Comes before a \<rule below\> before an \<a head\>. Has a "None" weight rule above to force things after the \<a head\> onto the grid. See \<a head\> for details. |
| | **Keys:** Control-- (part of the Control-F3 sequence) |
| \<rule below,rb\> | Comes before an \<a head\> and just after a \<rule above\>. See \<a head\> for details. |
| | **Keys:** Control-Shift-- (part of the Control-F3 sequence) |

**Table 9-2  Styles used in *Real World PageMaker*, continued**

| *Style Name* | *Notes* |
|---|---|
| <tip,t> | Starts with an 11-point Zapf Dingbats t (a down arrow). Tips always end with a half-point rule, 7.5 points (one half line space) down from the baseline of the last line of the tip, so there are several tip styles: <tip end para1>, <tip end para>, <tip end list>, etc. depending on what follows. If a tip end style precedes an <a head>, drop the rule at the end of the tip to avoid having two rules in a row.<br><br>ITC Garamd c 11/15, flush left (hanging indent places text—including second or, god help us, third lines—at 10p—8 points from the dingbat).<br><br>**Keys:** Control-T; Control-F2, when invoked from a text insertion point in the paragraph above, will style the <tip> and add the dingbat and the tab. |
| <table number,tn> | All tables, like figures, should have table numbers and be treated as if they were illustrations (that is, they can float slightly from their text reference—but, unlike the <figure number>, <table number> across the text column). Tables are numbered "Table 8-1," where "8" is the number of the chapter and "1" is the number of the table, counted from the first table in the chapter. On the same line (in the same style) as the table number, following an en space, there's a table title. Table numbers have 7.5 points space above, per the written spec. The spec also urges that the minimum width of space between columns should be 2p, the maximum; 3p6. There's a paragraph rule below (a hairline), 8 points from the baseline of the table number. 8 points more space below is added, per the written spec.<br><br>ITC Garamd c Bold 10/12, flush left.<br><br>**Keys:** Control-R |

**Table 9-2  Styles used in *Real World PageMaker*, continued**

| *Style Name* | *Notes* |
|---|---|
| \<table head,th\> | Heads, aligned flush left with each column in the table. \<table head\> has a rule 8 points below its baseline, with an added 4-point space after to push the first table entry down to 12 points below the baseline.<br><br>ITC Garamd c Bold Italic 9/12, flush left with however many columns we need.<br><br>**Keys:** Control-Shift-R |
| \<table,tb\> | Table body. ITC Garamd a 10/12, flush left in however many columns we need. 12 points space after each table entry.<br><br>**Keys:** Control-Option-Shift-R |
| \<table end,te\> | Table ends are the same as \<table\>s, but they have a hairline paragraph rule 12 points below their last line's baseline, and they put everything back to align to grid/15 points.<br><br>ITC Garamd a 10/12 |

We tracked all of our styles with the default track "Normal." If we'd had time, we'd have customized the tracks for the font. Similarly, we'd probably have used a slightly different spacing scheme. We used Word space Minimum 90, Desired 100, Maximum 110; and Letter space Minimum -1, Desired 0, and Maximum 30. Given what we now know about the fonts, those settings should probably be 95, 100, 105, 0, 0, 20.

## *Table of Contents*

We used PageMaker 4's new TOC features, of course. We had to change the styles for various elements through all the chapters to generate the various lists in the book. First we turned on "Include in table of contents" for the chapter titles, and created the short Contents. Then we turned it on for A-heads and B-heads, and generated the long table of contents. Finally, we turned it off for everything except tips, and generated the tip list.

## Index

Once we'd gotten through the production crunch and pages were off to the printer, we went back into the pages to build the index for delivery with bluelines. We created a topic list in Word and imported it into PageMaker. Then we started indexing at the beginning of the book, using the topics we'd imported and adding topics as necessary. We had to take turns working on the same live files, because there's no way to compile two separate topic lists.

## Imagesetting

Final page output was at 1270 dpi on Linotronic 300s with RIP IIs (one with version 49.3 PostScript ROMs and one with version 51) at Seattle ImageSetting. The color pages were printed to film at 2540 dpi. We printed the files to disk, then downloaded the files to the image-setters ourselves. When we weren't processing film or loading new film into the lino, we drank Ballard Bitter (what else?). We are extremely grateful to Chuck Cantellay, Peter Curry, and the staff of SIS for going above and beyond the call of duty, as usual, to help us out.

# *Resources*

This appendix lists the companies who make products discussed in this book (or at least make them available), sorted alphabetically by company. If you don't know which company made a product, you can either look up the product in the index (you'll find the company name in the text of the book.), or scan through this appendix quickly. It's not very long.

An asterisk following a product name indicates that the product is public-domain, freeware, shareware, or whateverwear—that it's available through user groups, online services, public-domain software libraries, etc. The addresses and phone numbers for those products and companies are provided merely as a reference. It's generally much easier to go through the underground than it is to get a copy from a harried philanthropist, or revenue-seeking corporation.

**Abbott Systems Inc**
CanOpener
62 Mountain Road
Pleasantville, NY 10570
800-552-9157

**Addison-Wesley**
*Inside LaserWriter*
*Inside Macintosh*
*Real World PostScript*
Jacob Way
Reading, MA 01867
617-944-3700

**Adobe Systems**
Adobe Font Downloader
Adobe Illustrator
Adobe PhotoShop
Adobe Type Manager
Art Browser*
SendPS*
1585 Charleston Road
PO Box 7900
Mountain View, CA 94039
415-961-4400

**Affinity Microsystems**
Tempo II
1050 Walnut Street
Suite 425
Boulder, CA 80302
303-442-4840

**Aldus Corporation**
Aldus FreeHand
411 First Avenue S., Suite 200
Seattle, WA 98104
206-622-5500

**Altsys, Inc.**
Art Importer
Suite 109
720 Avenue F
Plano, TX 75074
214-424-4888

**Apple Computer, Inc**
LaserWriter Font Utility
LaserWriter II SC
MacroMaker
ResEdit
20525 Mariani Avenue
Cupertino, CA 95104
408-996-1010

**Caseys' Page Mill**
Bullets & Boxes
6528 South Oneida Court
Englewood, CO 80111
303-220-1463

**CE Software**
DiskTop
LaserStatus
QuicKeys
801-73rd Street
Des Moines, IO 50312
515-224-1995

**Eric Celeste**
Macify*
358 North Parkview
Columbus, OH 45209

**Data Viz**
MacLink Plus
35 Corporation Drive
Trumbull, CT 06611
203-268-0030

**Dayna Communications**
DaynaFile
50 South Main Street
Salt Lake City, UT 84144
801-531-0600

**Edco Systems**
LetrTuck
PM Tracker
12410 North Dale Mabry
Highway
Tampa, FL 33618
813-962-7800
800-523-TYPE

**Emerald City Software**
Lasertalk
SmartArt
Box 2103
Menlo Park, CA 94026
415-324-8080

**GCC Technologies**
Personal LaserPrinter
580 Winter Street
Waltham, MA 02154
617-890-0880

**Goldstein & Blair**
*The Macintosh Bible*
189 Purdue Avenue
Kensington, CA 94708
415-528-3546

**Kenji Gotoh**
Neko*
co-op SenjuOhashi 105,
3-19-18 SenjuMidori-tyo
adachi-ku, Tokyo 120 Japan

**Linotype Company**
Linotronic Imagesetters
425 Oser Avenue
Hauppauge, NY 11788
516-434-2000

**Mainstay**
Capture
5311-B Derry Avenue
Agoura Hills, CA 91301
818-991-6450

**Peachpit Press**
*Learning PostScript: A Visual Approach*
1085 Keith Avenue
Berkeley, CA 94708
415-527-8555

**Preferred Publishers**
Exposure
5100 Poplar Avenue
Suite 617
Memphis, TN 38137
901-683-3833

**Preferred Software Inc.**
Vantage
5100 Poplar Avenue, Suite 706
Memphis, TN 38137
800-446-6393

**Lincoln Stein**
Quote Init*
44 Boynton Street
Boston, MA 02103

**Sybex**
*Encyclopedia Macintosh*
2021 Challenger Drive
#100
Alameda, CA 94501

**Taylored Software**
Xris-Xros
Box 1887
Aptos, CA 95001
408-688-3536

**Technical Publishing Services, Inc**
Color Calibration Software for PostScript Imagesetters
2205 Sacramento
San Francisco, CA 94115
415-921-8509

**Varityper**
FontConflicts*
FontMagic*
FontWizard*
PSFontFinder*
11 Mount Pleasant Avenue
East Hanover, NJ 07936
201-887-8000

**Hiroaki Yamamoto**
Boomerang*
Lawrence Berkeley Laboratory
1 Cyclotron Road
Berkeley, CA 94720
415-486-6407

**Zedcor**
DeskPaint
4500 East Speedway, #22
Tuscon, AZ 86712
800-482-4567

# Index

# Calling All Monsters

Just nailed a stack of pages and need to bellow in triumph? Want to share your latest face-melting PageMaker tips and tricks? Got a PageMaker-related product you'd like us to know (and talk) about? Enraged because something in this book didn't work? We'd love to hear from you.

Just drop us a line at one of the following addresses (Ole isn't online, and apologizes for being so backward; he'll still read it all):

Open House
6006 2nd Avenue NW
Seattle, Washington
98107

MCI Mail: 252-2575

BIX: sroth

CompuServe: 72261,1361

MacNet: rothsf

America Online: Sroth